Urban Vigilantes in the New South:
Tampa, 1882–1936

A Florida Sand Dollar Book

Robert P. Ingalls

# Urban Vigilantes in the New South: Tampa, 1882–1936

University Press of Florida
Gainesville/Tallahassee/Tampa/Boca Raton
Pensacola/Orlando/Miami/Jacksonville

Copyright 1988 by The University of Tennessee Press
First paperback edition 1993 published by University Press
of Florida
Printed in the United States of America on acid-free paper ∞
All rights reserved

**Library of Congress Cataloging-in-Publication Data**
Ingalls, Robert P., 1941–
    Urban vigilantes in the New South : Tampa, 1882–
1936 / Robert P. Ingalls.
      p.  cm. — (A Florida sand dollar book)
    Includes bibliographical references and index.
    ISBN 0-8130-1223-6 (pbk. : acid-free paper)
    1. Vigilantes—Florida—Tampa—History.
2. Violence—Florida—Tampa—History.  3. Tampa
(Fla.)—Social conditions.  4. Tampa (Fla.)—Race
relations.  I. Title.  II. Series.
F319.T2I64   1993
305.8'009759'65—dc20                      93-7217
                                                      CIP

The University Press of Florida is the scholarly publishing
agency for the State University System of Florida, comprised
of Florida A & M University, Florida Atlantic University,
Florida International University, Florida State University,
University of Central Florida, University of Florida,
University of North Florida, University of South Florida,
and University of West Florida.

University Press of Florida
15 Northwest 15th Street
Gainesville, FL 32611

For Marie-Joèle

# Contents

Acknowledgments / xi

Introduction / xv

1. The Southern Roots of Lynch Law / 1
2. The Origins of Antilabor Vigilantism / 31
3. "Pro Bono Publico": The Citizens' Committee of 1901 / 55
4. "The Cossacks of Tampa": The Citizens' Committee of 1910–11 / 87
5. From "Stern Repression" to Collective Bargaining / 116
6. "Tar and Terror" / 163

Conclusion: Violence and Hegemony / 205

Notes / 215

Bibliography / 263

Index / 277

# Illustrations

*Pages 6–9*
Florida peninsula, map
Florida and Cuba, map
Tampa Bay area, 1900, map
Tampa, 1880
John P. Wall
Confederate war memorial

*Pages 44–49*
Martínez Ybor cigar label
Vicente Martínez Ybor's portrait on a cigar label
Ignacio Haya
Workers preparing filler tobacco
Cigarmaker handrolling a cigar
First Sánchez & Haya factory in Tampa
Sánchez & Haya cigar label
A group of cigar manufacturers, 1895
José Martí with Tampa cigarworkers
Tampa, 1893

*Pages 64–68*
Cuban Club
Centro Asturiano
Italian Club
Ybor City homes, 1898
Ybor City's main street, c. 1898
Tampa policemen, 1899
Wallace F. Stovall
Donald Brenham McKay

*Pages 91–94*
Lynch victims, 1910
West Tampa, 1906
Selectors at the Sánchez & Haya factory
Hugh C. Macfarlane

*Pages 123–132*
Tampa's port, 1922
Staff of *La Traduccion*
Ybor City's Labor Temple, 1921
A *lector* reading to cigarmakers
Tampa, 1926
Two cigar manufacturers, 1921
Members of the Tampa Chamber of Commerce
Ybor City's new Labor Temple in the 1930s
Another *lector* reading to cigarmakers
Women cigarmakers
Workers at cigar-banding machines
Postcard protesting 1932 political convictions

*Pages 169–176*
Tampa, 1926
National Guard battery and Mayor Chancey
Robert E. Lee Chancey
Joseph A. Shoemaker
Ku Klux Klan rally, 1923
Billboard protesting tar-and-feathering
Klan circular
Ku Klux Klan rally, 1937
Cartoon of Klan flogger
Tampa, 1940

# Acknowledgments

The writing of history is a collaborative effort. Historians build on and profit from the work of colleagues who precede them. Footnotes provide one means of acknowledging debts to other historians, but citations reveal little about the amount of benefit derived from any particular source. This book is framed by two lynchings, one in 1882 and the other in 1935. I first learned about the former from Richard Maxwell Brown's study of vigilantism and the latter from David M. Chalmers' history of the Ku Klux Klan. I am grateful for the thoroughness of their research, which put me on the trail of Tampa vigilantes.

Much of the evidence I accumulated lay buried in repositories outside Tampa. The bibliography indicates the location of these collections, and in every one I received learned, prompt assistance from librarians and archivists, who readily accommodated the demands of a traveling historian. Several institutions and associations that appear nowhere else in this book deserve credit for allowing access to their important collections. These include the AFL–CIO Library and Archives in Washington, D.C., the Tamiment Institute at New York University, the New York Public Library, and the Tobacco Merchants' Association in New York.

Two Tampa libraries house much of the material that made my search for local vigilantes a successful one. The Tampa–Hillsborough County Public Library System contains a number of newspapers, books and photographs on local history that can be found nowhere else. The enthusiastic and knowledgeable librarians and staff at the University of South Florida Library assisted me throughout this project. The list of their names would read like the roster of a softball team, but they know who they are. I also owe a large debt to Paul E. Camp and J. B. Dobkin, whose command of local history and desire to preserve it have made the University of South Florida Library's Special Collections Department a special place.

I am grateful for financial support from two institutions. The University of South Florida, through the College of Social and Behavioral

Sciences and the Division of Sponsored Research, generously funded travel and research. A fellowship from the National Endowment for the Humanities made it possible for me to devote an entire year to this project.

Once I had collected the essential information about Tampa vigilantes, a number of colleagues and friends helped me put the story in its present form. Gary M. Fink, James R. McGovern and Tom E. Terrill endorsed the project at its inception. Steven F. Lawson has heard about it longer and more often than anyone else. I deeply appreciate his innumerable and invaluable contributions, which helped bring the project to fruition. I am especially indebted to Louis A. Pérez, Jr., for constant encouragement. His comradeship and probing questions inspired me to give substance and direction to this study. He also wields a sensitive, but incisive, pencil. A mutual fascination with lynch law, working-class history, and theater provided the basis of a friendship with Denis Calandra, who served as a sounding board and discerning reader. Nancy A. Hewitt has also been a sympathetic listener and insightful reader. Her own study of working women in Tampa promises to add a dimension that is missing from this investigation of collective action.

Patricia A. Cooper shared her extensive knowledge of the cigar industry and the sources that document the history of cigarworkers. I appreciate her willingness to give early drafts of the manuscript a careful reading. L. Glenn Westfall kindly provided access to relevant material in his research files. Helpful comments on portions of the manuscript also came from Charles H. Martin and Jacquelyn Dowd Hall. For almost thirty years, George H. Mayer has proven himself a rare mentor and friend who always seems to know what the situation, moment, paragraph or sentence calls for. Since none of these generous people read the entire manuscript in its final form, they are absolved of any responsibility for the result. They have, however, contributed materially to whatever strengths it may have.

All the words that follow were "processed" time and again by Michael G. Copeland, Nita Desai, Cecile L. Pulin, and Peter Selle. I am extremely grateful for their skill, dedication, and good cheer. Charles Pettis kindly translated a number of passages from Spanish into English. Joyce Bland and Susan McConnell took extraordinary care and interest in making photographic copies of most of the illustrations. Without ever seeing any of the manuscript, Peggy Cornett and Sylvia Wood made much of it possible through their successful efforts to facilitate smooth operation of the Department of History at the University of South Florida. I also greatly appreciate the encouragement and support provided by Cynthia Maude-Gembler of the University of Tennessee Press.

Permission to use previously published material was kindly granted by the *Florida Historical Quarterly*, the *Journal of Southern History*, and *Southern Exposure*. My essay "Radicals and Vigilantes: The 1931 Strike of Tampa Cigar Workers" was originally published in *Southern Workers and Their Unions, 1880–1975: Selected Papers, the Second Southern Labor History Conference, 1978*, edited by Merl E. Reed, Leslie S. Hough, and Gary M. Fink.

As any writer knows, the right environment makes work and life more productive and enjoyable. My children, Michèle and Marc, have shown remarkable understanding that much of my "work" is done at home—all around it and at all possible hours. As this project grew, my wife Marie-Joèle encouraged it, allowing it temporarily to take over my life and our house. In countless ways she has sustained me for twenty years. For that and much more I dedicate this book to her.

# Introduction

The American South has achieved special prominence for its history of blood-letting. "Beneath the image of a gracious, hospitable, leisurely folk has lurked that of a hot-tempered, violent, even sadistic people," notes the sociologist John Shelton Reed.[1] Although a general history of the South would require attention to both grace and violence, as well as to other traditions, this study focuses on the role of group violence in Tampa, Florida, from the 1880s through the 1930s. Tampa did not, however, exist in isolation.

Defined as damage or seizure of persons or property, violence has figured prominently in all of American history, and no region has escaped untouched.[2] Collective violence in the United States has also been characterized by a conservative bias. Instead of being directed by subordinate groups against those in power, it has been wielded primarily by dominant groups seeking to maintain their supremacy.[3] As Richard Hofstadter pointed out, violence in the United States "has been used ostensibly to protect the American, the Southern, the white Protestant, or simply the established middle-class way of life and morals."[4] Violence in defense of the status quo can be distinguished from revolutionary or reactionary violence, both of which are motivated by a desire on the part of less privileged groups to redistribute power.[5] The United States occasionally experienced both revolutionary and reactionary violence, as evidenced by isolated assassinations by anarchists at the turn of the century and by rebellious attempts of rural Americans to resist change. Most American violence, however, has been repressive, designed to control subordinate groups.[6]

Americans appear responsible for developing vigilantism, the consummate expression of conservative violence.[7] Although it may be simply defined as taking the law into one's own hands, vigilantism is more than that, since it also necessitates some degree of organization by a group of people. There is no agreement on the minimum number required, but in any case, it would exclude individuals acting alone. Moreover, vigilantes take the law into their own hands to reinforce existing power relationships, not to subvert them.[8]

Vigilantism has been characterized as "establishment violence." Two political scientists define it as "the use of violence by established groups to preserve the status quo at times when the formal system of rule enforcement is viewed as ineffective or irrelevant." This definition does not mean that vigilantes are necessarily members of an elite, but rather that they use violence to defend the established order against some perceived threat.[9] Operating outside the formal legal system, vigilantes engage in both overt acts of violence which actually harm people or damage property and threats of violence which rely on force to prevent the free movement of other persons.[10] Thus, vigilantism takes the form of extralegal coercion by a group of private individuals seeking to maintain the existing distribution of power.[11]

Although American vigilantism is commonly associated with the nineteenth-century frontier, it persisted well into the twentieth century as an urban phenomenon. The fixation on the role of the frontier long concealed the fact that most American violence has occurred in cities.[12] Vigilantism originally won widespread approval because it served as a means of controlling crime by horse thieves and other outlaws in sparsely settled areas which lacked effective law enforcement. However, long after the disappearance of frontier conditions and the imposition of a criminal justice system, establishment violence remained a popular method of repressing so-called "undesirables," a designation which included "Catholics, Jews, Negroes, immigrants, labor men and labor leaders, political radicals, advocates of civil liberties, and nonconformists in general."[13] Perceived as threats to dominant groups, these people were often victims of extralegal violence because they broke no formal law and, therefore, could be repressed only outside the law. Urban vigilantism flourished as early as the 1850s, when the San Francisco Vigilance Committee achieved national notoriety.[14] Although the setting and victims of such movements changed over time, this form of collective action remained an effective strategy for preserving the power and values of dominant groups.

Studies of southern violence have emphasized both its prominence and its manifold forms. From the defense of personal honor and slavery in antebellum days to the massive resistance against integration, southerners have individually and collectively resorted to lawlessness on a scale that has long attracted the attention of contemporary observers and scholars. The varieties of violence historically associated with the South include dueling, lynching, night riding, flogging, and tar-and-feathering.[15] Each of these could result in death, but southerners also have committed conventional homicide at rates consistently higher than those found in the rest of the country.[16] This fact led one observer to describe the region as "that part of the United States lying below the Smith and Wesson line."[17] In addition to causing injury to people, southern violence has also taken the form of attacks on property, occasionally reaching epidemic proportions.[18]

Much of the South's collective violence can be classified as vigilantism. From the days of "Judge" Charles Lynch in eighteenth-century Virginia to the Ku Klux Klan of the 1960s, southerners organized privately outside the law to repress groups and individuals who appeared to threaten the existing order. Indeed, the practice of lynching can be seen as one type of vigilante violence.[19] Other familiar expressions of southern violence, though not necessarily fatal, frequently had all the characteristics of vigilantism. For example, flogging and tar-and-feathering, sometimes known as "whitecapping," were often part of well-organized local efforts to defend established values.[20] Only by examining specific incidents of group violence, however, can historians determine their particular purpose and degree of organization, as well as those responsible. The difficulty is that many such movements were secret, and even when widely publicized, they often left too little evidence to reconstruct a reliable account of their activities. Historians have, nevertheless, successfully documented a number of vigilante movements that appeared in various southern localities.[21] The focus on an individual community permits analysis of collective violence over time in the context of group relations generally.

This study examines the history of vigilantism in Tampa over several generations. As early as the 1850s, Tampa experienced vigilante movements. The practice became an organized form of community justice in the 1880s, when Tampa emerged as a city, and it continued to claim victims until the 1940s. The varieties of vigilantism practiced by Tampans included lynching, flogging, tar-and-feathering, and the forced expulsion of so-called "agitators." The city's establishment violence was directed at workers, labor organizers, immigrants, blacks, Socialists, and Communists. By the 1930s, Tampa had become so infamous for extralegal group violence that the American Civil Liberties Union branded it as one of the worst "centers of repression" in the United States.[22] That very decade, however, also saw an end to this form of terror in Tampa.

Explanations of violence in general and southern violence in particular have divided most sharply on the question of causation. Studies of collective violence have tended to pursue either of two conflicting approaches. One theory views outbursts of group violence as a product of social disintegration and the breakdown of social control that accompanies massive structural changes, such as industrialization and urbanization. This interpretation argues that disorder and violence are the result of new expectations and frustrations generated by rapid social change, which also contributes to "the partial breakdown of systems of normative control, to the collapse of old institutions through which some groups were once able to satisfy their expectations, and to the creation of new organizations of the discontented."[23]

The competing theory presents collective violence as part of the "normal" political process. That is, group violence represents one organized response to the competition over power that occurs throughout society. "Far from being mere side effects of urbanization, industrialization, and other large structural changes, violent protests seem to grow most directly from the struggle for established places in the structure of power," Charles Tilly has observed. Thus, violence has been regularly used throughout history by those groups trying to gain or regain power, no less than those in power attempting to retain it.[24]

If collective violence were actually a result of rapid social change, the South should have experienced less lawlessness than other areas, since it was arguably the most stable region of the country, especially from the end of Reconstruction until World War II. This seeming paradox of lawlessness in a stable society may explain why some historians have drawn upon social-psychological theories, such as the concept of relative deprivation and the frustration-aggression hypothesis, in an attempt to understand the southern penchant for violence. While stressing cultural conditioning, including child-rearing practices, these studies suggest a number of possible triggering mechanisms for southern violence, ranging from the authoritarian personality to the fear of outsiders and "a siege mentality."[25]

Many historians have relied on political and economic analyses to illuminate the sources of collective violence in the South. From this point of view, the relative stability of southern society does not preclude the possibility that various groups resorted to violence in order to retain their power. In the general case of repression by dominant groups, "violence and stable institutions, instead of being opposites, become co-partners."[26] The study of southern violence as an outgrowth of group conflict naturally derives in part from theories of collective violence that have "emphasized the structural features of societies, particularly insofar as that structure is related to the distribution of power and its exercise."[27] This approach has been employed by historians investigating various types of group violence in the South.[28]

Vigilantism in Tampa was largely the product of a series of continuing power struggles over a sixty-year period. Collective violence emerged as a pervasive force in the 1880s, at the time that Tampa was undergoing transformation from an isolated, biracial village to an urban, ethnically diverse manufacturing center, and it thrived long after Tampa had grown into a large southern city. The level of violence actually peaked in the twentieth century, well into the process of urbanization. Institutional development, especially the expansion of the state and changes in the local economy, affected the course of vigilante violence, but the patterns of group conflict depended more on interpersonal power struggles than on the impersonal forces of modernization. However, group violence was only one form of collective action, and its use on a regular basis by members of the local elite suggests that violence found acceptance as a legitimate expression of community justice. The reasons for that lay deep in southern society, and the link between Tampa vigilantes and southern attitudes seems unmistakable. The city and its vigilantes were very much a part of the South—old and new.

The term "New South" is used here to distinguish the period after the Civil War from that preceding it. Despite its origins in the Old South, Tampa was largely a product of the New South. Institutions, values, and, in a few cases, particular individuals from the 1880s and 1890s dominated life in Tampa through the 1930s. Thus, the period from the 1880s through the 1930s forms a remarkably consistent whole, with the greatest changes occurring at the beginning and the end of the sixty-year span. The term "New South" accurately describes an era in Tampa which was characterized by a number of features, including pervasive violence, that the city had in common with other southern communities.[29]

The value of any community study depends in part on the representativeness of the locale. For a New South city, Tampa had some unusual characteristics, especially its high percentage of foreign-born residents, its reliance on skilled labor to manufacture expensive cigars, and, as a result, its relatively high wages. Nevertheless, Tampa had much in common with other boom towns of the New South. Its development into a manufacturing center was fueled by outside capitalists, many of whom remained absentee factory owners.[30] Commercial interests retained significant influence in the local elite, which was composed primarily of the larger merchants, bankers, and professionals, especially lawyers.[31] With the exception of some immigrant capitalists, Tampa's elite was also overwhelmingly composed of southern-born whites. The newcomers attracted to Tampa arrived primarily from other southern states. As was said of Atlanta in the 1880s, Tampa was a "Cracker city built by Crackers[,] . . . a city fashioned and controlled by 'native' men."[32] In addition to a class structure similar to that of other southern cities, Tampa had the same biracial caste system, despite the presence of many immigrants, including Afro-Cubans.[33] In short, Tampa's dominant institutions and values resembled in most cases those found in other southern cities between the 1880s and the 1940s.[34]

The chapters that follow are topically organized, but they progress in chronological order. Chapter 1 examines an 1882 lynching and the southern roots of establishment violence in Tampa. Chapter 2 covers the transformation of Tampa from a sleepy village into a cigar manufacturing center, where vigilante violence was first directed against workers during the years 1887–1892. Chapters 3 and 4 trace the continued use of establishment violence as a result of labor-management struggles in the cigar industry, principally during strikes in 1901 and 1910. The gradual decline of antilabor violence is examined in Chapter 5, which covers disputes in the cigar industry from 1918 through 1935. Chapter 6 focuses on Tampa's last vigilante incidents during the 1930s.

This work does not offer a complete history of Tampa from 1882 to 1936, or a full study of the city's ethnic, racial, and class relations in all their complexity. Instead, it uses "violence as a tracer of collective action."[35] Focusing on the flashpoints where conflicts among competing groups led to violence, it seeks to understand the process of interaction among various groups of people in Tampa and to explain why struggles over power resulted so frequently in violence. The ultimate purpose of the book is to expand our understanding of collective action in the New South.

Urban Vigilantes in the New South:
Tampa, 1882–1936

# 1
# The Southern Roots of Lynch Law

Vigilantism has aroused decidedly mixed feelings among Americans. While generally taking pride in being law-abiding citizens, Americans have, nevertheless, frequently taken the law into their own hands. Typifying this ambivalence, a leading Tampa citizen alternately denounced and endorsed lynch law over a century ago. In 1877, in the wake of a lynching in neighboring Polk County, the editor of Tampa's *Sunland Tribune* warned: "While the good people do all in their powers to suppress crime by bringing the guilty to justice, let them be careful not to allow their outraged sense of justice to induce them to violate the laws themselves by resorting to mob violence, known as Lynch law." Five years later, following a lynching in Tampa, the same newspaperman exclaimed that "in this and all similar instances we approve of Lynch law being executed in the most open and fearless manner."[1] Did these apparently contradictory statements indicate a change of mind or simple hypocrisy? Or was there some unexplained distinction that justified lynching in one case, but not in another?

Ambivalent attitudes toward vigilantism resulted in part from the fact that the practice raised a number of larger questions about the nature of law and society. For example, how did a community define crime? What constituted justice? How should law-breakers be punished? When, if ever, was the resort to extralegal or illegal methods justified? Communities continually grappled with such questions in theory and practice, but the moment of truth frequently came in the wake of a crime perceived as especially heinous. The public's reaction to an outrageous crime often forced a community to reflect on the nature of justice. In addition, the communal response could expose the actual workings of the law and the power that lay behind it.

Such an offense to local sensibilities occurred in Tampa in 1882, when a transient assaulted a prominent white woman. The attack was considered so unspeakable that newspapers printed only the barest details, and no Tampa paper divulged the victim's name. The crime occurred during the night of March 5, 1882, as a result of a break-in by Charles D. Owens, a white itinerant of about thirty. Owens had recently emigrated from England and worked at odd jobs around Tampa. After apparently stealing several small items from the home of John A. McKay, one of Tampa's leading businessmen, Owens attacked Ada McCarty, the twenty-six-year-old unmarried sister of Mrs. McKay.[2] News reports indicated that Owens committed "assault with intent to rape one of the most respectable young ladies of the community," but he was scared off "before consumating [sic] his hellish purpose." In making his hasty escape, the intruder left clues to his identity, including a knife found at the scene, which put Sheriff D. Isaac Craft and a posse on his trail the following morning. They soon caught the suspect, who was returned to Tampa at about one o'clock that afternoon and placed in jail to await trial.[3]

Despite initial attempts to conceal the nature of the crime, news of the "outrage" and the arrest of the "brute" spread quickly through the normally peaceful town of some one thousand people. It soon became clear that the expeditious action of the sheriff did not satisfy many Tampans, a number of whom began to gather immediately on a street near the jail. Within an hour the angry crowd grew to over one hundred people, and cries rang out to hang the prisoner. A group of about twenty men went to Sheriff Craft's home, where they reportedly took him by surprise and forced him to turn over the keys to the jail. The mob, growing larger by the minute, then marched on the jail, seized the prisoner Owens, and carried him to a large oak tree across the street from the courthouse. A rope was passed over a branch and a noose made while Owens' hands and feet were tied. The terrified man pleaded for mercy, begging for a trial. Turning a deaf ear, leaders of the mob placed the noose around Owens' neck and put him on a cart that was drawn up under the tree. When the cart was pulled out, the rope slipped, and the screaming victim fell harmlessly to the ground. Six men immediately grabbed the other end of the rope and pulled Owens up to his death. With its objective accomplished, the crowd slowly dispersed, but the dead body was left hanging directly in front of the courthouse until sunset.[4]

The sheriff's prompt arrest of the suspect and the presence of a jail and courthouse strongly suggest that the lynching of Charles Owens did not result from frontier conditions or the ineffectiveness of legal processes. Nevertheless, Tampa was a small community and still somewhat isolated in 1882. Located on south Florida's Gulf coast, the town had no rail connection to the outside world. From the north it could only be reached by stagecoach over rough trails or by steamer in an overnight trip from Cedar Key. Its rough physical appearance featured unpaved, sandy streets and unpainted, wooden buildings of at most two stories.[5] One contemporary visitor described Tampa as "quaint and old-fashioned in appearance."[6] In a more critical observation, writer Kirk Munroe called it "a sleepy, shabby Southern town."[7] Tampa had three small hotels, two saloons, and a number of merchants, but no bank. However, after several decades of actual decline in population, Tampa had begun to expand after the 1880 census had reported 720 residents.[8]

Despite its small size and somewhat primitive conditions, Tampa had advanced beyond the stage of a simple frontier town, particularly in its system of criminal justice. The circuit court for Florida's sixth judicial circuit, which had jurisdiction over capital crimes and all equity cases, served several counties on the state's west coast. Its chief officers were from Tampa, the county seat of Hillsborough County. When the lynching of Charles Owens occurred, the circuit court was scarcely overburdened with criminal cases in Hillsborough County. During all of 1881, the grand jury had handed down only one criminal indictment for the entire county of some 6,000 people.[9] "For several years past crime has been steadily on the decrease in the County," the grand jury reported.[10] Thus, the resort to lynch law in Tampa was not due to a crime wave or to the lack of constituted authorities. At the time of the lynching, the circuit court was meeting in Tampa, and it could have dealt promptly with the charges against Owens had local citizens so desired.

Contemporary observers had no difficulty explaining why it was necessary for Tampa citizens to take the law into their own hands. The tone was set by the editor of Tampa's *Sunland Tribune*, Dr. John Perry Wall, a forty-five-year-old practicing physician who was one of Tampa's leading citizens, editor of the weekly paper since its founding in 1876 and mayor from 1878 to 1880.[11] Wall claimed that it was not the absence of effective law enforcement machinery but rather the nature of the crime that dictated the resort to lynch law. "The public sentiment of this county may be relied on to protect the honor and defend the helplessness of the fairer sex from insult and outrage," Wall declared, explaining why "Lynch law may occasionally become a necessity."[12]

The defense of the lynching in terms of "honor" and the sanctity of "the fairer sex" reflected a commitment to a set of values that frequently led to violence. The code of conduct that governed southern communities before and after the Civil War required immediate, personal vindication of any violation of personal or family honor. This code often led to group violence. For example, white southerners frequently employed vigilante action to avenge the rape of white women, since the crime not only injured the victim but also stained the family's honor.[13] The paternalism of chivalry reduced white women to personal objects in need of the protection of white men.[14] Blacks were most often the victims of lynching for rape, but whites occasionally suffered the same fate. As a Louisiana attorney pointed out in 1906, the strongest unwritten law in the South effectively stated: *"Any man who commits rape upon a woman of chaste character shall, without trial or hearing of any kind, be instantly put to death by his captors or other body of respectable citizens."*[15]

Like other people ruled by an unwritten code of honor, southerners not only approved of resorting to violence to protect dominant values but also limited the role played by formal law. Distrust of the state and a preference for personal justice meant that southerners frequently employed extralegal, though not necessarily illegal, methods to enforce order. They believed strongly that community justice included both statutory law and lynch law. Indeed, southerners did not view vigilante violence as necessarily lawless. Whenever regular procedures seemed inappropriate or inadequate, local citizens employed lynch law, which was perceived as a legitimate extension of the formal legal system.[16]

Tampans certainly spoke and acted as if southern honor justified the lynching of Charles Owens. While refusing to identify the victim by name, the *Sunland Tribune* described her as "an accomplished and highly esteemed young lady of Tampa." She was, in fact, the daughter of Mitchell McCarty, one of the founders of Tampa. Owens, in contrast, was "a disreputable brute" and "a monster." He was given a further appearance of evil by news stories noting his remarkable resemblance to Charles J. Guiteau, the assassin who had killed President James A. Garfield the previous year.[17] In a newspaper editorial, John Wall declared that the honor of women precluded any reliance on the criminal justice system in cases of rape or attempted rape. "Let any man who thinks the lynching last Monday was wrong," Wall urged his readers, "contemplate his wife, sister or daughter in court reciting the filthy details of such an outrage in public under the gaze of a curious and to some extent indifferent public."[18]

A letter to the editor of the *Sunland Tribune*, signed "VOX POPULI," also stressed the inability of the courts to deal effectively with such crimes. "The people have every confidence that Judge [Henry L.] Mitchell, the State attorney and all the officers of the Court will do their whole duty in the future as they have ever done in the past," the writer declared; "what they do lack confidence in is the adequacy of the law, when enforced to its utmost extent to treat such cases as that of Owens." Claiming to speak for Tampans, the anonymous letter writer asserted the people's belief in a higher law based on the right to defend family and home. "Holding the protection of their loved ones and the sanctity of their homes to be above and beyond all law, they are determined to so deal with such outrages, that every wretch who may be capable of committing them shall feel and know that retribution, swift and terrible, hangs like the sword of Damocles, suspended over his head by a single hair."[19]

The defense of the Tampa lynching as both just and expeditious found support around the state. "The people of Tampa are an honorable and law-abiding people, and no man could be lynched there in the light of open day if he did not deserve it," asserted an editor in a neighboring county.[20] Due to the "heinousness" of the crime, the *Jacksonville Union* argued that the public would accept "the righteousness" of the punishment. "There are some crimes [so] dastardly and revolting as to fatigue public indignation," the paper observed, "and it is hardly surprising that in this instance the people of Tampa felt that the law's delay would be an unmerited luxury to the villain." In a more direct comment, the *Monticello Constitution* declared: "Served him right. Hurrah for the citizens of Tampa."[21]

These justifications, invoking higher law and righteousness, suggest that the lynching of Charles Owens was carefully planned and sanctioned by the community at large. In fact, news reports stressed that the hanging was well organized. In line with traditional republican values that in the South emphasized local collective action to enforce order, most citizens participated, and they followed certain procedures that gave the process an aura of legitimacy.[22] One witness related that "by the time the prisoner was safely behind bars, the people had about determined to take the law into their hands."[23] Before seizing Owens, the crowd also took a vote to decide whether or not to hang him. Once the group had reached its decision, only the sheriff and mayor protested. However, as the *Tribune* observed, Sheriff Craft was simply doing "his duty," and he "was as helpless as an infant in the presence of so large and determined a crowd of men led on by some of our most prominent citizens."[24] City officials took no subsequent action against any of the lynchers, and the circuit court completely ignored the lynching.[25] The local grand jury concluded its final report at the end of the month by congratulating the people of Hillsborough County on the "marked absence of crime in our midst."[26]

Tampa's resort to collective violence in defense of honor reflected the community's roots in the Old South. Founded as a trading center adjacent to Fort Brooke, a United States military post established near Tampa Bay in 1824, Tampa had prospered as a result of the settlement of south Florida by pioneers from neighboring states. As the last true frontier area east of the Mississippi River, south Florida attracted a wave of settlers in the 1840s after the temporary defeat of local Indians in the Second Seminole War. Lured by the federal government's offer of free land in return for taking up residence in the newly conquered region, southerners from north Florida and Georgia made up the bulk of the homesteaders. They brought with them their way of

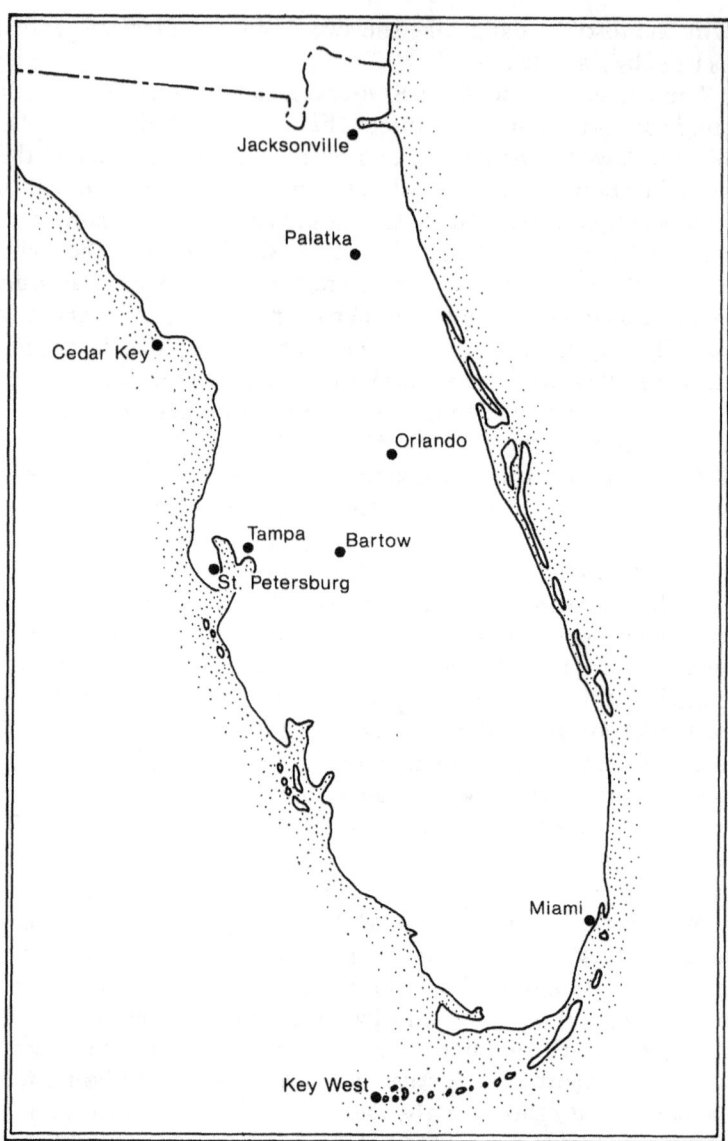

Florida peninsula

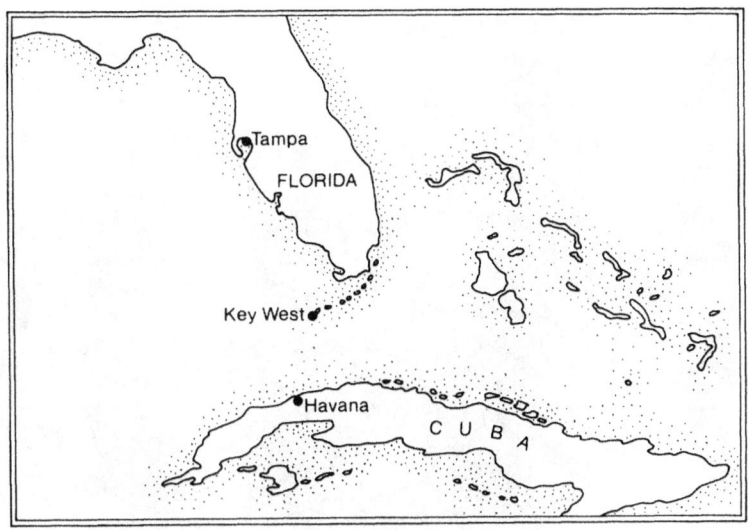

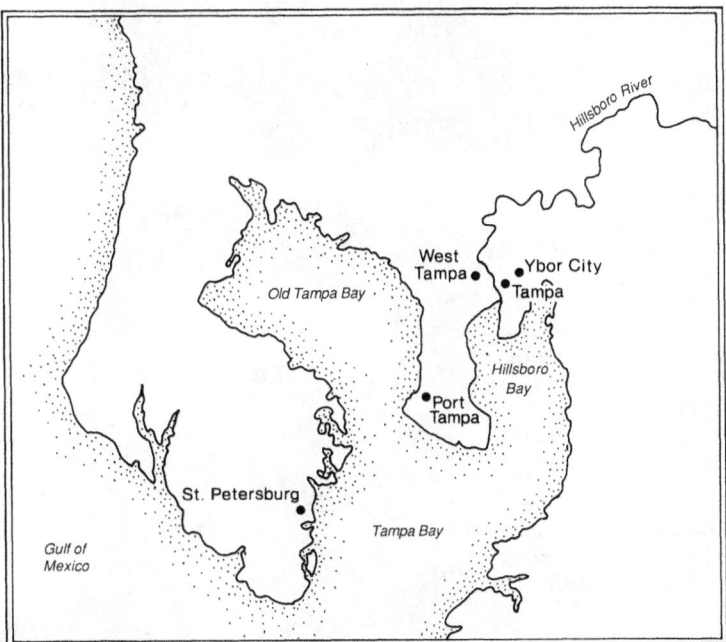

Florida and Cuba

Tampa Bay area, 1900

Tampa in 1880, viewed from the county courthouse. The oak tree in the foreground became known as "the hanging tree" after it was used for the lynching of Charles Owens in 1882. Tampa–Hillsborough County Public Library System.

Dr. John P. Wall, editor of the *Sunland Tribune* and a Tampa civic leader. University of South Florida Special Collections.

Tampa's Confederate war memorial was dedicated in 1911. University of South Florida Special Collections.

life, including slavery. A few even transplanted the plantation system, despite the inhospitable conditions. Several large sugar plantations with over eighty slaves each grew up along the Manatee River, thirty miles south of Tampa.[27]

It was cattle ranching that prevailed, however. The natural ground cover of various grasses and shrubs provided feed for cattle which could roam the open range. By 1850, Hillsborough already ranked fourth among Florida's twenty-eight counties in the number of cattle. Ten years later, Florida was second only to Texas among southern states in the per capita value of livestock, and Hillsborough topped all Florida counties in the number of cattle. At least 60 percent of Hillsborough County's farm operators in 1860 were ranchers producing a surplus for market, and the cattle industry dominated the area. Finding a market initially proved difficult. Some ranchers drove their herds as far as Savannah, over 300 miles away, but by the late 1850s, they had located a new outlet in Cuba. The Spanish colony could be reached by ships leaving from west coast ports, especially Tampa, which dominated the cattle trade and became the commercial hub of the region. With a population of 885 in 1860, Tampa was the second largest town in south Florida.[28]

Despite the general absence of a plantation economy, Hillsborough County was very much a part of the Old South. The county's population of 2,981 people in 1860 had originated largely in the southeast and included 564 slaves. As in the rest of the South, the vast majority of farm operators (73 percent) owned no slaves, and the typical slaveholder owned, on the average, fewer than five slaves. The county differed from the plantation South in that it contained only one slaveholder with more than twenty slaves. The cattle business did not rely on slave labor, but the typical cowman in Hillsborough County had at least one slave per household. Moreover, many of the county's richest and most powerful families, in and out of agriculture, held slaves in 1860. Captain James McKay, a Scottish immigrant and Tampa trader who had pioneered the export of cattle to Cuba, owned seven slaves. Many Tampa merchants and professionals also possessed small numbers of household slaves. Out of a total of sixteen city and county officeholders in 1860, nine owned slaves, and Tampa's mayor was the second largest slaveholder in the county.[29]

Further proof of Tampa's identification with the Old South came with the secession crisis. During the 1860 election campaign, Tampans were already threatening secession. The local Democratic party, headed by a committee of five, four of whom were slaveholders, resolved in March 1860, "That, as we believe the doctrines of the Black Republicans are intended to destroy our institutions and subject us to their will, the election of one of their members we would regard as open declaration of war upon the slaveowning States, which should be met by the South with an immediate severance of those ties that bind these States together."[30] After Florida did take this step and joined the Confederacy early in 1861, Tampans celebrated with "a day of rejoicing." All businesses closed, and citizens gathered at an overflow meeting, which showed "the beauty and chivalry of our section" and "stirred the heart of patriotism." The day's festivities ended "with three hearty cheers for Jefferson Davis and the Confederate States of America."[31]

Southern traditions and frontier conditions led to the use of vigilante methods by Tampans during the antebellum period. Incorporated as a city in 1855, Tampa had the ordinary framework of a municipality, including a town marshal, but it soon faced extraordinary pressures when the Third Seminole War erupted at the end of the year. Continuing until 1858, the last of Florida's Indian wars brought fighting to Tampa's doorstep. Along with it came criminals who plagued the town.[32] The editor of the *Florida Peninsular*, Tampa's weekly newspaper, recalled that "during the war and for a while after its close, there was but little security in our midst to peaceable citizens for life or limb. It is no reproach to our brave Volunteers, to say that . . . our City was infested with gamblers, No. 1 black legs, burglars, thieves, robbers, and cut throats."[33] As a result, Tampans formed vigilance committees, and local residents lynched several accused criminals. In 1858 the *Peninsular* reported that William Locke and a confederate had stolen two horses in Tampa and fled town. A group of citizens soon caught Locke and apparently lynched him.[34] The *Peninsular*'s editor noted cryptically, "On the way [to Tampa] the prisoner disappeared, and it is whispered, by knowing ones, will *never steal again!*"[35] Another group of vigilantes subsequently captured Locke's accomplice about sixty miles from Tampa. "The party brought him back some 50 miles, and *left him, like his comrade Locke, to steal no more!*"[36]

An anonymous letter writer justified this action by vigilantes, commonly called "regulators" in the antebellum period. Noting that some people "condemn all Regulators and their acts," he added that "some of our best Citizens have adopted this plan of ridding the State of an alarmingly increased number of murderers, gamblers, horse thieves, robbers, petty thieves, swindlers, and counterfeiters, and in spite of the declarations of some men, that the law is the best remedy, a large majority of our best citizens will not believe it." The community's elite accepted the necessity of vigilantism because of "the Law, and the manner in which it is administered." The problems were allegedly legal technicalities, combined with "dishonest Lawyers," who allowed the guilty to go unpunished. The remedy, this observer argued, was to simplify the laws, instruct judges "by law to keep justice at all times in view," and disbar lawyers who tried to clear anyone they knew to be guilty. "Let these changes be made, and you will not find a Regulating Company in Florida one year after the change."[37] Given this view of the role of statutory law, vigilantism was unlikely to disappear. Indeed, a formal "Vigilance Committee" continued to operate in Tampa during 1858.[38]

The supposed ineffectiveness of legal processes led to another outbreak of vigilante violence during the winter of 1859–60. In an interesting example of comparative justice, a slave and a white man were tried for separate murders. In an 1859 session of the circuit court in Tampa, the trial of the slave "Adam" for killing a white man took four days, whereas the trial of George Buckley for the murder of his father-in-law occupied but one day, since his guilt was "so patent." After juries found both men guilty, the judge sentenced them to be hanged on the same day.[39] When the appointed time arrived, Buckley was legally hanged, but the execution of the slave "Adam" was blocked by a state supreme court writ of error. Therefore, Tampa citizens took the law into their hands and lynched Adam on the day of his scheduled execution.[40]

In response to a Jacksonville editorial condemning this step, the *Florida Peninsular* defended the actions of local vigilantes. Reviewing the breakdown of law and order in the wake of the Third Seminole War, the editor of the *Peninsular* recalled: "One morning a man, a noted villain of the deepest die, was found swinging to a pine, by the neck. A few were whipped; others received orders to leave." As a result, in the opinion of this Tampan, "robberies ceased, gamblers fled, riotness [sic] disappeared, and we can now say, with pride and satisfaction, that there is not a town or county in the whole South, that can boast of a more peaceable, sober and law abiding people than the City of Tampa and the County of Hillsborough." Since any failure to punish criminals would have threatened this stability, Adam was hanged "after as fair and patient a trial as was ever witnessed in a court of justice." Distinguishing between "a mob" and "mature deliberation by the citizens," the Tampa editor concluded that "there ever will arise, in the best regulated state of society, circumstances calling forth the *ultima ratio populi*."[41] This view of vigilante justice, drawing on southern republicanism, clearly saw ultimate intervention by the local community as a reinforcement of the law rather than a subversion of it.

The Civil War temporarily turned Tampa into a virtual ghost town, but the small community survived largely intact. Even though located at the periphery of the South, Tampa could not avoid the war's impact. The town's port was blockaded, and the threat of invasion by federal troops led many residents to seek safety in the surrounding countryside. With the population dispersed and the economy disrupted, local government was suspended.[42] In 1878 a local newspaper observed that "the business men of Tampa found themselves at the close of the war bankrupt in everything save honor and integrity."[43] Census reports showed a town in decline. From a population of 885 in 1860, Tampa fell to 796 in 1870 and 720 in 1880.[44] Attempting to put the best face on local efforts to rebuild, a newspaper editor in 1878 noted "with pride the fact that Tampa owes less of her present prosperity to capital and men from the North since the war than any other place in the State."[45]

Tampa did not escape Reconstruction, but it did avoid the violence that swept much of the South, including north Florida. Reconstruction brought brief occupation of the town by federal troops, followed by the elevation of white and black Republicans to local offices. After restoring the city government in 1866, Tampa voters allowed it to lapse again in 1869, choosing to rely on county officials until 1873, when the town was again incorporated.[46] During the interim there were some complaints about crime. "We now have no Sheriff and are consequently at the mercy of the lawless, the rowdy and the drunkard," an 1871 editorial asserted.[47] This perception, however, was not reflected in the criminal justice system, even though Democrats had regained control of local courts by 1870. The circuit court grand jury concluded its mid-1871 term with a general condemnation of corruption among public office holders, but it declared, "Peace, harmony and good feeling prevail throughout the county."[48] Hillsborough County apparently never experienced any "outrage" that called for vigilante action during Reconstruction.

As a result, Tampa Democrats could decry radical Reconstruction and simultaneously counsel restraint by citizens. The *Florida Peninsular* called the Fourteenth and Fifteenth Amendments "frauds perpetrated upon the Southern people," but the paper asked rhetorically: "What's the use of fighting against a wrong that cannot be remedied?"[49] When vigilante violence broke out in neighboring counties in 1877, Tampa's Democratic newspaper appealed for law and order. "It is easy to talk of Lynch law," the *Sunland Tribune* observed after lynchings in nearby Hernando and Polk counties, "but very few really conscientious men can be found who approve it."[50] With Reconstruction having just ended and Democrats in control of the state government, the *Tribune* linked its crusade against vigilantism to economic development. "Let all good citizens uphold the supremacy of the laws and thus secure social order and stability," the *Tribune* argued. "This is the way to encourage immigration and promote the interests of the State."[51]

Despite changes wrought by the Civil War and Reconstruction, antebellum culture survived in Tampa. Customs associated with the Old South thrived in white society, especially among members of the local elite, who could afford to indulge their appetite for a traditional way of life after Reconstruction ended. Slavery had disappeared, but the culture built on unfree labor and the plantation system still held sway in the decades after the war. Indeed, the experience of Reconstruction may well have served to reinforce certain attitudes among upper-class Tampans.[52]

Classic southern romanticism was expressed in the staging of ring tournaments. Found throughout the South, this traditional festival gave leading Tampans and their counterparts elsewhere an opportunity to dress as medieval knights and test their skill as horsemen by trying to spear rings with their lances. Organized by the exclusive Knights of Hillsborough, the annual ring tournament gave the winner the honor of choosing the "Queen of Love and Beauty," who reigned over a ball which capped the festival.[53] After a lapse of several years, the tournament was revived in Tampa in 1877 to coincide with the inauguration of Florida's first Democratic governor since the war. The 1877 tournament gave "expression to the general rejoicing felt on this auspicious occasion of our deliverance from the rule of mal-administration and robbery by the carpet-bag and scalawag theives [sic]." The "First Maid of Honor" for that year's ring celebration was Ada McCarty, who five years later was the victim of the attack that led to the lynching of Charles Owens.[54] The Knights of Hillsborough continued to organize annual ring tournaments as late as 1887.[55]

Another popular ritual linked to honor and shame was the charivari, an ancient custom that persisted in the South. The charivari was a type of mob action that served a variety of purposes ranging from the punishment of deviant behavior to the ridiculing of unconventional marriages.[56] Tampa's Donald Brenhan McKay fondly remembered the charivari as a means "of greeting newly-weds whose marriage involved unusual features, such as the use of a shotgun as a persuader by a male member of the bride's family, unsavory reputation of either or both parties to the ceremony, great disparity in the ages of the bride and groom—and sometimes without any excuse."[57] This kind of charivari involved a group of men drawing attention to such a marriage by creating a deafening ruckus, with every imaginable noisemaking device, on the wedding night. McKay recalled participating in one such party, apparently in the 1880s, when Circuit Court Judge Henry L. Mitchell joined a crowd which gathered in front of a room occupied by newlyweds in Tampa's Orange Grove Hotel and "set up a din which could be heard a mile away."[58]

Another Tampa pastime associated with the Old South was gambling. Once again McKay remembered that during the 1870s and 1880s prominent Tampans frequently engaged in betting on horse races and cockfights. Although certainly not unique to antebellum southern society, medieval festivals, charivaris, and gambling were some of the customs that made the Old South distinctive.[59]

The continued strength of antebellum traditions in Tampa reflected the community's domination by native-born southerners during the postwar period. The 1880 census indicated that over 90 percent of Hillsborough County's population was born in the South. The origins of the 442 whites living in Tampa were somewhat more diverse than those of the county as a whole, but four out of five white Tampans were southern-born. The 10 percent of the town's white population from the North was slightly outnumbered by a heterogeneous mixture of foreign-born whites. The vast majority of Tampa's southern-born whites (78 percent) were Florida natives, with the remainder largely from the southeastern states of Georgia (7 percent), Alabama (5 percent), and South Carolina (5 percent).[60]

Although the dominance of southerners and their culture contributed to the lynching of Charles Owens, their view of honor and justice did not go unchallenged. The most vocal critic was James W. Locke, a transplanted northerner and federal judge. Born in Vermont in 1837, Locke had briefly practiced law in New Hampshire before entering the U.S. Navy as a paymaster in 1861. Stationed at Key West for much of the Civil War, he had remained there when mustered out of the service. Taking up the practice of law in Key West, Locke had become active in Republican politics and held the positions of county superintendent of education, clerk of the U.S. court, U.S. commissioner, county judge, and state senator. In 1872 he was appointed judge of the United States Court for the Southern District of Florida, and ten years later he took a stand against the lynching of Owens.[61] The resulting controversy revealed the depth of Tampa's commitment to certain southern values and the degree to which they conflicted with northern mores.

On the day of the hanging, Judge Locke was in Tampa to preside over a regularly scheduled session of federal court. Locke subsequently reported that when he had recessed his court for lunch at approximately one o'clock on March 6, 1882, he noticed a prisoner being brought to jail. Upon returning about an hour later, he found the dead body of the same man hanging from a tree in front of the courthouse. Later that afternoon, reliable witnesses informed Judge Locke that a leading Tampan, General Joseph Baisden Wall, had actively participated in the lynching. A resident of Tampa since 1872, Wall was a thirty-five-year-old practicing lawyer who had held the position of state attorney from 1874 to 1878. He had recently been promoted to the rank of brigadier general in the state militia and was commonly referred to by this title.[62]

As a federal court judge, James Locke had no jurisdiction over a lynching, but he found another means of disciplining General Wall. On Tuesday morning, March 7, the judge issued an order directing Wall to show cause within twenty-four hours why he should not be barred from practicing in federal court as a result of "his advising and encouraging" the lynch mob in which he had participated. General Wall immediately went into federal court, accompanied by his counsel, Stephen M. Sparkman, who as state attorney would be in charge of prosecuting any murder indictment resulting from the lynching. Wall and his attorney filed a motion for continuance of the federal show cause order until the local grand jury of the state court had met. Judge Locke took the motion under advisement.[63]

The following morning, March 8, General Wall and his attorney reappeared in federal court. They first withdrew their motion for a continuance and then directly challenged Judge Locke's show cause order. In a written statement Wall contended that the federal court had neither proof of his involvement in the lynching nor jurisdiction, since the alleged crime was not a federal offense. Judge Locke immediately overruled the challenge to his court's authority. To establish General Wall's role in the mob, Locke called to the witness stand United States Marshal Peter A. Williams, who testified to what he had seen on the day of the hanging.[64]

Marshal Williams depicted Joseph Wall as a ringleader. Williams had observed General Wall go into the sheriff's house with a group of unidentified men at about 2 p.m. When the group emerged from the house, the marshal had followed them to the jail, where he "saw Mr. Wall coming from the jail with the prisoner." Marshal Williams claimed that due to his excitement he did not notice who else was in the lynch mob, but he seemed certain about General Wall's prominent role. "When going from the jail to the tree, Mr. Wall, I think, had hold of the prisoner; he was beside him," Williams testified. At the time of the hanging, members of the mob had their backs to the marshal, and accordingly he did not see the faces of the people who actually pulled the rope stringing up Owens. "I did not see [Wall] afterwards until the hanging was over," Williams told the court; "then the crowd had increased, perhaps to 200 persons." Thus, the marshal placed Joseph Wall at the head of the mob just before the lynching and as part of the crowd immediately afterwards.[65]

General Wall turned down the opportunity to rebut this damaging testimony, declaring that he had nothing further to say. He chose to stand on his written response to the show cause order in which he denied "counseling, advising, encouraging or assisting an unlawful, tumultuous and riotous gathering or mob, in taking one John from the jail of Hillsborough County and causing his death by hanging, in contempt and defiance of the law." This denial, however, was seriously qualified because it was an unsworn statement.[66]

Judge Locke ended the hearing without calling any other witnesses. He later defended his action by stating that Sheriff Craft and Mayor George Bascom Sparkman, the only persons who had publicly protested the lynching, were out of town at the time of the federal court hearing. Furthermore, Judge Locke contended, "on account of the excited state of feeling existing at the time, the timidity of many, from the influential position of some of those engaged in the hanging, and the sympathy of others with the lynchers, it was not advisable to attempt to compel any resident of said City of Tampa who was found to have personal knowledge of the matter, to testify against said J. B. Wall."[67]

On March 10, two days after taking testimony, Judge Locke formally issued an order prohibiting Joseph Wall from practicing as an attorney before the federal courts of the Southern District of Florida. In a scathing indictment of lynching, Judge Locke declared: "Lynch law, stripped of all the sophistries with which it is surrounded by the ingenuity of its supporters, is, in its plain, naked self, not only a violation of the law, but an attack upon, and a flaunting insult to, its courts and officers." Whatever "possible excuse might be offered for mob or lynch law by a layman or ordinary citizen, there can be none for one in the position of an attorney," the judge argued. "Nothing, in my opinion, could seem more abhorrent to a lawyer, . . . than engaging in any such lawless outrage." Taking note of General Wall's denial that he had encouraged or advised the lynch mob, Judge Locke contended that due to Wall's "influence in this community [,] . . . his presence would be ample encouragement to others on such an occasion." On the question of the federal court's authority to discipline an attorney for misconduct in the absence of any formal criminal charges, Judge Locke rejected the view that his court was "helpless as against the local inactivity, neglect, or prejudice of the prosecuting officers or jurors of any one county." Given the "direct and positive" evidence of Wall's "participation in this act of lawless violence," Judge Locke disbarred him. This decision did not prevent Wall from continuing to practice in state and local courts, but he sought to reinstate himself in federal court by appealing Judge Locke's ruling.[68]

Joseph Wall had an outspoken defender in his brother John, the president of the city council, who wrote a series of blistering editorials in the *Sunland Tribune*. Reminding his readers that Judge Locke was "one of the thieving carpetbag crew who hied to this state at the conclusion of the civil war and was an active agent and participant in all infamies of the reconstruction era," John Wall declared that in "this whole [Wall] affair Judge Locke has managed to win the soubriquet of Judge Pecksniff, as well as the contempt of all good citizens of this community."⁶⁹ In less polite language, the editor dismissed Judge Locke as "an ignoramus" and a "Judicial imbecile."⁷⁰ Dr. Wall contended that "the U.S. Court for the Southern District of Florida, is at present nothing more nor less than a political engine working at full capacity." The *Tribune*'s editor claimed that Locke's action was part of a plan "to have numerous prominent Democrats in this and adjoining counties indicted on technical charges for the purpose of holding them over their heads to coerce them into the Republican ranks."⁷¹

Other Floridians also criticized Judge Locke. The publisher of the *Tribune*, Tampa businessman Thomas K. Spencer, contended that "if General Wall had promised to keep still in this county during the [1882] election, . . . the Judge would not have struck him from the roll." However, Spencer declared, "General Wall is too much of a Democrat to compromise with them, and hence had to go."⁷² Judge Locke's action aroused the ire of other Democratic papers in the state, such as the *Monticello Constitution*, which argued that the judge had "arbitrarily and illegally stricken Gen. J. B. Wall's name from the roll of attorneys in his court."⁷³ In defense of Judge Locke, a Republican paper, the *Tampa Guardian*, asserted that "*politics* had nothing to do whatever, in any shape or form, in the unfortunate affairs, which took place last week."⁷⁴

If political considerations figured in Locke's decision, they had little impact on Joseph Wall's public life. He did not lose his right to vote or run for office, and his popularity increased among Florida Democrats. Within weeks after his disbarment in federal court, Wall was widely touted as a possible Democratic candidate for Congress. Support for the idea came from several newspapers, including the *Bartow Informant*, which claimed that there could be no question about Wall's fitness for Congress. Wall did not become a candidate for any position in 1882, but he subsequently went on to hold a number of elective offices.⁷⁵

Judge Locke's denunciation of lynch law was primarily a result not of partisan politics but of an ethic that rejected honor as a code of conduct. Locke had grown up in the North, which by the mid–nineteenth century had developed a culture antagonistic to honor. Northerners had a strong sense of dignity which, according to one historian, encouraged them to look inward to their consciences as a guide for personal conduct, whereas devotion to honor led southerners to look outward to a communal standard of right and wrong. Reinforced by Puritanism and the development of capitalism, dignity was tempered in the North by an acceptance of written law as a means of assuring social order. In contrast, the southern concern with honor led to a regional preference for personal justice regardless of the law.[76]

This meant that Judge Locke and General Wall were lawyers with distinctly different conceptions of the law. Wall considered lynching a legitimate means of defending honor. Locke, in contrast, condemned lynch law as a criminal act and rejected any suggestion that honor could justify taking the law into one's own hands. Citing an unusual Tennessee case in which an attorney had been disbarred in 1829 for killing someone in a duel, Locke approvingly quoted the earlier decision's conclusion that such an act constituted "wicked and willful murder," rather than "an honorable homicide." This respect for written law led to Locke's conclusion that "the honor of this court and the [legal] profession" demanded the disbarment of General Wall for participating in the lynching.[77]

The sectional dimension of this conflict figured prominently in the reaction to comments apparently made by Judge Locke during the court hearing. John Wall reported that the Republican had associated the lynching of Charles Owens with "the *Rebel* spirit."[78] The *Key West Democrat* claimed that Judge Locke had "injured himself and outraged Southern people" by stating "that 'this act was the same spirit that fostered and encouraged the Rebellion,' or words to that effect."[79] No complete transcript of the court hearing survives, but in the process of disbarring General Wall, Judge Locke had clearly lectured Tampans about the illegality and immorality of lynch law. The *Sunland Tribune* complained that Locke had used the incident "to slander the people of Tampa, and assume the airs of great virtue and a superior civilization."[80] James T. Magbee, the Republican editor of the *Tampa Guardian*, stoked the sectional fires by condemning lynching as a "relic of barbarism" that was a peculiarly southern phenomenon.[81]

The *Sunland Tribune* tried to discredit this assertion by citing contemporary examples of lynchings in other parts of the country. The week following the Tampa hanging, the *Tribune*'s editor pointed to newspaper accounts of recent lynchings in Colorado and New Mexico, and he emphasized that "the crime charged in one case was of no higher grade than cattle stealing." After reprinting details of these mob actions, Dr. Wall asserted that "lynching is no uncommon thing in all new States and territories in the west, and as the population of these is derived principally from the older States of the North, it is somewhat ludicrous to see the carpet bag Radical from the same section putting on airs of a superior civilization and condemning the southern people for similar acts for much more grave and dastardly crimes."[82] This defense of vigilantism noted regional differences in the types of crime punished by lynch law, but it conveniently overlooked the fact that most southerners, unlike many westerners, had well-established criminal justice systems that could deal with lawbreakers. The question remained as to why lynch law persisted in the older states of the South.

As their actions and statements implied, the Walls and their leading supporters were products of the Old South. Joseph and John Wall were the sons of Perry G. Wall, a Georgia native, who had migrated to territorial Florida as a young pioneer in the 1820s. Staking out homesteads first in Hamilton County and then in nearby Hernando County, Perry Wall became a large landowner with seventeen slaves by 1850. He was also a prominent officeholder, serving successively as deputy marshal, clerk of the circuit court, and probate judge. After the Civil War, Wall relocated in Tampa, where he held the positions of probate judge and postmaster. Born in 1836, John P. Wall received a degree from the Medical College of South Carolina shortly before the outbreak of the Civil War, in which he served as a Confederate army surgeon, rising to the rank of major. After the war, Dr. Wall moved to Tampa, where he practiced medicine and became a leading citizen, serving a term as mayor and editing the *Sunland Tribune*.[83]

His half brother Joseph also volunteered for the Confederate army, though not until 1865, when he reached the age of eighteen. Following his military service, Joseph studied at the University of Virginia, receiving a law degree in 1869. After briefly practicing in Hernando County, he joined his father and brother in Tampa, entering a law partnership with Henry L. Mitchell. Joseph Wall soon built a profitable law practice that included clients such as the Jacksonville, Tampa and Key West Railway.[84]

The status of John and Joseph Wall was secured not only by their family background and professional degrees from leading southern institutions but also by marriages into local families of even higher social standing. Dr. Wall took as his second wife Matilda McKay, the daughter of one of Tampa's earliest and richest residents, Captain James McKay. After his first wife died in 1873, Joseph Wall also married into one of the area's wealthiest families, taking as his bride Frederica Lykes, whose brother, Howell T. Lykes, was one of Florida's "cattle kings."[85]

Joseph Wall's colleagues in Tampa's small legal fraternity had similar backgrounds. His first law partner, Henry Laurens Mitchell, was born in Alabama in 1831 but came to Hillsborough County with his parents as a teenager in the 1840s. After studying with a Tampa lawyer, Mitchell was admitted to the bar. In 1857 he was elected state attorney for the area encompassing most of south Florida.[86] Although neither he nor his father owned any slaves, Henry Mitchell was considered a champion of southern society. One supporter called him "a

Southerner in heart, soul, and body, and he glories in it, and when we need hard knocks instead of law phrases, he will be found ready, willing and able to do good service in the cause of the South."[87] Proof of his loyalty came in 1861, when he resigned his public office to volunteer for the army. Elected to the state legislature, Captain Mitchell returned to civilian life in 1864. With the end of Reconstruction, he was appointed judge of the circuit court for Florida's sixth judicial circuit. At that time, his former law partner, Joseph Wall, held the position of state attorney for the district.[88]

Wall was replaced in 1878 by Stephen M. Sparkman, who was born in Hernando County in 1849 and had studied law in the office of Henry Mitchell. Sparkman and Joseph Wall became partners in large land purchases. In addition, Wall regularly rode the circuit with his friends, Judge Mitchell and State Attorney Sparkman, and on the day Charles Owens was lynched, all three men were in Tampa for the opening of the regularly scheduled session of the circuit court for Hillsborough County.[89]

The common background and status of these men, combined with close personal and professional relationships, account for the lack of any criminal proceedings against General Wall for his participation in the lynching. These southerners had grown up on the Florida frontier, and all, except for Sparkman, who was too young, had demonstrated their firm commitment to southern cultural norms by volunteering to defend them during the Civil War. As lawyers, Confederate veterans, and public officeholders, these men became leading members of Tampa's small elite after the war. According to deep-seated southern traditions, the high status of these Tampans was reflected in the titles, such as "Judge" and "State Attorney," by which they were commonly addressed.[90]

Their status as guardians of traditions of justice was reinforced by military titles that carried even greater honor in the South. During the Civil War and Reconstruction, southern whites revered military officers and came to accept the right of such men to lead in civilian life as well.[91] In 1882, Joseph Wall proudly carried his militia title of "General," and his private counsel, State Attorney Sparkman, was frequently referred to as "Colonel," the rank he held in the Florida militia.[92] Southern honor and its continued influence among Tampans help explain not only why Charles Owens was lynched but also why the local community failed to take any action against leaders of the mob. In this case, as in many others throughout the South, lynch law represented the will of the community, which operated independently of statutory law.[93]

The strength of southern honor in the antebellum period was that it was sanctioned by local white communities and was rarely challenged by external forces. The Civil War and Reconstruction marked a turning point, as outsiders attempted to impose competing norms of behavior. Indeed, it was the war that brought James Locke to Florida and ultimately to Tampa, where he took his stand against lynch law. Representing an ethic that most Tampans probably did not understand, the Republican judge from New England took the only official action against any member of the lynch mob. If this outsider had not been present in Tampa on the day of the lynching, the entire incident undoubtedly would have generated little more than the initial newspaper reports, which simply recounted the actions of anonymous citizens and concluded that justice had been done.

Ironically, in the wake of Judge Locke's ruling that prohibited Wall from practicing in federal court, the general further undermined local autonomy by appealing the decision to the United States Supreme Court. General Wall's petition to the high court asked for a writ of *mandamus* directing Judge Locke to withdraw his order. The appeal explicitly did "not go into the question of Mr. Wall's guilt or innocence with respect to the charges for which he was disbarred." It simply argued that Judge Locke did not have the authority to disbar an attorney for an act that was under the jurisdiction of another court. Wall's petition went so far as to ask hypothetically, "Had he committed murder himself, instead of having mingled with the lynching party, far away from the presence of the court, will any lawyer say that such an act would have given the court jurisdiction to disbar him of his rights as an attorney?"[94]

In April 1883 the U.S. Supreme Court ruled on Wall's appeal. In a split decision the court upheld Judge Locke's jurisdiction. The country's highest tribunal also invoked northern standards to condemn the practice of lynching. Speaking for the majority, Justice Joseph P. Bradley, who came from New Jersey, where lynchings rarely occurred, referred to the charge against General Wall as "a very heinous offense."[95] Justice Bradley claimed that Judge Locke had understandably responded quickly, issuing a show order without first securing an affidavit stating the charge, because reliable information made Wall's participation in the lynching a "notorious" fact. The majority decision concluded that the initial court order against Wall, "though not strictly regular," did not violate any of his rights.[96]

In an extended discourse on the crime of lynching, Justice Bradley drew on a moral code that clearly conflicted with that of General Wall and his defenders. The Supreme Court justice called lynching "the prostration of all law and government; a defiance of the laws; a resort to the methods of those who recognize no law, no society, no government." Disposing of the usual defense of lynch law, Justice Bradley declared: "Whatever excuse may ever exist for the execution of lynch law in savage or sparsely settled districts, in order to oppose the ruffian elements which the ordinary administration of law is powerless to control, it certainly has no excuse in a community where the laws are duly and regularly administered." He emphasized that in this particular instance the resort to lynch law had occurred "with audacious effrontery, in the virtual presence of the court!" Warming to this subject, Justice Bradley argued that in Tampa "No respect for the dignity of the government as represented by its judicial department was even affected; the Judge of the court, in passing in and out of the place of justice, was insulted by the sight of the dangling corpse." This offense to his ethical sensibilities, which the Supreme Court justice apparently assumed were universal, led him to ask plaintively, "What sentiments ought such a spectacle to arouse in the breast of any upright judge, when informed that one of the officers of his own court was a leader in the perpetration of such an outrage?"[97]

On the question of the federal court's power to disbar a lawyer who was not first indicted or convicted of a crime, Justice Bradley cited a list of precedents that he contended upheld the lower court's authority. In "removing grossly improper persons from participation in the administration of the laws," the purpose was not to punish a lawyer but to preserve courts from persons unfit to practice.[98] The decision concluded that General Wall's act of misconduct, which "was as clear of all doubt as if [he] had expressly admitted his participation," justified his removal from federal court practice.[99] "Of all classes and professions, the lawyer is most sacredly bound to uphold the laws," the opinion declared. "He is their sworn servant; and for him, of all men in the world, to repudiate and override the laws, to trample them under foot and to ignore the very bands of society, argues recreancy to his position and office and sets a pernicious example to the insurbordinate and dangerous elements of the body politic."[100]

In a dissenting decision, Justice Stephen J. Field challenged both Judge Locke's authority and his procedure, but the jurist from California also denounced lynch law. Referring to "the lawless proceedings of the mob," he called the usurpation of law "the greatest of crimes, for which the actors should be held amenable to the violated laws of the State." Justice Field also dismissed the contention of General Wall's counsel that the resort to violence was somehow explained by the allegation that the lynch victim had attempted to rape a young woman.[101]

The rebuke by federal courts did not adversely affect General Wall's local reputation nor did it end his association with vigilantes. In 1886, he was elected to the state senate, and after reelection he served as senate president during the 1889 session. Meanwhile, he became the first president of the Florida State Bar Association in 1887. During the

1890s, he held a number of positions in the criminal justice system, including another appointment as state attorney before rising to become judge of the circuit court for Florida's sixth judicial circuit.[102] The *Tampa Morning Tribune* called Judge Wall "perhaps the best known lawyer in Florida" and "a gentleman highly esteemed by all."[103] Less well publicized, but certainly not unknown in Tampa at the time, was the fact that Wall had frequently participated in vigilante activities, which were locally perceived as legitimate extensions of the law. In both 1887 and 1892, he led formal vigilance committees that are examined in the next chapter.

Any lingering doubts about General Wall's role in the 1882 lynching were erased decades later by the reminiscences of an eyewitness. D. B. McKay, who subsequently became editor and publisher of the *Tampa Times* and a four-term mayor of Tampa, was thirteen years old in 1882. As he recalled:

> It wasn't until 1952 that I learned that Judge Joseph B. Wall was disbarred from practice in the federal courts, presumably on account of his participation in a lynching. . . . The victim, a white man, was seized from the sheriff who was taking him to jail, and hanged from a limb of an oak tree which stood in Lafayette street, directly in front of the court house. Circuit court was in session at the time. . . . He left the court room, joined the mob and tied the "hangman's knot," as no other man in the crowd knew how. I witnessed the lynching.

McKay failed to mention that it was an attack on his aunt in his home which led to the lynching. "The disbarment apparently did not become a matter of public knowledge," he noted, "as Judge Wall continued in practice and was elected to public offices subsequently." In fact, Joseph Wall's exclusion from federal court was highly publicized, but as D. B. McKay correctly remembered, "His standing in public esteem did not suffer."[104] General Wall's reputation was probably enhanced by his willingness to defend the community's standard of justice, which demanded swift retaliation against a deviant who dishonored a prominent white woman and her family.

Tampa's southern heritage, including the tradition of honor, remained a source of pride among leading white residents even after the turn of the century. Celebrations linked to the Confederacy provided an occasion to sing the praises of the Old South. When Confederate veterans gathered for one of their annual reunions, the *Tampa Tribune* declared that southerners would always remember these men as "brave, chivalrous and honorable."[105] In 1911, on the fiftieth anniversary of the birth of the Confederacy, 5,000 Tampans witnessed the unveiling of the city's monument to "those who fought and fell in the Lost

Cause."[106] Mayor D. B. McKay, the son of a Confederate soldier, called the monument a permanent "testimonial to our undying love for the cause that we of the South believe was right," and he claimed that southerners "feel great pride in the fact that we are of the same blood as the women and men who made glorious history under the Stars and Bars."[107] The featured speaker, a native Georgian who was state attorney for the district, recalled the ideals which the South had fought to defend: "The superiority of the moral to the material, the lofty sense of honor, the chivalrous courage, the knightly bearing toward woman, the refinement of the ancestral southern life . . . will, let us hope, characterize our lives as long as the world shall last."[108]

The continued commitment to honor was more than rhetorical, and it led to personal violence. As one observer stressed, the readiness of southerners to resort to deadly weapons was "not the result of individual depravity, but is the logical sequence of circumstances and social relations which for generations have been active factors, and of which the present generation feels the effect." This ethic meant that "no man can live respected in a Southern community and be a coward."[109] Aggrieved individuals did not hesitate to shoot offending parties with little or no warning. Community standards made it "an impossibility to hang a man of good family in the South for killing another man."[110] As a Jacksonville newspaper pointed out in the 1880s, "the verdict of Florida juries has been almost uniformly that murder is no crime when committed by respectable men; and a feeling has grown up that it is a good deal safer to kill a man than to steal a pig."[111]

Tampa shootings resulting from affairs of honor went unpunished, but they were usually not fatal. In 1886 a local businessman opened fire on a traveling salesman who had reportedly been "on too intimate terms" with the Tampan's wife. Although the offended party emptied his gun and the surprised salesman got off several shots, neither was hurt, and no arrests apparently resulted. The following year, a Tampa man was acquitted for shooting another in the leg during a fight resulting from "a misunderstanding."[112]

These incidents attest not only to the use of violence to settle disputes but also to the common presence of firearms. "Florida is one of the states whose laws prohibit the carrying of concealed weapons, but the practice is, nevertheless, quite as common here as in states where no such prohibition exists," the *Tampa Tribune* observed in 1895. The newspaper's editor added that the practice was "not likely to be broken up until men learn[ed] to rely upon the laws for which they are taxed, instead of looking to themselves and their weapons for safety."[113] Guns did not cause the violence, but they certainly made physical injury more likely in a society highly sensitive to personal slights. "If the habit of carrying deadly weapons could be suppressed in the southern states," one observer claimed, "it would diminish the number of homicides very largely."[114]

Another source of violence was racism, which was reinforced by Tampa's southern heritage. After the Civil War and the abolition of slavery, white Floridians looked "to the ruling class to see that those whom God has made their inferiors, shall not suffer from the misfortune."[115] The expectation that whites would continue to reign supreme over legally inferior blacks was, of course, upset by Radical Reconstruction. Indeed, under Republican rule, Tampa had several black officeholders, including a congressman. This redistribution of power sparked some complaint but no violence; the town's temporarily displaced leaders counseled forbearance while ridiculing blacks, so-called "XVth Amendments."[116] Whites, who made up 78 percent of Tampa's population of 800 in 1870, apparently did not suffer enough to resort to mob violence against blacks.[117] As soon as Republican rule ended in 1877, John Wall emphasized in an editorial that "the colored population of South Florida is in a small minority compared with whites," and moreover, "our colored people are, upon the whole, remarkably intelligent and honest, and possess but few of the lazy vagabond class."[118]

The paternalism implicit in this defense of local blacks dominated white attitudes during the years after 1877. With conservative white Democrats again in control of Florida politics, Tampa's traditional elite faced no threat from the town's black community, which was small and stable. Confined to an area at the edge of Tampa known as "the Scrub," blacks held a number of skilled jobs, operated several businesses and maintained a variety of social institutions, including churches and fraternal organizations.[119] "The colored population . . . number[s] about one-thousand, a majority of whom are industrious, thrifty and progressive," the *Tampa Journal* declared in an 1887 issue promoting the city. "Many of them own their own homes. Some are mechanics, others merchants. They have churches, schools and several literary societies, and withal are respectable, orderly and peaceable."[120] This positive view of blacks was seriously qualified during election campaigns, when white Democrats used racism to rally the party faithful. "A bloody shirt, a nigger and a high protective tariff constitutes the Republican party," a Tampa editor exclaimed in 1888.[121]

Leading Tampans stressed that blacks could progress only by looking to the traditional white establishment. "As a true native born Southron [sic] we believe that our judgment of colored people is just and fair and tempered by a sympathy that only the native of the South can feel," another local editor observed. "Take the colored man away from evil influences and he is a trusty and sympathetic friend and his zeal and impulsiveness will be toward the right. Subject him to the evil and his plastic nature carries him far in the opposite direction."

**Population of Tampa, 1880–1930**

| | Distribution (percent) | | | |
|---|---|---|---|---|
| | Native-born white | Foreign-born white | Black[a] | Total population |
| 1880 | 55 | 7 | 38 | 720 |
| 1890 | 45 | 26 | 29 | 5,532 |
| 1900 | 44 | 28 | 28 | 15,839 |
| 1910 | 50 | 26 | 24 | 37,782 |
| 1920 | 57 | 21 | 22 | 51,608 |
| 1930 | 65 | 14 | 21 | 101,161 |

Source: Tenth Census of the United States, 1880, Population Schedules, National Archives Microfilm Series T-9, roll 128; U.S. Census Office, Eleventh Census, 1890: Population of the U.S., Pt. 1 (Washington, D.C., 1895), 454; U.S. Census Office, Twelfth Census of the United States: 1900, Population, Pt. 1 (Washington, D.C., 1901), 612; U.S. Census Office, Thirteenth Census of the United States: 1910, Population, 2 (Washington, D.C., 1913), 330; U.S. Bureau of the Census, Fourteenth Census of the United States: 1920, Population, 3 (Washington, D.C., 1922), 195; U.S. Bureau of the Census, Fifteenth Census of the United States: 1930, Population, 4 (Washington, D.C., 1933), 421.

[a]"Black" includes both native-born and foreign-born.

As a result, this Tampan concluded, "They will yet learn that the Southern people are their best friends."[122]

Tampa's spectacular growth after 1885 was based largely on foreign-born immigrants, but the city's black population also increased significantly.[123] The number of black residents more than doubled in the 1890s and again in the first decade of the twentieth century. However, Tampa's total population expanded so rapidly that the city's proportion of blacks steadily declined from 29 percent in 1890 to 21 percent in 1930.[124]

The arrival of new black residents excited fears among local whites, who saw black men in particular as a social threat rather than an economic necessity. At the turn of the century, the *Tribune* complained that "Tampa is now infested with a large and increasing number of lazy Negroes, who prefer to stand about and pick up a living by their wits, rather than go to work."[125]

Like other southern communities, Tampa relied on a variety of legal mechanisms to control its black population. In the wake of Reconstruction, Florida had largely disfranchised and strictly segregated blacks. Beginning with the new 1885 state constitution, the state effectively barred most blacks from voting, through the imposition of the poll tax and the use of the white primary. Removed from the political arena, blacks were also rigidly segregated through a system of state codes which put existing social practices into law.[126]

Leading Tampans not only enforced the discriminatory laws, they also publicly expressed the racism that justified white supremacy. "The negro is not yet in condition to come in competition with the whites in society, schools or churches, and if forced to do so would be left far behind," the *Tampa Tribune* asserted in 1892.[127] This seemingly benign attitude concealed more virulent racism that frequently surfaced in the reporting of black crime. During a ten-day period in 1895, for example, a Tampa newspaper described a series of blacks accused of various crimes as a "wild-eyed Ethiopian," a "Hottentot beauty," a "dusky sneak-thief," and a "young coon."[128] One news summary of municipal court proceedings contended that "the most important cases were those drawn from the inexhaustible reservoir of the 'Scrub.'"[129]

As the city's black population swelled during the 1890s, white Tampans increasingly distinguished between good and bad Negroes, who could expect different treatment according to their behavior. "The negro who does his duty as a citizen, who obeys the laws of his country, who recognizes that there is a line of demarcation between the races which cannot be obliterated by all the laws that could be enacted, need have no fear of the white man," the *Tampa Tribune* lectured in 1899. "Such negroes will, on the contrary, have the help of the whites." However, the paper warned, "The negro who fails to realize his duty as a citizen and who commits a serious breach of the law, may expect to be punished."[130]

As in other southern communities, the rape of a white woman by a black man was perceived as the greatest threat to established values. "The South does not make a pretext of its white women's honor," the *Tampa Tribune* exclaimed in 1921. "The South protects its white women's honor; and the black brute that lays a finger on her body will continue to burn at the stake. . . . White supremacy will be maintained in the South; the honor of its white women will be maintained by the South."[131] This paternalistic view made lynching for rape a weapon of racial and sexual terror, designed to keep both black men and white women in their respective places.[132] However, the urge to use mob violence was increasingly counterbalanced by the fear among Tampa leaders that lynch law would spoil the city's reputation, which local promoters considered crucial to attracting new businesses.

After the turn of the century, spokesmen for the Tampa elite frequently counseled caution when they feared that an unthinking mob might resort to lynch law. For example, when a white man was charged with raping a young white girl in 1901, the *Tampa Tribune* tried to calm outraged citizens by successfully calling for a special session of the circuit court "in order that there might be no outbreak of mob violence to sully the fair name of Tampa."[133] While commending "the forbearance of the citizens of Tampa," an editor in a neighboring town suggested that had the accused "been a negro he would unquestionably have been lynched—not improbably burned—many people seeming to think a white brute entitled to more consideration than a black brute."[134]

Several months later, however, Tampans avoided lynch law when a white woman revealed that she had been attacked by a black man. The attempted rape was foiled, and the accused man quickly identified. Swift legal proceedings, combined with noninflammatory newspaper reporting, helped prevent mob violence.[135] In the wake of these two incidents, the *Tribune* echoed a common refrain when it observed: "Let the courts always be as prompt as they have been in these cases, and the people will leave to them the vindication of outraged law."[136]

In 1903, Tampa had its first lynching in twenty years when the law failed to punish a black man accused of an attack on a white child. The offense occurred on Egmont Key, an island in Tampa Bay that housed a federal military post. On December 1, 1903, a black civilian employee of the army base, Lewis Jackson, was brought to the county jail in Tampa after "the commission of an unmentionable act" on a three-year-old girl. Whatever the exact nature of the act, it was apparently not rape, because the county judge immediately ruled that the state had no statute covering the unspecified crime, which the *Tribune* described vaguely as "a peculiar one, without parallel in this part of the country and . . . [of] unprecedented brutality and obscenity." After relating this, the newspaper demanded, "WHAT WILL BE DONE?" As if to answer its own question, the *Tribune* reported talk of "another Houston party," in reference to George Houston, a black who had been castrated, but not killed, by anonymous Tampa vigilantes five months earlier after he had been seen embracing a fourteen-year-old white girl.[137]

When Jackson was released from jail because of the alleged absence of a law covering the offense, he was seized by a well-organized gang of fifty men. The vigilantes had been waiting at the edge of Tampa during the evening of December 4. "The spokesman of the mob informed [Jackson] that he was to become an example for all others of his race," the *Tribune* reported. In the absence of any spectators, the vigilantes "first Houstonized and then lynched" Jackson, who was discovered hanging from a tree by a passerby at about eleven o'clock that evening. A large crowd quickly gathered to view the body, which was left suspended until the next morning.[138]

The lynching of Lewis Jackson followed the pattern of ritualized murder that was becoming all too familiar in the South. Although the rape of a white woman by a black man was the alleged offense in only about one-third of all lynchings between 1881 and 1903, the myth of the black beast rapist was widespread in the South at the turn of the century. Moreover, the mob killing of blacks for a variety of offenses increasingly involved torture and mutilation, such as the castration of Jackson.[139] In taking this step, Tampans did not act in haste. The so-called mob was in fact a group of about fifty men that had been organized for two days, awaiting the outcome of official inquiries. In the absence of any indictment, the *Tampa Tribune* announced that punishment had been meted out by "the organization which had been effected for the purpose."[140] The objective was not only to punish Jackson but also to provide a lesson for the city's black community. Reports of the lynching noted approvingly that "practically the entire colored population of Tampa" had viewed Jackson's "lifeless body," which served as "the silent reminder of the power and effectiveness of the mob."[141]

The careful planning and the *Tribune*'s thorough knowledge of the vigilante operation suggest that the lynchers were known and that they included members of the local elite. Nevertheless, the coroner's jury quickly ruled that Jackson had met his death "at the hands of persons unknown." The *Tribune* correctly called this the "usual verdict . . . on lynching."[142] As another Tampan had pointed out a decade earlier in the wake of the lynching of eleven Italian immigrants in New Orleans, citizens did "not propose to kill a man and then hang themselves for it."[143]

A product of the Old South, Tampa's elite shared the cultural values associated with the plantation economy. Prominent among these mores was the concept of honor, which sanctioned community justice—including lynch law—to defend family purity, self-esteem, property, and white supremacy. These norms survived the Civil War and Reconstruction and contributed to lynchings in 1882 and 1903. Organized and defended by members of the local elite, lynch law enjoyed widespread support among white southerners who viewed extralegal punishment as a legitimate means of preserving order in a republican society. Between 1882 and 1903, Tampa underwent an economic and social transformation that turned the town into a burgeoning city. Instead of undermining lynch law, the resulting changes reinforced the tendency to rely on establishment violence to assure the continued dominance of the local elite and its traditional values.

# 2
# The Origins of Antilabor Vigilantism

By 1900 the list of offenses punishable by Tampa vigilantes had lengthened considerably as a result of economic and social changes. Beginning in the mid-1880s, the arrival of outside capital and foreign immigrants quickly transformed Tampa into a multicultural, urban manufacturing center. Based on the transplanted Cuban cigar industry, Tampa's growth was explosive not only in the pace of economic change but also in the social tensions that resulted. Immigrant capitalists relocated near Tampa in an attempt to create an environment where they could control rebellious cigarworkers. The immigrant craftsmen who came to Tampa brought with them both their cigarmaking skills and their traditions of labor militancy, which found expression in radical ideologies and trade unionism. Moreover, cigarworkers were overwhelmingly devoted to the cause of *Cuba Libre*.

In Tampa they had to contend not only with factory owners but also with local power brokers, who soon found the cigar industry a mixed blessing. Although the rapid expansion of cigar manufacturing increased the power and wealth of Tampa's leading businessmen and professionals, it created also conditions which threatened the hegemony of the ruling elite. Members of Tampa's establishment could accept and even endorse Cuban nationalism, but they recoiled at the workers' radicalism, which threatened the local economy, especially during periodic strikes. To counter the legal activities of cigarworkers, prominent Tampans relied on their vigilante tradition to protect their interests, which they identified with those of cigar factory owners.

During the 1880s, Tampa experienced an economic boom that was fostered by a combination of improved transportation, local promotion, new capital investment, immigration, and good luck. As in other parts of the country, a revolution in transportation provided the spark for Tampa's rapid development. Almost exclusive reliance on water transport for commerce ended in 1883 with the arrival of Henry B. Plant's South Florida Railroad, ultimately connecting Tampa with Jacksonville and cities to the north. "The advent of this railroad awoke the slumbering populace," a Tampa newspaper observed.¹ By 1886, Tampa had 2,376 residents, a total more than double the city's population only four years earlier. The local elite, composed largely of southern-born merchants and professionals, took immediate steps to exploit the opportunities provided by the initial boom. In May 1885, sixty-seven businessmen and professionals organized the Tampa Board of Trade to coordinate promotional efforts.²

Outside forces soon created an unexpected chance to lure Cuba's displaced cigar industry to Tampa. Several cigar manufacturers had first left Cuba during the 1860s, when their industry was disrupted by international trade restrictions and the Ten Years' War for Cuban independence. Immigrant capitalists were attracted to the United States by tariff laws which placed high duties on finished cigars but not on tobacco leaf. Seeking unrestricted access to the North American market, cigar manufacturers first found a haven in Key West, Florida, which had the right climate and proximity to Cuban tobacco and workers. However, the spread of unions and a wave of strikes in the 1880s, including a crippling month-long walkout in August 1885, prompted several Key West manufacturers to relocate their operations.³

Vicente Martínez Ybor and Ignacio Haya, two Spanish-born capitalists with factories in Key West, picked Tampa as the site for new plants. They were attracted by the town's port and rail facilities and the promise of cash subsidies and labor peace. In October 1885, the Tampa Board of Trade agreed to raise $4,000 to subsidize Martínez Ybor's purchase of a $9,000 tract of barren land just outside Tampa's city limit. Soon thereafter, Ignacio Haya bought adjacent property to construct a cigar factory for the New York-based firm of Sánchez & Haya.⁴

These Spanish entrepreneurs quickly built a new community, known as Ybor City, which had the essential characteristics of a company town. Perhaps influenced by similar endeavors, especially the celebrated model community built outside Chicago by George Pullman in the early 1880s, Martínez Ybor and Haya created development companies that soon had title to an area big enough for a small unincorporated city. Within a year after Martínez Ybor's initial purchase, his Ybor City Land and Development Company had accumulated over 100 acres in the heart of Ybor City, as well as a nearby tract of 1,000 acres. Meanwhile, the cigar firms of V. M. Ybor & Company and Sánchez & Haya had built two wooden factories, where the production of cigars had begun by May 1886. They also constructed houses to attract cigarworkers. The new dwellings could be purchased with interest-free installment payments and were considered superior to housing available in Key West and Havana. Martínez Ybor's development company also financed a number of community services, such as police and fire protection and a street railway which connected Ybor City with Tampa. As in other company towns, all of these "public" services were owned and operated by the community's leading employer, Vicente Martínez Ybor, who had invested over $300,000 in buildings and improvements by early 1888.[5] Ybor City lacked some of the more oppressive features of other company towns, such as company stores that charged inflated prices and deducted the cost of purchases from employees' paychecks. Nevertheless, it fit the pattern of communities built and largely owned by companies whose primary purpose was "to attract, hold and control labor." As one authority on employer-dominated communities subsequently noted, "it is the question of control which overshadows all other problems in the company town."[6]

The attempt of factory owners to control cigarworkers through the creation of a company town was part of a continuing struggle between capital and labor that was rooted in the production process. The manufacture of expensive handmade cigars in Ybor City was done by the so-called "Spanish hand process," which thrived in Havana and Key West and depended on "clear Havana" tobacco grown in Cuba.[7] Like other preindustrial craftsmen, cigarmakers learned their trade as apprentices over a period of several years. A Cuban cigarmaker who came to Ybor City in 1888 later recalled: "At 14 my father placed me in a cigar factory in Havana in order to learn the trade of cigarmaker. . . . Shortly after I had completely mastered the cigar trade, my uncle, Gonzalo Perez Guzman, brought me to Tampa with him. . . . I was 18 years of age."[8] Sitting side-by-side at long tables, referred to as benches, cigarmakers needed only a hardwood board and a curved knife to roll high-priced, clear Havana cigars by "the feel of the hand." The completed cigars were taken to departments in the factory, where they were sorted and boxed by other skilled workers who also viewed their "work as an art." "Pickers" put cigars of the same size and color together, and "packers" placed them in boxes.[9]

Cigarworkers exercised enormous control over the workplace, as a result of both the nature of the labor process and the traditions surrounding the Cuban handicraft. Wage rates for cigarmakers were determined by a system of piecework, according to which a specified "price" was paid for each one thousand cigars. Piecework could be used to exploit machine workers by forcing them to speed up their production, but it gave better paid cigarmakers the opportunity to set the pace of their handwork and to determine their hours. Individual workers arrived and departed when they chose. Custom dictated that coffee be served at the benches and that workers be permitted the unrestricted smoking of the company's cigars while in the factory. Moreover, at the end of the day, each male worker received three free cigars, which he could smoke or sell for added income.[10] By tradition, management also exercised little supervision over cigarmakers. As late as 1939, a study of Tampa's cigar industry emphasized that "the foreman is prohibited by custom from making but one inspection trip each day through the plant."[11]

The institution that best reflected the work habits and sentiments of Latin cigarworkers was the *lectura*, or system of reading in the factories. Paid by the cigarmakers to read while they performed their silent handwork, the reader (*lector*) sat on an elevated platform and read material chosen by the workers, who voted for what they wanted to hear. As one of Tampa's last readers recalled, "The *lectura* was itself a veritable system of education dealing with a variety of subjects, including politics, labor, literature, and international relations." In response to the expressed desire of cigarworkers, the *lectores* developed a routine. "We had four daily shifts. One was used to read national news stories. Another was devoted to international political developments. The third concerned itself entirely with news from the proletariat press. And, lastly, the novel." Significantly, as this reader emphasized, "almost all the novels involved serious themes, usually labor-related subjects."[12] Whatever their source, the readers' texts featured heavy doses of radical thought. Confirmation of the educational value of the institution came in the twentieth century from a leading anarchist who was a cigarmaker by the age of fourteen. "Oh, I cannot tell you how important [readers] were, how much they taught us. Especially an illiterate boy like me. To them we owe particularly our sense of the class struggle."[13] Vicente Martínez Ybor tried to insulate cigarworkers from outside influences by creating a company town, but his employees had hired a reader, José Delores Poyo, by December 1886. Poyo, a leading Cuban patriot, also published Ybor City's first Spanish-language newspaper, which was directed at cigarworkers.[14]

The control exercised by Cuban cigarmakers could be found in other factories relying on preindustrial craftsmanship. In the late nineteenth century, industrial capitalism was initially built through an expansion of preindustrial methods of production. This permitted experienced skilled workers to maintain greater control over the workplace than many economists have assumed. Preindustrial craft traditions provided skilled workers with a variety of means for resisting the subordination that early factory owners sought to impose. Methods of resistance included efforts to control the supply of labor and piece rates, the use of informal bargaining, and the defense of restrictive work practices. All of these techniques were utilized by Tampa's cigarmakers in the absence of formal union recognition during the late nineteenth and early twentieth centuries. The conflict between workers who wanted to preserve their control and employers who sought to reduce it resulted in a constant and dynamic power struggle over who exercised what authority in the workplace.[15]

Cigarworkers were clearly aware of their traditional rights and fought for generations to retain them. *El Internacional*, the official voice of local unions, boasted in 1921 that Tampa cigarworkers were guilty of "the terrible crime of being consciously workers who are always trying to defend their rights and never submit to the false cajolery of the cigar manufacturers."[16] A 1939 study commissioned by the Tampa Chamber of Commerce found that Latin cigarworkers "oppose[d] measures which are a part of the standard discipline in American plants." This report asserted that the "force of custom is the most powerful force in the Tampa industry." Once work-related practices "took on the status of customs, . . . nothing short of a revolution could change them." As a result, the study concluded that "hand cigar plants in Tampa appear to be operated in the same manner as they were twenty, thirty or fifty years ago."[17] Cigarworkers had in fact lost some rights and control in the fifty years after 1886, but labor-management conflicts during the period focused largely on issues related to authority in the workplace.

Ybor City was initially heralded as a workers' paradise developed by farsighted capitalists. In the months following production of the first cigars during the spring of 1886, Tampa newspapers issued glowing reports.[18] The editor of the *Tampa Guardian* claimed that the builders of Ybor City were "actuated not only by a desire to acquire wealth for their own coffery, but are inspired with the worthy disposition to render those around them comfortable and happy. If all capitalists would exhibit the same thoughtful and worthy consideration for the condition and prosperity of their employees, there would be less discord between capital and labor." The *Tampa Journal* also praised the developers of Ybor City for instituting practices "by which the usual conflict and clash between labor and capital can be happily avoided." Moreover, as this newspaper pointed out in December 1886, Tampa was "directly enjoying the benefits of the great capital and enterprise that is being expended [in Ybor City]. It is this enterprise that has contributed largely in keeping 'dull times' away from Tampa during the past year."[19]

The hope that Tampa's budding cigar industry could avoid labor-capital conflicts quickly evaporated. In a pattern that would repeat itself, workers organized competing unions that divided along both ethnic and ideological lines. Soon after production began in Ybor City, some Cuban and Spanish cigarworkers joined a mixed local of the Knights of Labor, the American union which had previously organized cigarworkers in Key West.[20] In December 1886, other Cubans in

Ybor City formed a branch of the Cuban Federation of Cigar Makers ("La Federación Cubana de Tabaqueros"), which was based in the émigré community in New York City. A local spokesman for the Knights contended that the Cuban Federation was "a political organization" which had "for its object the instillation of hatred in the Cuban mind against everything Spanish." This charge was undoubtedly due to the mounting anti-Spanish sentiment among Cuban nationalists, who sought to free their homeland from Spanish rule.[21]

The president of the Cuban Federation of Ybor City countered that his members believed that "all men are brothers, . . . and we do not repel, therefore, any nationality, race or color, though we uphold our right to keep alive the just and well known feeling towards our native country." He further asserted that the federation was "a trade union," whose members "struggle against 'bossism' as well as against the monopolies of the wealthy class of the world." The Cuban union leader concluded: "The only division that exists is a very natural one. The Spaniards who have controlled the cigar-making trade at New York, and several other cities, want to control it here, and we the Cuban cigarmakers of Ybor & Co., are determined not to let them control a trade that has been created and enlarged by us in this country." This focus on the issue of control and the linkage of national and international struggles in radical terms could scarcely have reassured either Spanish factory owners or their allies among Tampa's elite.[22]

Ethnic conflicts in Ybor City precipitated a strike and an outburst of violence early in 1887. With a small number of Spanish cigarmakers under increasing pressure from the predominantly Cuban work force, members of the Knights of Labor walked out of Martínez Ybor's factory in January 1887, demanding that the firm fire the Cuban foreman, Santos Benítez, because he had supposedly discharged a Spanish worker for no reason except his nationality. Eduardo Manrara, a Cuban who was Martínez Ybor's business partner and the factory's manager, agreed that the dismissal was without cause, but he refused to move against Benítez unless it could be shown that the majority of workers opposed his continuation as foreman. When representatives of Martínez Ybor's 450 workers attempted to compromise their differences at an evening meeting on January 20, shots were fired into the group. Four men, apparently all Knights or their supporters, were wounded, one fatally. On the basis of the mortally injured victim's dying declaration, two Cubans were immediately arrested and bound over for trial.[23]

The week after the shooting, the striking Knights returned to the Martínez Ybor factory, and several days later management fired Benítez. This in turn led to another strike as the firm's Cuban workers walked out, refusing to return until the popular foreman was reinstated. The voluntary departure of Benítez from the city quickly ended this strike, and the first crisis in Tampa's new cigar industry appeared over. A local newspaper reported on February 9 that "peace, quiet and work has been fully resumed at Ybor City."[24]

The atmosphere, however, remained highly charged. Workers continued organizing around issues of class and nationality, and interested observers tried to comprehend the nature of the first prolonged disruption of Tampa's infant industry. A tobacco trade journal, which spoke for manufacturers around the country, deplored the strike and related violence, but it expressed little surprise, given the battles that had already occurred in other cigar manufacturing centers, especially Key West. One reporter noted that aside from the issue of nationality, the focus of the Tampa dispute over the control of foremen resembled "the majority of similar disturbances throughout the country lately." With an air of resignation, this outside observer concluded that "Tampa is already beginning to acquire that notoriety which seems almost inseperable [sic] from an increased population."[25]

Tampa businessmen proved less understanding. The *Tampa Journal*, whose editor, William N. Conoley, was a real estate broker and a founding member of the Tampa Board of Trade, reflected the view of local entrepreneurs when it expressed surprise that cigarworkers struck over a nonmonetary issue—the control of foremen—having nothing whatever to do with wages or any other supposedly rightful concern of labor. The only explanation Conoley could find for such behavior was that "the entire trouble among these people at Ybor City is the result of evil men, agitators, revolutionists, and excited patriots, who gratify their morbid ideas of distinction, heroism and fame, by imposing upon the ignorant prejudices of the masses." Lest any reader doubt the economic impact of these disturbances, the *Journal* asserted that the "unsettled state of affairs, if allowed to continue, is sure to seriously affect the social and business interests of Ybor City, and Tampa as well." Given the seriousness of the situation, Conoley urged "the Cubans and Spaniards to stop . . . all agitation of political questions and engage only in your legitimate avocations."[26] After strikers had finally returned to the Martínez Ybor factory, Conoley's newspaper, hinting at the possible use of vigilante action to prevent future disruptions of production, stated that "any demonstration of terrorism will be promptly met with whatever means and methods required to put it down."[27]

When immigrant workers failed to heed such warnings, Tampa businessmen did not hesitate to carry out Conoley's threat. Several weeks following the return of cigarmakers to their benches, the Spanish owners of Ybor City's two cigar factories complained to the Tampa Board of Trade about continued "interference and attempted intimidation [by] a few Cuban outlaws now in Tampa."[28] The manufacturers specifically asked for "aid to rid them[selves] of obnoxious characters."[29] In response to this appeal, the Board of Trade convened a special meeting on March 8, chaired by Joseph B. Wall, the board vice president, who had recently been elected to the state senate. Those present at the special session of the board also included William Conoley, State Attorney Stephen M. Sparkman, and several elected city officials who were board members. After a lengthy discussion of the situation in Ybor City, the Board of Trade adopted a resolution assuring "Messrs. Ybor & Co. and Sánchez & Haya as well as the Citizens of Tampa, and Ybor City generally, that they will guarantee them full support and protection for their lives and property by every legitimate means."[30]

The board's subsequent actions made it clear that "legitimate means" included vigilante methods. Indeed, the Board of Trade immediately adopted this course by calling a public meeting of local citizens who "determined that for the best interests of all, the more prominent of the disquieting persons should be requested to leave."[31] Operating completely outside formal legal structures, but in a systematic way nevertheless, this gathering of leading Tampans drew up a list of eleven men, apparently all Cubans, "appointed a committee of fifteen citizens, composed of the best and most responsible business men, and gave them full authority to adopt and prosecute such measures as might be necessary to accomplish the purpose desired."[32]

This legalistic language represented an attempt to legitimize the process by which prominent citizens took the law into their hands to repress cigarworkers who had not violated any law. The process of creating a vigilance committee followed certain well-publicized procedures reflecting those southern republican values that had traditionally sanctioned private community justice to assure order and defend property. Tampa businessmen viewed their actions as an extension of the law when they called a public meeting of "local citizens" to establish a formal Committee of Fifteen and select two officers with the titles of "chairman" and "secretary" to head the vigilance committee. These posts went to leading members of the Board of Trade who had been outspoken supporters of vigilantism. Joseph Wall, a lawyer and the community's highest elected official, served as chairman, and William Conoley of the *Tampa Journal* became secretary.[33]

The Committee of Fifteen quickly implemented its charge. Upon its creation on the evening of March 8, 1887, the band of vigilantes went to Ybor City and ordered the designated "suspects" to leave town on the next boat to Key West. Eight Cubans named by the Board of Trade took the steamer that night. Two other Cubans on the list of eleven had been previously charged with the killing that had occurred on January 20. They were out on bail, and the vigilantes ordered them to return to jail to await trial at the next session of circuit court. The men complied, but the sheriff quickly transferred them to a jail in Key West, for fear that they might be lynched in Tampa.[34]

The final man targeted by the citizens' committee was Ramón Rubiera, the national secretary of the Cuban Federation of Cigar Makers. Rubiera had arrived in Tampa in February in an effort to settle differences between cigarworkers and employers. When ordered out of town by the Committee of Fifteen, he refused, insisting that the group reconsider its "unreasonable and unjust" request. The vigilantes agreed to reconsider, but the next morning the committee issued a written order, signed by Joseph Wall and William Conoley, which declared that "in obedience to the request of the citizens' meeting" the committee was "compelled to insist upon the original request that Mr. Rubiera leave these parts since the majority of his fellow citizens differ from his opinion." Two days later Rubiera took a boat to Key West.[35]

In addition to expelling nine union organizers, the Committee of Fifteen formally warned cigarworkers against further disruptions. At the request of the citizens' committee, the following notice was read in English and Spanish to employees in Ybor City's cigar factories.

> We are here as the representatives of the good people of this community to say that we intend to have order, peace and quiet prevail in our midst, and we give this notice that all disturbers and agitators must leave at once without further notice. If you are peaceable and law-abiding and wish to remain in our midst and pursue your legitimate avocation and business we will see that you are protected and in no way disturbed; but if you remain you must conform to our laws and customs.

Since eight of their number had already been forced out of town and the armed vigilance committee operated openly without any interference from legal authorities, immigrant cigarworkers learned quickly about local "laws and customs."[36]

Members of Tampa's establishment had no difficulty justifying vigilante methods, which they did not consider illegitimate or even illegal. The Committee of Fifteen was defended most eloquently by Thomas K. Spencer. A native of the area, a Confederate veteran, a founding member of the Board of Trade, and long-time editor and publisher of the *Tampa Tribune*, Spencer used editorial space to explain and excuse the forced expulsion of "a gang of bandits and dynamiters." To allay doubts about the guilt of the departed Cubans, Spencer contended that the Board of Trade had "the most positive evidence that every one of them were (sic) outlaws of the worst character." The men had extorted money from cigar manufacturers and threatened to blow up the cigar factories, according to Spencer, who invoked language that raised the specter of a repetition of Chicago's deadly Haymarket bombing the previous year: "These represented the very worst elements of society and if they had not been promptly throttled, the torch, the knife and the bomb *might* have laid Ybor City in ruin and filled her streets with blood." Considering the "devilish designs" of "these suspects," Spencer thought "every fair minded man . . . will agree that there was but one course to pursue and that was the one the committee pursued and the entire community backs them up for so doing."[37]

The 1887 expulsion represented the first use of vigilantism against Tampa workers. It won widespread acceptance in large part because of the community's tradition of establishment violence. A generation earlier, during the antebellum period, a formal Vigilance Committee had driven suspected criminals out of Tampa.[38] More significantly, there were strong echoes in 1887 of the traditional southern concern with honor, which had led to violence in the past. William Conoley, an Alabama native, disagreed with a Key West newspaper's contention that "Lynch Law at Tampa" might drive the cigar factories away. Regardless of the economic consequences, however, Conoley proudly proclaimed that "we will always protect our families and our property, and our neighbor's family and property against dynamite fiends, Cuban outlaws and cutthroats." Defense of family and property justified "our action as a community," according to Conoley.[39] What mattered most was not strict legalisms, but "the community's good," as another Tampan insisted in a public statement which concluded: "We are an order-loving people, and do not propose that any band of outlaws and desperadoes shall come into our midst and disturb our peace, order and business prosperity." For the Tampa elite, the dictates of honor and good business coincided in 1887, and outsiders were duly warned that the community would not permit shameful agitation that interfered with business. "Those who come for the purpose of disquieting and disturbing the peace of our citizens, or of injuring our business interests," a Tampa resident vowed, "may rest assured that they will not be tolerated but a few hours after their sin has been found out."[40]

The most direct connection to Tampa's vigilante tradition was provided in 1887 by Joseph B. Wall, who headed the Committee of Fifteen. As a well-known leader of the 1882 lynching, a former prosecutor, and a current state senator, Wall brought to the 1887 vigilance committee both experience and legitimacy. No direct evidence of his attitude in 1887 survives, but his numerous business connections and his position as vice president of the Board of Trade suggest that more than honor motivated Wall to lead the citizens' committee. In addition to any paternalistic belief that he and his associates were the natural guardians of the community's welfare, Joseph Wall had a stake in the success of Tampa's new cigar industry. During his career as a practicing attorney and public servant, he had accumulated sizeable land holdings. By 1885, Wall was among the twenty largest owners of farmland in Hillsborough County. Because the property was cleared and developed its value was enhanced. Local growth, stimulated first by the arrival of the railroad and later by the establishment of the cigar industry, had increased property values dramatically. Land outside the city limits previously selling for $10 an acre was going for $250 an acre. In September 1887 the *Tampa Tribune* contended that the growth of Ybor City's cigar industry had "caused an advance in value of all surrounding real estate, including the whole city of Tampa, of from fifty to one thousand per cent."[41] Palpable evidence that Joseph Wall had realized an increase in his wealth was his construction in 1887 of one of the first brick office buildings in Tampa. Men engaged in real estate, including Joseph Wall and William Conoley, could anticipate further accumulations of capital if the local economy expanded without any interference from militant cigarworkers.[42]

The only public denunciations of the 1887 expulsion of Cuban organizers came from the victims and their supporters living outside Tampa. A Key West newspaper condemned the "arbitrary and unlawful act of the self-constituted committee in ordering the indiscriminate expulsion of Cuban operatives."[43] The strongest protest was issued by the Central Labor Union of New York, composed of delegates from various local unions, including Ramón Rubiera, who was himself a victim of Tampa vigilantes. In a set of resolutions, the New York labor council attacked Tampa businessmen for exercising "arbitrary powers to expel by threats of personal violence a number of peaceful citizens." The New York trade unionists attributed the Board of Trade's action to "a desire of precipitating class conflict in this Republic." The resolutions also called on the federal government to protect "citizens engaged in the legitimate mission of organizing the working people."[44] A similar request was made directly to the United States Department of Justice by the Key West branch of the Cuban Federation of Cigar Makers. This led to a cursory inquiry by the United States attorney for the Southern District of Florida, who interviewed Ramón Rubiera in Key West and recommended to Washington authorities that no further action be taken.[45]

Official indifference by outside authorities permitted, perhaps even encouraged, the Tampa elite to strengthen local mechanisms of social and political control. As a form of collective action, vigilantism requires a certain degree of organization, which ordinarily rests on some common interest.[46] In 1887 the Tampa Board of Trade coordinated and led the movement to expel labor agitators. The board's formal guarantee to protect cigar manufacturers also committed it to a continuing role in policing the industry. In pursuit of greater cooperation and better coordination with cigar manufacturers, the Board of Trade expanded its membership to include immigrant owners for the first time. In the weeks following the 1887 expulsions, Ignacio Haya, Vicente Martínez Ybor, and his son Candido A. Martínez Ybor joined the association. In May 1887, William Conoley, who had served as secretary of the Committee of Fifteen, was elected president of the Board of Trade, and Eduardo Manrara, Martínez Ybor's partner, became vice president. Dr. John P. Wall, the group's outgoing president and half-brother of Joseph Wall, hailed the Board of Trade "as an exponent of the sense of the business interests of Tampa," and he called on members to "work individually and collectively as a band of brothers."[47]

In a related process of political consolidation, Ybor City became part of Tampa during the spring of 1887. Supported by the Board of Trade, annexation promised improved control over the immigrant district by extending the jurisdiction of Tampa agencies, especially the police and health departments. "The extension of our city limits is a matter of prime necessity to insure better law and order," Thomas Spencer stressed in the *Tribune* the month after expulsion of the Cubans.[48] Following annexation, Spencer called for the election of "our best men" to run the expanded city government. "Remember that capital will be slow to invest in a place that is subject to rag-tag municipal government," he warned.[49] Leading Tampans must have been pleased by the voters' selection of a city council that included C. A. M. Ybor to represent the new ward of Ybor City. At the request of Tampa's mayor, one of the first steps taken by the consolidated city council was to expand the police force temporarily from two to ten men. Such action provided some reassurance for local businessmen concerned about crime and agitation among immigrant workers, but it failed to prevent a recurrence of strikes or vigilante violence.[50]

Despite its political incorporation into Tampa, Ybor City remained socially a separate community. The arrival of additional cigar factories attracted more immigrant workers, who supported various Latin institutions, including Spanish-language newspapers and the "Liceo Cubano," a meeting place for social and political activities. By 1890, one-quarter of Tampa's population of 5,532 was foreign-born.[51] Most of the Cuban and Spanish immigrants worked in the cigar industry and lived in Ybor City, which became "a new Havana on American soil."[52] Physically and culturally isolated from Tampa's "Anglo" citizens, Ybor City's Latin cigarworkers formed part of a larger community that encompassed Key West and Havana. In addition to traveling frequently from one city to another to seek better employment or to visit family and friends, cigarworkers kept abreast of events in the extended community and joined organizations that linked the three cigar manufacturing centers.[53]

Following the 1887 expulsion of nine Cuban militants, ferment among cigarworkers briefly declined but then increased during the 1890s as Cuban and Spanish laborers organized in support of national and international causes. After several years of limited activity, the émigré movement for Cuban independence regained momentum, culminating in 1891 with José Martí's first visit to Tampa and the formation of the Cuban Revolutionary Party in 1892. It was this organization, supported by Tampa and other émigré communities, that ultimately brought unity and success to the struggle for Cuban independence from Spain. Cigarworkers also rallied behind various socialist and anarchist banners. At this point, ideological positions were rarely well defined, but their tenor was unmistakable.[54] *La Revista de Florida*, a Spanish-language newspaper published in Tampa and described by a contemporary as "principally concerned with modern labor philosophy and ideology," declared in 1889: "The banner of socialism is our banner. It signifies: Liberty, Equality and Fraternity."[55]

Despite general appeals for class solidarity, cigarworkers occasionally split along ethnic and ideological lines. The most obvious division of the early 1890s was between Cuban nationalists and Spanish anarchists. Both groups had outspoken supporters in Ybor City's cigar factories.[56] In 1891 the simmering conflict aroused the attention of Tampa authorities when Spanish anarchists paraded through the streets of the city in celebration of May Day. Carrying red flags and reportedly "marching to the beat of the drum in regular anarchist style," the Spaniards encountered hostility from both Cuban co-workers and Tampa's establishment. In a counterdemonstration, Cuban cigarworkers staged a parade two days later that prominently displayed the American flag. While emphasizing that "the people of Tampa . . . had nothing to fear from such loyal population as our Cuban friends show themselves to be," the *Tampa Tribune* warned Spanish demonstrators that "we hear from our best citizens that it will not do well for them to repeat it."[57]

The following year, prolonged turmoil in Ybor City again led to the intervention of vigilantes. With immigrant workers still divided, a strike at the factory of Sánchez & Haya resulted in a shootout between a few Spanish and Cuban cigarworkers in August 1892. Apparently no one was hurt, and police immediately arrested those involved on assault charges.[58] Two weeks later conflicts among workers culminated in a near riot when several hundred Cubans and Spaniards surrounded a saloon where five Spaniards sought refuge after allegedly attacking a Cuban. The crowd of workers threw rocks and exchanged shots with

A label for Vicente Martínez Ybor's most popular brand of clear Havana cigars, which were manufactured first in Havana, then in Key West, and finally in Tampa, beginning in 1886. Thomas Vance and L. Glenn Westfall Collection.

A 1902 cigar label produced by V. Martínez Ybor's Sons Company honored their father, one of the founders of Ybor City. Thomas Vance and L. Glenn Westfall Collection.

Ignacio Haya. Thomas Vance and
L. Glenn Westfall Collection.

Workers preparing filler tobacco for cigars at Tampa's Cuesta–Ray factory. Florida State Archives.

A Tampa cigarmaker handrolling a cigar in the twentieth century. Florida State Archives.

The Sánchez & Haya factory, where the first cigars were produced in Ybor City, as it looked in the 1890s. Tampa–Hillsborough County Public Library System.

A cigar label featuring the brick factory of Sánchez & Haya, who won the coveted right to call their firm "Factory No. 1," by winning the race with Martínez Ybor to produce the city's first clear Havana cigars in 1886. Thomas Vance and L. Glenn Westfall Collection.

Cigar manufacturers playing cards in Ybor City's Cherokee Club in 1895. Standing from left to right: Candido M. Ybor (son of Vicente); Arturo and Oscar Manrara (sons of Eduardo); M. Guonod. Seated from left to right: William Kline; Emilio Pons; F. A. Solomonson; and an accountant holding a child. Tampa–Hillsborough County Public Library System.

Tampa cigarworkers surrounded José Martí, with his suit jacket open and standing at the top of the steps of Martínez Ybor's factory, after the Cuban patriot delivered a speech in 1892. University of South Florida Special Collections.

Tampa in 1893 with the offices of the *Tampa Tribune* on the far left. Tampa–Hillsborough County Public Library System.

the cornered men. Again, however, no one was hurt, and the crowd dispersed when police started making arrests for disorderly conduct. The five men who had come under attack claimed that the "Cuban element hate us because we are Spaniards, and the [Spanish] anarchist element hate us because we are democrats and do not think as they think."[59] A thousand cigarworkers, including Cubans, Spaniards and Americans, disputed this charge in a public letter branding the five Spaniards as "scabs," who were "not only opposers of the working classes but were the real originators of all the labor troubles which occurred in the town."[60]

As this debate raged on, strikes continued to disrupt Tampa's cigar industry during August. Four days after Sánchez & Haya strikers won reinstatement of some fired workers and returned to their jobs, cigarmakers at Emilio Pons & Company walked out, demanding better material and higher wages. Within a few days the Pons employees also returned to work with a complete victory. Then a strike closed down the Martínez Ybor factory, which had 750 employees.[61]

The *Tampa Tribune* had a ready explanation and an expeditious remedy for these persistent disruptions. "Tampa cannot afford to have her business interests unsettled and two or three hundred men thrown out of employment every month or two at the caprice of ten or fifteen anarchists," the *Tribune*'s editor declared, "and the sooner the aforesaid anarchists are notified to leave this vicinity the better it would be for all concerned."[62] The newspaper later asserted paternalistically that "labor needs protection from anarchists." If weak or ineffective laws permitted anarchists to continue "poisoning the minds and misleading organizations of labor men," the *Tribune*'s editor feared that the United States would cease to be "a civilized and enlightened country where RIGHT is the rule." The message was clear: a higher law justified eliminating anarchists from the community.[63]

Another shooting incident brought increased support for this proposition. In late August 1892, two striking employees of Martínez Ybor exchanged shots on a street in Ybor City. Although neither was injured and police immediately arrested the alleged instigator, the *Tribune* asked rhetorically: "Can Tampa Submit To Such Outrages as This?" The newspaper answered emphatically: "It is Time for the American People to Take a Hand." The inflammatory news story described the shooting incident as an "attempted assassination," which was "a most dastardly outrage . . . that should not be quietly passed over in a civilized law-abiding community." The *Tribune* specified the form of community justice that should prevail by reminding its readers that five years earlier a committee of the Board of Trade had gone to Ybor City, "read a notice in each of the factories warning the men named to leave the city within twelve hours or suffer the consequences and within the time stipulated everyone of them had left Tampa forever."⁶⁴

The day following this renewed call for vigilante action, the *Tribune* reported approvingly that "a vigilance committee of a hundred members was formed last night to apprehend and mete out speedy justice in the future to all violators of the law and disturbers of the peace." Toward this end the vigilantes strung a huge banner across Ybor City's main street, declaring in Spanish:

> TAMPA VIGILANCE COMMITTEE . . . hereby gives warning to all — Cubans, Spaniards and all others — that lawlessness in Ybor City must cease. Whoever hereafter fires a pistol in this town except actually in defense of his life or commits any other unlawful act will be punished by this committee.

After detailing the formation of this anonymous group, the *Tribune* concluded matter-of-factly: "Of course all good and law-abiding citizens will deplore the *necessity* for the existence of a vigilance committee in this city, but as there is a *necessity* for some such action on the part of the citizens we believe the movement will be sanctioned by the people."⁶⁵

When the strike at Martínez Ybor's factory did not collapse under this pressure, the so-called Tampa Vigilance Committee was superseded by a more formal group that was created through familiar procedures. On September 6, 1892, cigar manufacturers appealed to the Board of Trade for assistance and furnished the board with the names of "five men who are responsible for most if not all the trouble in Ybor City." Invoking the 1887 precedent, leaders of the Board of Trade publicly called for "all citizens who have the best interests of this city at heart and who wish to put down the lawless set who are professional agitators and leaders in the late riot in Ybor City . . . to meet with the board of trade at the city hall . . . to consider the best action to be taken."⁶⁶ At this mass meeting of "representative business and professional men," the secretary of the board read the text of the association's 1887 guarantee of protection for cigar manufacturers. The gathering then adopted a formal motion creating a committee of five, headed by Joseph Wall, to investigate the complaints of factory owners. After hearing the committee's formal report the following day, leading citizens approved a motion introduced by Stephen M. Sparkman, a founding member of the Board of Trade, authorizing the chairman of the public meeting to select another committee of five which would take whatever action it considered necessary. In effect, this turned matters back to the Board of Trade, since a board officer, Thomas M. Weir, chaired the mass meeting. Weir, an Alabama native, and a Tampa real estate promoter, appointed himself and four other board members, including Joseph Wall and D. B. McKay, to the committee of five.[67]

With Wall again acting as chairman and D. B. McKay of the *Tampa Times* serving as secretary, the committee of five met and immediately expanded to form the Committee of Twenty-five to assist cigar factory owners. Surviving sources do not indicate precisely what form this assistance took, but the *Tampa Tribune* reported "a disposition to . . . forcing the anarchists to leave the place and the state, and if they do not go when ordered then the danger would come, as some favor swinging their carcasses at a rope's end." While expressing the hope that lynching would prove unnecessary, the *Tribune* reinforced the belief that a few radical agitators were responsible for all the disturbances. "The Cuban and the Spaniard are alike mercurial in temperament and quick to act, but they are not bad when no evil influences are working amongst them," the newspaper lectured derisively. "But when subjected to the devilish influence of even one unprincipled socialist, communist or anarchist, they are transformed into little less than madmen, and there is no peace, no order, until the cause is removed."[68]

Threats of lynch law, combined with the highly publicized presence of the Committee of Twenty-five, undoubtedly influenced the outcome of the strike. Cigarworkers refrained from any further violence, and they returned to the Martínez Ybor factory the following month without winning any of their demands. Even though the Committee of Twenty-five apparently did not resort to overt violence to break the strike, its very existence encouraged Martínez Ybor's management to hold out against strikers, instead of making concessions as other companies had done before the appearance of vigilantes on the scene. Striking cigarworkers were also put on the defensive as a result of the organization of a formal vigilance committee that operated openly and was headed by the same man, Joseph Wall, who had led the group which expelled nine Cubans five years earlier. A spokesman for cigar manufacturers reported that at least one strike leader had left Tampa the week following the formation of the Committee of Twenty-five in 1892. Those who remained suffered defeat in the strike against Martínez Ybor.[69]

The practice of antilabor vigilantism arose in Tampa as an extension of a continuing struggle between workers and factory owners over control in the cigar industry. Foreign capitalists created Ybor City as a company town in a concerted attempt to increase their authority and undercut the collective strength of skilled employees. When cigarworkers continued to defend their traditional rights by organizing and disrupting production in Ybor City, manufacturers appealed to Tampa leaders for assistance. With the city's booming economy increasingly dependent on the production of cigars, businessmen and professionals invoked their own tradition of vigilantism to protect factory owners. Unable to use legal methods to prevent organizing or to break peaceful strikes, Board of Trade members took the law into their hands in well-organized campaigns to repress cigarworkers, who represented primarily a threat to profits and stability. Leaders of the Board of Trade used occasional outbursts of violence among workers as excuses to justify extralegal action despite the fact that police easily handled such incidents.[70]

The targets of Citizens' Committees were all immigrants, but nativism rarely figured in the public justification of vigilantism. Indeed, Tampa's southern-born leaders resorted to vigilante action in defense of immigrant capitalists, who were increasingly integrated into elite organizations, beginning with the Board of Trade. The only public opposition to vigilante businessmen came from local cigarworkers and labor organizations in Key West and New York which included both immigrants and native-born Americans. Thus, vigilantism in Tampa largely followed class, not ethnic, lines. Although elite coercion did not eradicate militancy among cigarworkers, it did make organizing more difficult. It also enhanced the power of manufacturers in their ongoing struggle with workers over control in the cigar industry.

As the victims of vigilantism changed, so too did the reason for private community justice. Whereas the defense of personal honor had previously served as the primary justification for collective violence directed at common criminals, economic necessity emerged as the dominant theme in the pronouncements of antilabor vigilantes and their supporters. After 1887, appeals to southern honor faded from the elaborate defense of extralegal action directed at workers. Despite some changes in the operation of vigilantism, continuity with past practices explains the persistence of establishment violence. Above all, leadership remained in the hands of local notables, like Joseph B. Wall, who had deep roots in Tampa and the Old South. Wall's elevation to the presidency of the Florida Bar Association in 1887 demonstrated that southern attorneys considered his well-publicized vigilante activities legitimate and even legal. In the New South, as in the Old South, community justice encompassed both public and private actions. Despite improvements in urban services, including the police, prominent Tampans refused to allow government a monopoly over the use of force to assure order on their terms. Citizenship, reserved for white males, demanded that local property holders collectively enforce community standards. "Citizenship involves duties—sometimes unpleasant ones, but they are none the less sacred duties—that cannot be shirked lightly, nor can they be neglected without cost," the editor of the *Tampa Tribune* lectured in 1891. "Citizenship is not merely living as an individual, but it imposes a share in the common responsibilities of the community as well as its profits."[71] The only opposition to citizen vigilantes came from their victims and other workers who lacked the power to curb establishment violence.

# 3

# "Pro Bono Publico": The Citizens' Committee of 1901

The use of antilabor violence by Tampa's elite certainly did not inhibit the growth of the city. During the 1890s, Tampa's population increased by 286 percent to a total of almost 16,000 in 1900. This rapid expansion was fueled by cigars. "The cigar industry is to this city what the iron industry is to Pittsburgh," the *Tampa Tribune* observed.[1] Additional cigar companies were attracted by continued subsidies, especially free factory buildings, and by the promise of labor peace, guaranteed by citizen vigilantes.

When cigarworkers closed down the industry for prolonged periods, Tampa businessmen acted on their 1887 pledge to protect employers and their property. During a four-month strike in 1901, prominent Tampans organized a vigilance committee which used violence to defeat cigarworkers. A comparison with a strike in 1899 shows that cigarworkers could win a power struggle with employers if it did not involve union recognition and if vigilantes did not intervene. When the Citizens' Committee took the law into its own hands in 1901, it operated openly and with the tacit approval of public officials. Despite complaints from cigarworkers, establishment violence continued to enjoy widespread acceptance as a legitimate means of eliminating threats to the city's leading industry.

During the 1890s, the success of Ybor City led to the development of another company town adjacent to Tampa. The new community was largely the creation of Hugh Campbell Macfarlane, a Scottish immigrant who had come to the United States in 1865 at the age of thirteen. After establishing himself as a lawyer, Macfarlane arrived in Tampa in 1883 and quickly became a leading citizen, serving first as city attorney from 1887 to 1890 and briefly as state attorney in 1893–94. Like several other Tampa professionals, Macfarlane assured his success through real estate development related to the cigar industry. After purchasing several hundred barren acres west of the Hillsborough River across from Tampa, Macfarlane began in 1892 offering free sites and factory buildings to cigar manufacturers to locate in what became known as West Tampa.[2]

Connected to Tampa by a bridge financed by Macfarlane and his associates, West Tampa grew rapidly. By 1895, when it was incorporated as a separate city, West Tampa already had attracted several cigar companies from Key West, and it had some 2,800 residents, most of whom were immigrant workers and their families. Unlike Ybor City, West Tampa remained a separate municipality until annexed in 1925, but it was always socially and economically linked to Tampa. Many cigarworkers lived in Ybor City and worked in West Tampa.[3]

The rise of this new community reflected Tampa's development as a manufacturing center built on immigrant labor and the cigar industry. In addition to the continued influx of Cubans and Spaniards, Italians began arriving in large numbers during the 1890s. Originating in several Sicilian villages, many of Tampa's Italian immigrants followed a circuitous route, passing first through New Orleans before settling in the cigar city. In Ybor City and West Tampa, Italians joined Cubans and Spaniards to form the city's burgeoning Latin community.[4] Most of these immigrants migrated to Tampa for employment in cigar factories. By 1900, some 4,000 cigarworkers, almost all foreign-born, held jobs in more than one hundred factories, large and small, concentrated in Ybor City and West Tampa.[5] "The Cubans and Spaniards depend altogether on the cigar trade for employment," reported a government survey of Tampa's immigrant workers. "The Italians have shown themselves able to survive in other callings, but the majority of them are also dependent upon the industry."[6]

While living and working together, the various immigrant groups retained ethnic loyalties that in some cases were profoundly provincial. Sicilians organized L'Unione Italiana in 1894, and Spaniards divided along regional lines, forming first the Centro Espanõl in 1891 and then the Centro Asturiano in 1902. Cubans separated by race with Afro-Cubans creating La Unión Martí-Maceo in 1907, which was quite distinct from the larger Círculo Cubano, dating from 1899. All these local mutual aid societies built impressive club houses in Ybor City, and several followed in West Tampa. The clubs provided not only meeting places for social events, but also services, especially health care, that were difficult to obtain in Tampa's "Anglo" community.[7]

Despite the presence of competing ethnic organizations and occasional expressions of hostility, especially between Cubans and Spaniards, immigrant workers shared a strong sense of class solidarity that often transcended differences in nationality, race and gender. As early as 1892, Cuban and Spanish cigarworkers had joined together to confront employers, although no permanent union survived the first strikes in Tampa. The class consciousness of workers was most obviously expressed in the variety of radical ideologies, ranging from socialism to anarchism, which found increasingly wide support among cigarworkers. With Cuban and Spanish radicals already active in Tampa, the arrival of Italian immigrants brought a new wave of socialists and anarchists. Many of the Italians came from a section of Sicily which had experienced rural uprisings, led in part by socialists, during the early 1890s.[8] "When in 1902 I landed in Tampa, I found myself in a world of radicals for which I was prepared," one Sicilian later recalled. "In those days in Tampa, anarchists and socialists were many."[9]

During most of the 1890s, labor militancy was muted as a result of the preoccupation of cigarworkers with the intensified struggle for Cuban independence from Spain. The formation of the Cuban Revolutionary Party in 1892 marked the beginning of a new, unified effort of Cuban exiles to win independence for their homeland. For the next six years, Tampa cigarworkers devoted themselves to the cause of Cuban independence. By 1896, Cubans in Tampa had organized forty-one patriotic clubs, which raised money and supported filibustering expeditions to Cuba. Many leading cigar manufacturers, including Spanish-born Vicente Martínez Ybor, also endorsed the cause of *Cuba Libre*, as did a number of Italian cigarworkers, some of whom fought in Cuba. These efforts brought a temporary suspension of labor-management confrontations in Tampa's cigar industry. In 1896, for example, when a strike threatened in Ybor City, a Cuban émigré leader came to Tampa and successfully urged workers to forego a walkout. With the end of the Spanish-Cuban-American War in 1898, long-deferred class issues again disrupted Tampa's cigar industry.[10]

In 1899, Tampa cigarmakers confronted employers in a dispute that briefly closed down most factories in the city. The strike was precipitated by management's attempt to improve efficiency and control over cigarmakers. Rather than allowing workers to decide the quantity of tobacco for each cigar, as had been the custom, management of the Ybor-Manrara factory introduced scales to weigh the tobacco. The new system established a specified number of cigars to be made from a measured amount of tobacco. One industry journal observed that the scales were commonly used in the North "to prevent stealing by unscrupulous employees."[11] However, Tampa cigarmakers walked out of the Ybor-Manrara factory in May 1899, in defense of what they considered not only a tradition but also their right as skilled craftsmen to determine the quantity of tobacco for each cigar.[12]

Known as "the weight strike," the 1899 walkout is best described as a control strike. The dispute was not simply a matter of hours or wages, but rather constituted an effort by cigarmakers to maintain collective control over the production process. The specific issues in control strikes commonly included work rules, union recognition, removal of unpopular foremen, and regulation of layoffs.[13] In this case skilled cigarworkers were fighting to protect their traditional regulation of production.

Some historians have suggested that the 1899 strike marked a turning point in management's effort to introduce efficiency into cigarmaking. To be sure, changes were occurring in the industry following the deaths of Vicente Martínez Ybor and several other pioneer manufacturers, but the weight scales were introduced by Eduardo Manrara, a surviving partner who had managed the Ybor factory since 1886.[14] The weight strike was part of a continuing power struggle between cigarworkers and manufacturers that had led to the very first strikes in 1886 and 1887 over the control of foremen in Martínez Ybor's factory.

The 1899 strike was also typical in that cigarworkers demonstrated that they could bring enormous collective strength to bear. Their skills and sense of solidarity meant that striking workers were not easily replaced. Labor unity was so strong that cigarworkers did not bother to set up picket lines. Indeed, strikers did not even have a formal organization in 1899, although as the dispute dragged on, a committee was established to represent workers in discussions with employers and Tampa businessmen. Cigarworkers found financial and moral support in Key West and Havana. Some also located temporary employment in other cities. By the end of the 1899 strike, an estimated 1,400 idle workers and their families had gone to Key West and Havana. Even if few found jobs in Cuba's depressed cigar industry, they at least could move in temporarily with friends or relatives.[15]

Given the collective strength of cigarworkers, Tampa manufacturers attempted to shift the balance of power in their favor by formally organizing for the first time in 1899. Employers took this step two months into the weight strike when they created the Cigar Manufacturers' Association of Tampa "for protection against this labor trouble, and to end the strike."[16] Although initially directed at dealing with the strike in progress, the organization adopted a constitution and bylaws to bind all members into a common front. "The organization is a permanent one and will regulate all labor differences, no individual factory having any voice," declared one supporter.[17] The twenty largest Tampa manufacturers literally bonded themselves at the rate of $5,000 each to abide by the collective decisions of the association. This organization not only increased the power of large employers but also gave them the distinction of having the only trade association of cigar manufacturers in the country. In other cities, fiercely competitive firms failed to cooperate even on labor matters. Small manufacturers in other parts of the country commonly made concessions to unionized cigarmakers in order to avoid prolonged, costly strikes.[18] Large

Tampa employers with a specialized national market preferred to join forces and fight worker demands.

In their first group action members of the Cigar Manufacturers' Association agreed to lock out all employees until the strikers at the Ybor-Manrara factory returned to their benches with the scales in place. The lockout, which began on July 10, 1899, put almost 4,000 men and women out of work. This united effort produced optimism among employers. One sympathetic observer explained: "The general idea is that the fight will be won by the manufacturers, and that they will have no more trouble with their labor for years to come." The writer called this a "great source of satisfaction to everyone in the city but a few dissatisfied workmen who lead their brethren by the nose."[19]

Employers also received significant support from the local business community. At the beginning of the dispute over scales, the Tampa Board of Trade had publicly expressed concern "that certain agitators in Ybor City are . . . endeavoring to organize strikes in certain factories, to the detriment of the business of the city." This led the board to issue a formal warning: "The action of said agitators is condemned by the business community, and they are hereby warned to desist, and if said agitators do not desist they will be arrested and severely punished."[20]

Cigar manufacturers had another outspoken defender in Wallace F. Stovall, the owner/editor of the *Tampa Morning Tribune*. Stovall, a Kentucky native, had learned the newspaper trade after moving to Florida at the age of nineteen in 1886. As owner of the *Polk County News* seven years later, Stovall decided to try his luck in Tampa when the city became a one-newspaper town with the demise of the old *Tampa Tribune*. Backed by former newspaperman John P. Wall, Stovall started a new *Tampa Tribune* in 1893 to compete with the *Tampa Times*. Additional financial support for Stovall's paper came the following year when he incorporated the publishing enterprise. The original stockholders, whose interest Stovall later purchased, included cigar manufacturers C.A.M. Ybor, Emilio Pons and Sánchez & Haya.[21]

As an editorial writer and longtime member of the Board of Trade, Stovall was an aggressive city booster. He assumed that "the interests of the *Tribune* and the people of Tampa are one, and the same."[22] This philosophy, combined with extensive real estate investments, helped make Stovall one of Tampa's richest men. By the time he sold the *Tribune* for $1.2 million in 1925, he had become the city's largest individual property owner. He never held public office or served in the military, but Stovall was widely known as "Colonel," an honorary title conferred by several governors in recognition of his standing in the community.[23]

In 1899, at a time when three cigar manufacturers sat on the *Tribune*'s board of directors, Stovall's paper called for vigilante action against strike leaders.[24] The *Tribune* blamed the weight strike on "agitators, who are continually trying to bankrupt the city."[25] Stovall used the manufacturers' announcement of a lockout in July to call for "some radical measure" that would eliminate "the professional agitator." Aware that labor activists had been driven out of town in the past, Stovall suggested that it "would be eminently correct for the people of Tampa to force this undesirable element to abandon their abode in this city."[26] A month later, the *Tribune* renewed the threat of force. "Some warm talk is being indulged in by usually conservative citizens, and one remarked yesterday that the only remedy left available for the trouble now ruining Tampa's trade was to expel this [strike] committee," the *Tribune* reported on August 6. "The time is about ripe for the 'last resort,'" Stovall added.[27]

Disregarding these calls for repression of strike leaders, some twenty manufacturers yielded in mid-August. In addition to abolishing the scales and ending the lockout, employers agreed to a uniform list of wages for all different sizes of cigars. Other new shop rules included adequate supplies of ice water, monthly cleaning of the factories, and the use of coal, instead of wood, for heating in winter. The agreement also permitted a committee of cigarworkers to inspect factories to insure that employers observed these regulations. This settlement granted cigarworkers all their demands, which had not included official recognition of any union.[28] "The victory is claimed to be entirely with the cigarmakers, and so far as appearances go this is about the case," reported one manufacturers' journal.[29]

The cigarworkers' triumph attracted national attention among manufacturers since "the factory owners—for the time being at least—are at the mercy of the men." One tobacco industry journal claimed that manufacturers "were not prepared to withstand a long siege, having no heavy accumulations of stock on hand."[30] Summarizing the strength of strikers, another manufacturers' organ explained that workers had "formed an organization, obtained financial help from other sections, refused to entertain any advances toward a settlement, and finally began to deport their members to Havana, thus depriving the manufacturers of any fulcrum on which to work the lever object lesson."[31]

With orders piling up, factory owners surrendered to cigarworkers, but they gave up little. Only two factories had actually introduced scales in Tampa, and as the journal *Tobacco* emphasized, any increased cost resulting from acceptance of a uniform wage list could be passed on to cigar retailers and consumers.[32] Moreover, *Tobacco Leaf* stressed that manufacturers would not long accept the new regulations. "They claim to have the right—no extraordinary assumption surely—of determining the working rules of their factories, and it is pretty certain that they will yet exercise that right." In any case, *Tobacco Leaf* concluded, "the obvious lesson that the Tampa episode has taught is the worth of organization among factory owners."[33]

While focusing on the unexpected victory of workers, national trade journals overlooked the other unusual feature of the 1899 strike, which was the absence of violence in general and vigilantism in particular. However, the strikers' nonviolence did not go unnoticed in Tampa. "Not a single act of anarchy, violence or public demonstration has marked their conduct," stressed an anonymous letter to the *Tribune*.[34] Even the *Tribune* admitted that the strikers "conducted themselves, generally, in an orderly manner."[35] The peaceful conduct of the strike undercut the momentum the *Tribune* tried to generate for vigilante action. Despite threats and rumors of vigilantism published in the *Tampa Tribune*, local businessmen did not resort to violent methods, and cigarworkers won their demands. Yet this proved to be the last victory of Tampa cigarworkers in an industry-wide strike. It was also the last time citizen vigilantes did not intervene.

The setback of 1899 encouraged several manufacturers to join the national movement toward consolidation of the industry. In November 1899, a group of manufacturers specializing in domestic production of Havana cigars announced that they had formed the Havana-American Company, a corporation based in New York and capitalized at $10 million. The new company centralized ownership and control over eight leading producers with plants in New York, Chicago, and Florida, including three of Tampa's biggest and oldest firms—Ybor-Manrara, Seidenberg, and Julius Ellinger. The Havana-American Company immediately became the single largest manufacturer of handmade Havana cigars, but its control fell far short of a monopoly in an industry that remained very competitive. Although in existence for only eighteen months, the Havana-American Company marked a turning point in the cigar industry. Its creation enhanced the power of capital and placed the management of several Tampa factories in the hands of absentee owners. For cigarworkers the most distinctive characteristic of the new corporation was that all of its factories were nonunion.[36]

As owners became better organized, so too did Tampa cigarworkers. The Knights of Labor and the Cuban Federation of Cigar Makers had disappeared in Tampa, but competing unions still divided along ethnic and ideological lines. The Cigar Makers' International Union (CMIU), an affiliate of the American Federation of Labor (AFL), had established its first local in Tampa in 1892.[37] Built by AFL president Samuel Gompers, the CMIU's national organization bore the distinctive stamp of "pure and simple" unionism that stressed improvements in wages, hours, and working conditions for skilled workers. By focusing on immediate economic demands and rejecting political action, the AFL and the CMIU appeared to accept the existing order in return for a bigger piece of the pie.[38]

This brand of unionism had little appeal among immigrant cigarmakers in Florida. After talking to Cuban operatives in 1890, a CMIU organizer reported: "They are opposed to all American institutions. They cannot, nor will not understand reason, [and have] got no use for the International Union." This led the CMIU representative to abandon his mission in Florida. "Judging from what I have learned from the cigar makers of Tampa and Ybor City, I concluded that it was unnecessary for me to go to Key West," he wrote.[39] These observations were reinforced by the CMIU's subsequent experience with its Tampa local. For years after its formation in 1892, Local 336 attracted only a few dozen members, almost none of whom had a Spanish or Italian surname.[40]

Following the 1899 strike victory by cigarworkers operating without any union organization, the CMIU dispatched a Latin organizer to recruit members. After several months, he proudly reported that CMIU rolls in Tampa had grown from 57 to around 700. The organizer admitted that the CMIU had competition from a newly formed independent union of Tampa cigarworkers, but he failed to note that the CMIU local still attracted predominantly American members, who formed a small minority of the total work force of over 4,000 people.[41] The CMIU itself confessed several months later that "the great majority" of its Tampa members were American citizens.[42]

Created in the fall of 1899, the competing union was local, independent, radical, and Latin. Officially named "La Sociedad de Torcedores de Tampa," the union became popularly known as "La Resistencia," since its stated purpose was "to resist the exploitation of labor by capital." With dues of twenty-five cents a week, the union soon had enough money for its own newspaper, *La Federación*, which was published weekly in Tampa. Based in Tampa's cigar industry, La Resistencia also successfully organized other local workers, including bakers, waiters, bartenders, and laundry workers. Thus, it represented a dual union in the eyes of AFL leaders. More threatening to the CMIU was the fact that La Resistencia succeeded in signing up the workers in most of Tampa's cigar factories during 1900.[43]

Adding insult to injury, the radical leaders of the independent union heaped scorn on the CMIU for its conservative trade unionism. In a typical editorial *La Federación* charged: "The organization of labor that is not planted squarely on the class struggle can develop only in one direction—the direction of a buffer for the capitalist class, run by the

Labor Lieutenants of Capital. Pure and simpledom is the enemy born of the Working Class. [I]t is twin brother to the Capitalist Class."⁴⁴ In defense of its affiliate, the AFL's national journal falsely claimed that La Resistencia, "as its name implies, assists the employers in resisting the extension and influence of the *bona fide* organization of the cigar-making trade."⁴⁵

In late 1900, the competing unions confronted each other in a battle that produced labor violence. Flexing its muscle in the large factories owned by the Havana-American Company, La Resistencia initiated open warfare in November 1900, by demanding that management refuse employment to CMIU members. La Resistencia contended that the AFL union had precipitated the conflict by recently organizing a dual union for tobacco strippers, who removed the stems from tobacco leaves. Some 1,200 strippers, including many women, were already members of La Resistencia.⁴⁶ The independent union argued that its request for exclusivity in several cigar factories was "a purely conservative and defensive" measure designed to protect its membership from CMIU raids. La Resistencia had enrolled over 4,500 cigarworkers, including Cubans, Spaniards, Italians, and Americans.⁴⁷

Employers bowed to this reality and discharged several hundred CMIU cigarmakers and strippers. The compliance of management was also encouraged by the fact that the industry was in the midst of its peak season prior to the Christmas holiday and the loss of CMIU workers did not seriously affect production. "The manufacturers have no option in the matter," a trade journal acknowledged, since "with the exception of a few factories the Resistencia men are in the majority. . . . The manufacturer is obliged to accede to their wishes or close up."⁴⁸

Frustrated CMIU members marched through Ybor City demanding their jobs back. Reportedly composed of Americans, Cubans, and Spaniards, a crowd of some 200 men and boys confronted a small squad of police in front of the Seidenberg factory. "We want work!" someone yelled. "Bring out the Resistencia men from the factory, and we will disperse. We cannot work; they shall not work." In an attempt to prevent violence, Tampa's police chief persuaded Resistencia workers to leave the factory temporarily. The mob then marched to a factory unprotected by police, and shooting erupted. An American in the crowd later claimed that the factory's Italian doorkeeper had fired first, but the doorkeeper and other witnesses denied this. In any case, what followed was a fusillade from the CMIU men who had lined up in front of the factory. Hundreds of bullets were fired into the factory, breaking windows and lodging in walls and desks, while cigarworkers crouched on the floor of the brick building. Incredibly, no one was hurt, and the sheriff soon dispersed the crowd.⁴⁹

Responding to this incident, the *Tampa Tribune* showed its ambiva-

The clubhouse of L'Unione Italiana, or Italian Club, was built at a cost of $80,000 in 1917, and it is still in operation in Ybor City. Tampa–Hillsborough County Public Library System.

Ybor City's Círculo Cubano (Cuban Club) was built in 1918 and is still used. Tampa–Hillsborough County Public Library System.

The Ybor City clubhouse of the Centro Asturiano cost a staggering $110,000 to construct in 1914. It featured a 1,200-seat theater, a ballroom and a library for members. Tampa–Hillsborough County Public Library System.

The two-story home of José Arango, a cigar manufacturer, contrasts with the typical house of Ybor City cigarworkers seen on the left. A streetcar that ran between Ybor City and Tampa is also pictured in this 1898 scene. Tampa–Hillsborough County Public Library System.

Ybor City's main street in about 1898. The original wooden building of the Centro Español is on the right. University of South Florida Special Collections.

The Tampa police department in 1899. Tampa–Hillsborough County Public Library System.

Wallace F. Stovall, owner and editor of the *Tampa Morning Tribune* for over thirty years. University of South Florida Special Collections.

D. B. McKay, owner and editor of the *Tampa Daily Times* and four-term mayor of Tampa. University of South Florida Special Collections.

lence toward violence. On the one hand, the newspaper condemned this outbreak of so-called "mob law" as "very reprehensible" and "a species of anarchy." "Such lawlessness will not be tolerated in this city," Wallace Stovall asserted editorially. He even suggested that this injunction against collective violence applied to all classes. "When a body of men, no matter from which class it may originate, arm[s] itself and takes the law into its own hands, as did the mob of yesterday morning, constituted authorities should step in and make an example of the guilty parties." On the other hand, in his proposed desire "to see that those engaged in that [cigar] industry are not disturbed in the prosecution of their business," Stovall accepted a double standard that justified establishment violence in order to protect manufacturers from lawlessness.[50]

Soon after the formation of a citizen's committee to deal with Tampa's labor troubles, Stovall endorsed traditional vigilante methods. In a *Tribune* editorial he argued that "it should be the duty of the good citizens of Tampa to drive out of the city those agitators who are principally responsible for these troubles."[51] While Tampa businessmen attempted peacefully to resolve the interunion conflict, the *Tribune* kept up the pressure for expulsion of the nameless activists who were allegedly responsible for disrupting production. "The trouble between the two unions is costing Tampa, at a close and conservative estimate, $50,000 a week, and giving the manufacturers a world of trouble," Stovall lectured his readers. "The citizens of this city owe it to themselves to rise up en masse, [and] eliminate from the ranks of the workingmen the troublesome, obnoxious and much-despised agitator."[52]

Despite repeated appeals for citizens to take the law into their own hands, it was not clear who should be driven from the city. The *Tribune* specifically exonerated local CMIU leaders from responsibility for the labor violence, and the more radical union, La Resistencia, was not on strike. In fact, when "a few hot-headed young men" attempted unsuccessfully to form a committee to run the head of La Resistencia out of town, the *Tribune* expressed relief that the "unlawful" plan failed, since the targeted man had kept his men at work and cooperated with efforts to reach a compromise with CMIU strikers.[53] The local correspondent for *Tobacco Leaf* agreed. "Threats of lynching the leaders of the Resistencia have been openly made," he noted. However, he emphasized that La Resistencia had "acted with extreme moderation so far."[54]

Tampa businessmen intervened in the dispute, but they relied on mediation rather than violence or threats of violence. At a mass meeting the day after the shooting incident, Tampa businessmen created a "citizens' committee" with elected officers. The gathering also adopted two resolutions introduced by the head of the Board of Trade, Colonel

John B. Anderson, a leading banker. One resolution pledged the businessmen to support the police in enforcing law and order. The other recommended establishment of a mediation committee, composed of representatives of local businessmen, cigar manufacturers, and the two competing unions, to seek adjustment of the labor dispute. This committee quickly reached an eleven-point agreement that called for employment of cigarworkers regardless of union affiliation and union pledges to refrain from seeking members in the competing group. However, the CMIU rejected the agreement because it would have guaranteed the dominant position of La Resistencia. Failure to approve the pact left CMIU members without work.[55]

The intransigence of the CMIU further undermined the union's weak position. "Of the two unions," *Tobacco Leaf* observed, "the International seems to be the more idiotically pigheaded." The *Tampa Tribune* agreed. It denounced the AFL affiliate for its "unreasonable attitude," which left the CMIU "discredited by its leaders, criticized by its friends, [and] deprived of public sympathy." By contrast, La Resistencia won praise for accepting the compromise agreement and continuing to keep the factories operating. "Great is La Resistencia," the *Tribune* exclaimed in a rare moment of prounion sentiment.[56]

With little leverage in the cigar industry, the CMIU turned to fellow AFL craftsmen who were well organized in Tampa, especially among the building trades and the printers. In response to a direct appeal from the CMIU local, Tampa's Central Trades and Labor Assembly called a general strike to force the rehiring of AFL cigarworkers on their terms. Printers refused to cooperate, but over 3,000 union members stopped work on November 26, 1900, in a sympathy strike that effectively halted all construction projects in the booming city. "The object of the sympathetic strike is to . . . educate the Resistencia people of the deep love of liberty and right to work under American institutions," the CMIU proclaimed.[57]

The CMIU strike soon collapsed. La Resistencia refused to honor the sympathy strike, arguing that it had accepted "the pleas of the committee of citizens of Tampa" to continue working and avoid violence.[58] Cigar manufacturers also refused to bow to pressure from AFL unions for fear that the rehiring of CMIU members would lead La Resistencia to close the factories. After one week, the Central Trades and Labor Assembly ended the sympathy strike, and CMIU men gradually returned to some factories without winning equal status with La Resistencia.[59]

In the wake of the 1900 strike, a change in the ownership of leading cigar factories enhanced the collective power of management. In January 1901, the American Tobacco Company, which was a trust dominated by James B. Duke, entered the cigar business by organizing the American Cigar Company. Having already achieved a monopoly in the manufacture of most other tobacco products, such as snuff and cigarettes, the Duke interests sought similar control of the cigar industry. After first purchasing several northern firms that produced inexpensive cigars, the American Tobacco Company expanded into the luxury, clear-Havana business. In June 1901, Duke acquired the Havana-American Company, a move that transferred ownership of three of Tampa's largest factories, with some 1,000 employees, to the tobacco trust, with headquarters in New York.[60]

The 1901 acquisitions immediately transformed the American Tobacco Company into the largest single manufacturer of cigars in the United States, but without monopoly control. As one authority pointed out, "monopoly principles and conditions did not prevail" in the highly decentralized business based largely on hand production by skilled cigarmakers.[61] A decade after its formation, the American Cigar Company controlled less than one-sixth of the nation's cigar production, which remained a competitive business.[62]

The American Tobacco Company's ownership of the so-called "trust factories" in Tampa did, however, strengthen the hand of employers facing increasing demands from labor. A 1901 policy statement by a trust spokesman proclaimed bluntly: "No union shop will be permitted in Tampa."[63] This position, and the power behind it, led a national CMIU organizer to report several months later from Tampa that the trust was "to be more feared than any local organization which may spring up here in Tampa, as its object and aim is to reduce wages, humiliate its employees and teach children the trade."[64] The latter step never occurred, but the American Tobacco Company's widely publicized opposition to unions undoubtedly stiffened the resolve of other Tampa manufacturers to resist collective bargaining. Labor relations remained the one area in which otherwise competitive firms consistently cooperated, especially during strikes when the Tampa Cigar Manufacturers' Association served as the united voice of the largest employers. Local representatives of the American Tobacco Company also came to play a leading role in the manufacturers' association.

While the tobacco trust began acquiring cigar companies in 1901, La Resistencia continued to battle both employers and a small band of CMIU members. During the first half of 1901, Tampa's cigar industry experienced "amicable relations between employer and employee," according to one trade journal.[65] However, brief work stoppages by members of La Resistencia in individual factories produced increasing disgust among manufacturers, who described workers' demands as "preposterous" and "silly." In one case, for example, cigarworkers who missed four days' wages due to the unavailability of tobacco at one factory insisted that the firm pay them ten dollars each for the lost time.[66]

Its growing unpopularity among employers may explain La Resistencia's success in expanding its following among immigrant cigarworkers. In June 1901, a correspondent for *U.S. Tobacco Journal* reported that the leaders of La Resistencia had "gathered in all the members of the International Cigarmakers' Union, and if they succeed in getting the [cigar] boxmakers to join them, they will about have things their own way." Local CMIU officers continued to dismiss La Resistencia as a "band of trouble makers, Anarchists and [an] unlawful society."[67]

This interunion rivalry ended in a prolonged strike in 1901 which led to a crackdown by vigilantes. In a long-anticipated assertion of its growing power, La Resistencia issued an ultimatum on July 23 that contained two demands. Workers insisted that Tampa's cigar manufacturers pressure a local employer to abandon a branch factory in Jacksonville, and they called on owners to stop three named factories from employing members of any other union. If manufacturers did not comply within three days, La Resistencia threatened to close down all Tampa factories in support of an additional demand for a wage increase. The threatened walkout was, in effect, a sympathy strike in support of La Resistencia workers who had struck the Cuesta-Rey factory two weeks earlier in an effort to get the company to close down a branch factory in Jacksonville, where it was expanding operations in an apparent attempt to escape Resistencia's control. In addition to seeking protection of its power base in Tampa, La Resistencia was also renewing its campaign to secure the closed shop and eliminate the CMIU from the few factories which still accepted its members. In short, the issue once again was control, not wages or hours.[68]

La Resistencia members had every reason to anticipate acceptance of their demands. They had already won the ouster of CMIU members from most factories the previous year. Several Tampa manufacturers had also agreed to discontinue new or planned branch factories under pressure from La Resistencia. In addition, the militant union had expanded its membership to more than 5,000 in Tampa, some 4,000 of them in the cigar industry. Assessing the impressive strength of La Resistencia, the *Tampa Tribune* observed that the "federation is the most powerful influence in the city today, and, considered numerically, is the strongest organization in the State of Florida." The *Tribune* emphasized that the cigar industry was "in absolute dependence upon it, for there are not enough competent cigarmakers outside of it to run one big factory."[69]

Given its past success and its present strength, La Resistencia sought to prevent outside intervention by Tampa businessmen who had helped defeat cigarworkers in 1887 and 1892. Immediately after issuing its July ultimatum, La Resistencia requested a meeting with Board of Trade officials. At this gathering La Resistencia secretary José Gonzalez Padilla blamed the "continual unrest and disturbance in the cigar industry" on "a few men, claiming to be members of another union, but whom we do not recognize as union men." He argued that firing "these few disturbers" and discontinuing branch factories would assure the continued prosperity of the local cigar industry. Finally, La Resistencia appealed for a hands-off policy from Tampa businessmen in the event of a strike. "We will promise as a union," one leader pledged, "if we find it necessary to strike, to do so peaceably, and we ask the businessmen of Tampa, if they cannot help us, to at least occupy neutral ground."[70]

Cigar manufacturers quickly showed their determination to fight with every available means. Owners immediately rejected "the ridiculous demands" of the workers.[71] When La Resistencia members then walked out on July 26 as promised and expanded their demands to include a wage hike, manufacturers issued a manifesto explaining their position. Speaking through the Cigar Manufacturers' Association, factory owners dismissed cigarworkers' three demands as "impossible and unreasonable." Similar disputes over control, they claimed, had driven the clear Havana industry out of Key West and New York and could very well force a departure from Tampa. "We have now reached the point where we positively cannot stand this condition of things any more, and we will not open our factories until we can control and run our business to suit ourselves; otherwise they will not be opened again," the manufacturers asserted in an obvious attempt to frighten Tampa's business community. In conclusion, employers appealed to "the fair-minded people of Tampa, and [gave] them the opportunity of remedying the state of affairs." Manufacturers did not suggest any particular form of community intervention, but they had in the past, of course, received support from local businessmen who had forced union leaders to leave town.[72]

Threats of vigilante action circulated immediately. On the second day of the 1901 strike, the *Tampa Tribune* reprinted without comment an editorial from another Florida newspaper that concluded, "if Tampa would march about twenty of the [Resistencia] leaders out of the city with orders not to return, the city would not be kept in confusion by a few hot headed fools."[73] Three days later a *Tribune* news story reported a rumor that " a committee of citizens was being organized to wait upon the leaders of the strike and invite their immediate and final departure from the city." The paper noted that José Padilla was "the particular target of this alleged committee's displeasure." An additional report of possible vigilante action came from the Tampa correspondent for *Tobacco Leaf*, who wrote at the end of the first week of the strike that "there is a strong probability that if things don't change pretty soon, Judge Lynch will take a hand—not to hang anyone, but a few leaders may find it expedient to change the base of their operation."[74]

On August 6, with local businesses "becoming seriously affected by the strike," Wallace Stovall assured *Tribune* readers that an end was in sight. "The method of settlement, while slightly different from those hitherto adopted, promises to be much more decisive," the editor declared in an oblique reference to vigilantism. "It has been very carefully considered and arranged, and by people who have the welfare of the city at heart."[75]

In fact, vigilantes were implementing a carefully orchestrated plan at the very moment Stovall published his inside information. During the night of August 5, an armed Citizens' Committee began seizing La Resistencia leaders. The roundup continued quietly throughout the next day until the vigilantes held fifteen men whose names appeared on a list of twenty-one "cigar strike agitators." The *Tribune* later reported that the kidnapped men included "all the conspicuous leaders of the Resistencia except for one [José Padilla], who has succeeded in eluding the vigilance of the committee of citizens and the large corps of officers who have been on the lookout for him."[76] After holding their victims incommunicado at a secret location outside the city, the Citizens' Committee released two and placed the remaining thirteen on a chartered schooner. Under cover of darkness, the ship departed on the morning of August 7 with eight to ten men guarding Resistencia leaders.[77]

The kidnapping and expulsion occurred so surreptitiously that relatives and friends had no idea what had happened to the missing men. Initial inquiries brought the response that the strike leaders had been arrested, but supporters could not find a Tampa attorney who would investigate. Once the ship had sailed, the *Tampa Tribune* indicated that the men had been "banished by force of arms," but the paper gave no destination for the deportees.[78] Despite remarkably accurate news stories in national tobacco journals, local confirmation of the victims' fate took two weeks. On August 23, the *Tribune* reported that a chartered boat had just returned from Honduras, where it had dropped the kidnapped union leaders on a deserted beach. The thirteen men were warned: "Be seen again in Tampa, and it means death."[79]

Referring to themselves as representatives of "The People of Tampa and Surrounding Country," the anonymous vigilantes claimed in a published declaration to have acted "in the interest of the entire community." Their attempt at self-justification was complicated by the fact that strikers had not engaged in any violent or illegal activities. Indeed, a statement from the vigilance committee referred to cigarworkers as "industrious, peaceable, and law-abiding." The vigilantes claimed that they could not "afford, however to have you tyrannized and terrorized by anarchists and professional labor agitators, who can only succeed . . . by creating dissensions between you and your employers." They would not permit such troublemakers "to destroy this prosperous city." The members of the Citizens' Committee further warned organizers who remained in Tampa, "if you have regard for your safety, you will shake its dust from your feet."[80]

Wallace Stovall expressed similar views in justifying "the forcible deportation." The day after La Resistencia leaders disappeared, the editor noted that "the strikers never give the authorities any trouble." The problem was that "worthy operatives" were "easily hoodwinked by designing labor agitators." Accordingly, asserted Stovall, "The business people of Tampa are to be commended for taking the matter in hand," since the "anarchists" and "professional foreign agitators" had to be eliminated from "the ranks of the honest workman." Stovall applauded "deporting those who are responsible for the trouble," because it seemed the only way of ending the strike and keeping cigar manufacturers from relocating elsewhere.[81] To counter any possible legal objection to the vigilante action, the *Tribune*'s editor invoked higher law: "No wellintentioned citizen is disposed to grumble over the banishment of the Resistencia leaders, because public policy, in some cases, must rise superior to strict legality."[82]

Members of the vigilance committee successfully concealed their identity, but general descriptions of the group emphasized its elite origins. The Citizens' Committee was most commonly identified with the Tampa business community. "The very best business sentiment of the city actuated and executed the step," the well-informed *Tribune* reported four days after the deportation. "This movement was quietly planned by the business men of the city," the Tampa correspondent for *Tobacco Leaf* confirmed. "Business men of Tampa decided that the removal of these agitators would settle the labor troubles, and a committee of 100 was organized," another national trade journal revealed. A Jacksonville newspaper report from Tampa similarly declared that "the best men of the city" had deported strike leaders.[83] None of these sources directly linked the Citizens' Committee to the Tampa Board of Trade, which had organized antilabor vigilance committees in the past. However, one of the victims claimed that the Board of Trade paid "1,000 pesos" to have Resistencia leaders deported to Honduras.[84]

A connection with one previous vigilance committee was provided by Board of Trade member D. B. McKay, the owner/editor of the *Tampa Times*. Nine years earlier he had served as secretary of the Committee of Twenty-Five. McKay's interest in the cigar industry was strengthened by his 1900 marriage to Aurora Gutiérrez, the daughter of one of Tampa's leading cigar manufacturers.[85] Nearly a decade later, McKay freely admitted to having participated in the 1901 Citizens' Committee. While campaigning for mayor in 1910, he defended his role in deporting union leaders. A newspaper reporter present at a 1910 campaign rally related that McKay explained he "had placed his life in jeopardy" in 1901 but "felt that he was doing the duty of a man and a citizen and, under similar stressful circumstances, with the very existence of this city alike involved, he would do so again."[86]

McKay's reasoning reflected the motivation of other Tampa businessmen. The deportation of La Resistencia officials was part of a well-organized effort to retain the cigar industry in Tampa and revive the local economy, which depended heavily on the factories' average weekly payroll of $80,000.[87] Considering the high stakes, businessmen easily equated their interests with the community as a whole, but they acted in behalf of the city elite. As one sympathetic observer pointed out, "the so-called Vigilance Committee really means every leading citizen of Tampa, although only a small number actually participated in the capture and isolation, as it were, of the more violent of the strikers, whose words and acts *threatened* to break the public peace."[88] No member of the Tampa elite publicly criticized the deportation. One local reporter asserted that "the overwhelming preponderance of public sentiment condones the action, and is in readiness to take still more drastic measures if the occasion warrants it." A Tallahassee newspaper claimed that "the business people of Tampa [felt] they are justified in anything almost, except the taking of human life, to bring an end of the conditions prevailing there."[89]

Cigar manufacturers certainly appreciated the intervention of the Citizens' Committee. "They make no comment whatever about the kidnapping," one reporter noted, "but the gleam in their eye tells how they feel about it."[90] National tobacco journals openly praised the vigilante businessmen. *Tobacco Leaf* asserted that "the action of the citizens of Tampa deserves national recognition and a national following."[91] Another trade spokesman resorted to xenophobia, rarely so explicit in Tampa. Describing La Resistencia as "foreign in its origin, foreign in race, foreign in tongue, and antagonistic to our laws, customs and government," this New York editor concluded: "Had the Cuban workmen assimilated themselves with the American citizens, public opinion would not have tolerated such a summary proceeding as the kidnapping and deporting of the strike leaders. But remaining merely aliens, it is being justified on the ground of 'Public Welfare'

(Pro Bono Publico).... Indeed, the public welfare of Tampa required some drastic measures."⁹²

La Resistencia's enemies in AFL locals also supported the vigilantes. Tampa's Central Trades and Labor Assembly of AFL-affiliated unions formally adopted a resolution endorsing the action of the Citizens' Committee. According to one report, local AFL officials thought the deportation of La Resistencia leaders was "in the interest of organized labor and would be beneficial to the entire labor situation."⁹³ This position expressed the enmity that often existed between the AFL and competing dual unions, but it also gave Tampa businessmen the opportunity to claim that the expulsion of La Resistencia members was not antiunion because Tampa's AFL leaders had endorsed it.

National officials of the CMIU contended that La Resistencia was not a *bona fide* union, but they publicly condemned the deportation. "While we have no use for the leaders of this so-called organization, we cannot and do not endorse the methods employed by this self-appointed committee of kidnappers," the *Cigar Makers' Official Journal* declared. The CMIU also denied that its members had in any way been involved in the vigilante action. Admitting that "some suppose . . . benefit for the International Union," CMIU officers asserted that they were "glad to be able to say that none of our members participated in this plan of deporting the strike leaders."⁹⁴

Florida newspapers overwhelmingly approved the illegal crackdown on La Resistencia. "This may be a little outside the law and constitutional rights, but the end justifies the means," declared one editor in a familiar defense of establishment violence.⁹⁵ Leading Floridians accepted a version of republicanism that claimed for property-holders in each community the ultimate right to protect their economic interests even if it required taking the law into their own hands. "In Tampa we have seen a flourishing city threatened with ruin and its business practically destroyed, because labor and capital could arrive at no agreement: did law require that the suffering be indefinitely prolonged till the stagnation and privations of a siege fell like a funeral pall on the city?" a Jacksonville paper queried. In defense of Tampa's vigilante action, the editor explained, "The court failed us—[and] the people have acted as the Anglo-Saxon has always claimed the right to do in self-protection."⁹⁶ A Pensacola newspaper declared that Tampans had understandably employed "unlawful yet effective means" in order "to prevent the unprincipled leaders of the [Resistencia] union from further interference with *the real interests* of the city and its only industry."⁹⁷ Echoing this argument, another editor asserted, "Capital has the advantage of labor, and any attempt on the part of workingmen to do injustice to employers will be quickly resisted."⁹⁸

Observers around the state also contended that the Citizens' Committee had acted with restraint. That is, the lawlessness did not threaten to get out of hand. As one newspaper put it, "In any other city in this country such lawlessness would breed lawlessness and would lead to retaliation of a like violent kind, but Tampa is largely a law unto itself, and had apparently hit upon the way to effectually hold its foreign labor element in check."[99]

One popular justification of antilabor vigilantism was that it worked. "The Tampa method of dealing with unreasonable strikes is harsh and unlawful, but it seems to be effective," a Savannah, Georgia, newspaper pointed out with a nod of approval.[100] The Citizens' Committee had so carefully selected its targets that continuation of the 1901 strike was difficult. The kidnapping eliminated La Resistencia's principal leaders, including its treasurer, who had charge of strike funds. Gone too was the editor of the union's newspaper, *La Federación*. The head of La Resistencia, José Padilla, escaped capture, but he was forced to flee Tampa with vigilantes hunting for him.[101]

Despite these setbacks and the resulting confusion in the wake of the deportations, La Resistencia continued the strike. New leaders immediately assumed the positions of departed comrades, and they expressed the determination to hold out "until our abducted leaders are restored to us, safe and sound."[102] Threatened with additional deportations, the union's new secretary declared: "We have so arranged our organization that, for every set of officers that may be removed, another set stands ready to step into their places."[103] Similar resolve was expressed by other striking cigarworkers and their supporters. "Forward Comrades! Long Live Solidarity!" cried one manifesto in response to the kidnappings.[104] "The bourgeoisie of Tampa are not accomplishing anything else but injecting in the minds and souls of the workers a most tenacious and long lasting resistance," asserted a local Italian-language paper in defense of "the dignity and self-respect of the workers who have been so brutally mistreated by the oppression of these gangsters."[105] Hundreds of cigarworkers demonstrated their willingness to continue the strike by leaving Tampa for Key West and Havana, where there was little hope of employment. Those who remained in Tampa received food in soup kitchens run by La Resistencia.[106] Despite shrinking local funds, strikers got "eloquent encouragement" in the form of financial assistance from cigarworkers in Key West and Havana.[107]

The Tampa elite responded to the continued labor resistance by increasing the legal and illegal pressures on strikers. In mid-August 1901, less than a month into the strike, landlords organized and began evicting cigarworkers who could not make rent payments. This unprecedented step further underscored the collaboration among Tampa businessmen in support of cigar manufacturers. Emboldened by the numerous endorsements of vigilantism, the anonymous members of the Citizens' Committee continued to direct force at selected targets. Vigilantes ordered another seventeen leaders of La Resistencia to leave town on August 20.[108] Most complied immediately, but the union's acting secretary defiantly crushed the written warning under his heel and exclaimed, "Damn the Americans; they cannot make me go."[109] Six days later he and the new editor of *La Federación* disappeared after having been "arrested." It became clear that the missing men had been abducted and driven out of town by vigilantes, who were probably also "special officers" empowered to make arrests.[110] In announcing the disappearance of two more strike supporters several days later, *Tobacco Leaf* assured manufacturers that "the deportations will only cease when the strike is settled, or when every cigarmaker who is addicted to the speechmaking habit has departed for other fields."[111]

Vigilante businessmen repeatedly warned that they would not tolerate peaceful, legal activities in support of the strike. When the illegal expulsion of several editors failed to prevent La Resistencia from publishing its newspaper, the Citizens' Committee finally raided the office of *La Federación*, dismantled the press, and carted it away along with other material from the office. In mid-September the Citizens' Committee also destroyed La Resistencia's soup kitchens, dumping food and breaking equipment.[112]

Despite such provocation from vigilantes, strikers remained peaceful. "There has been no disorder on the part of the striking element," a manufacturers' spokesman admitted in late September. "No doubt it is best that this policy was adopted by them, for it is no hard matter to conjecture what would have happened had violence been used by them at any time, if one takes into consideration the temper of the citizens during this trouble."[113] In part to avoid confrontations, La Resistencia continued to use its limited funds to buy tickets for hundreds of cigarworkers to leave Tampa each week. This policy served at once to relieve the financial burden on strikers remaining in Tampa and to reduce the potential for union violence against strikebreakers or company property. This did not, however, prevent the systematic use of establishment violence against strikers.[114]

Convinced that cigarmakers would return to their benches if offered protection, the Citizens' Committee organized a highly publicized back-to-work campaign during September 1901. In a one-sided agreement with the Cigar Manufacturers' Association, the Citizens' Committee pledged on September 19 to protect any worker who accepted employment in Tampa's cigar factories. Owners guaranteed jobs "under the present rules and regulations," which excluded either a wage increase or a closed shop.[115] "Every man is taken back with the same understanding—no union, no committee, the manager to control the business," one insider explained.[116] Manufacturers threatened "to fill every factory in this city with imported labor," if workers did not immediately accept these terms.[117] To back up this warning, factory owners circulated word that they had agents looking for German, Bohemian, and American cigarworkers in northern cities.[118]

When strikers still stood firm with most refusing to surrender, they became targets for another wave of repression. Vigilante violence was a reaction not only to the stubbornness of cigarworkers but also to the assassination of President William McKinley in Buffalo, New York. Verbal attacks on La Resistencia became even more vicious after a self-proclaimed anarchist killed the President in early September. "Considerable criticism has been indulged in of the Tampa method of dealing with the lawless and tyranneous [sic] Resistencia organization which threatened to destroy that city's chief industry," a Pensacola newspaper observed, "but since the Buffalo tragedy the peculiar characteristics of the Tampa organization have been much more intelligently appreciated, and the necessity for the drastic measures resorted to by citizens has been fully realized."[119]

After McKinley's assassination the *Tampa Tribune* became rabid in its appeals for vigilante violence. "Shoot the anarchists. Then the strike will come to a sudden halt," one *Tribune* editorial declared. "Exterminate the anarchists and labor agitators," another suggested.[120] After the back-to-work movement failed to attract a large number of cigarworkers, the *Tribune* called on vigilantes to move against strike leaders who supposedly kept men and women idle against their will. "The Citizens' Committee should turn its attention towards [t]he few anarchists who are left in the city," an editorial argued in October. "Wipe them out of existence and the strike will be broken."[121]

The next day vigilantes kidnapped a strike leader known to have strongly opposed any return to work.[122] The fate of the victim was unclear, but a reporter sympathetic to manufacturers confided: "It is presumed that he has gone off for his health."[123] The disappearance of this man brought to seventeen the number of La Resistencia men who had been kidnapped by vigilantes and expelled from Tampa since the strike began. In addition, at least fifteen others had fled with the Citizens' Committee looking for them.

During October 1901, with factory doors open and the strike in its third month, Tampa authorities tried another tactic to force cigarworkers to resume their jobs. Using the vagrancy law, police began making mass arrests of strikers. Brought into police court, cigarworkers were quickly found guilty of vagrancy and given a choice.[124] "Those who are willing to go to work in the factories are escorted by an officer to the one in which they desire employment, and those who do not want to work are given 30 days on the street cleaning gang," one observer explained.[125] The Citizens' Committee not only endorsed this practice but also participated in the arrest of strikers.[126] Tampa businessmen, including those in the Citizens' Committee, were sworn in as special officers and policed the city with the power to make arrests. "Almost every reputable citizen is a sworn officer," reported *Tobacco Leaf*, "and the town is thoroughly patrolled every night and all night by these citizens and the police."[127]

Under these monumental pressures the strike gradually collapsed. Throughout October cigarmakers slowly returned to work. No further vigilante violence occurred, but the threat remained ever present. "The Citizens' Committee will see to it that no one is allowed to interfere with the men at work," one industry journal vowed.[128] The final blow came in November. Unable to find a sufficient number of workers in Tampa to operate factories at full strength, employers chartered a ship to provide free passage for cigarmakers who wished to return from Havana. Despite a sympathy strike by cigarworkers in Cuba to block this strikebreaking effort, some thirty unemployed cigarmakers immediately sailed for Tampa. More were reportedly ready to follow. When the first group arrived in Tampa, they were met by members of the Citizens' Committee, who provided an escort to Ybor City.[129] Lest strikers interfere with this operation, the *Tampa Tribune* warned that "any utterance or action tending to hinder the complete restoration of pleasant and profitable relations would be fatal."[130]

With as many as 2,000 cigarworkers back in the factories, La Resistencia officially called off the strike on November 23, 1901. The decision was ratified in a unanimous voice vote by over a thousand union members. Their return on terms set by the manufacturers represented a complete defeat for La Resistencia.[131] "This was a bitter pill for 'La Resistencia' to swallow," a CMIU organizer pointed out, "but there was not anything else for them to do, as their funds were exhausted and their ranks broken." The independent, radical union never recovered and soon disappeared.[132]

Antilabor vigilantism figured prominently in the failure of the 1901 strike and the demise of the union. The presence of a competing union which did not observe the strike complicated the situation, but CMIU membership was too small to determine the outcome. Kidnappings and illegal deportations, not the CMIU, decimated the leadership of La Resistencia and hampered its ability to function effectively, especially in the midst of an industry-wide strike. The expulsion of several editors of *La Federación* and the destruction of its presses by vigilantes also deprived the organization of spokesmen who could rally workers. Although vigilante violence weakened the structure of La Resistencia, it also occasionally provided a temporary boost to the strikers' determination to remain firm in their demands. However, such short-term benefits failed to compensate for the loss of leaders and the disruption of strike activities. The intervention of the Citizens' Committee also encouraged manufacturers to stand firm and fight rather than surrender to worker demands as they had in 1899 and 1900.

Strikers rarely won prolonged struggles, since they had fewer resources than employers to sustain themselves during a shutdown. With union leaders removed and vigilantes patrolling the city, La Resistencia could ultimately do little to prevent strikebreakers, including some of its own members, from returning to work under the protective arm of the Citizens' Committee. With its resources exhausted, La Resistencia capitulated after four months. Bankrupt and in disarray, the rudderless union never regained its following among Tampa cigarworkers, who temporarily remained largely unorganized.

The use of illegal coercion to intimidate workers was encouraged not only by its success in 1901 but also by its acceptance from public officials. Since local authorities had cooperated with the Citizens' Committee in helping seize La Resistencia leaders, the victims and their supporters had appealed to state and federal officials for legal protection and punishment of the vigilantes. Several wives of the abducted men complained to Florida's governor that their husbands "were ignominiously kidnapped from our homes, and on the streets, by the police, contrary to the laws of any civilized country." Emphasizing that their husbands' "only guilt is that they're strikers," the women called for a state inquiry and "justice."[133] Despite other protests and petitions from cigarworkers, nothing came of the governor's promise to investigate.[134]

A perfunctory federal inquiry also served to legitimize establishment violence. In response to complaints about violations of federal laws, the Department of Justice ordered the U.S. attorney in Jacksonville to look into the deportations.[135] After meeting with Tampa Board of Trade members, including Congressman Stephen M. Sparkman, and with the executive committee of La Resistencia in October 1901, the U.S. attorney admitted that "a number of the most prominent agitators of the strike had been compelled to leave Tampa." However, he concluded that "it was impracticable to secure any evidence which would justify a criminal prosecution in the Federal Courts."[136]

One incident during the 1901 strike revealed clearly that elite attitudes toward collective violence depended on who wielded it and for what purpose. While Tampa strikers avoided violence, their supporters in Key West had resorted to force in late October 1901, to prevent a group of Tampa citizens from recruiting strikebreakers. The Tampa delegation, which included several businessmen and the chief of police, had gone to Key West in behalf of the American Cigar Company to recruit cigarworkers. The so-called "Importation Committee" was met in Key West by a jeering crowd of over 1,000 cigarworkers who reportedly threatened violence if the Tampans did not leave immediately. The group left when Key West authorities stated they could not guarantee them safety.[137]

This produced an outcry in Tampa. Peter O. Knight, the local lawyer for the tobacco trust, who as state attorney had taken no action against Tampa vigilantes during the strike, now demanded that the governor order the arrest of anyone in Key West who even incited violence.[138] The governor immediately complied with this request in a telegram to the sheriff in Key West.[139] Nothing further came of the incident, but the editor of the *Tampa Tribune* called it "a disgrace to the people of Florida." In contrast to his approval of establishment violence in Tampa, Wallace Stovall lectured Key West: "No community can thrive or flourish that permits open violations of law and order."[140] With a call to "Stop This Mob Rule," Stovall demanded that state and federal authorities "act in a decisive manner" to prevent violence in Key West.[141]

The irony of such rhetoric was not lost on cigarworkers. An observer sent secretly to Key West by the governor reported that "Cubans, and the Citizens generally, are very bitter against Tampa and complain at your action in trying to protect the Tampa Committee against the Cubans [in Key West], when the Tampa people had a free hand with the Cubans in Tampa."[142]

As in the past, elite coercion to repress cigarworkers encouraged further cooperation and organization among factory owners and Tampa businessmen. Toward the end of the 1901 strike, cigar manufacturers reorganized their local trade association into the Clear Havana Cigar Manufacturers' Association of Tampa, which an insider called "the strongest organization that has yet been in existence among the manufacturers."[143] This move also reflected a renewed commitment to remain in Tampa. As a result of the concerted action by the Citizens' Committee to break the strike, the city had endeared itself to manufacturers. A gratified representative of the American Cigar Company, who was visiting Tampa when the first deportations had occurred, told a reporter that "he did not think that there was another place in the Union where it could have happened so smoothly and easily."[144] The response of Tampans to the strike had shown factory owners that they had "the aid and sympathy of the citizens and the officers of the law."[145] This alliance, dating from 1887, was based on the guarantee of the Board of Trade to repress militant cigarworkers in order to insure the uninterrupted production of cigars and keep the industry from relocating.[146]

Tampa's method of dealing with strikers became a model for other communities. In a 1901 article entitled "Shanghai The Leaders—A New Solution of the Strike Problem," the *New York Herald* noted that Tampa's forced expulsion of Resistencia leaders provided "a peculiar contribution to labor history in this country." The National Association of Manufacturers (NAM) also publicized the deportations. "A few years ago the leading citizens of Tampa made up their minds that there could be no industrial peace in their city so long as certain labor agitators, members of a cigarmakers' union, were allowed to remain there," the NAM related in a 1903 issue of its official magazine. Emphasizing that cigar strikes in Tampa "interfered greatly with business," the NAM explained that union leaders were deported to Honduras. "The action of the leading citizens was illegal, but it pacified Tampa," the association informed employers. "The kidnapped agitators have not deemed it advisable to make any more trouble in that city." The NAM also reported that a town in Idaho had adopted the Tampa example with similar success.[147]

Following the collapse of La Resistencia, Tampa vigilantes tried to prevent cigarworkers from reorganizing even as part of a more conservative American union. A year after the end of the 1901 strike, a local CMIU officer reported optimistically to AFL president Samuel Gompers: "There is a great change in the Tampa situation and the entire Spanish movement has resolved to enter the C.M.I.U. of A."[148] When the AFL affiliate sought to take advantage of this opportunity, it too was threatened with vigilante violence. On March 2, 1903, James Wood, a CMIU organizer who had been in Tampa since late 1902, received the following warning:

> You are hereby commanded to leave the city at once and never return. Our men have been watching you since your arrival here and we are convinced that you are a troublemaker. Leave the city and save yourself the trouble of our being compelled to remove you which we will do if you are in the city twenty-four hours after receiving this letter. Take your big guard and leave the city under pain of death for we will not have [to] tolerate any more strikes in this city. Leave or you die.[149]

Similar threats were sent to four local CMIU leaders who were accused of inviting Wood to Tampa and "conspiring with the anarchists in Ybor [City] to bring on a strike." The anonymous vigilantes called themselves the "Committee of Tampa and Surrounding Country," the same name used by the group that had kidnapped and expelled La Resistencia leaders in 1901.[150]

The CMIU's international president, George W. Perkins, immediately demanded protection for his members and defended his union against charges levelled by the vigilance committee. In a letter to Tampa's police chief, Perkins argued that James Wood had gone to Tampa "to bring about a harmonious feeling in the cigar making trade." The CMIU also had "some control over the members and a perfected system of discipline, all of which . . . prevent hasty and ill advised strikes." In a condemnation of vigilantism, Perkins claimed that "a state of anarchy exists in the City of Tampa," because "men who owe allegiance to no one except themselves, have taken it upon themselves to enforce edicts of their own creation which are in plain violation of the . . . laws."[151] As a further precaution, Perkins sent copies of this letter to Florida's governor, the United States attorney general and President Theodore Roosevelt. The covering letter to the President argued that American citizens deserved federal protection "against the unwarranted, unlawful and outrageous threats of this self constituted vigilance Committee."[152]

Tampa's police chief denied these charges. He suggested that the threatening letters were fakes, "gotten up by one of the very men who received them for the sole purpose of unnecessarily agitating the laboring people."[153] Samuel Gompers then pointed out that the 1901 kidnappings gave credence to the "belief that the present threat is serious and emanates from a capitalistic organized banditti." The police chief countered that the 1901 committee was "composed of substantial men without regard to class or condition." Indeed, he claimed that local AFL members had approved the earlier expulsions of La Resistencia men.[154]

Deciding that "to leave under fire would be dangerous to the cigar makers union," James Wood remained in Tampa, but vigilantes pursued him when he left at the end of March 1903.[155] At his first stop in Palatka, Florida, Wood was approached by two men who called, "Hello, Wood! When you going back to Tampa?" After a brief exchange of words, the men grabbed Wood. In the ensuing struggle one of the assailants fired a gun, and then the men fled. One bullet struck Wood in the left arm, and another probably would have killed him had it not lodged in a watch in his left vest pocket.[156] Wood could not identify the attackers, but it was widely assumed that they had followed him from Tampa to carry out the earlier threat against his life.[157] The CMIU called the assault "a cowardly and criminal attempt on the part of the trust and other non-union manufacturers to prevent the organization of the workers of the South."[158]

The shooting of James Wood demonstrated that neither American citizenship nor membership in a conservative AFL union protected outsiders attempting to organize Tampa cigarworkers. Following the assault on Wood, the CMIU's national leadership concluded that three obstacles slowed organizing in Tampa. In addition to employer resistance, especially on the part of the tobacco trust, and the difficulty of attracting immigrant workers to an American union, George Perkins emphasized that in Tampa, unlike Key West, the CMIU had "to reckon with the Citizens' Committee, as well as the employers."[159]

By the time the CMIU focused its attention on Tampa, the Citizens' Committee had become a well-established tradition. As early as 1887, members of the local elite used the mechanism of vigilance committees to mobilize businessmen and professionals to repress cigarworkers and break strikes. Members of the 1901 Citizens' Committee clearly constituted "the best men of the city." They took the law into their own hands not because of criminal acts by workers or ineffective law enforcement but rather because the perfectly legal, nonviolent activities of striking cigarworkers undermined the local economy and threatened to drive out the cigar industry. As a New York newspaper pointed out, Tampa businessmen decided that the removal of La Resistencia leaders "was demanded by public policy and self-preservation."[160]

The defense of antilabor vigilantism relied on appeals to higher law reinforced by southern republicanism and the practice of community justice. These traditions gave the local elite the right to protect the city's "real interests" by whatever means necessary, including lynch law. The leadership of the 1901 strike by immigrant radicals undoubtedly explains some of the support for vigilante methods. Even local AFL leaders endorsed the deportation of La Resistencia leaders. However, the 1903 attack on an American organizer from the CMIU demonstrated that any challenge to the power of cigar manufacturers could result in vigilante violence. As long as these employers collectively resisted union recognition, they found Tampans willing to organize vigilance committees to repress workers and restore order on terms dictated by manufacturers.

The effectiveness of establishment violence depended on the complicity, or at least the tolerance, of public officials. Tampa police may have actually cooperated in the kidnapping of La Resistencia men, but in any case local officials took no steps to investigate the activities of the Citizens' Committee. The failure of state and federal authorities to move against Tampa's citizen vigilantes reinforced the dominant belief that community justice could continue to encompass illegal coercion as a legitimate means of protecting existing power relationships.

# 4

# "The Cossacks of Tampa": The Citizens' Committee of 1910–11

Following their defeat in 1901, Tampa cigarworkers remained largely unorganized. Sporadic organizing efforts by the Cigar Makers' International Union (CMIU) added several new locals and raised membership to about 1,000 by 1907, but this represented a mere 10 percent of Tampa's cigarworkers.[1] After almost a decade of relative calm in the industry, cigarworkers finally revolted in 1910. Once again, they challenged the power of factory owners, who fought back. When the conflict resulted in a strike that brought local production of cigars to a halt, manufacturers again found powerful allies in the business community, who organized another Citizens' Committee that engaged in more violence than ever before. Anonymous vigilantes also lynched two Italian immigrants in the midst of the strike. Reactions to this campaign of terror demonstrated that local and state officials still considered establishment violence a legitimate means of repressing workers.

During the first decade of the twentieth century, Tampa continued its spectacular growth. In a 1907 tour of the South, the journalist Walter Hines Page found Tampa "an exceedingly energetic city," observing that Tampans were "making money and enjoying themselves, extending the city, building beautiful homes, feeling proud of themselves, and enjoying life."[2] By 1910, the city's population had passed 37,000, more than double its size in 1900, and West Tampa contained another 8,258 people. Almost half of Tampa's residents (45.7 percent) were immigrants or had at least one foreign-born parent. The cigar industry remained the backbone of the local economy. Over one hundred cigar factories, concentrated in Ybor City and West Tampa, employed 10,500 workers, 84 percent of them foreign-born. The industry's average weekly payroll of $200,000 represented 75 percent of the city's total payroll. Producing over 250 million cigars annually, Tampa had become by 1910 the world's leading supplier of clear Havana cigars.[3] "The industry at present shows a degree of prosperity never equaled in its history," concluded a contemporary government study.[4]

While Tampa's cigar industry prospered, the conditions of employees deteriorated. Reflecting on the previous decade, a local union spokesman observed in 1910 that cigarworkers, "in their state of inertia, had been demoralized and had become careless of the defence of their rights leaving them in the care of the selfishly ambitious manufacturer."⁵ In the absence of effective organization, cigarworkers had failed to enforce the 1901 scale of wages. Pay varied widely from one factory to another, with some firms paying ten dollars less for each thousand cigars than competitors. Some Tampa employers also abused the apprenticeship system in order to hire cheaper workers to displace skilled craftsmen. "The condition of the cigarmakers during the last ten years has gone from bad to worse," the CMIU's international president, George W. Perkins, reported in late 1909. "Skilled clear Havana Spanish style workmen are receiving less wages in Tampa today than the average union cigarmaker receives for making [less skilled] mold work or the ordinary American style of handwork, in organized cities."⁶ Fearing a continuing decline among the clear Havana workers would undermine wages and conditions in other sectors of the industry, Perkins argued privately that "Tampa must be organized."⁷

The Cigar Makers' International Union mounted an organizing campaign in 1909 that met with immediate success in Tampa. After years of slow accretion in union strength, CMIU membership suddenly tripled from 2,000 to 6,000 during the winter of 1909–10. Tampa cigarworkers were enrolled in locals divided along craft lines for cigarmakers and other skilled workers—such as selectors, who graded tobacco leaves. These locals formed a Joint Advisory Board (JAB), which published its own newspaper, *El Internacional*.⁸ The CMIU's willingness to take such steps as temporarily reducing its initiation fee to one dollar helped attract new members, but Tampa cigarworkers were ripe for collective action. During a two-week visit in November 1909, George Perkins found "a vast change for the better in the attitude of the average cigarmaker of Tampa toward the International Union, compared with ten or even four years ago." The union's president attributed this "genuine interest" to the immigrant workers' realization that their situation had declined "because of lack of organization."⁹

Aware of past labor struggles in Tampa, Perkins tempered his elation with words of caution. He called on Tampa cigarworkers to convince "employers that you will refuse to countenance or sustain hasty or ill-advised strikes and that you will and can settle all wage and other disputes by the more rational and satisfactory method of conference." Warning against radicals, "the alleged leaders who seek to plunge you into discord," Perkins pleaded with Tampa operatives to "be guided by fearless and conservative leaders." The CMIU's president argued that to succeed, cigarworkers had to "win the respect at least of the employers and the citizens generally."¹⁰ The latter group was critical because, as Perkins reminded the union's national leadership, "One of the drawbacks to organization in Tampa, formerly was the 'Citizens' Committee.'" Since the city's economy was based largely on the cigar industry, "the 'Citizens' Committee' [was] ever ready to back the employers in any effort to stifle the growth of unionism," Perkins pointed out. "The citizens through their committee were always ready to fight for the maintenance of their property."[11]

During 1910, Perkins' worst fears were realized in the form of a six-month strike which was finally broken with the aid of a revived Citizens' Committee. Before the walkout the solid organization of most cigarworkers brought success in negotiations between the union's Joint Advisory Board and Tampa's Clear Havana Cigar Manufacturers' Association. The latter group represented thirty-eight of the city's largest employers, collectively controlling 90 percent of Tampa's production of cigars. Early in 1910 these manufacturers agreed to abide by a new scale of wages for some 107 cigar sizes. After cigarmakers won this pay increase without a strike, unionized selectors pushed first for a reduction in the number of apprentices and then for a union shop and formal recognition. The call for union recognition was endorsed by cigarmakers, who also complained that employers were not paying the recently approved scale of wages.[12]

After manufacturers refused to negotiate these issues, the CMIU struck a few selected factories, beginning in July 1910. Employers responded by temporarily laying off many workers. This escalating power struggle led the CMIU to declare a general strike of Tampa's entire cigar industry in early August. The walkout halted most cigar production, but a number of factories, especially smaller ones which were not in the Cigar Manufacturers' Association, remained open with a token force of nonunion workers.[13]

The 1910 shutdown was another control strike in which the primary issue was power rather than wages. *Tobacco Leaf* called the strike "an attempt to install the workmen in the place of the employer."[14] Tampa factory owners took the position that they would discuss wages but would not negotiate the union shop or formal union recognition. "There is only one question at issue," the Cigar Manufacturers' Association asserted in an open letter to "the Citizens of Tampa," and that was the workers' demand "that the International Cigarmakers Union be recognized and that none but members of this union be employed in the factories of Tampa." Emphasizing that employers would meet with representatives of cigarworkers to discuss other issues, as they earlier had in arriving at a new wage agreement, manufacturers declared that they did "not propose to enter into any negotiations having in view a recognition of the international or any other union." Factory owners warned that they would stick to this position, "even if it becomes necessary to close every factory belonging to our organization indefinitely."[15] A New York spokesman for a firm with interests in Tampa declared bluntly: "President Perkins and other officials of the International are out for blood. We must have their blood or they will have ours. . . . We are going to win, but we will have to fight to win."[16]

In an attempt to counter such arguments, the president of Tampa's Joint Advisory Board, José de la Campa, declared that workers had joined the CMIU to protect themselves from "the encroachments of those who would oppress us and treat us unfairly." He claimed that the organization of cigarworkers was designed to counterbalance the organization of employers and to "put an end to the convulsive movements in the cigar industry." Addressing himself to "the American people" in Tampa, de la Campa emphasized that the JAB had operated "in a very peaceable way." "The least the cigarmakers can ask for is recognition of their union," he concluded.[17]

Support for this demand came from other trade unionists in Tampa. At the start of the strike, local members of AFL affiliates showed their solidarity with cigarworkers by joining in "the greatest international labor demonstration in the history of Tampa." Nearly 1,000 unionized construction workers, printers, machinists, and longshoremen marched with more than 2,000 cigarworkers to a huge rally in Ybor City that attracted 5,000 people. The integrated audience heard speakers endorse the strike in English, Spanish, and Italian.[18] Similar expressions of sympathy came several weeks later when marchers in the annual Labor Day parade carried placards declaring that many Tampa workers already had the union shop.[19] This display forced the *Tampa Tribune* to admit that "the manufacturing of cigars is the only industry of consequence in this city which is not conducted under the union recognition plan." However, the cigar industry was also the largest business in Tampa and the only one dominated by well-organized employers, including many absentee owners, who collectively opposed union recognition.[20]

The Tampa Board of Trade tried unsuccessfully to bring a peaceful end to the strike. By 1910, the board's membership of almost 300 men represented "the bone and sinew, the push and hustle, of [Tampa's] entire business community."[21] On August 13, the Board of Trade appointed a committee of ten local notables to mediate the dispute. This group included three bank presidents, an officer of a fourth bank, and two real estate developers. Other committee members were Perry G. Wall, the Florida-born nephew of Joseph B. Wall and co-owner of one of the largest mercantile companies in Florida; Matthew B. Macfarlane, the brother of Hugh Macfarlane and the collector of customs; and Howell T. Lykes, a Florida native and president of Lykes Brothers,

Angelo Albano and Castenge Ficarrotta, still handcuffed together, on the morning after they were lynched in 1910. University of South Florida Special Collections.

West Tampa in 1906. The large building in the upper left is the Tampa Bay Hotel which was constructed in the late 1880s and opened in 1891. Tampa–Hillsborough County Public Library System.

Selectors at the Sánchez & Haya factory, choosing tobacco leaf for use as cigar wrappers. Florida State Archives.

Hugh C. Macfarlane, the founder of West Tampa and a leader of the 1910 Citizens' Committee. University of South Florida Special Collections.

a large cattle-raising and import-export firm based in Tampa.²² Committee member Wallace Stovall reflected the sentiments of local businessmen when he expressed the wish in his newspaper that "the present trouble will be settled in an amicable way before it has . . . very seriously hamper[ed] the growth and prosperity of the city."²³ The cost of the strike was estimated at $200,000 in weekly wages, "directly lost to the cigar factory employes and withdrawn from the channels of local trade."²⁴ After ten days of consulting with representatives of both sides, the Board of Trade committee offered a plan which the union rejected because it excluded both recognition and the union shop.²⁵ Local CMIU leaders complained that Tampa businessmen "failed because they went at it considering things from the staind point [standpoint] of their private interest."²⁶

On September 3, members of the Cigar Manufacturers' Association made a show of locking up their factories, which had been officially open, and coupled this step with talk of temporarily expanding production at branch factories in other cities. Such a threat was clearly designated to exploit persistent fears among Tampa businessmen that the industry might relocate permanently.²⁷

After the failure of initial attempts to settle the strike peacefully, momentum gradually built for invoking the vigilante tradition. The *Tampa Tribune* had already argued that most strikers would probably return to their jobs, "were it not for the presence of a few agitators, who keep the employed in a constant state of excitement working harm to the city." Support for this view came from a national tobacco journal which called de la Campa "an incendiary agitator whose only purpose seems to be to prolong the strike."²⁸ Toward the end of August, the first reports of strike-related violence sparked threats of a vigilante crackdown. "If the authorities prove incapable of handling the situation, citizens should organize and insure peace and order," the *Tribune* declared after a worker was "roughly handled" by strikers.²⁹

In mid-September several alleged shooting incidents were used to incite further feeling against strikers. On September 13, shots were reportedly fired at a cigar factory owner and at a foreman in separate incidents.³⁰ Neither man was hit, but exaggerated reports circulated of "murderous assaults" and "the reign of terror which has been created among the cigar makers by mobs led by De [la] Campa and his associates."³¹

On September 14 came an outburst of violence that triggered deadly lynch law. J. F. Easterling, the bookkeeper at a West Tampa cigar factory, was shot and severely wounded as he stepped from his car to go to work. Easterling did not see who fired at him, but he claimed that the shots came from a crowd of strikers. Stressing that Easterling was "the first American to be attacked," the *Tampa Tribune* argued that the shooting proved that members of "the lawless element ... have the temerity to assault an American who happens to incur their displeasure."[32] Six days after the attack, as the victim lay seriously injured in a hospital, police arrested two Italian immigrants and charged them with the attempted murder of Easterling. The arrest of Angelo Albano and Castenge Ficarrotta, however, failed to satisfy a group of Tampans, who immediately took the law into their hands.[33]

Within hours after their arrest, Albano and Ficarrotta were seized by a well-organized gang of vigilantes and hanged. The lynchers were given their opportunity by a curious set of circumstances that aroused suspicion of official complicity. After being taken into custody by police at about 6 p.m. on September 20, Albano and Ficarrotta had been placed in the West Tampa jail. That evening the county sheriff sent a deputy to transfer the prisoners to Tampa's county jail, which was considered more secure. Despite this show of concern for the safety of the prisoners, the sheriff's deputy enlisted only one friend, a Tampa fire captain, to assist. The two men took a horse-drawn hack to West Tampa, where they picked up Albano and Ficarrotta, and started back to Tampa at about 9 p.m. The sheriff's deputy later reported that the hack went only a short distance before it was suddenly stopped by twenty to thirty armed men who were lying in wait along a dark, deserted stretch of road. The vigilantes grabbed the prisoners, who were handcuffed together, and fled in automobiles. Unable to follow the faster cars, the deputy returned to West Tampa to sound the alarm.[34]

Officials soon found Albano and Ficarrotta. Still handcuffed together, they were hanging from a giant oak tree in a wooded area near where they had been abducted. Albano had been shot in the abdomen, but the coroner ruled that both men had died as a result of broken necks, "the members of the mob having allowed the bodies to drop the necessary four to six feet."[35] Pinned to Albano's clothes was a note, signed "JUSTICE," which declared: "BEWARE! OTHERS TAKE NOTICE OR GO THE SAME [W]AY. WE KNOW EVEN MORE. WE ARE WATCHING YOU. IF ANY MORE CITIZENS ARE MOLESTED, LOOK OUT."[36] Backing up this warning, anonymous letters were soon received by José de la Campa and other CMIU officials, who were threatened with similar violence if they did not leave town.[37]

No member of the lynch mob was ever identified, but this did not prevent the circulation of several explanations of the double lynching. Tampa authorities and the establishment press emphasized the criminal background of the two immigrants. Ficarrotta, a naturalized citizen in his forties who had lived in Tampa for some time, had been tried the previous year for the murder of his cousin. Although a jury had found Ficarrotta innocent, the state attorney declared in the wake of the lynching that Ficarrotta should have been convicted and legally executed for killing his cousin. Albano, a twenty-four-year-old alien, had at one time worked in the local cigar industry, but the *Tribune* stressed rumors about his alleged involvement in various criminal activities.³⁸ Labeling Ficarrotta "a professional murderer" and Albano his "assistant in his homicidal trade," the *Tribune* claimed two days after the lynching that "the victims of this expression of public indignation were fortunate in escaping the noose as long as they did." This defense of lynch law tied it to a form of crime control. "There will probably be a suspension of 'Black Hand' activities in Tampa," the *Tribune's* editor concluded optimistically. A Miami newspaper, describing the victims as "professional murderers" who previously "had managed to escape justice," further supported this view. "The whole community, in fact, the whole state, is better off because the two men have been removed," the paper argued.³⁹

A more widely accepted justification of the double lynching linked it directly to the cigarworkers' strike. In an editorial entitled "A Lynching and a Lesson," the *Tampa Tribune* noted that the "corpses swinging in the moonlight" represented "the verdict that the people of this city will not tolerate . . . assassination for hire." While admitting that the victims were not directly connected with the strike, the *Tribune* contended that "they were acting as agents of a certain element of the strikers in their attempt to end the life of Mr. Easterling."⁴⁰ Worker violence would force manufacturers to leave Tampa, just as they had earlier moved from Key West "on far less provocation." Therefore, Tampa's economic survival was at stake. "The magnificent industry which has been built up in this city by its business men, through liberal concessions to the manufacturers and by giving them protection when their interests were attacked, is on the verge of disintegration," Wallace Stovall lectured in the *Tribune*.⁴¹

After raising the specter of economic ruin and invoking the tradition of intervention by businessmen, Stovall argued that "it was certainly time for strong hands to intervene and do conclusive and unmistakable work." Without actually admitting that community leaders had killed Albano and Ficarrotta or ordered it done, Stovall left no doubt that he considered the double lynching part of an effort by the Tampa elite to reassert its control:

> The ban of condemnation was placed upon the hired assassin and the influences behind him. The sturdy and determined citizenry of Tampa asserted itself. The people who have built up this city and who have protected its interests and its welfare in the past are not to be found wanting at this critical juncture. They have served notice that *the control and direction of this community is to be retained by its*

*law-abiding, representative and reputable citizens*—and that its future is not to be blasted through the malevolent combination of the hired assassin and the transient agitator.⁴²

Speaking for Tampa's largely southern-born elite, which had used similar arguments to defend vigilante action in the past, the *Tribune's* editor typically portrayed lynch law as a legitimate form of community justice designed to protect dominant local interests.

Interpretations of the lynching as an expression of establishment violence came from a variety of sources. The CMIU pointed out that the lynchers' use of automobiles, which few people could afford in 1910, strongly suggested that the so-called mob was composed of men "with boiled shirts, high collars, diamonds and kid gloves."⁴³ One national tobacco journal claimed that the shooting of Easterling and the hanging of the accused by "a self-appointed vigilance committee" were "the logical fruits of the many incendiary utterances from the lips of José de [la] Campa and his associates—the agitators who have fomented the present strike in Tampa."⁴⁴ *Tobacco Leaf* declared that the "recent 'necktie party' . . . suggests that the citizenship of Tampa are at last fully aroused to the fact that the commercial interest of the city is in jeopardy."⁴⁵

The Cigar Makers' Union, while vehemently denying that the lynch victims were either practicing cigarworkers or involved in the strike, nonetheless agreed that the two Italians were "lynched due to the strike."⁴⁶ Spokesmen for cigarworkers saw the lynching as an attempt to intimidate strikers. The union paper, *El Internacional*, noted that the hanging "clearly reveals what our enemies are capable of doing to defeat us" but added that such violence would not frighten workers who had justice on their side.⁴⁷

Further support for the view that the lynching was an example of class violence came from an Italian official who visited Tampa to investigate the double murder. This inquiry resulted from the apparent unwillingness of local and state authorities to pursue the matter despite official complaints from the Italian embassy in Washington. Florida's Governor Albert W. Gilchrist tried to deflect protests from Italian officials by claiming that Ficarrotta was a naturalized citizen and that Albano had been born in the United States. However, the Italian ambassador soon supplied indisputable evidence that Albano was a native of Sicily, and the ambassador ordered an Italian vice-consul to make a personal investigation of the killings.⁴⁸ After interviewing a number of people in Tampa, the vice-consul reported privately that he could uncover "no direct evidence against the principals in the lynching, as the Americans will not incriminate themselves and the Italians will not speak from fear of retaliation, they being terrorized by the lynchers themselves." Nevertheless, the Italian official concluded from indirect evidence that the lynching was a well-coordinated effort to intimidate strikers and simultaneously eliminate two undesirable immigrants:

> From the opinion of the Italian colony at Tampa and from the result of my inquiry I have reason to believe that the lynching itself was not the outcome of a temporary outburst of popular anger, but was rather planned, in cold blood, to the most trifling detail, by some citizens of West Tampa with the tacit assent of a few police officers, and all with the intention of teaching an awful lesson to the strikers of the cigar factories who had passed from quiet protest to acts of violence against the manufacturers and, at the same time, of getting rid of two "terrible ruffians," one, a professional cutthroat, and the other a suborner and schemer.[49]

Given the unpopularity of the lynch victims, the conservative nature of the violence, and the probable complicity of the police, local authorities showed little interest in finding the guilty parties. When the governor inquired about the progress of the investigation, the Hillsborough County sheriff responded simply that Albano and Ficarrotta "came to their death at the hands of parties unknown." Minimizing the double murder, the sheriff stressed the previous criminal activities of the two Italian victims, "both of whom the people believe should long ago have either been sent to the penitentiary or hanged."[50]

Official indifference to the lynching encouraged another wave of vigilantism. Soon after the mob killing, leading Tampans created a new Citizens' Committee which ultimately helped crush the strike through extensive violence. The public campaign for organization of a vigilance committee was spearheaded by Wallace Stovall, who used the pages of the *Tampa Morning Tribune* to arouse the "good people of Tampa . . . in defense of their city and its welfare."[51] In an editorial entitled "SELF-PRESERVATION THE FIRST LAW OF THE CITY," Stovall declared that the strike threatened "PRESERVATION OF TAMPA'S CHIEF INDUSTRY." He blamed the prolonged work stoppage on "the interference of fanatical leaders," and he stated flatly that "the agitator has prevented amicable settlement."[52] Accusing Tampa businessmen of "evasion and even of downright cowardice" for failing to confront this threat to "the very life-blood of the town," Stovall concluded that "the time has come for the best people in Tampa to take charge of things and banish all those who are conspiring against the city and its interests."[53]

Manufacturers also appealed for a crackdown on strikers. In late September, when the cigar industry traditionally began its busiest season of the year, several factory owners issued complaints from their offices in New York. "We manufacturers believe that the substantial citizens of Tampa are in sympathy with us, but in spite of this fact, shooting, killing and general disorder prevails," one anonymous employer observed in an inverview. "Therefore," he warned, "the future of our business in Tampa . . . is not very encouraging to the manufacturers."[54] A similar threat to leave Tampa came from another factory owner, who wrote to *Tobacco Leaf,* "The manufacturers have appealed to the citizens of Tampa for protection [of] their lives and property, and while I believe the best people in the city are in sympathy with us, we have not received the protection asked for." He feared that "the manufacturers will find it necessary to scatter."[55]

Two fires in Tampa, set by unknown arsonists during the night of October 1, provided additional momentum for vigilante action. The perpetrators escaped detection, but the destruction of a cigar factory and minor damage at the *Tribune's* offices were used by Wallace Stovall as "evidences of the presence in this community of an anarchistic, law-defying element, who stop at nothing to accomplish their hellish purposes." The fires proved to the *Tribune's* owner that "neither the Mayor nor any other duly elected and constituted authority has any appreciable hand in the direction of affairs." Faced with "a condition bordering on anarchy," Stovall declared in a *Tribune* editorial that the community would not be safe "until Tampa's civic sentiment is aroused to the point of asserting itself and eradicating the ruinous and destructive agencies."[56]

That morning the Tampa elite began organizing a Citizens' Committee. At 10 a.m. on October 4, 1910, "an assemblage of determined men," in the words of one reporter, filled the main chamber of the county courthouse. The meeting attracted hundreds of Tampans from "every line of business and industry and every profession."[57] Mayor D. B. McKay, who had admitted during his recent campaign for office that he had participated in the illegal deportation of strike leaders in 1901, called the 1910 meeting to order and explained that the purpose was to save the city from the most serious crisis it had ever faced. The mayor then nominated Colonel Hugh Macfarlane as chairman. Macfarlane was immediately elected by acclamation. Clyde Glenn, owner of an advertising agency and local correspondent for *Tobacco,* was elected secretary.[58]

Upon taking the chair, Macfarlane reviewed the course of the two-month-old strike. In addition to detailing "outrages," allegedly committed by union men and "assassins for hire," Macfarlane claimed that both he and Wallace Stovall had received death threats. However, Macfarlane assured the gathering that he would not be deterred from continuing to do his duty to Tampa as he had for twenty-six years. "With every dollar I am worth and every drop of blood in my body, I will protect the future of Tampa," he boasted.⁵⁹ "Are you going to stand idly by and permit such a reign of anarchism and lawlessness or will you protect your lives and property even if it becomes necessary for every one of us to shoulder a gun?" This call to arms was greeted with shouts of approval.⁶⁰

Colonel Peter Oliphant Knight then took the platform. Like Macfarlane, Knight was a lawyer who had once served as state attorney, and through his many investments, especially in local banks and utilities, he had become one of the richest men in Florida. His birth in a northern state (Pennsylvania) made him an exception among members of Tampa's predominantly southern-born elite, but Knight had lived in Florida since 1884, when he took up residence at the age of eighteen. In a tribute to his acculturation, a reporter once observed that "Colonel Knight is a Floridian by adoption, investment and inclination."⁶¹ His close association with the cigar industry dated back to the beginning of the enterprise in Tampa, when he served as attorney for the Ybor City Land and Development Company. He later became local counsel for a number of corporations, including the American Tobacco Company and its trust factories in Tampa.⁶² "His influence, though not appearing on the surface, is a power in the land," a Hillsborough County editor pointed out.⁶³

Knight, therefore, appeared before the organizational meeting of the 1910 Citizens' Committee as a preeminent community leader. He introduced seven resolutions that he had previously drafted with the assistance of John P. Wall, Jr., a former city attorney and the nephew of Joseph B. Wall, the head of the vigilance committees of 1887 and 1892, who was still circuit court judge.⁶⁴ Emphasizing that the production of cigars accounted for 65 percent of the city's total income and provided "a basis for several other millions of dollars being paid in wages annually," the resolutions claimed that the continued existence of this industry was seriously threatened by widespread lawlessness, fomented by "agitators among the working classes of this city." The resolutions pointed out that Tampans had "always pledged the manufacturing interests that in any and all events the industry will be protected." Following this precedent, the resolutions held individual members of the cigarworkers' Joint Advisory Board personally responsible for acts of lawlessness in the community. Enforcement of these pledges was left in the hands of "a committee that has been already appointed by the business interests of this city to devise ways and means of settling this strike." The document concluded with an endorsement of any future actions taken by leaders of the Citizens' Committee.⁶⁵

These resolutions were formally adopted. After Colonel Macfarlane announced that anyone in disagreement should depart, only one lone dissenter left. The remaining group of over 400 men unanimously endorsed the resolutions by voice vote, followed by a roll call in which all present agreed to sign the document.[66]

The formation of the 1910 Citizens' Committee again demonstrated the class origins of establishment violence. In describing the public meeting, one report pointed out that the "best citizens of Tampa" had expressed "absolute support" for "certain plans for the settlement of the strike." The *Tribune* accurately observed that an "idea of the character of the meeting may be gained from a perusal of the names of the men composing it." Initiated and led by residents of substantial wealth and political power, including Tampa's mayor and the founder of West Tampa, the Citizens' Committee also obtained the endorsement of 432 local officials, businessmen, and professionals, who publicly signed their names to the enabling resolutions.[67] "It is an impressive and strong column of names and embodies the backbone of the business community," the local reporter for a tobacco journal emphasized.[68]

The membership of the 1910 Citizens' Committee also revealed clearly what Tampa's establishment meant by the much-used term "citizen." Scarcely any of the signatories could have been considered part of the working class.[69] Nevertheless, the *Tribune's* owner, who had affixed his own name to the resolutions, concluded expansively that it "would be difficult to get together a more representative body of Tampa citizens." Drawing on traditional republican theory, this claim based citizenship on property and position, rather than on place of birth, nationality, or residence. Wallace Stovall implicitly made a distinction between "citizen" and "resident." On the morning after "the solid citizenship of Tampa" had taken its collective stand, he asserted in an editorial that "every *resident* must be for Tampa or against it and labor union men, like all other men, must take one side or the other." Next to this editorial, the *Tribune* reprinted a column from an Ocala newspaper which suggested that "the law-abiding citizens of Tampa . . . suspend the rules for awhile, form a mafia of their own, round up the agitators, load them into a steamboat, the more leaky the better, head them for the open sea and establish a shotgun quarantine against their return." In justification of vigilantism, this Florida editor concluded: "It's what an American community generally does when all other means fail."[70]

The organization of Tampa "citizens" to break the cigar strike was part of a growing antiunion movement in the city. Four days prior to the mass meeting, a Tampa printer unilaterally ended his employment of union printers under an International Typographical Union contract. Hailing the benefits of the open shop, this employer bragged that he would "no longer suffer the ills of arbitrary constructions of a contract with the union." The *Tribune* reported that the printer had been assured the support of Tampa businessmen, who deluged him with new orders.⁷¹ Building contractors, the primary employers of workers under union contract in Tampa, also defended the open shop after formation of the Citizens' Committee.⁷² The *Tribune* claimed that the resolutions creating the Citizens' Committee stood "unequivocally for the 'open shop.'" Calling Tampa "the strongest organized union city in the south," Wallace Stovall expressed doubt that "unionism will ever be as strong again in Tampa as it was at the beginning of the present trouble."⁷³

Recognizing the threat to all workers posed by the new vigilance committee, Tampa trade unionists remained united in their support of cigarworkers. The week after creation of the Citizens' Committee, Tampa's Central Trades and Labor Assembly renewed its pledge of financial and moral support for strikers. This step angered the secretary of the Citizens' Committee, who warned that the city's "best citizens are standing firmly together . . . to make Tampa an open town in the future, and forever rid it of union domination."⁷⁴

The Citizens' Committee focused its attention on ending the strike by cigarworkers. In mid-October, leaders of the vigilance committee met privately with a number of cigar manufacturers who were called to Tampa by Enrique Pendas, the president of the local Cigar Manufacturers' Association. As a result of this conference, thirty-six of the city's largest factory owners, who dominated local production, agreed to reopen their factories on Monday, October 17.⁷⁵ This decision was encouraged by the belief that many of their workers were prepared to return. In addition, the *Tampa Tribune* noted that "manufacturers have been also prompted to this action by the assurance from the citizens' organization that they will be protected to the utmost extent, and that agitators will not be permitted to interfere in any way with workers who wish to return to the factories." Wallace Stovall warned "agitators to understand [that] they will not have the [police] officers alone to deal with, but an organization of determined citizens."⁷⁶

The well-organized and well-armed vigilantes wasted no time in attempting to intimidate strikers. Led by Hugh Macfarlane, the Citizens' Committee moved into action on the day before the scheduled reopening of the factories. After learning that cigarworkers were meeting at the Labor Hall in West Tampa, Macfarlane headed a delegation from the Citizens' Committee that went to the hall and demanded a hearing. He informed workers that the strike was over, and he pointedly told José de la Campa and other union officials that they would no longer be permitted to damage the interests of the city.⁷⁷

Later that same day the Citizens' Committee prepared for battle. At a huge meeting, over 200 Tampa businessmen were sworn in by

Mayor McKay as special policemen to patrol the community upon the reopening of the cigar factories the following morning.[78] These "citizen-policemen" operated under the guise of the law, but this did not prevent them from violating the law. Indeed, it probably encouraged them. In a further attempt to legitimize its strike-breaking activities, the Citizens' Committee also distributed leaflets in English and Spanish with the following message:

### NOTICE

> To the Cigar Workmen and all Citizens of Tampa, Ybor City and West Tampa:
> We, the Citizens' Committee, guarantee absolute protection to any one, who desires to go to work in any of the cigar factories of this community both in going to and from work and to their homes.
> CITIZENS' COMMITTEE
> Guaranteed by Court House Committee.[79]

The so-called "Court House Committee" referred to the public meeting that had adopted enabling resolutions for the Citizens' Committee on October 4.

Several hundred members of the Citizens' Committee were deployed before dawn for the reopening of the factories. The *Tribune* reported that the "serious-minded men were lawyers, doctors, bankers, manufacturers, brokers, merchants and other classes of business men . . . [who] represented the bone and sinew of Tampa's commercial and industrial life." Colonel Macfarlane led the group assigned to West Tampa. The Ybor City contingent was commanded by another lawyer, Colonel Charles C. Whitaker, a Florida native and former Tampa city attorney. The heavily armed vigilantes, empowered as special policemen to make arrests, patrolled in fifty private automobiles, and they vigorously enforced a proclamation from Mayor McKay that prohibited strikers from gathering near the cigar factories.[80]

The Citizens' Committee members let the desired end dictate the means. When a group of strikers resorted to silent protest by wearing cards with the Spanish word meaning "defiance," Colonel Macfarlane ordered the men to remove the badges. Vigilantes also emptied the Labor Hall in West Tampa, nailed the door shut, and left a sign reading, "This Place is Closed For All Time." Despite such clear violations of the law by the Citizens' Committee, the *Tampa Tribune* insisted that it "will be a mere technicality if any of the actions of any of the squads of citizen deputies are declared illegal."[81]

These heavy-handed tactics failed to achieve the immediate objective. A Citizens' Committee member who was also a correspondent for *Tobacco Leaf* reported that the group wanted to demonstrate "to the disturbing element that the men who own property and have a regard for the interest of the city propose to take care of the destinies of the city, even if it becomes necessary to handle a few undesirables without gloves."[82] However, only 100 of the more than 9,000 strikers returned to work the first day. Undeterred by this setback, the *Tribune* promised "no lagging on the part of citizen deputies . . . [who] will not lay down their arms and give up their badges until the city's most important industry is again on safe ground, in the hand of its owners."[83]

As vigilante squads patrolled the community and intimidated workers, prominent members of the Citizens' Committee also used the courts in an attempt to suppress strike leaders. On the basis of warrants sworn out by Wallace Stovall, CMIU officials were charged with conspiring to incite riots. Most of the accused men, including José de la Campa, were members of the union's Joint Advisory Board. De la Campa and four others were arrested on the Monday the cigar factories officially reopened. When cigarworkers cheered several leaders as police escorted them from the Labor Temple in Ybor City, Stovall drew a revolver and directed fellow vigilantes to clear the hall. Authorities could not locate five other union men who remained at large.[84]

On the second day of the back-to-work movement, eight of the same union officers were also charged with the more serious crime of conspiring to cause the death of J. F. Easterling, who had been allegedly shot by Albano and Ficarrotta. After signing warrants for the arrest of the eight men, three of whom were already in jail, the county judge ordered police to seize CMIU records to find evidence to support the conspiracy charge. Mayor McKay also ordered the Labor Temple in Ybor City closed. Since the building housed the offices of other AFL unions, as well as the Central Trades and Labor Assembly, its temporary closing interrupted the operation of many Tampa unions.[85]

Once CMIU leaders were in jail, vigilantes did their best to keep them there. After bail was set at $3,000 each, a member of the Citizens' Committee declared: "It was intimated to the prisoners that any effort on their part to be released might not meet with the approval of some of the more nervous citizens, and they, realizing that there was safety and protection in jail, decided to remain at the county boarding house until the atmosphere had cleared."[86] Tampa workers feared that vigilantes might lynch jailed strike leaders, and a number of labor people stood guard one night to protect the prisoners.[87]

The *Tampa Tribune* failed to mention Wallace Stovall's personal involvement in some of these highly questionable activities. This made it easier for the publisher to defend the Citizens' Committee. "Everything done so far has been by authority of law and on warrant from constituted authority," Stovall contended on October 19. "If the exercise of this authority has seemed to involve harshness, it is because the evil proceeded against demanded severe remedies."[88] While claiming that these "activities are directed against the agitators rather than against the workers," Stovall warned all strikers that the "next steps in the movement to place the cigar industry again in full operation will doubtless be eviction and the vagrancy law."[89]

The initial crackdown by vigilantes and the courts brought fewer than two hundred cigarworkers into the factories, but it produced a flood of protests from trade unionists. Locally, the JAB's newspaper, *El Internacional*, referred to the Citizens' Committee as "the Cossacks of Tampa," who were motivated by "the craving for money that has caused a number of heartless, innoble [sic] citizens to disregard Freedom, Justice, . . . and even the Constitution of their own country."[90] The union paper complained that the vigilantes directed their violence at nonviolent workers. Organized cigarworkers found themselves aligned against "that Trinity composed of the three distinct persons, manufacturers, citizens and officers of the law," and this "crowd of narrow minded men" had failed to understand the fundamental causes of the conflict.[91] "The economic differences are the sources of all trouble in society and . . . when the capitalist oppresses the laborer the most [,] these conflicts are . . . the natural result of oppression," *El Internacional* argued.[92]

Local Socialists also denounced the Citizens' Committee. One spokeswoman observed that the "life and liberty of men is not safe in Tampa if they are not capitalists or their allies."[93] The Tampa chapter of the Socialist Party of America formally condemned "the present high handed and unlawful act of His Honor, Mayor McKay, and the city government, by arming hundreds of able bodied men, filled with malice and hatred, and commissioned . . . to intimidate and abuse our peaceable and law-abiding citizens." Calling on the governor to defend the rights of all citizens, Tampa Socialists claimed that this was unlikely "until the wealth of the Nation is collectively owned and controlled."[94]

More moderate but equally ineffective protests came from Samuel Gompers. After receiving several complaints from trade unionists in Tampa, the president of the AFL asked Governor Gilchrist to provide protection for workers' rights and lives.[95] Gompers was especially concerned about a report that both a secretary of one of the CMIU locals and his son had been arrested by members of the Citizens' Committee, who "carried them to the depot in an auto and made several threats [about] what would become of them if they came back."[96]

These charges elicited denials from Tampa officials. Defending the legality of Citizens' Committee activities, Mayor McKay declared, "The citizens of Tampa have been acting . . . as sworn officials of the city and county, [and] they have been carefully instructed to conform strictly to the law and have done so; there [have] been no threats and no intimidation."⁹⁷ Such statements, however, only reinforced the belief of cigarworkers that Tampa's "city and county governments are absolutely at the beck and call of the noble 'Citizens' Committee.'" The CMIU explained that "Tampa's big business men have shown more than once that when their income was affected they would not hesitate at lawlessness to gain their point."⁹⁸

Appeals to federal authorities also failed to generate any outside pressure on Tampa vigilantes. As part of a national letter-writing campaign organized by labor and directed at President William Howard Taft, central labor councils around the country protested "the outrages committed upon the striking cigarmakers by the authorities and violators of law and order generally, at Tampa."⁹⁹ This resulted in a routine inquiry by the U.S. attorney in Jacksonville, who privately assured the Department of Justice that "there is nothing that calls for Federal intervention."¹⁰⁰

With the state and federal governments assuming a hands-off policy, vigilante businessmen continued to patrol Tampa streets, "armed with Winchesters day and night," as one of them bragged.¹⁰¹ Unable to point to significant results, the secretary of the Citizens' Committee explained to cigar manufacturers that "it is a slow proposition, for the reason that the agitators that have terrorized [workers] were of their own race and the Citizens' Committee are Americans, foreign to the cigar makers."¹⁰²

Vigilantes also cooperated in the effort to convict strike leaders on vague and shifting conspiracy charges. Several trials featured members of the Citizens' Committee as prosecutors and prosecution witnesses.¹⁰³ In November, after several trials on different charges, a jury found three CMIU leaders—José de la Campa, Brit Russell, and Joseph F. Bartlum—guilty of conspiring through speeches to prevent cigarworkers from returning to work. Emphasizing the impact of this alleged conspiracy, one prosecutor told the jury that the "strike probably is the most disastrous one in the history of the State of Florida or of the South."¹⁰⁴ The convicted men received the maximum penalty—a year on the chain gang.¹⁰⁵ Confident that the guilty verdicts would have "a very salutary effect upon the local situation," the *Tampa Tribune* heralded the fact that "these agitators were not made the victims of summary punishment; they were not handled by a mob or in defiance of constituted authority; they were given due process of law."¹⁰⁶

The supposed commitment to due process did not last long. As his newspaper was congratulating the community for its reliance on legal procedures, Wallace Stovall joined vigilantes who paid a visit to a national CMIU organizer and told him to leave town. J. C. Johnston, who was in Tampa assisting strikers, had been charged with criminal conspiracy in October, but a judge had dismissed that charge. On November 25, two days after the conviction of de la Campa and the two other local union leaders, a delegation from the Citizens' Committee went to Johnston's hotel room. The group included Colonel Charles Whitaker, Colonel Stovall and Colonel T. M. Weir, organizer of the 1892 Citizens' Committee.[107] Whitaker informed Johnston: "We are here representing the citizenship of Tampa. We are here to tell you that there is considerable feeling against you in Tampa and we are of the opinion that *if you stay here violence will be done you.* We are not telling you this for your sake but because we don't want the fair name of Tampa reproached because you are killed or injured while here, and in order to avoid this *we want you to get out and get out immediately.*"[108] The leaders of the Citizens' Committee stressed that they could no longer guarantee Johnston's personal safety after 10:30 that morning, when the next train was scheduled to leave town. Johnston took the hint and the train.[109] Nevertheless, the *Tribune* insisted, "No threats were made."[110] Weir added defensively that the warning to Johnston was intended "to preserve the law."[111] However, Wallace Stovall captured the spirit of the committee when he referred editorially to "Town-cleaning days," and bade "Goodbye, Mr. Johnston."[112]

Organized labor depicted Johnston's expulsion as another example of the lawlessness of the Citizens' Committee. The AFL, which was meeting at that moment in St. Louis, adopted several resolutions condemning the repressive tactics of Tampa vigilantes and public officials. Accusing the Citizens' Committee of "having transgressed law and order by constituting itself as an armed authority," AFL delegates charged that the group's aim was "to disrupt the organization of the Cigar Makers as well as that of every other organization of labor in that city, particularly the organizations of the building trades, the purpose being to establish in Tampa the nonunion shop."[113]

Samuel Gompers wired Governor Gilchrist to express "the deepest indignation that . . . Mr. J. C. Johnston has been ordered deported by a 'vigilance' committee or so-called Citizens' Committee of Tampa." Depicting Johnston as "a peaceful and law-abiding citizen, and exile, expulsion, or deportation [as] . . . an outrage," Gompers demanded that the governor protect the constitutional rights of all American citizens in Tampa.[114] With national attention focused on Tampa, Governor Gilchrist decided to investigate personally.

In advance of the governor's announced visit to Tampa, the Citizens' Committee held a mass rally at the courthouse to repudiate "the slanders of Gompers."[115] After hearing Colonel Hugh Macfarlane report how the Citizens' Committee had saved Tampa, the group adopted another set of resolutions, which defended the legality of vigilance committee actions.¹¹⁶ The resolutions declared that Tampa citizens had organized to assist "the officers of the law in the preservation of peace and good order." Contending that the three CMIU officials had been tried and convicted according to law and that J. C. Johnston had left Tampa "of his own volition," the resolutions insisted that the Citizens' Committee had operated "in a thoroughly lawful manner."¹¹⁷ Nevertheless, Wallace Stovall admitted in a *Tribune* editorial that the members of the committee had been "denounced as law-breakers, disturbers, violators of the rights of citizens, as a 'vigilance committee.'"¹¹⁸

The governor's inquiry in early December exonerted Tampa officials and the Citizens' Committee. After spending a week in Tampa and collecting testimony from representatives of government, business, and organized labor, Gilchrist issued a formal report in which he reviewed the specific charges of illegal action. While emphasizing the conflicting evidence, the governor generally downplayed the workers' version and failed to find that any law had been broken. He agreed that both a local union officer and J. C. Johnston had left Tampa "on account of fear for [their] personal safety," but he did not find that anyone had forced them to leave. Gilchrist contended that "more manufacturers and persons associated with them left Tampa on account of fear of personal violence to themselves." On the question of the closing of union halls in Tampa and West Tampa, the governor simply stated that it had been done by "officers," with the implication that it was legal. While observing that acts of violence had been committed by strikers and "by some citizens opposed to them," Gilchrist failed to link any of the violence directly to the Citizens' Committee. Indeed, he concluded that violence by workers had necessitated the use of the Citizens' Committee members as special policemen. Because of this action, "the city of Tampa has been as peaceable and as orderly as any city of its population in the world."¹¹⁹

This sweeping endorsement of the Citizens' Committee brought predictable reactions. Mayor McKay hailed the report, which he claimed "completely justifies the authorities and the citizens in their course throughout the trouble."¹²⁰ The *Tampa Tribune* reprinted copies of the governor's report so that local businessmen could give it the widest possible circulation around the country.¹²¹ Samuel Gompers dismissed the official findings as "biased."¹²²

For more radical workers, the governor's whitewash confirmed their view of the law and the role of the state. Following the conviction of three union officials and the expulsion of J. C. Johnston, the CMIU's local newspaper had argued, "The explanation of the whole thing is that the Law in Tampa is like a funnel: the larger end of w[h]ich is of equal dimen[s]ions to the Roman Coliseum and the smaller . . . with a diameter like a lady's ring. The larger entrance is for the manufacturers, citizens and officers of the law, the small for the working people."[123] The Joint Advisory Board claimed that cigarworkers could have easily won their struggle if not for their employers' alliance with government authorities and Tampa's elite: "The hostility of the Association of Manufacturers would have little meaning to us if the officers of the law, administrators of justice and other important factors of this community were impartial as they should be."[124]

The continued resistance of cigarworkers, combined with official acceptance of establishment violence, led to another wave of vigilantism. Several days after the governor issued his report exonerating the Citizens' Committee, 150 of its members conferred and unanimously reaffirmed their support for cigar manufacturers and the open shop throughout Tampa. Two weeks later the Citizens' Committee again acted.[125] On New Year's Day, 1911, strikers were "surprised . . . by the vigilance of the Citizens' Committee," according to a spokesman. When cigarworkers attempted to assemble in Ybor City on January 1, "a special officer telephoned to the Citizens' Committee headquarters, and in less than 30 minutes there were 40 automobiles, each containing five members of the Citizens' Committee, on the ground, and the meeting was prohibited and the crowd dispersed."[126] Vigilante squads also continued armed patrols near the factories to prevent picketing or any gathering of strikers. The committee was so well organized with district captains that it claimed it could quickly muster an armed force of over one thousand men if necessary.[127]

In January the Citizens' Committee also raided the offices of the JAB's official newspaper, *El Internacional*. Several weeks earlier, police had arrested its editor, J. M. Gil, on charges of conspiring to prevent cigarworkers from returning to the factories, but the newspaper had continued to publish its weekly edition while Gil languished in jail with bail set at $5,000.[128] On January 12, vigilantes from the Citizens' Committee went to the offices of *El Internacional*, where they found a journeyman printer. "After threat[e]ning him with horrible death and dismemberment, this delegation of Tampa's 'best citizens' smashed a pres[s] and cut a section from the belting, and proceeded to beat the poor man mercilessly," reported the union paper. "The Committee left orders that *El Internacional* should cease publication."[129] The JAB responded defiantly that "the Manufacturers tyrannical Association, . . . the Citizens Vigilance Committee, conscienceless unscrupulous newspapers, prostituted authorities, hostile Courts, and Mayor McKay—the whole kit and Kaboodle [sic] of them are powerless to prevent victory, can we but get the money to relieve the distress of the victims of this seven months struggle."[130]

The rising debt of union locals led to a vote by cigarworkers to call off the strike at the end of January 1911. The CMIU national office paid strike benefits to union members, but Tampa locals had sustained the strike by voluntarily providing weekly benefits to several thousand nonunion workers, at a cost of about $6,000 per week. When Tampa's CMIU locals exhausted their funds and began running into debt, they called for the membership vote which ended the strike on January 25, 1911.[131]

Despite their failure to win union recognition or any other concession, cigarworkers did not consider their return to work a total defeat. "Our fight in this long struggle was for the union, and although the manufacturers have not agreed to recognize us, we have won the union, as we are going back to work organized," the secretary of the Joint Advisory Board declared.[132] Two international union representatives who had assisted Tampa cigarworkers agreed that "the long struggle of the boys . . . while not successful as a whole . . . has been so in a great measure."[133] Unlike La Resistencia in 1901, the CMIU locals survived the strike. President George Perkins emphasized that the strike "demonstrated the ability of the International Union to discharge all of its financial obligations [to union members], and at the same time . . . taught the manufacturers a lesson they will never forget."[134] The local JAB secretary, an American who had replaced the imprisoned de la Campa, also thought that the strong support of the CMIU had dispelled the "old beliefs that the International Union does not come up to the aspirations of the Latin element."[135]

The CMIU's first industry-wide strike in Tampa may have made the organization more acceptable to immigrant cigarworkers, but the experience did little to endear their leaders to the international president of the union. Following the strike, George Perkins publicly attacked "radicals," who had seized control of the Tampa locals and precipitated the dispute. "If the old conservative Joint Advisory Board had remained in control of the board the big strike and lockout probably would not have taken place, but the workers would have been in practically the same, if not better condition than they are to-day and without enormous cost to the International Union," Perkins complained. "The conservative members of the board were either dropped or quit because of abusive criticism, and the control of the board went into the hands of the so-called radicals, and then the 'fireworks' commenced."[136] However, these tensions between national and local union leaders had no noticeable impact on the course of the 1910 strike, which received the full support of the CMIU.

Both radical and conservative union leaders agreed that the Citizens' Committee and its vigilante tactics had prevented the cigarworkers' ultimate victory. "There never has been a strike in the whole history of the International Union where we had to fight against greater odds and in which we had greater obstacles to overcome than the one at

Tampa," George Perkins observed.¹³⁷ Vigilante businessmen had failed to stampede a significant number of strikebreakers into the reopened factories, but they had thwarted a negotiated settlement by encouraging cigar manufacturers in their refusal to deal with union representatives or recognize the union in any way. "If it had not been for this, the strike could and would have been settled," Perkins contended, with the knowledge that cigarmakers in northern cities, such as Boston and New York, enjoyed recognition by employers other than the American Tobacco Company.¹³⁸ Local union leaders attributed the harsh treatment in Tampa to "the stubbornness of the manufacturers, the abuses of the citizens committee and the slanders of the press."¹³⁹ The Tampa JAB explained to other CMIU members that "owing to the fact that this city depends for its economic life on the one industry of cigar manufacturing, the manufacturers are considered as gods." This meant that cigarworkers had "two enemies—the employers and the citizens."¹⁴⁰ The JAB especially criticized the *Tampa Tribune* and *Tampa Times*, which "by suppression of facts, exploitation of every falsehood, misrepresentation and downright prevarication have created an antagonism against us."¹⁴¹ In fact, the two newspapers did serve as organs of the Citizens' Committee. Wallace Stovall and D. B. McKay, the owners of the papers, were not only leading members of the Citizens' Committee but at one point were also formally placed in charge of securing favorable national publicity for the group.¹⁴²

The precise impact of antilabor vigilantism is difficult to measure, since it was used in tandem with other methods of repression, especially the arrest and prosecution of strike leaders. Moreover, violence affected workers in different ways. Union officers claimed during the strike that the abuses of the Citizens' Committee had served to radicalize workers and encouraged them to hold out. Warning vigilante businessmen that "your methods . . . will get results opposite to what you expect," the editor of *El Internacional* suggested in the midst of the strike that "a few acts of conciliation would have done more to restore peace tha[n] all the three months of violence."¹⁴³

Vigilantes failed to drive the workers back into the factories, but they succeeded in severely crippling union operations. The daily patrols of vigilante squads during the last two months of the strike effectively prevented picketing or any meeting of strikers. The closing of union halls interrupted the payment of strike benefits and "caused a great deal of disturbance and confusion."¹⁴⁴ Union leaders who were not imprisoned or expelled had to meet in secret, and they could not hold rallies without having them broken up by the Citizens' Committee. Finally, the JAB had its printing press smashed. In a blunt justification of such action, one Tampan explained that "600 of the best citizens of this community . . . form[ed] themselves into a vigilance committee in order to protect the lives and properties in Tampa, from the machinations of the rabid and ill-advised mob."[145] While taking the law into their own hands, vigilantes had done more than protect life and property. They had also played a crucial role in defeating the cigarworkers' demand for union recognition.

Members of the Citizens' Committee considered their intervention so effective that they transformed their temporary organization into a permanent one after the strike ended. In January 1911, Wallace Stovall had pointed to "the formation of the citizens organization" as "the most important development" in the city during 1910. This observation led the *Tribune's* publisher to declare wistfully, "Tampa and its best citizens—may they ever remain on top!"[146] As spokesman for the disbanded Citizens' Committee, Mayor McKay called a special meeting of former members in March 1911.[147] The more than 300 men who answered the call approved a constitution which created a permanent "Citizens' Association," open to all members of the 1910 Citizens' Committee and other Tampans who sympathized with their purpose. The constitution's carefully drafted preamble acknowledged that the group's aim was essentially antiunion. The document asserted that "the future growth and material prosperity of this city largely depends upon . . . the employer to employ and the employee to be employed . . . without . . . hindrance on the part of any person or organization," adding that "strikes, lockouts and all other like troubles . . . are detrimental and demoralizing to good citizenship." The constitution empowered an executive committee of thirty to use "all honorable means to . . . carry out the true objects of this association."[148]

The composition of the executive committee showed the continuity with the 1910 vigilante group. The new Citizens' Association elected Hugh Macfarlane, the head of the 1910 committee, to serve as president. Mayor McKay became vice president. In addition to other prominent businessmen and lawyers who had enlisted in the Citizens' Committee during the 1910 strike, such as Wallace Stovall, Charles C. Whitaker, Kenneth I. McKay, Howell T. Lykes, and Julius A. Trawick, the new executive committee included several owners from the cigar industry, notably Enrique Pendas, the head of Tampa's Cigar Manufacturers' Association and a director of the Board of Trade.[149]

Explaining the new association to *Tribune* readers, Stovall argued that the 1910 Citizens' Committee had "certainly demonstrated its value to the city during the cigar strike." He contended that "it can be of vastly more service to the best interests of the community as a permanent body, devoted . . . to *the preservation of peace and order* and the protection of Tampa's interests from the designs of the unscrupulous and irresponsible." Stovall's silence on the question of law implied that preservation of order might in the future again require going beyond formal legal processes.[150] The Citizens' Association held publicized monthly meetings for several months, and then it disappeared from newspaper reports. It may have suspended activities, but it remained a threat to cigarworkers.[151]

The creation of a permanent vigilance committee to protect "Tampa's interests" was the culmination of twenty-five years of power struggles in the cigar industry. Beginning in 1887, when organizing among cigarworkers first disrupted production, Tampa's business and professional elite formally guaranteed that it would protect manufacturers through "every legitimate means." Fulfillment of that pledge had resulted in the periodic formation of Citizens' Committees. The most common method employed by successive vigilante groups was the illegal expulsion of labor organizers and union leaders. The 1910 lynching and defenses of lynch law by the local elite proved that community leaders still condoned violence as a means of eliminating "undesirables" and intimidating strikers.

Well-organized businessmen violated the law on numerous occasions, but Tampa vigilantes generally did not consider their actions illegal. Indeed, local lawyers, including several former prosecutors, led the 1910 Citizens' Committee and the Citizens' Association of 1911. In conformity with southern traditions of community justice that perceived vigilantism as a legitimate extension of the legal system, supporters of the Citizens' Committee stressed that a higher law, the so-called "law of self-preservation," justified the removal or repression of union leaders who threatened the city's biggest industry. Labor organizers were normally beyond the reach of the law because they operated in a legal and peaceful manner, even during prolonged strikes. Hence the defense of property and Tampa's cigar industry required prominent citizens to take the law into their own hands to restore political order and economic production.

Despite the apparent ethnic dimension to a conflict that in 1910 pitted American vigilantes against predominantly immigrant cigarworkers, the opposing sides generally depicted the struggle in class terms. Cigarworkers, who won the united support of American trade unionists in Tampa, viewed their opponents as greedy capitalists acting for selfish economic reasons. "A large part of Tampa's big business men have shown more than once that when their income was affected they would not hesitate at lawlessness to gain their point," Tampa's Joint Advisory Board asserted during the strike. "This collection of excellent gentlemen is now organized into a so-called 'Citizens' Committee,' ... armed with pistols and rifles, clubbing and threatening strikers in their frenzied efforts to drive them back into the factories."[152] Cigarworkers were certainly not surprised by class violence. "Capital and labor are two antagonistic armies doomed to fight against each other eternally . . . as long as the present social system exist[s]," *El Internacional* observed.¹⁵³

Members of the vigilance committee appropriated the word "citizen" to distinguish themselves primarily as a class. Tampa newspapers owned by spokesmen for the 1910 Citizens' Committee rarely engaged in nativist attacks even in their most virulent condemnations of strikers. Xenophobic arguments were difficult to make, since the purpose of vigilantism was to defend cigar manufacturers, many of whom were themselves immigrants and some of whom were members of the Tampa elite.¹⁵⁴ The vigilantes' use of the term "citizen" reflected an older, class-based conception that equated citizenship with ownership of property and a stake in the community. It was this class that supposedly retained the ultimate right under traditional republican theory to restore order and prevent chaos.

Establishment violence flourished in part because vigilantes were neither prosecuted nor punished in any way. During the 1910 strike, the activities of citizen vigilantes, as well as the names of many perpetrators, were well publicized, but local officials either overlooked the offenses or actually cooperated with the Citizens' Committee which Mayor McKay helped organize and lead. The failure of state and federal authorities to take effective action, despite frequent appeals from union officials, reinforced the view that the ends justified the means. Reflecting on the nation's lynching record for 1910, which included the death of Albano and Ficarrotta, the *Tampa Tribune* pointed out that the data "naturally show that the larger number of lynchings occur in the South, but that is merely because Southern people have more provocation for such appeals outside the law than the people of other sections."¹⁵⁵ The record of 1910 also demonstrated that no external government authority challenged Tampa's tradition of community justice.

# 5

# From "Stern Repression" to Collective Bargaining

The state has always shaped the contours of relations between employees and employers. In the United States prior to World War I, government authorities sided consistently with employers. Officials often claimed to follow a hands-off policy in labor disputes, since a neutral state served the interest of employers able to control their employees without direct intervention from public authorities. However, when workers successfully organized and threatened to win struggles with influential employers, government officials assisted in defeating labor, most notably during effective strikes against large corporations. Government intervention took a variety of repressive forms, including antilabor injunctions enforced by troops, but it rarely encompassed any positive action in support of workers until World War I.[1]

During 1917–18, the federal government briefly shifted its weight toward labor in an effort to avoid strikes that would hamper the war effort. Alexander M. Bing, a prounion businessman who served in Washington during the war, observed that the Department of Labor and a number of temporary federal agencies "evolved a body of war labor principles which represented the most enlightened attitude toward labor which the nation [had] ever attained."[2] National support for labor produced significant gains in wages and union membership, and it left many employers with "the impression that the Government truckled to labor during the war and gave it everything it asked."[3] Washington's commitment to workers was in fact less sweeping. It also proved temporary. "During the post-armistice period, when the extreme emergency was over, the Government's attitude radically changed," Bing pointed out in 1921.[4] Indeed, Washington reverted to its traditional role of effectively assisting employers through a hands-off policy, backed when necessary by measures to break strikes. Not until the depression of the 1930s did the balance between employees and employers decisively change, in part as a result of the federal guarantee of collective bargaining rights under the New Deal.[5]

These policy shifts, combined with changes in the cigar industry, brought a new era of labor relations to Tampa. The assertion of federal power and the election of Florida governors sympathetic to labor ultimately forced Tampa's elite to find nonviolent ways of influencing the outcome of labor-management conflicts. The disappearance of antilabor violence was also encouraged by a sharp decline in cigar production, which reduced the importance of the industry to Tampa's overall economy. The willingness of community leaders to abandon vigilantism evolved gradually and fitfully after 1917. When the threat from militant cigarworkers seemed great enough and state and federal officials appeared complacent or cooperative, Tampa businessmen reverted to violent methods. Nevertheless, as a result of economic and political changes, Tampa joined the rest of the country in the 1930s and accepted a new social equilibrium that included union recognition for organized workers and generally excluded violence as a means of repressing workers.

The first signs of change appeared in Tampa during World War I, when worker militancy produced another crisis in the cigar industry. After their setback in the 1910 strike, cigarworkers had deserted their union in large numbers. By 1913, local membership in the Cigar Makers' International Union had fallen from a peak of 6,000 to 2,500, and it continued to drop. However, when real wages suddenly declined as a result of the rising cost of living after 1914, Tampa cigarworkers soon flocked back into the CMIU, which had 3,600 members by 1917. The reinvigorated union petitioned cigar manufacturers for recognition, but they refused.[6]

Factory owners had the full backing of the Tampa Board of Trade. In 1917, this association established the Cigar Manufacturers' Bureau of the Board of Trade to facilitate improved cooperation between board members and owners of cigar factories. Representatives of both groups constituted the new bureau, whose declared purpose was "to attend to any misunderstanding between a manufacturer and his workmen."[7] One of the group's first actions was to reject the CMIU's request for union recognition, and leaders of the Board of Trade formally endorsed the decision because "they wanted Tampa to be an Open-shop town."[8] In response to continued pressure from the CMIU, the Board of Trade issued a warning to cigarworkers in September 1917. A leaflet printed in English and Spanish proclaimed that the board was "interested in the prosperity and the stability of the cigar industry of this city [because] property owners and business men of Tampa . . . have put up hundreds of thousands of dollars to secure the location of factories here, with the view of course, that they would bring prosperity to the community." As a result of their financial stake, local businessmen were "getting tired of the continued efforts of agitators to stir up strife and turmoil." This warning to "the masses" to disregard or get rid of the "comparatively few agitators" went unheeded.⁹

Businessmen and cigarworkers soon discovered that the federal government took new interest in Tampa labor disputes. When cigarmakers struck briefly in April 1918, for an average 8.5 percent wage increase, the Department of Labor dispatched a mediator to assist in ending the work stoppage. The increased use of government mediators, who relied on voluntary compliance, was part of the Wilson administration's national campaign to prevent any disruption of production during wartime. After several days in Tampa, the federal mediator reported to Washington that neither side desired "governmental interference."¹⁰ Since the mediator was the former head of the Georgia State Federation of Labor, the resistance of employers was understandable.¹¹

Cigarmakers also had good reason to be suspicious of government intervention. Both their experience and politics convinced cigarworkers that the state served the interests of factory owners. "Especially have the cigar makers suffered because of the open hostility or placid indifference of public officials in almost every conflict with their 'masters,'" observed *El Internacional,* the voice of Tampa's CMIU locals.¹² "Capitalism enslaves the wage workers and the mayor, governor or senator who represents a capitalistic form of government and society can, at best, serve the masters of industry," *El Internacional* argued in another context.¹³ Cigarmakers also had little need for outside assistance in the spring of 1918 because they had already won complete acceptance of their wage demand from several manufacturers and they probably felt they could wear down other employers without compromising.¹⁴ A leading Tampa manufacturer privately admitted that he was "in a fair position to accept the demands of the workmen without suffering any losses whatsoever."¹⁵

Pay was not the only issue, however, and workers continued to disrupt production throughout the summer of 1918.¹⁶ During the second week of August, manufacturers reported that more than 1,500 cigarworkers had struck several factories over "minor and petty difficulties." As in the past, employers and their allies in the business community blamed the trouble on a handful of so-called agitators who were now accused of being agents of the Germans or the Industrial Workers of the World (IWW), a radical American union.¹⁷ A spokesman for manufacturers asserted that "there are men of the I.W.W. type, if not actually members of the organization, who are constantly making some pretext for agitation so the workmen can be stirred up against the manufacturers."¹⁸ Pointing to "Hun Propaganda at Work," the Tampa reporter for *Tobacco Leaf* claimed that "the labor troubles for the past eighteen months have been purely and simply the work of I.W.W. and German propaganda."[19] Well aware that the Board of Trade had organized the expulsion of alleged agitators in previous disputes, a group of cigar manufacturers complained to the board that "labor agitators" were going "unchallenged" and warned that "should this condition of affairs be allowed to continue, the result cannot be other than disastrous for our city."[20]

The manufacturers' appeal did not fall on deaf ears. Indeed, members of Tampa's establishment had already started preparations for vigilante action. On August 11, Board of Trade leaders, Mayor D. B. McKay, and law enforcement officials held a highly publicized meeting with a small group of dissident cigarworkers, principally Americans, who were described in the press as "conservative workers." These men complained about alleged disloyalty in the cigar factories, fomented in part by readers. The "patriotic" cigarmakers charged that labor disturbances prevented collections for war bonds and the Red Cross. "There are men in this town who ought to be hanged," an American cigarworker reportedly told Tampa leaders. "It was the same way in 1910, and is still worse now. They think the American people are afraid of them."[21]

This dramatic appeal gave prominent Tampans the excuse to issue public threats. "You may have to become martyrs and put yourselves up to be shot at," Mayor McKay exclaimed, "but if you take that stand others will come to you in a hurry." Dr. Louis A. Bize, a Georgia-born physician who had become a Tampa bank president and head of the Board of Trade, said the occasion reminded him of 1776, when a few Americans took matters into their own hands and won because their cause was just. "If you have backbone, it is just a matter of time before you will win," Bize exhorted the gathering. "It may come as it did in 1776, with either guns or rope, but you will win." Matthew B. Macfarlane, an attorney and the brother of Hugh Macfarlane, assured the group of cigarworkers that they had "the law of self-defense" behind them. In an apparent endorsement of vigilante action, Tampa's police chief argued that there were "men in Tampa who should be gotten rid of, and that there would be no peace here until they were."[22] Following this public meeting, leaders of the Board of Trade, including Mayor McKay, met privately with fifteen cigar manufacturers, and all agreed that "the industry could not continue, as it has been doing, with strikes so numerous, and that some action should be taken by the business interests."[23]

That evening a group of Tampa citizens announced the formation of a vigilance committee. Municipal Judge J. Thomas Watson became spokesman for "a committee of citizens of Tampa, who are entirely unconnected with the cigar industy." Watson, a native of Virginia who had previously worked for the American Tobacco Company, told a public gathering at the courthouse that "we are after . . . the element that is making for disorder and is undertaking to convert our cigar industry into a place for strikes and anarchy." He declared that his group had drawn up a "blacklist" of eight men, "known to be agitators and troublemakers," and "when we are through with them they are going to leave Tampa."[24] The local correspondent for *Tobacco Leaf* reported that the committee would take "summary action."[25]

The following morning, August 15, 1918, the front page of the *Tampa Tribune* blared: "LABOR AGITATORS TO BE FORCED FROM CITY—VIGILANCE COMMITTEE TO ACT ON BLACK LIST."[26] Defending the right of "the level-headed people of this community" to protect workers from "anarchistic agitators," Wallace Stovall's *Tribune* invoked the vigilante tradition as a practical and legitimate means of dealing with people who had "no place in any well regulated community." "Tampa has dealt with the I.W.W element before," the *Tribune* emphasized. "The remedy has always proved effective."[27] In a similar vein, the local reporter for a national tobacco journal assured manufacturers that a "committee of loyal Americans is ready to protect property and stamp out Bolshevikism among the workers of the city."[28]

While leading Tampans stressed the need for order, even if enforced by vigilante methods, organized labor appealed for equal enforcement of the law. *El Internacional* pointed out that cigarworkers had broken no law, and the city had no need for Judge Watson's "ill-advised committee." The union paper argued that all violators of the law should be legally prosecuted, including "those who would curtail the freedom of thought and action of the workmen."[29] In a show of solidarity, Tampa's Central Trades and Labor Assembly also publicly protested against the threats made by the vigilance committee.[30]

The intervention of federal officials helped prevent the 1918 Citizens' Committee from carrying out its threat to expel labor leaders. On the day Judge Watson announced the formation of his vigilante group, a local CMIU official reported to Samuel Gompers that eight union men were targeted for expulsion from Tampa. As president of the American Federation of Labor, Gompers had unsuccessfully appealed for federal action against Tampa vigilantes in 1903 and 1910, but by 1918 organized labor had greater influence in Washington, where Gompers himself served on one of the government's wartime agencies.[31] Gompers got a receptive hearing from the Department of Labor, which sent an investigator "to ascertain the truth of the situation [in Tampa], and if necessary prevent violence and illegal action." The federal official, Grace E. Coates, reported that soon after organization of Judge Watson's vigilance committee, most strikers had returned to the cigar factories, "with their demands satisfactorily met." However, in light of the history of antilabor violence in Tampa, she noted that "the mention in 1918 of a citizen's committee aroused disturbing thoughts." One union leader had gone into hiding after Judge Watson issued his threat.[32]

Coates found some basis for workers' anxiety. In an interview with Mayor McKay, who she reported "is credited with participation in previous deportations," she heard a defense of vigilantism. McKay "declared that if the agitators persisted in trouble-making, no tangible evidence could be found for court prosecution, and so a 'voluntary action of citizens' would be the only recourse." Clearly unsympathetic with this view, Coates privately described Tampa's tradition of "lawless violence" as "the natural expression of the autocratic spirit, united for selfish ends." She added that whatever the present danger of violence, "the Latin employee was not conquered."[33]

In an attempt to avert further work stoppages and any accompanying violence, Coates persuaded union leaders and some employers in the cigar industry to submit future disputes to the War Labor Board, a temporary federal agency. Nevertheless, she left Tampa convinced that both sides in the industry, as well as leading citizens, had much to learn if additional conflicts were to be avoided.[34] Despite the lack of significant results from Coates' inquiry, AFL officials were certain that prompt federal intervention after the creation of the 1918 vigilance committee had "prevented the carrying out of drastic acts by that committee."[35]

Tampa emerged from World War I more populous and more prosperous than ever. The war effort had boosted the city's shipbuilding industry and expanded the use of its port. However, the production of cigars still dominated the local economy. The industry employed some 12,000 workers, who represented almost half the local labor force. In 1919 the output of cigars reached a record of 410 million. By 1920, Tampa had a population of 51,608 and ranked among the twenty-five largest cities in the South. West Tampa contained an additional 8,463 people.[36]

In 1920, Tampa experienced its longest cigar strike, which again demonstrated the state's ability to curb antilabor vigilantes. The ten-month cigar strike that began in 1920 was the culmination of an ongoing power struggle that had produced intermittent work stoppages in Tampa throughout 1919. Focusing on demands for increased wages to cover the rising cost of living, these union-led strikes brought higher wage scales, which helped expand union membership to the point where Tampa had more organized cigarworkers than any other city in the country. By the end of 1919, the CMIU had enrolled over 7,000 cigarmakers and selectors, who composed about 90 percent of the Tampa workers in those trades.[37]

Increased union strength and worker militancy brought more red-baiting. Reflecting the tone of the Red Scare then sweeping the country, a spokesman for Tampa factory owners charged that "the favorite mental pablum dispensed by the factory readers is Bolsheviki literature, and the average cigarmaker here is well-posted and deeply impressed with the radical movement in the United States."[38] The *Tampa Tribune* denounced labor activists in similar terms. "The crowd of reds operating in this city under the guise of anarchists, bolshevists, socialists, or anything else they may call themselves, are put on notice that the first aggregation of them caught attempting to hold a . . . protest meeting May 1—or any other day—is going to be awfully sorry," the *Tribune* warned in April 1919. "We are 'fed up' on that stuff. We want to get back to business."[39] The *Tampa Times* argued that local citizens "must not allow any sentimental considerations of free speech to blind us to the imminent peril of allowing treason and anarchy to be preached openly on our streets." Several months later, Wallace Stovall published "A Cure for Bolshevism," suggesting that IWW leaders "should be promptly hung before the masses of the people . . . as a warning to those others of the bolshevist tribe that none of their action was wanted in this country."[40] Speaking for the business community, the entrepreneur Peter O. Knight condemned "flannel-mouthed, pin-headed, brainless, anarchistic, bolsheviki labor agitators."[41]

Tampa cigarworkers continued to express radical ideas, as well as sympathy for the Russian revolution, during the postwar period. Cigarworkers' plans to celebrate May Day in 1919 revealed the sharp ideological division in Tampa. When local authorities learned that a May Day rally and parade were scheduled, they banned all demonstrations on that day. Local officials also called out the paramilitary Home Guards, a unit of volunteers formed during World War I, to enforce the ban.[42] The cigarworkers' union newspaper branded this suppression of free speech and free assembly "the most cowardly act committed in Tampa since the raid of the 'Citizens' Committee' nine years ago."[43] In a subsequent editorial, *El Internacional* observed that those "who recognize that a class struggle exists and must be fought to a finish for liberty, are not greatly surprised at the growing tendency of both big and little rulers to suppress freedom of speech in America."[44] *El Internacional* also pointed sarcastically at the class bias underlying the dominant view of the Russian revolution. "In the United States a capitalistic government is making the working-class behave, and we call that 'Maintaining Law and Order,'" *El Internacional* noted. "In Russia a working-class government is making the capitalists behave, and we call that a 'Reign of Terror.'" Defending the crackdown in Tampa, Wallace Stovall declared in the *Tribune*: "A reign of determination, NOT terror, has been created."[45]

Tampa's port in 1922.
Tampa-Hillsborough County Public Library System.

Cigarmakers in Tampa's Corral–Wodiska factory in 1929, with a *lector* reading from his platform in the upper right corner. Tampa–Hillsborough County Library System.

The staff of *La Traduccion*, one of Ybor City's Spanish-language newspapers. Florida State Archives.

Ybor City's Labor Temple in 1921. Tampa–Hillsborough County Public Library System.

Tampa in 1926 with the Hillsborough River in the center.
Tampa–Hillsborough County Public Library System.

Two cigar manufacturers pose with their new Westcott cars in front of their West Tampa factory in 1921. Tampa–Hillsborough County Public Library System.

Members of the Tampa Chamber of Commerce in front of the Board of Trade Building in 1930. Tampa–Hillsborough County Public Library System.

Ybor City's newest Labor Temple was the scene of the aborted rally celebrating the anniversary of the Russian Revolution in 1931. Florida State Archives.

Men and women cigarmakers perform their silent work while they listen to a *lector* reading from his elevated platform in Tampa's Cuesta-Rey factory in 1929. Florida State Archives.

Tampa's workforce of skilled, hand cigarmakers included many women by the 1930s. Tampa-Hillsborough County Public Library System.

Cigar-banding machines run by semi-skilled women displaced one group of skilled workers in the Tampa industry after 1935. University of South Florida Special Collections.

A postcard showing one of the fifteen people convicted for their involvement in the banned Communist rally on November 7, 1931. The reverse side of the postcard contained a printed message appealing to Florida's governor for a pardon. The state supreme court reversed the convictions in 1933. University of South Florida Special Collections.

In December 1919, cigar manufacturers precipitated a showdown with their employees. At a time when employers around the country were reversing advances made by unions during the war, the seventy-seven members of Tampa's Cigar Manufacturers' Association had the necessary cohesiveness to confront employees. The association's member firms, many of them based outside Tampa, were responsible for 95 percent of local production. The group was headed by Enrique Pendas, the local manager for the American Tobacco Company, which had recently purchased his cigar factory.[46] After several months of preparation, the Manufacturers' Association fired so-called "shop collectors," cigarmakers who also served as union representatives by collecting dues for the CMIU in the factories.[47] Local union leaders interpreted the dismissal of shop collectors as an "attempt to strangle the life out of the International by starving its members."[48] Employer opposition to the CMIU was certainly not new, but as *El Internacional* emphasized in January 1920, "Times have changed since 1910, and conditions have changed, also." Pointing to the impact of the World War on labor-management relations in the United States, the union paper asserted: "Collective bargaining by employees with employers is an accepted basis for the successful operation of any industry in America." *El Internacional* argued that "the manufacturers of cigars in Tampa would be doing a duty as well as a service to the city by accepting [collective bargaining] and by dealing honorably and fairly with their employes."[49] Union workers refused to strike immediately over the firing of shop collectors, but they warned that they "can not and will not continue indefinitely to tolerate the blacklisting of 200 of their members by the manufacturers."[50]

After delaying almost four months, the cigarworkers' Joint Advisory Board finally issued an ultimatum. On April 12, 1920, the board of five CMIU unions locals formally demanded that manufacturers rehire shop collectors and permit them to perform their same duties. The JAB also insisted that employers recruit only union members as *new* employees in the future.[51] Although acceptance of this demand would have permitted a small number of unorganized cigarmakers to continue working without union cards, the Cigar Manufacturers' Association immediately rejected the proposal which it equated with "the principle of the closed shop." The employers' group further argued that its constitution explicitly barred negotiations with union representatives or discrimination in hiring on the basis of union membership.[52] Following the manufacturers' rejection of the union shop and union recognition, the Joint Advisory Board called its members out of Tampa's thirty largest factories on April 14, 1920. In response, the Cigar Manufacturers' Association declared a lockout five days later, and both sides prepared for a prolonged siege involving over 12,000 cigarworkers.[53]

The participants correctly saw this struggle as another control strike in which the primary issue was power. "We are engaged in a struggle which is vastly more than a bread-and-butter proposition," *El Internacional* declared. Though denying that cigarworkers sought to control the industry, the paper affirmed that they did seek to "control [their] lives as workers and producers." Such a goal necessitated "organization and cooperation for our preservation and protection."[54] *El Internacional* also stressed that "the solidarity of the workers is founded upon the rock of class consciousness."[55]

Manufacturers agreed that power was at stake in the 1920 dispute, but they blamed a handful of so-called agitators for raising the issue. *Tobacco Leaf* claimed that the strike was "not a matter of lower wages but a refusal to turn over the management and control of their business by the manufacturers to a set of radicals and unresponsive leaders."[56] Linking the strike to the fight for the open shop then being waged across the country, Tampa's cigar manufacturers wrapped themselves in the mantle of "fairness, justice and Americanism."[57] In a series of advertisements in Tampa newspapers, the Cigar Manufacturers' Association repeatedly identified the closed shop with radicalism and un-American ideas. "The radical labor agitator gains his point when he is able to dictate to the employer whom he shall hire," the factory owners asserted. "When he dictates who shall not have the right to labor, he becomes at once un-American."[58] One spokesman for the manufacturers went so far as to accuse the strikers of intending "literally to sovietize the Tampa factories."[59]

Adhering "to the policy of strictly open shop in its broadest conception," the Cigar Manufacturers' Association refused even to talk with union representatives during the ten-month strike.[60] "Cigar manufacturers will never meet the Joint Advisory Board, or ever recognize the Joint Advisory Board," employers announced.[61] Claiming that the strike had national implications because it was an effort by "the radical unionists to get complete control of the cigar industry," *Tobacco Leaf* declared that "cigar manufacturers in Tampa are fighting the battle of the entire cigar industry."[62]

As the stalemate continued for months, both sides drew heavily upon their traditional sources of strength. Direct aid for union members came from their international union in the form of strike benefits, which ultimately amounted to $1 million.[63] Cigarworkers also successfully appealed for financial assistance from organized labor generally, using the argument that "the cigar manufacturers have the aid of organized capital."[64] In a display of solidarity, leaders of a Tampa local of the International Typographical Union assessed each of their members fifty cents a week to support the strike.⁶⁵ "The strength of the movement here has been due in large part to the liberal support of the American labor movement," *El Internacional* emphasized.⁶⁶ Except for the CMIU, the biggest contributions came from cigarworkers in Cuba, who were sending $10,000 a week to Tampa by July 1920. The funds were used principally to support about 2,000 nonunion strikers who were ineligible for CMIU benefits. The Tampa Joint Advisory Board also paid the transportation for over 3,000 strikers to go to Havana and other cigar centers in the United States, where many could find jobs.⁶⁷ These monumental efforts to sustain the strike reflected both worker solidarity and the conviction of AFL leaders that victory in Tampa was essential "for the purpose of defeating the open shop drive that has been inaugurated with a vengeance in that section of the country to destroy the organized labor movement."⁶⁸

Once cigarworkers made it clear that they were prepared for a prolonged struggle, cigar manufacturers increased the pressure for intervention by Tampa businessmen. After three months of watchful waiting, factory owners tried to rally community support by orchestrating a back-to-work campaign. The Cigar Manufacturers Association announced that factories would reopen July 8, 1920, on an open-shop basis but with no reduction of wages. *Tobacco Leaf* admitted that the move would attract few workers and that it would take three more months to resume normal production.⁶⁹ Nevertheless, when only a few dozen people entered the reopened factories, which did not even have picket lines around them, the manufacturers' association publicly charged that "assaults have been committed and open threats have been made that [strikebreakers] will be assassinated." Clearly directing their appeal to the Tampa business community, which had traditionally gone to the rescue of employers, factory owners argued that "all men who have material interests in the city are concerned in this struggle." Manufacturers stressed that "this great industry, which has been such a powerful factor in the development of the city, is in jeopardy."⁷⁰

Responding to this appeal and to vague complaints about "abuses by the strikers," the Tampa Board of Trade renewed its historic commitment to cigar manufacturers. On July 26, 1920, the association's board of governors adopted a set of resolutions that had been drafted by a special strike committee headed by D. B. McKay, who had just completed three terms as mayor. Other board officials on the 1920 strike committee were Louis A. Bize, J. Arthur Griffin, Thomas Carson Taliaferro, and J. Edgar Wall. Bize, Griffin, and Taliaferro were all southern-born Tampa bankers who had served on the 1910 Citizens' Committee. Wall, a Tampa native and nephew of the leader of the 1887 and 1892 Citizens' Committees, was a prominent local merchant.⁷¹ The resolutions proposed by the 1920 strike committee, and approved by the Board of Trade, asserted that Tampa citizens had "always pledged the manufacturing interests that in any and all events the industry will be protected." Aligning themselves with cigar manufacturers, board officials called on "the workmen to lay aside all demands for a closed shop, this demand in our opinion being impossible, unreasonable and Un-American." In apparent recognition that this appeal would go unheeded, the board reiterated its guarantee to protect the cigar industry "to the fullest extent possible to the end that property and life may be safe." The board also requested "all good citizens, either business men, professional men, merchants, manufacturers or workmen to aid and assist in preventing intimidation, threats, boycotts, or acts of lawlessness."⁷² The form that this assistance would take was unclear, but Louis Bize declared that businessmen were "ready to meet intimidation with firm resistance."⁷³

The reaction to the board's highly publicized declaration followed class lines. With the cigarworkers' strike costing over $250,000 in weekly wages that ordinarily went into "the various channels of the commerce of the city," Tampa business groups and civic associations, such as the Rotary and Kiwanis clubs, formally called for an end to the walkout.⁷⁴ In a typical resolution, the Wholesale Grocers' Association "viewed with alarm the demands of unwise and radical labor leadership," and it pledged "full support" to all men who wanted to work.⁷⁵ "Tampa as a whole is back of the manufacturers," Wallace Stovall declared in the *Tribune*.⁷⁶

Organized labor, however, strongly dissented from the position of the Board of Trade. CMIU locals ridiculed the idea that the board or the *Tampa Tribune* spoke for the public.⁷⁷ On the contrary, *El Internacional* argued that "the moneyed members of this community, claiming to represent the feeling of the people at large, have gone on record as bitter enemies of the workers."⁷⁸ Expressing "unalterable opposition to the 'open shop' policy," the local typographical union condemned the Board of Trade for deciding "to inject itself into the fight that is being made by the foreign manufacturers against the bread-and-butter producing people of our community."⁷⁹ Richard B. Lovett, president of the Florida State Federation of Labor and leader of a Tampa local of railway carmen, charged that the Board of Trade "had come out from under cover and acknowledged itself to be the tool of the [cigar] manufacturers' association." Following the board's offer of protection to factory owners and strikebreakers, Lovett feared "repetition of the atrocities of 1910 . . . with the tactics used by the famed 'Citizens' Committee' of that period." Given the outrages directed against strikers in 1910, Lovett argued that "they are the only ones who are in danger."⁸⁰

Suspecting an imminent outbreak of vigilante violence, union leaders took steps to prevent it. An AFL organizer, who arrived in Tampa four days after the Board of Trade's pledge of protection, appealed directly to Florida's Governor Sidney J. Catts, a political maverick who had aligned himself with organized labor.[81] Catts rejected the request to send in the militia to protect striking cigarworkers, but he insisted that the state no longer sided with the Tampa elite. In a private meeting with Sol Sontheimer, a national CMIU representative, the governor observed: "I know these people much better than you may think I do, [and] I fully understand what you are up against." Sontheimer left the meeting convinced that Catts "was in sympathy with our struggle."[82]

In addition to his private assurances, the governor asked the Hillsborough County sheriff to provide Sontheimer with "protection in all his rights." Catts also emphasized in a letter to the sheriff that he knew Sontheimer was "up against an aggregate of money interest which is tremendous and which will stop at nothing if they once get started."[83] The *Tampa Tribune* reported that Catts was prepared to send in the militia if necessary. The governor's unprecedented support for striking cigarworkers served notice to Tampa businessmen that they would be held accountable for vigilante violence. When no violence occurred during the month following the appeal to Catts, an AFL organizer concluded privately that the governor's actions had been "the balance wheel in keeping down the citizens committee."[84]

Intervention by the federal government also placed cigar manufacturers and Tampa businessmen on the defensive. At the beginning of the strike, CMIU president George W. Perkins had quietly alerted the Secretary of Labor that it might become necessary to send a federal mediator to Tampa. "Unless this is done the stirring times of 1910 may be repeated," Perkins had warned in May. Two months into the strike, Perkins confidentially requested the Department of Labor to look into the situation, which he described as "even more tense and acute."[85] The Labor Department sent Joseph R. Buchanan, "one of its oldest and most experienced conciliators" from the Division of Conciliation.[86] With only the power of persuasion to encourage a settlement, Buchanan arrived in July just as the Tampa Cigar Manufacturers' Association officially ended its lockout. "This association has assumed a stiff attitude of opposition to the Cigarmakers' Union and is attempting its destruction," the mediator quickly concluded. "Business interests and the public generally appear to be upon the manufacturers' side in the controversy—unjustly, however," he reported confidentially to Washington.[87]

The federal official's initial impressions were reinforced by subsequent developments. CMIU locals welcomed government assistance, but Buchanan learned "that the Manufacturers' Association would not accept the services of the Labor Department or any other agency in settling the strike; that there was no one in officialdom, 'from President Wilson to the Mayor of Tampa,' who would be accepted by the Association as an adjuster of the strike."[88] In defense of the hard line taken by employers, a local cigar manufacturer claimed that "we are merely defending ourselves from what we consider an unjust and untimely demand of a handful of labor agitators here to take control of our business and establish *soviet* rule."[89]

Support for this position came from former Mayor McKay, who spoke for the Board of Trade's strike committee. In an effort to have Buchanan removed from Tampa, McKay complained to one of Florida's United States Senators that the federal conciliator "has delayed the settlement of the trouble very materially, that he has encouraged the strikers, and that his attitude is virtually that of an agent of the International Union." Buchanan responded that "the Board of Trade has taken the lead in this community in supporting the determination of the Manufacturers Association to destroy the Cigarmakers' Union." After a month in Tampa, he concluded: "We might just as well abandon our attempts here."[90]

The federal conciliator failed to bring the two sides together, but his presence helped discourage establishment violence. Buchanan was in Tampa when the Board of Trade and other business groups passed their resolutions which, he noted, were "so constructed as to give the impression that the cigarmakers are employing methods of intimidation to restrain their own members and others from returning to work." He reported, however, that the strike was most unusual in that "there is *not a single Union picket on duty*," nor was there "any gathering of strikers or sympathizers anywhere outside the rooms of the Union." Nevertheless, as a result of the 1910 violence by the Citizens' Committee, Buchanan found "some here who believe that the employers are endeavoring to stir up that lynch-law sentiment again." Buchanan saw little reason to fear for the safety of strikers, but he was "convinced that the employers are perfectly willing that the labor men should get the idea that they are in danger of receiving the same kind of treatment that was administered to the leaders ten years ago."[91] The avoidance of vigilante violence was undoubtedly a result of the growing impression, as the attorney for the Cigar Manufacturers' Association acknowledged, that federal officials like Joseph Buchanan allowed "the influence of the Department of Labor to be perverted into an instrument of oppression."[92] Combined with the prolabor stance of Governor Catts, this meant that for the first time, Tampa businessmen felt constrained by both the state and federal governments.

After the departure of Joseph Buchanan in early August, the deadlock continued. "The manufacturers continue their policy of completely ignoring the cigar workers, and since no other alternative presents itself the workers are forced to pursue the same course," a labor newspaper observed.[93] The stalemate favored strikers, for employers could not recruit replacements even in the absence of picket lines.[94] In mid-August, an AFL organizer sent to Tampa by Samuel Gompers reported that "everything at present is looking most favorable for the strikers [as] they are still maintaining a solid front and all is going on peaceable [sic], and if that decorum can be pursued for only a few weeks longer there is no question . . . the workers will win out in this struggle."[95]

In an effort to break the strike, Wallace Stovall used the pages of his *Tampa Tribune* to incite vigilante action against union leaders. Knowing from past experience the effectiveness of antilabor violence, Stovall repeated the same arguments in 1920 that he had used in 1901 and 1910 to justify establishment violence. A week after the departure of the federal conciliator, Stovall informed his readers that "the rank and file desire to return to their labors, but are prevented by the professional agitator from doing so." Invoking "true Americanism and good citizenship," he asked rhetorically, "How much longer are the people who have made Tampa going to permit this great injustice to the business interests and the people who desire to return to their labors?"[96] For anyone who wondered what could be done, Stovall reminded *Tribune* readers of the city's historic pledge to protect the cigar industry and of the fulfillment of that guarantee: "the citizens of Tampa have been called on for protection several times, and they gave it, notably in 1900 [sic] and 1910."[97] Emphasizing that the 1920 strike had already cost over $6 million in lost wages, which would have gone into local commerce, the *Tribune* warned on August 23, "The people of Tampa are not going to tolerate this situation many days longer."[98]

Well aware that vigilantes could defeat the strike, organized labor persuaded state officials to reprimand Stovall. As an AFL organizer explained to Samuel Gompers, the *Tribune's* editorials showed "clearly a covert intent to promote 'mob violence' by arousing the so-called 'Citizens Committee' to take matter[s] in their own hands and bring the situation to a crisis as was the case in the 1910 strike." AFL representatives appealed to state attorney Charles B. Parkhill to take action on the "incendiary articles." Already enjoined by Governor Catts to enforce the law impartially during the strike, Parkhill agreed to meet with the *Tribune* owner. Accompanied by AFL organizers and the attorney for the Tampa JAB, the prosecutor met with Stovall for an hour on August 24. One of the AFL men present reported that Parkhill informed Stovall that the state attorney's duty was "to see to it that a repetition of former tragedies was not committed to mar the name of Tampa and the state of Florida." In view of Stovall's "continued editorials, and persistent effort to stir up strife against the workers," the prosecutor warned that Governor Catts would "send the Adjutant General in with the militia to preserve order," if the *Tribune* printed any more editorials along the same line. "I have no objection for you to discuss the open shop to your heart's content," Parkhill declared, "but don't incite violence by your articles [because] that's against the law and order and we won't tolerate it."99

This warning not only provided palpable evidence of a shift in the role of the state, but it also had a noticeable impact on *Tribune* editorials. After the visit by the state attorney, Stovall redirected his published comments to a general defense of the open shop as a "clean American doctrine."100 His editorials attacked unions and the "uneconomical, illegal, unfair and un-American" closed shop, but they largely avoided any suggestion that citizens should take action to end the strike.101

While state officials—at workers' insistence—watched for violations of the law by anyone, the Department of Labor tried again in September to break the deadlock. The five-month-old strike by 12,000 cigarworkers was the largest single labor dispute in the country.102 However, when a Department of Labor official inquired about concessions employers would make to end the strike, he was informed by the Tampa attorney for the Cigar Manufacturer's Association that factory owners would concede nothing because the "sole demand of strikers is for [the] closed shop, to which manufacturers as well as citizens of this community in general are unalterably opposed."103

The strike continued, with each side predicting victory. "So far as the manufacturers are concerned the strike is over," the employers declared in September. "Our factories are open, people are working."104 By October, manufacturers claimed that their factories had 15 percent of the normal workforce. A trade magazine announced "with great pleasure that the *United States Tobacco Journal* records indications of the approaching end of the cigar strike in Tampa."105 However, at the same time, an AFL organizer wrote to Samuel Gompers, "The strikers are very confident that they will gain an ultimate victory and they are not discouraged with the prospects . . . of having to continue the strike for several months to come."106

When employers' predictions of a union defeat failed to materialize after seven months, support for vigilante methods again mounted. In late November, following weeks of preoccupation with national, state, and municipal elections, the *Tampa Tribune* asserted that "the next task that waits the attention of the people is ending the hindrance to Tampa's cigar industry." Although "not advancing any lynching bees nor any deportation parties," Wallace Stovall declared that "the time is here for the people of this city to say to those responsible for the hungry mouths and poverty-pinched families of the greatest industry the city has, 'Get out! and leave us and our people and our affairs alone!'" Clearly targeting union leaders as the source of the problem, Stovall demanded, "How much longer are the citizens of Tampa going to see 15,000 honest workers intimidated and bullied by a score of so-called representatives of any organization in the world?"[107]

The following week, the *Tampa Tribune* issued a call to action. Stovall charged that "over-paid and corn-fed agitators are gloating over the fact that they intend to absolutely annihilate the cigar industry in this city." Indeed, the *Tribune's* owner claimed that the strike was led by "radicals who seek to achieve aggrandizement through the physical overthrow and destruction of our republican form of government." Equating republicanism with "the right of the individual citizen to work where and when he pleases," Stovall asserted: "The law of the land guarantees that right, yet the Joint Advisory Board attempts to say that it is mightier than the law." After employing tortured arguments to depict the strike as a battle between republicanism and radicalism, Stovall called on "every stalwart American citizen, both in and out of the unions, to curb radical agitators." He did not specify how this should be done, but in the past republicanism had been used to justify vigilantism directed at persons who challenged the prevailing distribution of power. Appealing directly to "the business interests of Tampa," Stovall concluded, "We must uphold our established institutions and fight for their preservation and the maintenance of the existing order of society."[108]

Two days later a Citizens' Committee was organized. The vigilante group was created ostensibly in response to a minor fracas in which union men fought with a small group of workers who supposedly sought an end to the strike. Union leaders claimed that an agent provocateur, acting on behalf of manufacturers, had precipitated this disruption of an otherwise peaceful strike. Subsequent court proceedings lent credence to this charge when it was revealed that the instigator was a special police officer who had not worked in the cigar industry for a number of years.[109] Nevertheless, "a general representative body of men, responsible for the upbuilding of the city and protecting its interests," according to D. B. McKay's *Tampa Times*, used the incident as an excuse to form a Citizens' Committee of fifty businessmen.[110] The group was headed by J. Arthur Griffin, a Tampa banker and treasurer of the Board of Trade, who had served on the 1910 Citizens' Committee.[111] A month before assuming leadership of the 1920 committee, Griffin had privately reported to fellow board officers about "the seriousness of the situation, asking every man present to use his influence to bring this [strike] to a speedy end, which could be done by showing the strikers that the people of Tampa were solidly behind the manufacturers."[112]

Toward this end, the Citizens' Committee tried to intimidate strike leaders. On December 1, vigilante businessmen stormed into Ybor City's Labor Temple. In the presence of some 200 strikers, J. Arthur Griffin of the Citizens' Committee confronted Sol Sontheimer from Chicago, whom businessmen "regarded as the 'brains' of the strike." The *Tribune* reported that Griffin told the union organizer "a recurrence of violence or attempts at intimidation would cause Sontheimer to be held personally responsible to the businessmen of this city." The Tampa banker added that his committee would guarantee protection to anyone returning to the factories. A supporting statement came from Charles Angus McKay, who was a native Tampan, a brother of D. B. McKay, a founder of the Tampa Retail Merchants Association, and vice president of the largest department store in south Florida.[113] The Citizens' Committee then left the Labor Temple, but the secretary of the Cigar Manufacturers' Association reported that the delegation of businessmen had given "these agitators and radicals to clearly understand that this useless strike had to end."[114]

Defenders of the Citizens' Committee invoked familiar arguments to justify prominent businessmen presenting themselves as enforcers of public order, independent of the police. Above all, union leaders were represented as a radical minority who used intimidation and fear to prevent resumption of work. The demand for the so-called closed shop meant "the sovietism [sic] of the industry," according to spokesmen for cigar manufacturers.[115] As part of this red-baiting, the *Tampa Tribune* charged: "To make the world a closed shop to all . . . is the desire of all, from Lenine [sic] down to the local 'labor skate' who is *particeps criminis* to having the worker . . . beaten and mistreated." Emphasizing that the walkout had worked "to the serious detriment of all business interests of the city," the *Tampa Times* argued that the strike was lost and that "the agitators who are keeping it up are covertly advising violence and intimidation as a last resort."[116] The *Tribune* claimed that the Citizens' Committee, "composed of fifty of the leading commercial and business men of the city, men of conservative, intelligent and patriotic characteristics," had acted in defense of "personal liberty" and "republican institutions," when it confronted strike leaders, "who through their coercive methods have hampered the progress and business interests of this city." In this endorsement of private community justice, the *Tribune* concluded: "What is wanted to end this destructive conflict is not arbitration, but the *stern repression* of violence."[117]

Tampa's labor press dismissed these arguments as fallacious and self-serving. The *Tampa Citizen*, which identified itself as "An Organized Labor Paper without a Muzzle, Published in the Interest of the Working Class in Tampa," stressed that the spokesmen for "the notorious 'citizens' committee'" had failed to cite any act of violence or intimidation by union members. Indeed, "the fact that the strike continues in full force and the criminal dockets of the state, county and municipal courts remain free of union men is convincing proof of the law-abiding intent of those charged with the responsibility of leadership in the strike."[118] Declaring that "the courts are the foundation of all civilization," the labor paper demanded: "Then why did not the 'citizens' committee' call upon the courts to impose a verdict upon these [union] men if they were guilty of committing any wrong?" There was "but one logical conclusion — that the 'citizens' committee' sought selfish gains at the expense of organized law and order."[119] This meant that "certain classes in this city are willing to lay aside all laws and courts and take the reins of government into their own hands to accomplish the defeat of a worthy cause."[120] However, the *Tampa Citizen* lectured, "The public interest is never defended through mob rule or threats of violence."[121]

The appearance of the Citizens' Committee failed to intimidate cigarworkers or their leaders. The warning given to Sol Sontheimer was similar to one that had forced a CMIU organizer to flee Tampa a decade earlier, but Sontheimer refused to budge. Instead, labor representatives alerted Governor Catts. Charging that "a Vigilente [sic] Committee composed of bankers and merchants and their agents" had ordered Sontheimer to leave town, Samuel Gompers appealed to the governor to prevent "so gross and violent a denial of American citizen rights."[122] Sontheimer met with state officials, and a Tampa newspaper reported that he had asked for a declaration of martial law.[123] It is not clear what specific action, if any, Governor Catts took, but the highly publicized appeals to a prolabor governor may have once again inhibited the Citizens' Committee from any overt violence. Certainly the continued peaceful conduct of strikers was not a sufficient cause to explain the restraint of Tampa businessmen who in the past had used vigilante violence even when cigarworkers broke no laws. Avoidance of violence in 1920 reflected the awareness of the Tampa elite that the state and federal governments were prepared to hold vigilantes accountable for violations of the law. Indeed, when threats from the Citizens' Committee failed to bring any change in the strike situation, employers fell back on the law.

On December 17, 1920, cigar manufacturers sought a federal court injunction for the first time in a Tampa cigar strike. Complaining that threats and intimidation by strike leaders had illegally interfered with their interstate businesses, factory owners won a temporary injunction prohibiting such action.[124] However, this court victory was largely symbolic, since strikers denied that they had ever engaged in such activities or even needed to in order to sustain the walkout. The Joint Advisory Board interpreted the legal maneuver "as an attempt on the part of . . . the Manufacturers' Association to further cement public opinion against the strikers."[125] As it turned out, neither the injunction nor public opinion determined the outcome of the strike.

In early 1921, with the strike entering its tenth month, the Department of Labor made a final effort to settle the dispute. For two weeks during January, a federal conciliator tried to bring the two sides together, but the Cigar Manufacturers' Association rejected any compromise short of its previously announced terms for a return to work. At a meeting of the Manufacturers' Association attended by the federal conciliator, the membership adopted a resolution declaring that it "refuse[d] to meet or have any dealings whatsoever with the Joint Advisory Board."[126] Employers were more confident than ever of victory because production normally decreased at the end of the busy holiday season.[127]

On February 4, 1921, two weeks after the Department of Labor failed to win any concessions from manufacturers, Tampa cigarworkers voted to end their ten-month strike. Factories had attracted less than 20 percent of the usual workforce, but local unions called for a referendum by the membership when funds dried up to pay strike benefits to nonunion cigarworkers. Some 1,500 unorganized strikers, ineligible for benefits from the CMIU, had received weekly payments from donations raised in other cigarmaking centers in Cuba and the United States. The flow of funds, amounting to about $10,000 a week, practically ceased in January 1921, as a result of a financial crisis in Cuba and slowed production in the United States. Unable to sustain the strike financially, union workers voted to end it by a margin of 2,514 to 1,054, with about a third of the strikers in Tampa refusing to cast a ballot.[128]

Each side claimed victory. "The manufacturers are victors in the fight to keep the industry on an open [shop] basis," the *Tampa Tribune* trumpeted.[129] However, the official voice of local cigarworker unions countered: "The manufacturers have not defeated us. Just the contrary. They are defeated, because we have walked into the shops more firmly united than ever before."[130] Insisting that Tampa workers had not lost the strike, the national leadership of the CMIU argued that the ten-month walkout "demonstrated the solidarity of the workers [and] . . . the ability and willingness of the International Union to meet its financial obligations."[131] More to the point, *El Internacional* observed, "The halt is only temporary and there shall never be peace in the local cigar industry until the rights of the workers are recognized by the bosses."[132]

Although the war over union recognition would continue, the 1920 strike showed that manufacturers could win a battle without the use of overt violence against workers. For the first time since 1899, Tampa vigilantes failed to use physical coercion to break a prolonged cigar strike. Nevertheless, the threat of vigilante violence loomed large over cigarworkers during 1920, especially after the formation of the new Citizens' Committee and its raid on the Labor Temple in December. The failure to carry out threats against union leaders was largely due to the unprecedented intervention of state and federal authorities, who were perceived as sympathetic to labor. More important, they also made it clear that Tampa businessmen would face legal penalties if they violated the law. Under this outside pressure, establishment violence was averted.

Any hope that the 1920 strike marked a permanent end to antilabor vigilantism soon disappeared. Despite cigar manufacturers' promises to the contrary, workers encountered wage cuts and discrimination in hiring after the ten-month strike ended.[133] Many owners also suspended the practice of reading in the factories. Weakened by the strike and a drastic decline in membership, the CMIU locals did not resist employers who, according to international president George Perkins, pursued Tampa cigarworkers "with merciless vengeance."[134] Finally, without any union backing, workers started a wildcat strike. At the height of production for the holiday season, a group of cigarmakers walked out of a West Tampa plant on November 17, 1921. Strikers demanded a restoration of the wage scale in effect at the end of the long strike and a return of the readers. The spontaneous action led to some property damage and arrests after windows were broken in several factories. The next day the walkout spread to Tampa's Ybor City after 4,000 cigarworkers voted in a referendum to strike for better wages and return of the readers.[135]

The Cigar Manufacturers' Association rejected both demands. Employers contended that increased wages would prevent Tampa products from competing successfully and that the practice of reading to workers had been abused by readers who used it as a platform for propaganda. Indeed, manufacturers blamed labor agitators for the strike which occurred with no warning in November 1921.[136]

Tampa's two daily newspapers immediately reinforced the view that agitators had caused the strike and should be expelled from the community. Two days after the walkout began, the *Tribune* declared that Tampa was "not going to have a repetition of what it suffered during previous, unjust, villainous attempts to dominate industry [even] if it has to take steps of extreme nature." This threat of vigilante action was followed by the assertion that the city was "amply prepared and able to crush beneath its heel any snake that seeks to strike its fangs into the body of business comity [sic]."[137] Although this was not a union-led strike, subsequent editorials stressed that AFL organizers were "again in our midst accomplishing their hellish deeds." Claiming that AFL representatives in other parts of the country had "resorted to violence and lawlessness, even to the extreme of murder," the *Tribune* called on "every stalwart American citizen, both in and out of the unions, to curb radical agitators." Support for this call to action came from D. B. McKay's *Tampa Times*, which argued that "the strike will work great injury to the city." Blaming "undesirables" for the disturbance, the *Times* concluded that "the time is past for temporizing or half-way measures. This strike is planned to destroy the cigar industry in Tampa. It is our chief industrial interest, and it must be protected."[138]

In the wake of these appeals, unknown vigilantes forced a strike leader to leave town. At about ten o'clock on the evening of November 22, several men representing themselves as police officers seized Luis Díaz, a cigar union leader, and took him away in a large touring car. Local police stated the next day that they had no knowledge of the whereabouts of the man who had disappeared in West Tampa. That city's police chief, Amazon C. Logan, dismissed the abduction as a hoax, probably "framed" to permit Díaz to leave town while engendering sympathy from workers.[139] However, when Díaz soon surfaced in Jacksonville, he reported that he had been kidnapped in West Tampa and threatened with lynching by vigilantes who had taken him to a neighboring town, put him on a train to Jacksonville, and warned him never to return to Tampa.[140]

Reports that two other strike leaders had also disappeared produced laudatory editorials in the local press. The *Tampa Tribune* kept "urging the people of this city to rid it of the radical agitator."[141] Invoking republican ideals to condemn a handful of strike leaders who threatened public order, the *Tribune* called "those who make war on the orderly processes of life and business enemies to the common cause, and traitors to the principle of majority rule." In addition, the newspaper equated "minority tyranny" with Bolshevism and chaos: "The rule of microscopic minorities is Lenineism; Lenineism [sic] is mob rule is chaos." While the *Tribune* used red-baiting to justify repressing strike leaders, the *Tampa Times* relied on familiar economic considerations to explain "WHY AGITATORS MUST BE DRIVEN FROM TAMPA." D. B. McKay's newspaper claimed that "the community has a proprietary interest in the [cigar] industry." This meant that "all who have the welfare of the city truly at heart [have] to protect the industry and insure its permanence and prosperity *by whatever means may be at their command.*" Pointing specifically at Luis Díaz, who was "conspicuous as an agitator," the *Times* contended that it still considered the expulsion of labor agitators a legitimate means of protecting the cigar industry. "It is the duty and to the interest of the business men and property owners, and all who desire to see the city prosper and expand, to expel them and to see that they remain away."[142]

Protests against the latest use of establishment violence came from the cigarworkers' union newspaper. *El Internacional* complained that Díaz and other militant workers were long-time Tampa residents who were guilty only "of the terrible crime of being consciously workers who are always trying to defend their rights." As the expelled men had broken no laws, *El Internacional* reflected that "guarantees the constitution of the United States of America offers to all its citizens does [sic] not exist for the cigar workers of Tampa." Moreover, the union paper pointed out that "those who consider themselves masters of the city, are guilty of gross transgressions of the law." *El Internacional* blamed in particular the "agitator-editor" of the *Tampa Tribune* and "the despicable writers of the 'doped' daily press" for stirring up violence against peaceful workers.[143]

With several strike organizers missing from the city and others in hiding, cigarworkers soon returned to the factories on manufacturers' terms. "We've got to have a leader," one cigarworker observed as strikers milled around the streets. "What we want is some leader capable of taking charge and dealing with the manufacturers."[144] In the absence of any spokesmen for unorganized strikers, several thousand cigarmakers returned to work by the end of the first week of the dispute, and within two weeks the strike was over.[145]

Spokesmen for Tampa's establishment attributed the quick defeat of strikers to the expulsion of their leaders. "The main cause of calling off the strike was the stand the press, public and the workers themselves, took regarding the agitators who were in town disturbing the industrial and social peace of the community," the *Tribune* declared. "These agitators were waited on, and without being hurt, were told to leave town; some of them reported to have been gently escorted part of the way out."[146] Looking to the future of the cigar industry, the *Times* warned: "Some of the men who promoted this strike are still in Tampa. They are undesirables, and the settlement of the strike should not in any wise abate the determination to drive them out." The *Tribune* even suggested that "Tampa should have some kind of a deportation ordinance, which would allow it legally to get rid of these vermin." Placing the need for order above constitutional guarantees of free speech and association, Wallace Stovall contended that "unless communities are given the right by law to rid themselves of incendiary revolutionists, and destroyers of the very fabric of the government, there will some day come a time when some community will become a law unto itself and make a riddance of rats such as will stand out [as] a warning to the vermin."¹⁴⁷ In fact, that time had long since arrived in Tampa. With the establishment of the cigar industry, businessmen led by the Board of Trade had initiated the tradition of using vigilante violence to repress workers.

A month after the end of the brief strike in November 1921, Tampans again took the law into their own hands to eliminate union leaders who supposedly threatened the cigar industry. On December 28, a cigar firm announced that it was closing its Tampa factory and moving production to Detroit. In an extended interview, a company vice president attributed the plant closing to "a spirit among the cigar factory workmen, which . . . makes it impossible to do business here successfully." The departing executive predicted that the cigar city "will lose other manufacturers if the situation is not regulated."¹⁴⁸ Tampa newspapers immediately appealed for suppression of "these agitators . . . [who] have slipped back into Tampa and [are] secretly working to start trouble again." The *Tribune* claimed that interference by labor agitators "must be put down or Tampa must give up its manufacturing and its ambition to be a city of varying resources." The *Times* agreed that the city fathers had "to rid the community of the anarchists and agitators before they succeed in their plans to destroy the cigar manufacturing industry."¹⁴⁹ Invoking historical precedent, D. B. McKay's newspaper noted that "The business men of Tampa have never failed in the past to meet any crisis or attack which threatened any material and desirable interest of the community."¹⁵⁰ Thus, Tampa notables continued to equate organizing among cigarworkers with anarchism whenever it threatened the material interests of the city. Moreover, defense of those interests justified community leaders taking the law into their own hands.

While the press sounded the alarm and defended private justice to repress so-called "agitators," the police chief of West Tampa threatened two cigar union officials. On December 27, Chief Logan went to Ybor City, where he had no jurisdiction, in search of the editors of *El Internacional*. Unable to locate either Francisco Fuente or Pietro Bianco, who also served as president of the union's Joint Advisory Board, Logan threatened bodily harm to both men if he found them. Moreover, he warned printers at the office of *El Internacional* not to publish anything about him. Fearing for his safety, Bianco fled town.¹⁵¹ From CMIU headquarters in Chicago, George Perkins complained to Samuel Gompers that Bianco had "never been arrested and the only charge against him is that he is a union man and that he fights for union principles and uses language that is vigorous and displeases our antagonists." Reminding Gompers that Tampa had an "Invisible Government," Perkins concluded, "Things in Tampa are done without warrant and with no regard to the rights of the workers or any citizen who is not submissive to the manufacturers and powers that be."[152]

Both Gompers and Tampa's JAB protested the "unwarranted intimidation" of Bianco and called on the governor to protect the rights of trade unionists in Tampa. However, the new governor, Cary A. Hardee, proved less sympathetic to labor than his predecessor, Sidney Catts. Hardee refused to take any action, claiming that he had "no authority whatever over City Police Officers."[153] The lesson of the 1921 expulsions was that defenders of the Tampa establishment could still drive peaceful union leaders out of town and get away with it.

Spokesmen for cigarworkers had no trouble explaining the revival of antilabor vigilantism. In the wake of these most recent attacks, *El Internacional* argued that "somebody in Tampa is trying to push the city back to the times when they used to lynch some workers, and when it was fashion to deport and commit other outrages against the workers, even if the law had to be violated." *El Internacional* claimed that the force behind such "terrorism" was Tampa's Cigar Manufacturers' Association, which was dominated by the American Tobacco Company, the largest single employer in Tampa. The editor of *El Internacional* charged that those responsible for the illegal repression of law-abiding cigarworkers "know they are exempt from the law and can do as they please, because they will know they are the only masters of the city."[154]

Strikes by cigarworkers erupted in the 1920s, but they were brief, isolated and peaceful. Reflecting the relative harmony of the period was the return of readers to the factories in 1927. The decade ended with a record year in Tampa's production of cigars. At that time, the city's largest single industry employed almost 12,000 workers, only a small percentage of whom were members of the Cigar Makers' International Union. During the 1920s, Tampa also continued its dramatic growth, almost doubling its population to 100,000 people, as a result of both the arrival of new residents and the annexation of West Tampa.[155]

After a decade of prosperity, the depression hit cigarworkers hard. Reduced demand for their luxury product led to a 17 percent decline in output and a 30 percent drop in payrolls between 1929 and 1931. Cigarworkers also faced displacement as a result of the increased use of machines to perform a variety of operations, including banding, stripping, and bunch-making. "The cigar-making machines are at the root of all the evil in Ybor City," a former cigarmaker reflected.[156] As early as 1930, a local CMIU official reported "a large number of cigar makers walking the streets." For those still employed, wage rates also fell. In January 1931, Tampa's Cigar Manufacturers' Association announced that the pay scale would be cut by 10 percent.[157] In an attempt to explain the inability of labor to prevent these reversals, a CMIU officer observed, "The workers are disorganized."[158]

Despite declining production, cigar manufacturing remained the foundation of Tampa's weakened economy.[159] Cigarworkers had dropped to only 25 percent of the city's total labor force by 1931, but the Chamber of Commerce reported that "cigar manufacturing continues to lead the industries of Tampa from the standpoint of number of factories and employees, internal revenue paid, capital invested and quantity of production."[160] Mayor D. B. McKay, who had been returned to office for another four-year term in 1927, declared in 1930, "The prosperity of the cigar industry is vital to the city."[161]

The worsening economic situation, coupled with the radical heritage of cigarworkers, predisposed many of them to welcome Communist party organizers during 1931. As part of its new policy of creating dual unions to compete with the American Federation of Labor, the Communist party formed the Tobacco Workers Industrial Union (TWIU) in April 1931. Affiliated with the Communist party's Trade Union Unity League, the TWIU soon gained a wide following among Tampa cigarworkers.[162] The Cigar Makers' International Union observed that "cigar makers of Tampa, Florida, were never satisfied with the slow (?) pace of the International Union." As a result, the CMIU claimed, the Communists succeeded "in poisoning the minds of the workers and weaning them away from the International Union."[163] In fact, the CMIU had few members in Tampa by the end of the 1920s, and the TWIU quickly signed up several thousand members in 1931.

Communists made their presence in Tampa known in other ways. During the summer and fall of 1931, they campaigned for improved unemployment relief, led protests against evictions, held rallies, and staged plays with titles like "Downfall of the Classes." Many of the programs were conducted in Spanish at Ybor City's Labor Temple. An undercover Tampa policeman, who spent several months secretly observing these meetings, later testified that they featured appeals for racial equality and much waving of red flags.[164]

Communists soon encountered opposition from police and vigilantes. On October 31, three Communists protesting an eviction in Ybor City were arrested and charged with vagrancy, interfering with an officer, and inciting a riot, even though no violence occurred when an angry crowd of over a thousand gathered.[165] Four days later, Frederick Crawford, a local painter and Communist party member, was kidnapped from his home, shortly after he had attended an Ybor City rally called to protest the arrests on October 31. The five kidnappers, claiming to be policemen with a warrant for Crawford's arrest, hit their victim over the head, blindfolded him, and dumped him in a car. Crawford was then taken to a deserted spot and flogged with leather straps. He later told police he recognized some of the floggers, but he refused to name them, for fear of another beating.[166] Explaining the reason for the attack, Crawford concluded that it was because of his "taking part in Communist meetings."[167]

Tampa authorities also used the law to suppress radical activities. When representatives of cigarworkers requested a parade permit to stage a march celebrating the fourteenth anniversary of the Russian revolution, the city denied permission.[168] Justifying his decision, Tampa's recently elected mayor, Robert E. Lee Chancey, said that the proposed parade from Ybor City's Labor Temple to City Hall would have passed through Tampa's black neighborhood. Although Mayor Chancey claimed that "our Negroes are probably the most peaceable citizens" and "fairly treated," he later explained that "the very thought of a parade marching through the Negro section in celebration of a soviet holiday is abhorrent to the minds of the southern people."[169]

At a last-minute meeting on November 7, 1931, a committee from Ybor City warned officials that workers might march without the required permit. Tampa's police chief responded by calling on the American Legion to send volunteers to serve as special deputies. By that evening, the city's small police force had swollen to one thousand men after hundreds of war veterans answered the call to arms.[170]

Meanwhile, plans went ahead for a rally at the Labor Temple. Handbills printed in Spanish and English widely advertised the proposed celebration of the Russian revolution. The occasion led one local Spanish-language newspaper to reflect: "The Russian people have evolved from the despotism and extreme misery of the czars to their current relatively prosperous situation. . . . Here in the United States the capitalist regime seems to have developed as much as it can and now it goes toward misery. . . . As the Russian Republic progresses . . . , the world will look toward Russia as the new hope."[171] Ybor City's celebration on November 7 attracted an overflow crowd that packed the Labor Temple and spilled out into the street. As the speech-making began inside, a spark ignited the highly charged atmosphere in the street, where police faced workers. Police later claimed that they came under attack from the crowd, but workers countered that policemen had struck the first blows.[172]

No matter who provoked the outburst, the results were unmistakable. When fighting broke out, shots from an unknown source struck a patrolman and wounded him seriously. Police reinforcements quickly restored order, and arrests followed. In addition to seizing a number of people on the street, police entered the Labor Temple and arrested leaders of the meeting. Along with fifteen prisoners, police carted off a Soviet flag and Communist literature. Later that evening, Tampa police, acting without a warrant, raided the home of Frederick Crawford, the Communist worker who had been flogged earlier that week.[173] Officers seized more Communist literature and arrested Crawford and six others found in his home, which was described in the local press as "headquarters of the communists." The twenty-two people taken into custody that evening were temporarily held without bail while local authorities decided what charges to file.[174]

The aborted November 7 demonstration brought a new wave of repressive measures. Mayor Chancey expressed regret that violence had occurred but argued that "the conflict apparently was the result of activities by paid organizers." He promised "no compromise with these outside agitators."[175] Toward this end, the city barred further use of the Labor Temple for "communistic meetings."[176] In support of city officials, the *Tampa Tribune* declared: "Demonstrations of this character should be squelched in their incipiency. The best emergency treatment for a riotous 'red' is jail."[177] However, the *Tribune* added in an editorial "Reminder" that the community had also used forced expulsions ("involuntary excursions") in the past. "When it has been found that authorities were not sufficiently powerful, the American manhood of the city has always risen to the occasion."[178]

This threat of vigilante action was reinforced by local war veterans on Armistice Day, which fell just four days after the aborted rally by cigarworkers. The keynote speaker, who was a Congressman and former state commander of the American Legion, told his audience that veterans were "ready to stamp under foot these human vermin, commonly known as Communists." As part of the Armistice Day program, a disguised Legionnaire with long, unruly hair leaped onto the platform and began spouting radical ideas in broken English. When the audience demanded his neck, the supposed "red organizer" pulled off his wig and launched into a speech denouncing communism.[179] He called "upon every American to rise against the bolshevistic movement in this country."[180]

Meanwhile, local authorities filed formal charges against those arrested at the November 7 rally. Upon undertaking his investigation, the county solicitor declared his office would "do everything in its power to put a stop to the red activities," because, he argued, "The Communist organization in the county and state constitutes a grave menace."[181] After a two-day inquiry, the prosecutor filed blanket charges of unlawful assembly, rioting, and assault to commit murder against seventeen of the prisoners who remained in jail. Each of the accused was held on $10,000 bond, which, though soon reduced to $6,500, no one could raise. Defense lawyers, however, were supplied by the International Labor Defense, an organization which often assisted people arrested in connection with activities of the Communist party.[182]

Cigarworkers also immediately began organizing on behalf of the accused. Employees in several factories walked out, protesting that factory owners interfered with attempts to collect defense funds. In addition, strikers demanded release of the prisoners arrested at the November 7 rally.[183]

As labor unrest continued to interrupt production in a number of large plants, cigar manufacturers counterattacked. At a mass meeting on Thanksgiving Day, November 26, employers agreed to remove the readers from the factories. Pointing to "a decided feeling of unrest in the cigar industry of Tampa," the manufacturers contended that "all of the trouble is originating from the readers' stand where fiery Communistic translations from anarchistic publications have been constantly poured into the workers." This claim overlooked the fact that the workers selected the material to be read, but the factory owners voted "to immediately withdraw the privilege of reading any matter whatsoever."[184]

When cigarworkers arrived at the factories the following morning, they found the readers' platforms dismantled. Although taken by surprise, the workers immediately staged a walkout. Several thousand gathered at the Labor Temple and voted to strike for seventy-two hours. The protest was directed at both the removal of the readers and the continued imprisonment of the people arrested on November 7, but sympathy for those in jail became the predominant issue. In a show of solidarity, over 7,000 strikers closed down all but a handful of Tampa's cigar factories. The three-day demonstration remained peaceful. It also assumed the proportions of a general strike in Ybor City and West Tampa, where other Latin workers, including bakers and barbers, joined in the sympathy strike.[185]

When the seventy-two-hour strike ended, cigarworkers returned to the factories only to find themselves locked out. The TWIU charged that "the bosses want to starve the cigar workers."[186] A spokesman for manufacturers admitted that "the attitude in the industry is to remain closed until the present unrest blows over."[187] Manufacturers could afford to cease production because the Christmas rush had passed when the lockout began on November 30. Although cigarworkers signaled their willingness to return to their jobs, factory owners remained silent, refusing to reopen their plants or indicate any conditions they expected labor to meet.[188]

Cigar manufacturers again received support from local vigilantes. On the third day of the lockout, three hundred leading Tampans met in a closed meeting and decided to form a Citizens' Committee of twenty-five men, whose identity was carefully concealed from the public.[189] Described in the press as composed of businessmen, the so-called "secret committee of 25 outstanding citizens" was created to help cigar manufacturers "wash the red out of their factories," according to the local correspondent for *Tobacco Leaf*. The *Tampa Tribune* reported that members of the secret committee were convinced that most local workers did not sympathize with the Communists, who were dismissed as "outside agitators." Nevertheless, the *Tribune* insisted that the Citizens' Committee "was formed for the sole purpose of driving out the Communists, whether they are Communists freshly arrived *or long here.*"[190]

By its very secrecy and its identification with "outstanding businessmen," the committee of twenty-five evoked memories of previous Citizens' Committees. In the past, of course, such groups had resorted to violence. "In many quarters [of Tampa] there was the recollection of another citizens' committee that served in a strike many year ago," the *Tribune* trumpeted. D. B. McKay's *Tampa Times* reported ominously that the 1931 committee was "authorized to take any steps deemed necessary to end the agitation of paid communist organizers here."[191]

Several other local groups enlisted in this effort. The United Spanish War Veterans and the Elks offered their assistance, "even unto the bearing of arms," in the words of the Elks. The American Legion stationed one hundred armed men in Ybor City and West Tampa.[192] "The whole town was going about this business of being rid of the vicious element that had come here for trouble," the *Tribune* bragged. "The spirit of the secret committee became the spirit of the people — to finish the job themselves, quickly and peaceably."[193] A Communist newspaper, however, complained that the Citizens' Committee had whipped up "a lynch spirit against the Tampa strike leaders."[194]

The day after the formation of the secret committee, police moved against cigarworkers. When the TWIU led about a thousand members to several factories where banders and packers were preparing cigars for shipment, police tried to disperse the crowd, and fighting erupted. Ten workers, including three women, were arrested for rioting. Several were held for possible deportation. Following the arrests, Tampa police raided the Ybor City headquarters of the TWIU, apparently without a warrant, and seized all the union records, along with a box full of cash and a union official who happened to be at the office. Membership cards showed that 5,000 local cigarworkers, half of the industry's labor force, had joined the Communist union. The raid was organized by Tampa's new police chief, Amazon Logan, the former police chief of West Tampa who had threatened CMIU officials in 1921.[195]

The day after these arrests, Mayor Chancey warned cigarworkers that the city would not tolerate Communist activities. Chancey told a delegation of workers that their seventy-two hour strike in sympathy with jailed radicals was "a strike against constituted law and order." Although the mayor said he could not force anyone to work, he strongly advised cigarworkers to divorce their union activities from the Communists. "This government of ours does not countenance such teachings as have been poured into your ears by these foreign disturbers of our peaceful city," the mayor lectured. "The peace will be preserved in this city, regardless of what it costs." Within hours after this warning, the Tampa city council passed an ordinance authorizing the appointment of special policemen with the same powers as regular officers, including the right to bear arms.[196]

The following day, December 6, cigar manufacturers received the powerful support of a sweeping federal court injunction that effectively outlawed the TWIU. The order came in response to a complaint filed by Jerome Regensburg, an official of E. Regensburg & Sons, Inc., a large cigar corporation with two factories in Tampa and headquarters in New York City. Regensburg's petition charged that peace had reigned in the local cigar industry until paid agents of the Communist party, allegedly on orders from the Soviet Union, had come to Tampa to organize cigarworkers for the purpose of overthrowing by force the government of the United States. On the basis of this information, U.S. Judge Alexander Akerman of Tampa, a Georgia native and a director of Tampa's Chamber of Commerce, immediately issued a temporary federal injunction. Akerman's order barred 140 individuals, including leaders of the TWIU and publishers of two Spanish-language newspapers in Ybor City, from interfering in any way with the peaceful conduct of the cigar industry. In addition to forbidding "seditious literature or speeches," the federal court order specifically enjoined the TWIU from operating in Tampa.[197]

Once again, Tampa's system of community justice, encompassing both legal and illegal methods, reinforced order from above. The *Tampa Tribune* contended that three decisive acts during the first week of the lockout firmly restored "that law and order which was menaced by Communistic agitation." In addition to the mayor's warning to cigarworkers and the federal court injunction, the *Tribune* applauded the organization of the secret committee of twenty-five, emphasizing that "the suppression of sedition and anarchy is the business of all good citizens of Tampa." The *Tampa Times* reported that a "double fear" gripped TWIU leaders: "first of the meaning of the injunction and its effect . . . ; second, a fear of 'unofficial violence.'" In defense of both forms of intimidation, D. B. McKay declared in an editorial, "The unpatriotic must expect to reap as their kind have always reaped."[198]

During the second week of the lockout, the Citizens' Committee brought about the reopening of the cigar factories on manufacturers' terms. With their employees silenced by both the federal injunction and the threat of vigilante violence, cigar manufacturers agreed to reopen their plants, "provided the factories can be operated upon a basis of true Americanism and loyalty to our city, state and federal government." The owners spelled out "true Americanism" to include the open shop, nonrecognition of the TWIU or any other group with "Communist affiliation," removal of the readers, and a ban on collections of any kind within the factories.[199] Cigarworkers indicated a willingness to accept these conditions, but only if all employees were rehired, without discrimination, to share existing work. Cigarworkers appealed to Mayor Chancey for support. He demurred, stressing that negotiations were in the hands of the secret committee of twenty-five. Rather than consult with labor, the Citizens' Committee simply endorsed the position of cigar manufacturers, including the understanding that workers would be rehired on an individual basis. With the full backing of the secret committee, manufacturers reopened their factories on December 14, under the terms they had previously announced.[200]

Cigarworkers showed their willingness to return, but only about 70 percent of those who had originally walked out in the seventy-two-hour sympathy strike were rehired. "Reds had been weeded out, and only the old faithful workers . . . were on the job," declared one industry spokesman.[201] Gone too were the readers' platforms and any sign of the Communist union.[202]

A powerful alliance of local forces defeated the Tobacco Workers Industrial Union. As soon as the TWIU showed its strength among cigarworkers, it came under attack from city officials, a federal judge, and Tampa businessmen, all of whom went to the aid of cigar manufacturers. Leading Tampans justified their actions by depicting the struggle as more than a labor-management dispute. "It was not essentially a cigar strike, but a red revolution, into which the cigar industry was drawn," claimed *Tobacco Leaf*. In the view of the unidentified chairman of the secret committee of twenty-five, "The paid representatives of Communism had sought to disrupt [the cigar industry] and the community."[203] Reflecting on the response of the Tampa elite, Judge Alexander Ackerman observed:

> Two weeks ago we were all sitting over a powder keg. The monstrous doctrines of Communism were being preached in our midst, . . . and it was feared that our streets would run with blood. There developed a spirit of cooperation among our officers, who, in conjunction with a committee of clear-headed citizens, began to prepare plans for defense, and the paid agitators began to leave Tampa like rats deserting a

sinking ship. I can in mind's eye see that big, bold Negro in a red Packard with an Illinois tag, exceeding the speed limit on his way back to Chicago.[204]

Depicted in these terms, the need to eliminate the Communist threat justified using any means necessary. Community leaders argued that they had employed only lawful means to defeat "the red menace," but vigilantism played a significant role in breaking the TWIU. After a group of vigilantes had flogged Frederick Crawford for engaging in Communist activities, the secret committee of twenty-five used the threat of violence to intimidate cigarworkers. The police also resorted to raids without search warrants to suppress Communists. This resulted in a judge's dismissing charges against Frederick Crawford because police had broken into his home without a warrant.[205]

The final blow to the argument that strictly legal means had defeated the TWIU came in a 1933 court decision. The ruling by Florida's Supreme Court overturned the convictions of fifteen demonstrators previously found guilty on several counts, including unlawful assembly at the rally on November 7, 1931.[206] In May 1933, after most of the fifteen defendants had served their full sentences of one year in prison, the Florida State Supreme Court unanimously reversed the convictions on the ground that those arrested at the November 7 rally could not be charged with unlawful assembly because police had not first ordered them to disperse, as required by law.[207] The American Civil Liberties Union hailed the decision as "a judicial rebuke to those in Tampa who have sought to use police and court machinery to crush a labor union fighting for decent conditions in the cigar industry."[208]

The real lesson for the Tampa elite was that vigilantism still worked. None of the perpetrators of establishment violence went to jail. Moreover, under pressure from vigilantes, the TWIU disappeared, and so too, for the moment, did outward signs of worker militancy. "Labor is tranquil and more amenable to reason, and is showing a desire to cooperate and eliminate the waste absolute customs have imposed in the past," one manufacturer observed in the wake of the strike.[209]

The well-orchestrated repression of worker militancy in 1931 led to more formalized cooperation between cigar manufacturers and prominent Tampans. In January 1932, *Tobacco Leaf* emphasized that the cigar industry was "closer to other interests in Tampa than it has been in years, as a result of the united front put up by all interests to the threat of revolutionary communism displayed in the recent strike." On the basis of this improved relationship, the Cigar Manufacturers' Association of Tampa took the unprecedented step of electing "three leading citizens" to its board of directors. The purpose, according to

*Tobacco Leaf,* was "to keep a permanent bond between the industry and the city." This goal, along with the men selected, strongly suggests that the three citizens had earned the appreciation of manufacturers during the 1931 strike, perhaps as members of the secret committee of twenty-five. The men so honored included D. B. McKay, "a friend of the industry for almost half a century," who had been publicly identified with every Citizens' Committee since 1892.[210] The other two "outsiders" were a past president of the Chamber of Commerce and an attorney who was also a local bank director.[211]

The victory of cigar manufacturers in 1931 did not prevent the further decline of the industry. Production of luxury hand-rolled cigars continued to plummet due to a variety of national and international forces, including the depressed economy, the increased popularity of cigarettes, and competition from inexpensive machine-made cigars.[212] Faced with these conditions, the tobacco trust abandoned Tampa. In 1932, the American Tobacco Company closed its cigar factories in Havana and Tampa and opened a new plant in Trenton, New Jersey, which featured a climate control system and a newly-trained labor force of "deft-fingered girls [to] replace the traditional Cuban cigarworkers." Pointing to the advantages of these operatives, company executives explained that women "have the finger dexterity; don't mind the monotony and therefore don't need story readers; they are more tractable."[213] Plant closings and removals eliminated the jobs of over 4,000 cigarworkers in Tampa during the early 1930s, as local production of quality cigars fell from 504 million in 1929 to 294 million in 1933.[214] "The cigar making machines are ruining, not only the cigarmakers, but the manufacturers as well," Enrique Pendas observed. "The [Tampa] factories must compete with other factories in the country. This competition is ruinous."[215]

Facing the threat of extinction, as well as continued worker militancy, most of Tampa's remaining manufacturers agreed to union recognition under the New Deal in 1933. Following passage of the National Industrial Recovery Act with its promise of collective bargaining rights for employees, cigarworkers flocked into the "Local Independent Union of the Cigar Industry of Tampa."[216] In August 1933, the independent union led a strike which closed most of Tampa's factories for a week until cigar manufacturers agreed to sign a temporary code of fair competition, approved by the National Recovery Administration (NRA). The code for Tampa's cigar industry provided for a minimum wage, which brought an immediate pay increase to many workers. This agreement did not extend union recognition, but the AFL took immediate steps to insure that its affiliate, the Cigar Makers' International Union, would win the right to represent Tampa workers. With support from the AFL's president, the CMIU mounted a campaign to recapture the allegiance of Tampa cigarworkers. This effort succeeded, and by December 1933, the CMIU had enrolled over 5,000 members in Tampa.²¹⁷

For the first time, cigar manufacturers cooperated with the CMIU in an attempt to bring stability to Tampa's industry. In August 1933, a spokesman for factory owners, complaining to the NRA in Washington about "labor trouble agitated by communists," appealed for government assistance.²¹⁸ Once the CMIU had signed up the majority of Tampa's workers, it called for the Department of Labor to mediate an agreement with employers. When Commissioner of Conciliation Thomas M. Finn went to Tampa in December 1933, he found both sides willing to talk.²¹⁹

The central issue was not wages, but union recognition. At a conference with factory owners and leading Tampans, including D. B. McKay and Howell T. Lykes, the international vice president of the CMIU assured cigar manufacturers that if his union received formal recognition, "a stability would come about in the industry here [in Tampa] such as has been unknown heretofore."²²⁰ A committee of manufacturers soon agreed to union recognition and collective bargaining according to NRA principles. In return, the CMIU gave up the right to strike. Both sides agreed to abide by a system of arbitration to settle any disputes. The three-year agreement also continued the existing ban on readers in the factories.²²¹

Most of Tampa's large manufacturers signed the 1933 agreement. This established a mechanism for collective bargaining, subject to arbitration, to settle wage and other disputes. Spokesmen for labor and management attributed the approval of this unprecedented document to federal intervention and the mutual desire for stability in the midst of economic decline and radical agitation.²²² Calling the pact "a great step forward in cooperation," the Tampa correspondent for *Tobacco Leaf* declared that "the leadership of the Federal Government was essential."²²³ In an attempt to explain the new attitude of employers, a former president of Tampa's Cigar Manufacturers Association subsequently observed, "We have to consider the workers if we want to survive."²²⁴

The primary opposition to collective bargaining came from Hav-A-Tampa Cigar Company, a large Tampa-based firm which did not belong to the Cigar Manufacturers Association. Hav-A-Tampa produced low-priced, machine-made cigars with a work force of about 800 employees, of whom "only six or seven [were] Latins," according to federal mediator Thomas Finn. "All their employees are women who come from little towns near Tampa," a retired cigarmaker complained.²²⁵ Facing little pressure from these employees, the company refused to sign the 1933 agreement or in any way extend union recognition. Finn privately described the general manager of Hav-A-Tampa, Daniel Hoyt Woodbery, as "obdurate, and [he] informed us . . . that Union's [sic] led to 'Mob Rule' etc."[226]

Union recognition by most of Tampa's large cigar companies did not eliminate worker militancy or labor-management disputes, but it marked the end of vigilante violence to break strikes. After 1933, when conflicts over new work rules occasionally led cigarmakers to walk out in violation of their no-strike pledge, Tampa businessmen still took an interest, but they looked to federal officials to resolve disagreements in the declining industry.[227]

Reflective of this new attitude was the response of Tampa business leaders to a 1935 strike by several hundred cigarmakers in one plant. The dispute arose in a factory operated by the Schwab-Davis Company. Cigarmakers formally complained that the firm had introduced the production of cheap cigars by a system of teamwork in violation of the union contract. Under the terms of the 1933 agreement, an arbitration committee of workers and manufacturers ruled in favor of cigarmakers and levied a $400 fine against Schwab-Davis. From his headquarters in New York City, the company's president, Fred J. Davis, announced that he would not pay the fine. When his employees then refused to return to work, Davis threatened to close the idle factory and expand the company's operations in other cities.[228]

The impasse forced Commissioner of Conciliation Thomas Finn to return to Tampa. He met with union representatives, members of the Cigar Manufacturers' Association, and a "citizens committee," composed of two Tampa bankers and D. B. McKay. Although ever since 1892, McKay had been involved in a series of Citizens' Committees that had used vigilante violence to break strikes, in 1935 he accepted the suggestion of Commissioner Finn and personally paid the $400 fine assessed against Schwab-Davis.[229] Finn reported that McKay and the two other members of the Citizens' Committee made it clear that "they would do all in their power to co-operate with the representative of the Department of Labor in an endeavor to save the factory for Tampa."[230] Whereas in the past the same concern of local businessmen had led to establishment violence against workers in the absence of any intervention by outside authorities, the presence of the commissioner of conciliation encouraged a peaceful resolution of the 1935 strike in accordance with the terms of the 1933 agreement. McKay paid the fine, cigarmakers returned to Schwab-Davis, and disputes in the industry continued to be argued within the framework of union recognition, collective bargaining, and arbitration. Without revealing that the chairman of its editorial board had played any role in the "amicable settlement" of the four-week strike, the *Tampa Times* noted approvingly that there had been "no demonstration of any type during the strike, and peaceful relations are expected to continue."[231]

D. B. McKay's generosity in 1936 failed to endear him to cigarworkers. When manufacturers suggested that McKay arbitrate a subsequent dispute in 1935, local CMIU leaders denounced him as someone who "can not be impartial," because he had consistently sided with cigar factory owners against workers.[232] Similarly, when elderly cigarmakers were invited to a 1936 dinner celebrating the fiftieth anniversary of Tampa's cigar industry, one refused to attend because McKay was a guest of honor. Eighty-year-old José García, one of the first Cuban cigarmakers in Ybor City, explained that "it was a terrible affront to the early settlers in giving them a banquet now almost when life is about to expire, after they had been considered little more than dogs by McKay and many others in prominent positions."[233]

This symbolic protest in the form of a rejected dinner invitation reflected both continued class antagonism and a change in the arena of conflict. As Thomas Finn of the Department of Labor observed privately in 1935, cigar manufacturers still encountered "demands made upon them by the Latin workers of Tampa who are bound hand and foot by beautiful traditions and who prize their workmanship above money." However, Finn added, "The fault does not lie alone with the workers[;] employers are equally to blame[;] in day's [sic] past, workers were underpaid, unfairly and unjustly dealt with."[234] The difference was that by the mid-thirties the federal government provided a forum for resolving long-standing disputes. Collective bargaining under government supervision did not guarantee resolution of conflicts, let alone survival of the luxury cigar industry, but it did discourage the use of violence to repress workers.

The 1930s marked a turning point in the struggle over control in Tampa's cigar industry. The depression brought economic disaster, and the New Deal promised a measure of stability in labor relations through collective bargaining. The 1932 closing of Tampa factories owned by the American Tobacco Company had also removed a powerful obstacle to union recognition, and most remaining cigar companies agreed to bargain with representatives of the conservative CMIU in return for a no-strike pledge. But Tampa cigarworkers were in retreat. Decimated by the depression, displaced by machines, and dispersed by the search for work or welfare, they no longer represented the same threat to employers. "The people of Ybor City are orphans, not only of father and mother, but of everything in life," a retired cigarmaker mused in the 1930s. "They cannot find work at the cigar factories because of the machines."[235] "Families after families are leaving for the North," another former cigarmaker pointed out. "This exodus is chiefly observed among the younger generation, who finding themselves without work, migrate to New York where they find many opportunities."[236]

Prominent Tampans, led by D. B. McKay, accepted the new equilibrium. With the cigar industry in danger of disappearing and the city under growing external pressure to end its tradition of establishment violence, many Tampa leaders sought a new image and new businesses to fill the gap left by departing cigar companies.

These changes did not elicit unanimous support among members of the Tampa elite. Indeed, they produced for the first time significant disagreements over the appropriate means of maintaining existing power relationships. Among cigar manufacturers, Hav-A-Tampa Cigar Company resisted union recognition. Its less skilled and unorganized work force meant Hav-A-Tampa could successfully oppose unionization and collective bargaining. Its owners also continued to support some forms of establishment violence, as they soon demonstrated by their response to the 1935 lynching of Joseph Shoemaker, discussed in the next chapter.

The decline of antilabor violence in the wake of union recognition was part of a national pattern. During the 1930s, industries and communities that had long been a law unto themselves came under increasing outside pressure, especially from state and federal governments, to conform to standards of conflict resolution that excluded violence. This was particularly evident in the case of employers who were covered by New Deal collective bargaining laws. As in the cigar industry, employers around the country discovered that union contracts could be used to discipline militant workers. Conflicts between labor and management did not disappear, but union recognition eliminated the leading source of industrial violence. As a result, this form of collective violence declined dramatically throughout the United States after the changes in collective bargaining wrought during the 1930s.[237]

The end of establishment violence against cigarworkers did not bring vigilantism to a sudden halt in Tampa, however. Lynch law had always been directed at a variety of groups and individuals, not just cigarworkers, and some of the city's worst collective violence occurred in the 1930s after peace reigned in the economically devastated cigar industry.

# "Tar and Terror"

During the 1930s, Tampa's "reign of terror" came to an end, but not before it claimed two more lives in separate incidents. A black prisoner was lynched in 1934, and the following year a white radical was flogged to death. Reactions to the 1934 lynching clearly showed that public attitudes toward mob violence were changing, especially among community leaders, who uniformly condemned the killing. The lynchers, however, went unpunished. Then, in 1935, vigilantes flogged and tarred and feathered three Socialists, one of whom died. This political murder generated a prolonged local and national campaign to punish the perpetrators and halt Tampa's violent repression of radicals and labor organizers. The unprecedented crusade finally led to the first indictments and convictions of vigilantes in Tampa. Although the convictions were ultimately overturned, they helped end Tampa's vigilante tradition. By the end of the decade, economic and political considerations, similar to those that had encouraged leading Tampans to support peaceful collective bargaining for cigarworkers, drove them to suppress vigilantism aimed at other targets, including blacks and radicals.

A change in elite responses toward lynch law directed at common criminals became evident during and after World War I. "The *Tribune* deplores mob rule of all kinds," Wallace Stovall observed in 1920. D. B. McKay claimed that "it would be difficult to find an apologist for lynching in these days."[1] When tested, this view proved more than rhetorical.

In 1917, Tampa officials prevented the lynching of a black prisoner. The twenty-one-year-old man was accused of killing a white woman and her baby and raping a fourteen-year-old white girl. These crimes had occurred some thirty-five miles from Tampa in a small town located in an adjacent county, but Tampa police had found the suspect hiding in the city's black section. Soon after his arrest on April 20, 1917, the suspect confessed to the double murder and the rape. "Any one of these crimes would have resulted in [the accused] being quickly lynched by the people of this city and section a few years ago, but the lynch spirit seems to be passing," the *Tampa Times* observed. The city's two leading newspapers called for an immediate trial "in order to prevent talk of lynch law."[2] Emphasizing the importance of outside opinion, the *Tribune* argued that if the "fiend" could be "promptly convicted and executed, it will save the State the stigma of a mob." As these appeals to public-spirited citizens were being written, a crowd of some 1,000 people gathered in front of the county jail in Tampa during the night of Saturday, April 21. The mob of would-be lynchers and curious spectators confronted one hundred National Guardsmen, in addition to city police, sheriff's deputies, and civilian volunteers, all of whom were clearly determined to protect the black prisoner. This show of force, combined with several arrests, cooled the ardor of the crowd, which gradually dispersed as dawn approached. "It was apparent the mob lacked a real leader," noted one reporter.[3]

This time community leaders had taken a firm stand against lynch law. First, they had encouraged the sheriff to request the National Guard as a precaution, and then they had joined the force protecting the prisoner until he was secretly transferred to a Jacksonville jail after the mob had dispersed.[4] The sheriff subsequently revealed that he might have been less firm without the pressure applied by leading Tampans. When asked by a reporter if the confessed murderer-rapist deserved lynching, the sheriff admitted, "I would like to see him dealt with, but it is my duty to enforce the law, even against my personal feeling in any matter." In a similar vein, the commander of the National Guardsmen, Captain Sumter L. Lowry of Tampa, observed that it seemed "unjust to be forced to call out the boys to protect a negro murderer and rapist, but we are forced to do it under orders of the state."[5] The fact that these militiamen had just returned from active duty in Mexico and were preparing to serve in the World War may have heightened Captain Lowry's sense of duty and awareness that he was responsible to a higher authority. In any event, the black prisoner escaped lynching and lived to be legally tried and executed several months later.[6]

In 1927, Tampa officials, backed by the National Guard and a vigilance committee, crushed another attempt to lynch a murderer. The killer, Benjamin Frank Levins, was a thirty-eight-year-old white transient who confessed to the ax murder of a Tampa family of five that he had mistaken for a family against whom he held a grudge. Arrested immediately and held in the county jail in Tampa, Levins soon declared, "I done it. I killed 'em. God knows why. I was just crazy on dope."[7] On May 29, 1927, two days after discovery of the grisly crime, a mob of some 1,000 people stormed the county jail. Repulsed by police and sheriff's deputies, the crowd gathered again the following night. Despite the announcement that Levins had been transferred to another jail, a group of about fifty men made two separate armed assaults on the Tampa jail, leaving eleven people, including two policemen, wounded by bullets. The second night of violence ended with the arrival of National Guardsmen, requested by the sheriff and commanded again by Sumter L. Lowry, now a colonel who had seen combat in World War I.[8]

Prominent Tampans immediately denounced the people who formed the mob. Reports circulated that the crowd included delegations from surrounding towns and even other counties. Whatever their origin, the rioters were "the enemies of organized society" in the eyes of D. B. McKay, who condemned the violence in editorials. "The mob and the organized forces of society met and clashed in Tampa last night," the *Tampa Times* observed. "Organized society won."[9] Civic associations, such as the Kiwanis Club, immediately adopted resolutions deploring the "misguided efforts of ill-advised elements of the community."[10]

Neither appeals for order nor the presence of 500 National Guardsmen prevented a third night of rioting, in which six civilians were killed by soldiers protecting the jail with machine guns.[11] This led Mayor Perry G. Wall to call on "all law abiding men" to join a citizens' committee to assist in quelling "the spirit of violence held by lawless elements." Colonel Lowry, the owner of a Tampa insurance company, reinforced the idea that the local elite should lend a hand in restoring order. "Men of standing in the community can do an immense service by reporting agitators and by quieting groups likely to become unruly," he declared.[12] Some 600 "leading citizens" answered the call to arms and "organized a vigilance committee to patrol Tampa and combat mob violence." The sheriff deputized the "citizen vigilantes," who included "representatives of every civic organization and business and professional men," as well as "some of the community's most prominent citizens." The cooperative effort of the National Guard, sheriff's department, city police, and vigilance committee successfully restored order, and Mayor Wall asserted proudly that "hoodlumism" had ended.[13]

The prevention of a lynching in 1927 demonstrated once again the growing concern of city fathers that certain types of collective violence adversely affected dominant class interests. As in 1917, prominent Tampans seemed most concerned about the composition of the mob and the effect "a lynching horror" would have on the city's reputation.[14] The *Tampa Times* argued that the community's "civilized people" should not allow an "unthinking" mob "to bring our city and its citizenship into disrepute."[15] Pointing out that Florida had amassed the country's worst lynching record during the previous year, the *Times* contended that "Florida's shame" required the state "to shut down the mob's activity, no difference how desperate the means."[16] In the midst of the three days of rioting, the *Tampa Tribune* warned that a lynching would do "great harm to the community . . . [by] placing it on the list of communities where the law is flouted and the mob reigns."[17]

The means of restoring law and order had, of course, included the use of "citizen vigilantes." This irony was overlooked because they were recruited from "the better element of Tampa" and had the blessing of law enforcement officials. As soon as the rioting had ended, the *Tribune* even suggested that the 600 vigilantes remain organized to suppress the dope traffic. "They can rid Tampa of this evil, which our regularly constituted officers have failed to check," the newspaper's editor asserted in a ringing endorsement of vigilante action by the establishment.[18]

Changes in elite attitudes toward lynching did not signal any weakening of segregation. "White supremacy in the south will be maintained," the *Tampa Tribune* proclaimed in 1921.[19] The paper warned that "'no sane negro' will demand so-called 'social equality,' for it becomes a source of friction between the two races that is quite certain to culminate in trouble."[20] A 1927 study of Tampa's black community concluded that "orthodox Southern traditions as to race relations prevail in Tampa."[21]

The one tradition increasingly opposed by Tampa leaders was the use of mob violence against blacks. The city's 23,000 black residents represented no threat to powerful whites, who perceived black labor as an economic necessity. "Everyone must recognize the need of negro labor in this city as in other cities of the South," the *Tampa Tribune* emphasized in 1926 after a mob of fifty men burned the local field offices of a company developing a black subdivision. "No matter how great a city Tampa may become, it will still have need of the labor service of negro men and the domestic service of negro women."[22] This argument obviously appealed to the upper class, but it may have been lost on white Tampans who competed with blacks for jobs or who did not hire maids.

The deadly suppression of the 1927 riot discouraged large lynch mobs from ever forming again in Tampa. However, it did not prevent the recurrence of lynchings at the hands of small, well-organized groups which concealed their activities from public view. Although increasingly common in the South after 1935 as resistance to mob violence mounted, secret vigilante executions had been the typical form of lynching in Tampa since 1903.[23]

Nonetheless, Tampans were shocked by the 1934 lynching of Robert Johnson. The murder came as a surprise, in part because the alleged offense that precipitated the summary execution had not even merited press coverage. Johnson, a black of about forty, was arrested on January 29, 1934, for questioning about an assault on a local white woman.[24] Despite intensive interrogation of Johnson, Tampa police failed to find any evidence linking him to the beating of the woman, whose attacker had fled when a group of blacks had come to her rescue. In the middle of the night following his arrest, Johnson was released into the custody of Thomas M. Graves, who represented himself as a deputy constable ordered to transfer the black prisoner to the county jail to face charges of stealing chickens. Graves later reported that soon after leaving the city jail with Johnson at 2:35 a.m., he was stopped by three cars in downtown Tampa, thrown into the back seat of his own car by three unmasked men, and driven in a procession of about twelve automobiles to a deserted area outside the city, where the lynchers used his gun to shoot Robert Johnson four times in the head and once in the body. The vigilantes allegedly left Graves to report the lynching. His version included the claim that Johnson had confessed to attacking the white woman.[25]

News of Johnson's death caused an uproar. The nation's second lynching of 1934 and the first in Florida since 1932, the Johnson case provided a test of the state's willingness to uncover and prosecute those responsible for the summary execution of blacks. Toward this end, organized opponents of lynching immediately put pressure on Governor David Sholtz, a New York-born, Yale-educated Democrat who had won election in 1932 with pledges of reforming Florida.[26] The Association of Southern Women for the Prevention of Lynching reminded Sholtz that only a week before Johnson's murder, he had promised to use his power to assure the apprehension and punishment of anyone involved in a lynching. In fact, the governor did take immediate action by ordering the local sheriff and state attorney "to detect and bring to speedy justice those guilty of the lynching."[27]

Given Tampa's record of complete inaction in the aftermath of previous lynchings, the sheriff and state attorney for Hillsborough County appeared unusually diligent. In a surprising display of frankness, Sheriff Will C. Spencer publicly expressed doubts about the guilt of Robert Johnson and stated his belief that a white man had attacked the white woman in question. Spencer privately expressed his conviction that Thomas Graves knew all the lynchers and should have been indicted as an accessory to murder.[28] State Attorney J. Rex Farrior, a Florida native and recent appointee to public office, also suggested Graves' probable complicity by telling reporters that Graves had no legal authority to serve as a law enforcement official or to carry a pistol, his various commissions and permits having expired. "In other words," Farrior explained, "I can't find a bit of evidence to show that T. M. Graves had any more authority than a private citizen when he appeared at the Police Station at 2:35 a.m. . . . and demanded the prisoner to be turned over."[29]

Nevertheless, no indictments were forthcoming. After examining fifty-six witnesses over a three-week period, the local grand jury issued a report which condemned "the lack of precaution, diligence, and courage on the part of T. M. Graves," who "was not at the time a duly authorized or commissioned officer." The grand jury concluded, however, that it had "insufficient evidence to indict T. M. Graves as an accessory before the fact for the murder of Robert Johnson."[30] State Attorney Farrior confided to the governor that a large majority of the grand jurors voted against indictments "either because they did not understand the circumstantial evidence, or because one or two of them may have been in sympathy with lynching a negro charged with such an offense."[31]

As late as 1934, even suspicion of assaulting a white woman, no matter how unfounded, could lead to the lynching of a black man, especially if it appeared that no one would be legally punished for the offense. "The crime justified severe punishment," a Tallahassee newspaper editor asserted. "We will waste no sympathy on the victim. He probably deserved what he received."[32] The lynching of Robert Johnson, after police had cleared him of the assault charge, was an example of repressive justice, according to which any black would serve as an object lesson for the entire community.[33] Above all, it demonstrated that summary execution by self-appointed vigilantes still occurred not only in rural areas of the South but also occasionally in large cities like Tampa, which had over 100,000 people by 1934.[34]

Tampa's 1934 lynching revealed again the growing local concern over the impact of mob violence on the city's image. The widely publicized killing of Robert Johnson occurred just as cigar manufacturers were bringing a measure of order to labor relations and local promoters were seeking new businesses to boost the sagging economy. "A lynching is deplorable; it reflects on the county," State Attorney Farrior exclaimed. He later added that the community "must not tolerate such a happening that spreads a blot on Tampa's history."[35] While pushing for prosecution of the "Tampa lynchers," one local newspaper expressed the fear that "the lynching of Johnson might develop into a case of nationwide importance, second only to the famous Scottsboro case in Alabama."[36] At a meeting of the local Kiwanis Club on the day after the lynching, former Governor Doyle E. Carlton complained, "This act gives a black eye to Tampa.... It will draw no people to Florida or the west coast."[37] When the grand jury failed to indict anyone, the *Tampa Tribune* concluded that the unsolved murder of "this helpless and friendless negro" had left "another black mark on the record of Tampa and Florida."[38] However, the spotlight originally focused on Tampa had already faded, and the grand jury's typical response generated little publicity, let alone protest, outside the local

Tampa in 1926. Tampa–Hillsborough County Public Library System.

Joseph A. Shoemaker. P. K. Yonge Library of Florida History, University of Florida.

The local National Guard battery in front of Tampa's city hall posed with Mayor Robert E. Lee Chancey in 1932. Tampa–Hillsborough County Public Library System.

Tampa's Mayor Robert E. Lee Chancey posing with two Junior League members in 1931. Tampa–Hillsborough County Public Library System.

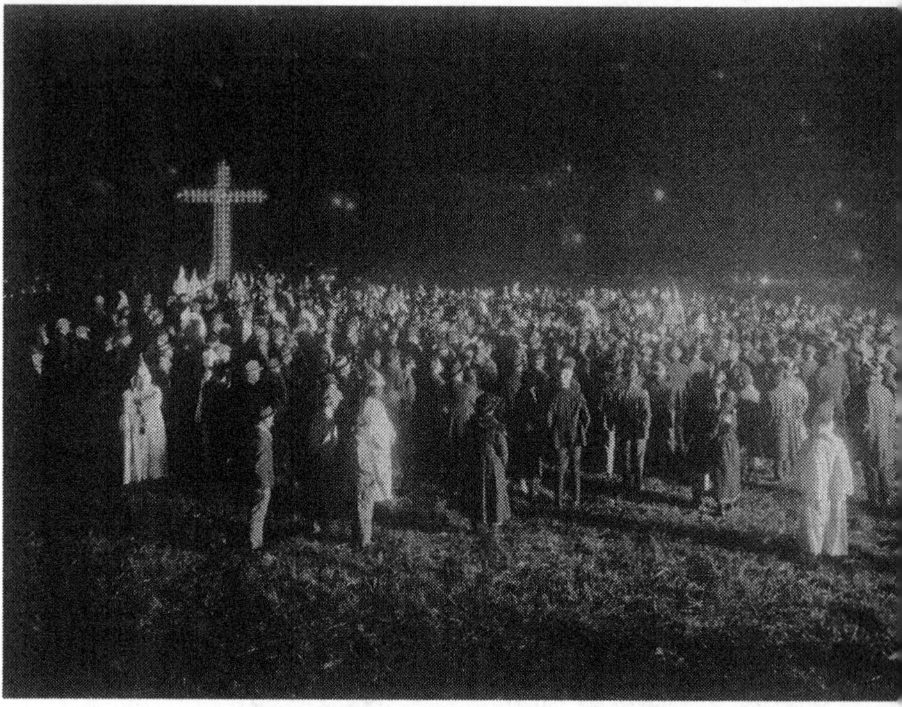

SOUTHERN LUMBER & SUPPLY CO.
TAR.. TODAY
WHITEWASH TOMORROW
TAMPA: THE YEAR ROUND CITY

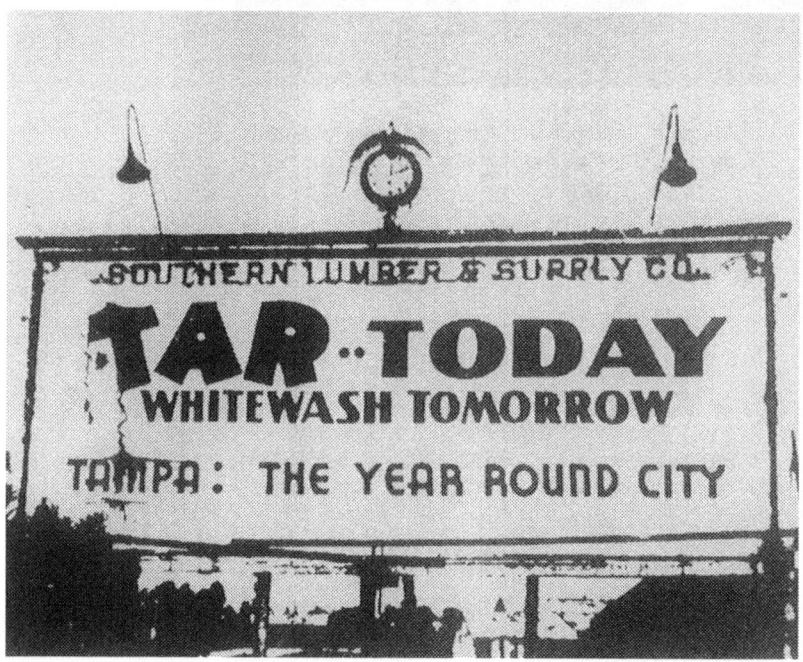

The Klan circular that was distributed in Tampa after the flogging of Joseph Shoemaker. University of South Florida Special Collections.

A Ku Klux Klan rally held in Tampa during November 1923. Tampa–Hillsborough County Public Library System.

A billboard erected by a Tampa businessman after the tar-and-feathering of three Modern Democrats. University of South Florida Special Collections.

A Ku Klux Klan rally held in Tampa on February 23, 1937. *Tampa Morning Tribune*, February 24, 1937.

A 1936 cartoon depicted a Klan flogger with a gun and a bucket of tar protecting gambling in Tampa. *St. Louis Post–Dispatch,* January 13, 1936.

Tampa in 1940. Tampa–Hillsborough County Public Library System.

area.[39] It took the vigilante murder of a white man the following year to end this form of collective violence in Tampa.

The flogging of Joseph Shoemaker in 1935 was a product of a power struggle that had disrupted the city for several years. At stake was control of the city's political machinery, notoriously corrupt and, therefore, profitable. The battle focused on local elections, which divided the Tampa elite in the 1930s and led to widespread violence between the opposing forces.

The city's dominant political faction was headed by Patrick Crisp Whitaker, a Georgia native. After graduating from law school, Pat Whitaker had moved to Tampa in 1916. His brother Thomas joined him in establishing a law partnership, and the two built up a successful criminal practice during the 1920s. Pat's persuasive speaking ability made him an attractive political candidate, and in 1924 he won election to the Florida House of Representatives. Two years later local voters sent him to the state senate, and by 1931 he was president of that body.[40]

In 1931 the Whitakers' family machine captured control of Tampa with the election of Pat's brother-in-law, Robert E. Lee Chancey, as mayor. Chancey was also a Georgia-born attorney who had relocated in Tampa as a young man and then gone into politics. After arriving in Tampa in 1905, Chancey became the law partner of Matthew B. Macfarlane. First in 1917 and again in 1925, Chancey was elected Hillsborough County solicitor, the official who had responsibility for prosecuting all state offenses except capital crimes. He also served as president of the Hillsborough County Bar Association.[41] Chancey's election as mayor in 1931 was effectively achieved when he won the nomination of Tampa's "White Municipal party," which had been organized in 1910 to eliminate blacks from any meaningful role in the city's electoral politics.[42] However, Chancey's 1931 victory came amidst widespread charges of vote fraud and the arrest of a hundred people suspected of cheating at the polls.

The faction opposed to the Whitaker machine controlled the county government during the 1930s. This meant that each side could muster law enforcement officers to do battle on its behalf, especially during elections, when muscle often determined the outcome. During the 1931 primary, sheriff's deputies at one point arrested a group of city policemen.[43] "For a time it looked as though Tampa would have a civil war," according to one observer.[44]

In the municipal primary four years later, the opposing factions engaged in open fighting. The 1935 campaign for the nomination of the White Municipal party pitted Mayor Chancey against former Mayor D. B. McKay, who had served four terms, from 1910 to 1920 and from 1927 to 1931. As Tampans went to the polls on September 3, 1935, gun-toting county deputies confronted city policemen, who were backed by over a thousand special policemen armed with clubs and shotguns. After several people were wounded early in the day, Governor David Sholtz sent in the National Guard, which he had already mobilized, in order to prevent further bloodshed during the primary election.[45]

Despite the presence of 300 National Guardsmen, intimidation of voters and rampant fraud once again plagued the primary, won by Mayor Chancey. "Since the Chancey boys were inside the polls, they were able to control things pretty well," recalled a reporter who covered the election. "The poll clerks were appointed by the mayor or the City Election Board, so their people were on the tables."[46] One woman who wanted to vote in the primary could not get a taxi to take her to the polls. She then tricked a cab driver into going to an address near the polling place. Upon realizing the ruse, the driver exclaimed, "Gosh, I may get killed for this, we are not allowed to take people to vote." When asked who told him that, the driver responded, "They got us all together last night and the police gave us the orders and said they came from the Chief." Some people, however, obviously had no trouble casting several ballots. D. B. McKay's poll watchers counted less than 7,000 people entering polling places, but official returns reported more than 14,000 votes cast. Reacting to such practices, Kenneth I. McKay, the candidate's brother and a long-time attorney for the Cigar Manufacturers' Association, declared privately that Tampa's "responsible citizens" were tired of being "outraged, robbed and governed by thieves and gunmen."[47]

Several prominent Tampans seemed most troubled by the national coverage of the "wild election" which brought "nationwide discredit" to the city.[48] The head of the Junior Chamber of Commerce complained that "Tampa has received a lot of unsavory publicity from the primary, and it isn't doing the city any good."[49] The morning after the 1935 primary, the *Tribune* warned that "Tampa must get away from this sort of thing—when, with no important issue or interest at stake, the selfish rivalry of competing factions of politicians and of grasping gambling syndicates, each fighting for control of the offices and the law-breaking privileges, can involve the city in a heated, disrupting and discreditable fight."[50]

The *Tribune's* reference to gambling syndicates was not simply political hyperbole. A 1935 study by Tampa's Junior Chamber of Commerce concluded that "past election frauds can be attributed directly to a fight for control of the gambling industry in the community." The civic group estimated that the numbers racket, known locally as "bolita" because it involved drawing a numbered little ball to choose the winners, took in over $1 million a month and employed approximately 1,000 people. This meant that the annual take from just one form of gambling was greater than the local cigar industry's annual gross sales of $10 million.[51] Thus, the *Tribune* accurately called gambling "Our Biggest Business."[52] A 1936 report in the *Tampa Times* charged that local gambling had become "commercialized" over the years. "From the humble wheel of fortune or dice game in the back room of a corner cigar store or sidestreet cafe, the business grew to . . . large well-appointed establishments, heavily financed by syndicates each controlling from half a dozen to fifty such places."[53]

Gamblers and greedy politicians formed a natural alliance. In return for campaign contributions and other payments, local officials allowed gamblers to run their illegal games openly. The *Tampa Times* reported that gamblers succeeded "on many occasions in obtaining nominations at the primaries for 'safe men,' some of them highly respected citizens who took the extremely liberal view that there was no occasion to interfere with the gamblers since gambling was what the public wanted." In a somewhat backhanded compliment, the *Times* added that except for "this winking at violations of the law, some of these candidates were otherwise reasonably conscientious public officials."[54]

One close observer of the 1935 primary was Joseph A. Shoemaker, who earned five dollars serving as a poll watcher for the city administration. A forty-seven-year-old Pennsylvania native, the unemployed Shoemaker had moved to Tampa from Vermont in May 1935. He lived with his brother, Leroy T. ("Jack") Shoemaker, who had resided in Tampa for several years, managing a furniture store. During the September primary, Joseph Shoemaker had been assigned to count voters entering one polling place. At the end of the day, he discovered that there were 104 more ballots cast than people who had appeared. When he complained to policemen on duty, he was told to change his count to make the totals come out even.[55] Disturbed by the obvious fraud, Shoemaker organized a reform group to challenge the city machine in November's general election.

Although he had lived in Tampa only a few months, Shoemaker had been active in third-party politics in Bennington, Vermont. For several years he had been a member of the Socialist party and had written numerous letters to Norman Thomas, the party's national leader, who met with Shoemaker on one occasion. Thomas remembered Shoemaker as "very well meaning but not too clear headed."[56] Certainly, he was no revolutionary. Shoemaker had given a speech in 1934, attacking the Communist party, which he branded "the bitterest enemy the Socialist party has to contend with." Shoemaker wanted to "inaugurate socialism peacefully, gradually, sanely, by education and use of the voting power."[57] In the 1934 elections he had endorsed the New Deal and Democratic party candidates as a practical means of advancing his kind of socialism. This step led to his expulsion from Vermont's Socialist party.[58]

Following the 1935 primary election in Tampa, Joseph Shoemaker created an organization he called the Modern Democrats. Although not actually a political party with a place on the ballot, the group endorsed three independent candidates who got their names on the municipal ballot in the general election and pledged themselves to support the Modern Democrats' plan for reform. Drawing on the ideas of moderate socialists such as Upton Sinclair, the Modern Democrats offered a ten-point program that promised clean government and increased political democracy through use of the referendum and abolition of the poll tax. Their platform also appealed for economic reforms such as public ownership of all utilities, a minimum wage for city employees, and a system of "production for use instead of profit" to provide jobs for the unemployed.[59] Joseph Shoemaker, as chairman of the Modern Democrats, publicized the plans of the reformers and drew attention to himself in a series of letters to the editor published in the *Tampa Tribune* during October and November, prior to the general election on November 5.[60]

Shoemaker's folksy appeals included rambling discussions of "political economics," in which he attacked capitalism as "the greatest enemy of true democracy."[61] In a weak attempt to defuse inevitable charges of communism, Shoemaker offhandedly observed, "The biggest cooperative enterprise in the United States is our postoffice. Is that communism? If so, we want more of it."[62] He also promised a "new deal" for Tampa if voters elected Miller A. Stephens, a marine mechanic and Tampa native running against Mayor Chancey. The Modern Democrats also endorsed two independent candidates who were known Socialist party members. Charles Homer Roberts ran for city tax assessor, and Charles E. Jensen, state secretary of the Socialist party, was a candidate for the board of aldermen.[63]

Shoemaker's Modern Democrats worked closely with local members of the Socialist party. Ybor City had been a stronghold of the party since at least 1900, when Eugene V. Debs visited Tampa. The depression brought a revival of local interest in the Socialist party, especially among the unemployed. In 1931 the Socialists offered a write-in candidate for mayor who received 138 votes.[64] During 1935, Tampa Socialists formed a branch of the Workers Alliance of America, a national organization of the unemployed, which was aligned with the Socialist party. The Workers Alliance of Florida was headed by Eugene F. Poulnot, a thirty-nine-year-old unemployed Florida native who was a printer by trade and had once served as president of the local pressmen's union. During the depression, Poulnot had joined the

Socialist party and taken the lead in organizing the city's unemployed. In 1934 he was arrested by Tampa police for breach of the peace as a result of an "incendiary" speech he gave at a rally of relief workers demanding higher payments from the city.[65] The charge was subsequently dropped, but Poulnot's activities had earned him a reputation as a "communist and trouble maker" in the view of local officials.[66] "From the time Tampa's local Relief Work Council was organized in 1931 and until the present time, Eugene Poulnot has been an agitator, consistently trying to stir up strife among relief clients," Mayor Chancey complained in 1936.[67]

In 1935, Poulnot joined other Socialists in campaigning for the Modern Democrats.[68] Poulnot's "right-hand man and first lieutenant" was Samuel J. Rogers, also unemployed and active in the Workers Alliance.[69] Although a trained physician, the fifty-six-year-old Rogers had not practiced medicine since 1925, when he left his native South Carolina due to failing health. After recovering somewhat in Florida, Rogers had worked at odd jobs and joined the Socialist party.[70] During the 1935 municipal campaign, the Modern Democrats certainly did not attempt to conceal the Socialist background of their leading spokesmen and candidates for office. While attacking the "corruption, chicanery, dishonesty and dictatorship" of the "brazen politicians" in control of Tampa, the Modern Democrats contended that "wherever Socialists have been elected to public office they have earned the admiration and respect of their constituents."[71]

The Modern Democrats' challenge of the White Municipal party captured plenty of publicity and about 10 percent of the vote. Most Tampans were apparently willing to accept the results of the September primary as final. Even though it had earlier refused to endorse anyone in the factional battle over party nominations, the *Tampa Tribune* strongly defended the principle of the white primary. "Every person who voted in the primary is in honor bound to vote today for the nominees . . . who have opposition," an editorial argued on the morning of the general election in November.[72] In the balloting, Mayor Chancey handily defeated Miller Stephens by a vote of 10,768 to 919. The two other candidates of the Modern Democrats lost by similar margins.[73]

Although defeated at the polls, the Modern Democrats remained active and retained a high profile. During November 1935, they held public rallies and formed a permanent organization in preparation for county and state elections the following year. Joseph Shoemaker also continued to have letters published regularly in the *Tampa Tribune,* using the readers' column to explain a new cooperative system of production based on the ideas of the American Commonwealth Federation.[74] "So far the people here are not backing my plan the way I had been led to believe that they would," Shoemaker confided to an editor in New York. "However, I shall keep right on trying for results."[75] This persistence clearly annoyed some Tampans, who took steps to suppress the Modern Democrats.

A carefully planned vigilante attack on the Modern Democrats began with a raid by Tampa police on Saturday, November 30, 1935. At about nine o'clock in the evening, police barged into a home where Joseph Shoemaker, Eugene Poulnot, Samuel Rogers, Charles Jensen, and Walter Roush were holding a meeting. Except for Shoemaker, all were members of the Socialist party. The police raid was led by Sergeant Charles A. ("Smitty") Brown, head of the traffic squad, who acted without any warrant of any type. Brown was accompanied by four officers from his division, including John P. Bridges and F. W. Switzer, and two other city employees, Carl W. Carlisle and Robert L. Chappell, who also held commissions as special policemen.[76] As the intruders grabbed papers and searched the Modern Democrats, the owner of the house, who was not involved with the group, asked Sergeant Brown, "What's this all about?" Brown replied that they were looking for Communists. When told that there were none present, Brown volunteered, "I'm mighty sorry about this, but it's on orders."[77]

The five Modern Democrats were taken to police headquarters in the center of Tampa for questioning about alleged "communist activities."[78] A sixth man taken into custody, John A. McCaskill, was a Tampa fireman who had apparently spied on the Modern Democrats while pretending to be sympathetic. When Poulnot had initially failed to attend the fateful meeting, McCaskill had gone after him, and upon their return police had raided the house. At the police station, McCaskill, the son of a policeman, was booked under a false name and then released.[79] The five Modern Democrats were individually interrogated by Sergeant Brown in the presence of other officers. Rogers was asked if he was a Communist or if he believed in racial equality, and he denied both assertions. After brief questioning, the men were released one at a time over the next hour.[80]

As they left the police station, between 9:40 and 10:15 p.m., Poulnot, Rogers, and Shoemaker were forced into waiting cars. Poulnot, the first to be released, was accompanied to the street by a policeman, who helped push him into a car with the assistance of two other men. When Poulnot's screams attracted a crowd, the officer claimed that the man being restrained was crazy so they were transporting him to a mental hospital. The car sped away, and another soon picked up Rogers, who was placed in the back seat by a special policeman joining the two other men already in the car. Finally, men in a third automobile seized Shoemaker as he left the police station. The three victims, their eyes covered, were taken to a remote wooded area in Brandon, about fourteen miles east of Tampa.[81]

There Rogers, Poulnot, and Shoemaker were savagely beaten, one after the other. With their pants pulled down, they were bent over a log with men holding their arms and legs. Then they were flogged with an assortment of chains, straps, and hoses. Poulnot, accused of being "a leader of radical groups," later recalled losing consciousness. Rogers related that Shoemaker was lashed for about five minutes, and one of his assailants muttered, "So you will write letters to the *Tampa Tribune*." After the beatings, the vigilantes applied warm tar and feathers to the victims' exposed bodies.[82] They may have also burned Shoemaker's foot in the fire used to heat the tar. As the floggers departed, they warned the three Modern Democrats to "get out of town in twenty-four hours or we'll kill you."[83]

As it turned out, Joseph Shoemaker soon died from his wounds. After being left at the deserted site, the three victims put on their clothes and started walking along a road, but Shoemaker quickly collapsed. Poulnot speculated that his friend had received the worst beating, including severe blows to his head, because he had recognized one of the kidnappers as a Tampa policeman and had addressed him by name. Poulnot and Rogers tried to carry Shoemaker, who weighed over 220 pounds, but they were forced to leave him and slowly make their way back to town. There they immediately contacted Jack Shoemaker, who drove out and at daybreak found his brother near death.[84] Rushed to a hospital, Shoemaker was in such bad condition that a doctor reported three days later: "He is horribly mutilated. I wouldn't beat a hog the way that man was whipped. . . . He was beaten until he is paralyzed on one side, probably from blows to the head. . . . I doubt if three square feet would cover the total area of bloodshot bruises on his body, not counting the parts injured only by tar."[85] In a desperate attempt to save Shoemaker's life from the rapidly spreading gangrene, doctors amputated his left leg, but to no avail. He died on December 9, nine days after the flogging.[86]

Joseph Shoemaker became Tampa's sixth lynching victim since 1882, but his murder attracted more attention than the previous cases. His race naturally explains some of the concern. Although the fourth white man killed by Tampa vigilantes since the Civil War, Shoemaker was the only white man lynched in the South since 1933. The other thirty-three victims during 1934 and 1935 were blacks, including Robert Johnson.[87] However, as the *New Republic* pointedly observed: "When Southern white men lynch a Negro, that's not news. When Southern white men, under the eyes of local police and apparently with tacit approval, kidnap a white man and beat him so badly he dies, that is perhaps something else again."[88] The brutality of the violence that took Shoemaker's life also undoubtedly accounted for some of the ensuing uproar. "Even callused minds might flinch from a thing so horrible—tar and feathers, a gangrenous leg, amputation and death that closed mumbling lips," noted one Florida newspaper.[89]

The sadistic treatment of vigilante victims was not, however, unusual in the South. Lynch mobs had all too frequently mutilated blacks and even burned them alive.[90] Southerners had also long employed nonfatal forms of punishment, including flogging and tar-and-feathering, to discipline both blacks and whites outside the law. Dating back to pre-Christian Europe, these techniques were part of the practice of charivari, designed both to hurt and to humiliate the victim for the purpose of defending traditional values.[91] The Tampa area in particular had been plagued by various shaming rituals associated with lynch law. In 1920, Tampa newspapers reported that a "trio of vigilantes" tarred and feathered a Spanish immigrant accused of exposing himself in a downtown park. Detained by police, the victim was placed on display in a jail cell. Over 2,000 people viewed the "feathered bird" before he was allowed to remove the marks of shame.[92] Three years later anonymous vigilantes wearing Klan regalia kidnapped and flogged three Tampa men suspected of trafficking in liquor.[93] Between 1929 and 1935, at least two more whites and two blacks were flogged in Hillsborough County and neighboring Pinellas County.[94] Five vigilantes also kidnapped a St. Petersburg attorney in 1935 and castrated him "for fooling around with the wrong person." Subsequently charged with participating in the crime was F. W. Switzer, one of the policemen who raided the meeting of the Modern Democrats.[95]

The flogging death of Joseph Shoemaker, however, was unusual in that it was widely perceived as a political crime. "In the first few days after the flogging," the *Tampa Times* later reported, "it was freely whispered around where political handymen congregated freely that these three floggings were only the beginning of a series that would 'put the fear of God' in political and social agitators and deter them from attempting to interfere with machine politics in next June's primary."[96] Several journalists described the Shoemaker killing as a "political murder," and the case raised fears of fascism in some minds.[97] "All Florida has awakened, temporarily, at least, to the realization that an Americanized Fascism has come to the land of orange groves," claimed a Socialist newspaper.[98] While some observers linked the crime to the Nazi terror rising in Europe, others tied it directly to the American tradition of vigilantism. The American Civil Liberties Union (ACLU) branded it a "vigilante attack," as did the Communist party, which called Shoemaker "another victim of vigilantes."[99]

The flogging of the three Modern Democrats was clearly an expression of establishment violence, given the involvement of Tampa police and the support they gained among certain members of the local elite. Although the first reports of the November 30 attack contained no hint of police complicity, by December 3, Tampa newspapers had learned from Eugene Poulnot and Samuel Rogers that they had recognized policemen among their kidnappers. The resulting headline in the *Tampa Times* blared, "POLICE IMPLICATED."[100]

Fearing that this fact would prevent Tampa authorities from pursuing the case, friends and associates of the victims immediately sought outside help. "It was police from beginning to end," a Tampa Socialist wrote to David Lasser, head of the Workers Alliance. "All the protest that you can get sent in will help."[101] A similar appeal came from Frank McCallister, a twenty-seven-year-old Socialist who served on the party's state executive committee. Born in Illinois, McCallister had lived in St. Petersburg, Florida, for several years. After losing his job as an insurance salesman during the depression, he had dedicated himself to democratic socialism and become active in the Tampa Bay area, defending the civil liberties of the unemployed, workers, and blacks.[102] When he learned of the Tampa flogging, McCallister immediately notified Norman Thomas in New York and appealed for help because local Socialists had "absolutely no funds." Thomas sent telegrams to Mayor Chancey and the Hillsborough County sheriff, demanding legal action against the floggers.[103]

Norman Thomas also took the lead in organizing a campaign to keep the national spotlight on Tampa and put pressure on law enforcement officials. Even before Shoemaker died, Thomas had brought together a variety of labor and left groups to form the Committee for the Defense of Civil Rights in Tampa. Based in New York, the defense committee was headed by Thomas, who quickly enlisted a remarkable coalition of sponsors, including various Socialist organizations, several New York City garment worker unions, the American Civil Liberties Union, the National Association for the Advancement of Colored People, and the International Labor Defense. The committee mounted a fund-raising and letter-writing campaign designed to "bring down upon the heads of government in the city of Tampa the full force of public indignation everywhere."[104]

Other national groups brought additional leverage to bear. Two days after the floggings, the ACLU offered a $1,000 reward for information leading to the arrest and conviction of the guilty persons. Support also came from the American Federation of Labor, which had scheduled its 1936 convention for Tampa. Following Shoemaker's death, president William Green issued a statement saying it was "altogether probable" that the AFL would transfer its convention to another city unless those responsible were tried and, if found guilty, punished.[105]

As outside pressure mounted, many Floridians condemned the floggings. In communities across the state, newspaper editors deplored the crime. The Tallahassee *Daily Democrat* found the attack "so revolting that no civilized community or state can permit it to go unpunished." The *Miami Herald* declared that the gang responsible was "as venomous as a mad dog, and its leaders should be dealt with just as dispassionately as we would a rabid animal."[106]

Tampa's two largest newspapers took a strong and consistent stand against the floggings, even before Shoemaker died. Immediately after the attack, the *Tampa Times* worried about the impact of "another large blot on the reputation of Tampa for lawlessness." As Shoemaker lay in a hospital, the *Times* argued that if Tampa were "to regain a reputation as a law-abiding community it must ferret out and punish the perpetrators of this outrage."[107] The *Tribune* also expressed concern about "the damage that has been done to Tampa's good name," especially after Shoemaker died.[108] The paper claimed that the floggers had not only "brutally murdered an inoffensive citizen, innocent of any crime or wrongdoing, but they have inflicted upon this city in injury which it will take years to overcome." The city had to "clear itself by convicting and punishing these public enemies."[109] Explaining the stand taken by local newspapers, the Committee for the Defense of Civil Rights in Tampa pointed out that the *Tribune* had previously "supported the cigar manufacturers in their ruthless suppression of unionism, in their frame-ups, kidnapings and deportations of labor men," but vigilante violence had begun to take its toll on the city's fortunes. "Unfavorable publicity has hurt Tampa," the New York-based committee emphasized. "It is keeping industry from the city. It is keeping tourists from the city."[110]

The growing price of lynch law, combined with the brutality of the attack on an "inoffensive" white man, explains the unprecedented outcry of protest in Tampa. Resolutions deploring the crime poured from a variety of local groups, including the Central Trades and Labor Assembly, the cigarworkers' unions, the teachers' federation, the Junior Chamber of Commerce, the American Legion, and the Hillsborough County Bar Association.[111] Citing "the blot which has been placed on the good name of the city of Tampa," the board of aldermen offered a $2,500 reward for the arrest and conviction of those responsible for Shoemaker's death.[112] Four days after Shoemaker died, a Tampa attorney reported to the ACLU that "public sentiment is boiling, and the people of Tampa have actually gone into the matter for the future of our city." Noted the *Tribune*, "No crime in recollection of old timers here ever stirred the community to greater indignation."[113]

The biggest local protest was orchestrated by Tampa ministers. Although clergymen had remained noticeably silent in the wake of past violence, they found a new voice in the person of the Reverend Walter Metcalf, an Englishman who was the minister at Tampa's First Congregational Church. The local church had been established in 1885, but as a leader of the church observed a century later, "The liberal Northern flavor of Congregationalism failed to flourish in the reconstructed South."¹¹⁴ The Reverend Mr. Metcalf, however, held a position of prominence in the community, since he was also president of the Tampa Ministerial Association at the time of the floggings. While Socialists worked behind the scenes to bring pressure on local authorities, Metcalf "allowed himself to be used as the spearpoint," according to Frank McCallister. In 1936, Metcalf confided that he had "risked a great deal during the past year in advocating free speech and demanding the punishment of the Tampa floggers."¹¹⁵ At the time Metcalf stepped forward, David Lasser found a pervasive "feeling of terror" in Tampa.¹¹⁶

Metcalf took a variety of actions to arouse and mobilize local sentiment. The week after the floggings, he used his Sunday sermon to call for "a powerful investigation . . . into this latest social outrage."¹¹⁷ On the Sunday following Shoemaker's death, Metcalf and the Ministerial Association organized a public memorial service, held in the municipal auditorium. The "service of public penitence" was attended by about a thousand people and broadcast over a local radio station. Listeners heard Metcalf call on the city to "take cognizance of circumstances and conditions which brought this civic calamity upon it."¹¹⁸ With encouragement from Socialists in New York, Metcalf became chairman of a local group, which called itself the Committee for the Defense of Civil Liberties in Tampa. The committee's other officers included several local Socialists.¹¹⁹ Working in cooperation with the national Committee for the Defense of Civil Rights in Tampa, the local group announced that its purpose was to expose "the unholy alliance of the police with criminals engaged in floggings and murders" and to insist that "floggers and murderers be strongly prosecuted."¹²⁰

The reaction of Tampans surprised many outsiders. A Texas attorney who visited the city several times on behalf of the New York defense committee observed that "an unusual, surprising and almost unique feature in the Shoemaker case . . . [was] the vigorous protest that the citizens and the papers of Tampa have made."¹²¹ Norman Thomas publicly applauded the community's strong stand.¹²²

Despite the extraordinary reaction to the floggings and Shoemaker's death, most people expected a whitewash by Tampa authorities. "There is little liklihood [sic] of the city officials doing anything to apprehend these criminals," the head of a Tampa civic association confided to the ACLU.¹²³ David Lasser of the Workers Alliance observed privately during a December visit to Tampa, "I can't see the city officials allowing themselves to be stripped of their power through a first class exposure." As one Florida editor sarcastically asserted after Shoemaker's death, "indications are that . . . the whitewash barrel is being prepared and will be used."[124] Publicizing this view, the owner of a Tampa lumber yard used a huge billboard to proclaim:

TAR TODAY
WHITEWASH TOMORROW
TAMPA: THE YEAR ROUND CITY.[125]

City officials did at first attempt a coverup, but political pressures and public protests soon brought indictments. The initial inquiry was made by Tampa's police chief, Richard G. Tittsworth, an attorney and a close friend of the mayor, having served as his assistant in the county solicitor's office during the 1920s.[126] On December 5, 1935, Tittsworth reported that "no member of the police department had any participation directly or indirectly with the flogging."[127] Although the city seemed reluctant to press the case, county and state officials pushed ahead under orders from Governor David Sholtz, who publicly called for prosecution of "the perpetrators of this dastardly outrage."[128] The new sheriff of Hillsborough County, Jerry R. McLeod, had no political ties to the city administration. Formerly managing editor of the *Tampa Times* and district director of the Works Progress Administration, McLeod had been recently appointed to office by Governor Sholtz, who had dismissed the previous sheriff, Will Spencer, for "drunkenness, incompetency, and neglect of duty in office."[129] Since the floggings of the Modern Democrats had occurred in his jurisdiction, McLeod began collecting evidence as soon as he learned of the crime.

Sheriff McLeod worked in cooperation with State Attorney Rex Farrior, who had responsibility for prosecuting capital crimes. During the two-week period after the floggings, McLeod and Farrior officially questioned some seventy-five people, and on December 12, Farrior reported to the governor that the investigators were "leaving no stone unturned."[130] Four days later, the state attorney began presenting evidence to a special session of the grand jury. In his charge the circuit court judge called for "a wholesome revival of civic accountability" in order to restore the reputation of the city. "It has been said by some of our business men," the judge pointedly told the grand jurors, "that important industries have purposely avoided their establishment here because of the reputation of this city with respect to law enforcement."[131] In the course of their investigation, McLeod and Farrior revealed to the press pieces of incriminating evidence indicating that the attack was carefully planned by city employees.[132]

As evidence of police involvement mounted and demands for arrests increased, Mayor Chancey took action. On December 9, the mayor started his own inquiry, and he threatened to discharge any police officer who withheld information. He then suspended John McCaskill, the city fireman who had joined the Modern Democrats, reportedly to spy on them for the police. Soon thereafter, the mayor also suspended the five city policemen and the two other city employees with commissions as special policemen who had raided the meeting of the Modern Democrats. In the wake of the suspensions, Police Chief Tittsworth announced that he was taking an indefinite leave of absence.[133]

On December 18, Sheriff McLeod made the first arrests in the case, and indictments soon followed. After a day of questioning by State Attorney Farrior, five of the seven officers in the raiding party, including Sergeant Brown and the two special policemen, were arrested and charged with the murder of Joseph Shoemaker.[134] Another Tampa policeman, Sam E. Crosby, was also charged with murder. Crosby had been recently reinstated in the department after being found innocent of charges of vote fraud in the September primary. The week after their arrests, the four policeman and two special officers were indicted for kidnapping the three Modern Democrats, assault with intent to murder Poulnot and Rogers, and second-degree murder in the death of Shoemaker. A month later Tittsworth was indicted as an accessory after the fact for attempting to block investigation of the kidnappings and murder.[135]

As the probe continued, strong evidence surfaced pointing to the involvement of the Ku Klux Klan in the crime. Joseph Shoemaker's brother revealed that shortly before the floggings he had received a telephone call with the warning: "This is the Ku Klux Klan. We object to your brother's activities. They are Communistic. Tell him to leave town. We will take care of the other radicals, too."[136] Jack Shoemaker thought he recognized the voice as that of a local justice of the peace who was a known Klansman. The same man was spotted at police headquarters by Modern Democrats just before the kidnappings.[137] A journalist who visited Tampa in December concluded on the basis of interviews with local officials and newspapermen that "the City Hall and the Police Department were hotbeds of Ku Kluxism, that the former chief of police was either a member of the Klan or was dominated by it, and that four of the six policemen who have been arrested . . . are Klansmen."[138] A local attorney privately called Tampa "a very pro-Klan community."[139]

In the wake of the floggings, a Klan circular was widely distributed in Tampa. Declaring "Communism Must Go," the leaflet proclaimed, "THE KU KLUX KLAN RIDES AGAIN." The Klan pledged "to fight to the last ditch and the last man against any and all attacks on our government and American institutions." The circular concluded with an appeal for help and gave a Tampa post office box for a mailing address.[140]

As a result of the continuing investigation, three reputed Klansmen were charged with participating in the floggings. On December 21, Sheriff McLeod went to Orlando, a city eighty miles northeast of Tampa, and picked up Arlie F. Gillian, the caretaker of an orange grove, and Edward Spivey, a typewriter repairman. Both men had worked as special policemen in Tampa's infamous September primary election, and after their arrest in December, they were indicted on the same charges as the six Tampa policemen in connection with the kidnapping and beating of the Modern Democrats.[141] When the Orlando men were taken into custody, Sheriff McLeod announced, "The two men arrested are members of the Ku Klux Klan, and Gillian told me he was a former state officer in the Klan. Spivey told me that the call for special policemen for the armed city primary on September 3 was made at an open meeting of the Klan."[142] Another Orlando man, an electrician identified as a Klansman who had also served as a special policeman in the primary election, was subsequently indicted on the same three charges of kidnapping, murderous assault, and second-degree murder.[143]

The final arrest in the flogging case came in February 1936, and it brought to eleven the number of men charged. The last man indicted was Manuel A. Menendez, who had been a police stenographer and was charged with being an accessory after the fact, along with former Chief Tittsworth.[144] All eleven of the accused men were linked by their formal ties to Tampa's police department. At one time or another in 1935, each man had been employed by the department, six full-time and the five others as special policemen. The eight Tampa residents under indictment had all worked for the city government at the time of the floggings, but none, except perhaps for Police Chief Tittsworth, could have been considered a member of the local elite. However, their alleged crimes clearly qualified as establishment violence, since they were designed to reinforce the existing distribution of power.

In addition, some prominent Tampans went to the aid of the accused. The chief defense attorney was Pat Whitaker, who was backed by his brother Tom and two other lawyers, including one who had rented the Tampa post office box used by the Klan.[145] Bail bonds for the accused floggers, amounting to almost $100,000 in all, were provided by a group of Tampa businessmen, including Eli B. Witt, owner of Hav-A-Tampa Cigar Company; D. Hoyt Woodbery, secretary-treasurer of Hav-A-Tampa; Eugene L. Rotureau, president of Tampa Stevedoring Company; and Edward W. Spencer, owner of Spencer Auto Electric, Inc., one of the largest distributors of automotive parts in the southeastern United States.[146] These businessmen were native-born southerners (except for Spencer, who was from Indiana), and their public association with the accused floggers suggested that the beatings might have been connected with the city's tradition of antilabor violence. Hav-A-Tampa was the only large cigar company to have resisted the tide of union recognition during the 1930s, and Hoyt Woodbery had privately complained in the past about unions bringing chaos and "mob rule."[147] The Committee for the Defense of Civil Rights in Tampa charged that bail for the accused policemen was *"supplied by labor-hating, anti-union cigar manufacturers."*[148]

Circumstantial evidence emerged suggesting that the attack on the Modern Democrats might have been designed in part as a warning to a union organizer in Tampa. Frank Henderson, a representative of the AFL's International Longshoremen's Association, had quietly arrived in Tampa in an effort to unionize black stevedores in Florida ports. On the night of the floggings, Henderson was arrested and brought to police headquarters, where he witnessed the interrogation of the Modern Democrats.[149] "Threat of similar treatment was used by the police in an effort to drive him out of town," according to one observer, who charged that Klansmen had done the dirty work, "but the anti-union employers they serve in Florida are the *real* criminals."[150] Significantly, the president of a Tampa stevedore company helped provide bail bonds for several of the accused floggers.

The indictments in the flogging case brought praise from Socialists who had campaigned for justice. During a visit to Tampa, a Texas attorney for the Socialist party called the arrests a blow "against anti-labor mob violence and the Klan."[151] Socialists had no doubt that their concerted efforts had forced local authorities to take action, but they also paid high compliments to Sheriff Jerry McLeod for pursuing the case.[152]

To maintain pressure on the community, Norman Thomas went to Tampa in January 1936 and addressed a rally sponsored by the local Committee for the Defense of Civil Liberties in Tampa. Speaking to a cheering crowd of 2,000 on January 19, Thomas attacked the "men higher up," who "protect and maybe order [floggings]; the politicians who profit by such things; the economic interests who are intent upon putting fear in their workers." Yet he also praised the community's response. "This is the first time in American history," he declared, "that any floggers ever have been brought to justice, and perhaps some higher-ups reached." Thomas attributed the indictments to the courageous efforts of the Reverend Mr. Metcalf, Sheriff McLeod, the *Tampa Tribune*, and the *Tampa Times*.[153] Returning the compliment, both Tampa papers applauded the visit and speech of Norman Thomas. This praise of a radical outsider demonstrated the enormous change that had occurred in the public attitudes of some members of Tampa's establishment since the days when local newspaper editors incited vigilante violence against so-called "outside agitators."[154]

Despite the indictments, most observers expected the accused to avoid conviction. A "'Kommon Kwestion,'" a central Florida newspaper observed, was "will the jury find that they 'Kant Kwite Konvict.'" In a report to Norman Thomas's committee, an investigator found "the general notion in Tampa is that the men charged are likely to get loose."[155] Nevertheless, the Tampa businessman who had earlier used a billboard to predict a "whitewash" changed the huge sign to read "The Boys at the Old Town Hall ARE NOT SO K-K-KLANNISH THESE DAYS."[156]

Two deaths, officially ruled suicides, raised questions about a possible conspiracy to silence witnesses. On January 24, 1936, Robert P. Fariss was found dead in his car. Fariss had died from inhaling carbon monoxide from the automobile's exhaust, which was connected to the inside of the car by a garden hose. A justice of the peace ruled the death a suicide, but events surrounding the case made it appear suspicious. Fariss was one of the Klan members who had rented the post office box given as the address of the local Klan on circulars. Ten days before he died, Fariss was questioned by the county solicitor about his whereabouts on the night of the floggings. Investigators also examined specimens of pillow feathers at the Fariss home after finding a paper grocery bag with the name "Fariss" on it at the scene of the floggings. After talking to the county solicitor in response to a subpoena, Fariss began receiving anonymous telephone calls at home and at work.[157] Moreover, the justice of the peace who ruled his death a suicide was identified as "a leading Klansman," who had issued the warning to Joseph Shoemaker before the floggings.[158] Mrs. Fariss told reporters she did not believe her husband had committed suicide. "He had no reason to kill himself," she claimed. She then reported being threatened by an unidentified telephone caller who said, "We got Bob. We'll get you next."[159]

A month later, another witness died. Police Sergeant H. Carl Tomkins reportedly jumped to his death from a Tampa hospital room, where he was recovering from wounds received in a fight with a prisoner. On the night of the floggings, Tomkins had been on duty in charge of the desk at police headquarters. He had subsequently testified before the grand jury investigating the floggings and was described as "an important witness." Although his doctor reported Tomkins had been despondent and a nurse saw him leap to his death, some observers found the suicide of a second witness hard to believe.[160] "Another Tampa flogging witness ended his life," the *Miami Herald* declared. "Looks like they control trials over there as delicately as they do elections."[161]

In preparation for the first trial, Governor Sholtz strengthened the prosecution team by putting State Attorney Farrior in charge. Farrior had gotten the indictments, but his office did not have jurisdiction over the prosecution because none of the accused was charged with first-degree murder, a capital crime. However, considering the "grave importance" of the flogging cases and "in an earnest desire to bring about an early conclusion of these matters, *because of the public interest,*" the governor directed Farrior to take the place of the county solicitor in county criminal court proceedings.[162]

As the prosecution team prepared for battle, defense attorneys engaged in a series of delaying maneuvers. Beginning in late February 1936, Pat Whitaker filed motions first attacking the nature of the information accompanying the charges and then requesting a four-month postponement to allow the "inflamed passion and mind of the people to subside and cool." After the criminal court judge denied these motions, Whitaker asked for a change of venue due to "a feeling of mob spirit" against the accused in Tampa.[163] When the judge denied this request and set a trial date for March 23, Whitaker waited two weeks and then filed a motion asking the judge to disqualify himself from presiding over the scheduled trial because he was reportedly a candidate for governor in the upcoming June primary. Having no discretion on this motion, the judge removed himself.[164]

Governor Sholtz immediately assigned another judge, who attempted without success to try the case in Tampa. The new trial judge was Robert T. Dewell, a criminal court judge from neighboring Polk County, who had often served in Hillsborough County courtrooms.[165] Dewell, a fifty-year-old Florida native with a law degree from Yale University, privately expressed appreciation for this "plenty hot" assignment, and he promised the governor to do his "darnest [sic] to try this case right plum down the middle of the road . . . [so] this will bring additional credit to the present [Sholtz] administration."[166] When the trial commenced on March 23, Pat Whitaker renewed his formal request for a change of venue, claiming that a fair trial was impossible in Tampa due to the intensive local "campaign of vilification" against the accused policemen. Judge Dewell reserved ruling on the motion until potential jurors were examined, but after a week of failing to seat an acceptable six-man jury, the judge granted the change of venue.[167]

Judge Dewell moved the trial to Bartow, the county seat of Polk County. Located forty-five miles east of Tampa in the heart of an area devoted to citrus groves and phosphate mining, Bartow was a small city of some 4,000 people. Given the depressed state of the local economy, one local newspaper looked forward to the celebrated trial, hoping it would produce "a minor boom in Bartow among hotel and restaurant folks, while additional wire services . . . are being installed to care for the . . . news agencies."[168]

After almost two months of delay due to defense motions and the failure to seat a jury in Tampa, the trial of seven of the accused finally got underway in Bartow on April 13, 1936. The defendants were five policemen—John Bridges, "Smitty" Brown, Sam Crosby, F. W. Switzer and R. G. Tittsworth—and two former special policemen, C. W. Carlisle and Robert Chappell. All except Tittsworth were tried on four counts each related to the kidnapping of Eugene Poulnot. Tittsworth was charged with being an accessory after the fact. Lasting six weeks, the trial attracted few spectators to the remote, three-hundred-seat courtroom. However, the proceedings had a national audience through daily accounts in northern newspapers from New York to St. Louis.[169] The events in Bartow also received front page coverage in Tampa. To the surprise of everyone, the defense and prosecution quickly agreed on a six-man jury, composed of a PWA relief worker, two mechanics, a machinist, a retired locomotive engineer, and a dragline operator in a phosphate mine.[170]

Most of the trial was devoted to the examination of thirty-four prosecution witnesses. Several Modern Democrats testified to their activities leading up to the police raid on November 30, 1935, and Eugene Poulnot and Samuel Rogers described their kidnappings and the floggings. After detailing his arrest and questioning by police, Poulnot testified that C. W. Carlisle and John Bridges had forced him into a car driven by F. W. Switzer. Near the end of the trial, the jury visited Tampa police headquarters and the scene of the flogging.[171]

The defense strategy became clear at the opening of the trial. Faced with compelling evidence that policemen had raided the meeting of the Modern Democrats without a warrant and then kidnapped the three men who were flogged, Pat Whitaker tried to paint the victims as Communists who threatened American civilization and the southern way of life. Beginning with his questioning of jurors, Whitaker attempted to turn the case into "the State vs. Moscow."[172] The first red herring materialized when Whitaker asked prospective jurors if they had heard any speeches by Norman Thomas, "a nationally known communistic propagandist." State Attorney Farrior objected to this line of questioning, but Judge Dewell permitted it to continue. Nevertheless, he admonished potential jurors to disregard the mention of Thomas's beliefs, explaining that "Norman Thomas is not on trial."[173]

Taking advantage of the wide latitude granted by the judge, the chief defense counsel proceeded to give a civics lesson. As he questioned prospective jurors, Whitaker inquired, "Do you believe in our form of government in its entirety?" Upon receiving an affirmative answer, he added, "Then you don't believe or subscribe in any respect to the principles of Communism which seeks to destroy our form of government?"[174] He also asked if a potential juror understood that "the Communists advocate the destruction of churches . . . and the destruction of home life."[175] Raising the bugaboo of racial equality, Whitaker exclaimed, "Communism stands for social equality of all races, between Negroes and white people as opposed to Anglo-Saxon American institutions."[176]

During the cross-examination of prosecution witnesses, Whitaker used red-baiting in an effort to destroy the credibility of the Modern Democrats. Charles Jensen, one of the men arrested in the police raid preceding the floggings, was questioned about ties the Modern Democrats may have had to the American Civil Liberties Union. When Jensen tried to explain that the ACLU was a nonpolitical organization, Whitaker asked if it was "the same American Civil Liberties Union that sent the defendants' counsel down to Scottsboro?" This reference to the Alabama trial of a group of blacks accused of raping two white women brought an immediate objection from the prosecution, which Judge Dewell sustained.[177] "Then you don't know if it's a political, Communistic organization?" Whitaker inquired, returning to the ACLU. Jensen once again asserted that it was not, but the defense had managed to imply that Modern Democrats equaled ACLU equaled communism equaled race-mixing equaled the rape of white women by black men.[178] Similarly, Whitaker asked Samuel Rogers if he had once lost a job for selling liquor and for "relations with Negro women." Rogers vigorously denied the accusation, but the desired impression was left with the jurors.[179]

Pat Whitaker pulled out all the stops in his cross-examination of Eugene Poulnot, whose kidnapping was the crux of the charges against the defendants. Ostensibly in order to test Poulnot's credibility, the defense counsel was permitted to pose a variety of questions seemingly irrelevant to the kidnapping charge. During the two-hour interrogation that brought some sixty objections from prosecution attorneys, Whitaker declared that his purpose was to show Poulnot's "illegal activities from birth to the present time." Typical questions included "Do you believe in the overthrow of our government by force and violence?" When Poulnot responded negatively, Whitaker asked whether the witness had ever "cursed the United States Government, the flag, the White House and praised the Government of Russia?" Whitaker persisted. "Didn't you say, 'I am a Communist and I'm damn proud of it?'" Poulnot forcefully responded to several such questions with the simple declaration, "That's a lie."[180]

Turning to the explosive issue of race, Whitaker inquired, "Did you state that you believe in social equality among Negroes and whites?" Again, Poulnot denied having said that. The defense attorney then asked Poulnot if he was acquainted with Angelo Herndon, the black Communist, whose conviction for sedition in Georgia had generated enormous publicity.[181] Rex Farrior cut off this question by raising an objection and pointing out that Herndon "may have been convicted of everything in the world, but it has nothing to do with this case."[182]

Over strenuous objections from defense lawyers, the prosecution managed to introduce records showing that the Modern Democrats had advocated peaceful change through legal political methods. While members explained the organization's widely publicized ten-point program, the group's secretary produced minutes of meetings which revealed that the Modern Democrats regularly sang "America" and read excerpts from the United States Constitution.[183]

The most damaging testimony against the accused came from Tampa policemen who confirmed Poulnot's version of his arrest and kidnapping. Police Lieutenant J. L. Eddings, a fourteen-year veteran of the force, related that he was in the desk sergeant's office when Sergeant Brown and the other members of the raiding party brought the Modern Democrats to headquarters for questioning. Eddings also placed Brown and three other defendants in or near a car parked in front of the station house at the time of Poulnot's kidnapping. W. D. Bush, chief of detectives at the time, testified that when he went outside headquarters after hearing cries of distress, he saw Brown and Carlisle closing a car door. Another policeman testified that he observed Carlisle escort Poulnot out of headquarters and soon thereafter saw John Bridges in the rear seat of a car with his hand over Poulnot's mouth. A fourth police officer said that he was eight feet from the car when it pulled away with Sam Crosby in the front seat and John Bridges in the rear, holding Poulnot.[184]

In vigorous cross-examination, Pat Whitaker tried to present police witnesses as liars because they had originally told different stories. However, this tactic backfired. Each policeman said that he had remained silent at first because he feared for his job. Lieutenant Eddings related that former Chief Tittsworth had downplayed the floggings. "He said he didn't know whether they had even been flogged, and if they had, it was probably no more than they deserved," Eddings related.[185] Bush testified that when he informed Tittsworth of the facts, the chief "blew up and got mad about it and that was the end of it." Once Tittsworth had left the department on a leave of absence, the policemen claimed that they had then told the truth to investigators.[186]

After the prosecution had consumed a month presenting its case, defense attorneys took little time for rebuttal. They first moved for directed verdicts of acquittal for their seven clients on a variety of grounds, including claims that the indictments were defective, no evidence of a conspiracy had been presented, and Poulnot's testimony was perjured. After hearing the arguments, Judge Dewell acquitted two defendants, R. G. Tittsworth and Robert Chappell, because of insufficient evidence. The judge also reduced the four charges against each of the remaining five defendants by eliminating counts related to an alleged conspiracy to kidnap Poulnot. Left with a single charge of kidnapping, the defense provided only twenty-six minutes of testimony, all designed to attack the credibility of Eugene Poulnot.[187]

Final arguments took two days, as four attorneys spoke for the state and three for the defense. Prosecutors emphasized that the activities of the Modern Democrats were legal and had nothing to do with communism. One attorney for the state claimed that the crime committed by the former policemen struck "at the roots of our Constitution and Anglo-Saxon civilization." Prosecutors argued that the kidnapping was carefully planned and began with the raid on the Modern Democrats, who had been infiltrated by "a despisable rat." Attacking vigilante methods, one state attorney called on jurors to convict the former policemen in order to uphold the rule of law. "If men are permitted, regardless of the purity of their motives, to take the law into their own hands," he warned, "our government cannot exist."[188]

Defense attorneys still contended that the Modern Democrats were a Communist group that had to be fought by whatever means necessary. "The fight on communism . . . has just started," one lawyer asserted. "The answer is the American people will stamp out these foreigners with a perverted idea of government." Urging jurors to disregard outside opinion, the Bartow attorney concluded: "This is imperial Polk County, and we are able to manage things here pretty well ourselves."[189] Pat Whitaker claimed that the charges against his "friends" were part of a political frame-up, designed to advance the careers of politicians and certain Tampa police officers who were "self-seeking perjurers." In summation, Whitaker argued that the issue facing the jury was communism, not constitutional rights.[190]

At the end of the six-week trial, the jury deliberated less than three hours and found the five remaining defendants guilty of kidnapping Poulnot. "The verdict came as a complete surprise," observed a Polk County newspaper. Even prosecutors expected at best a hung jury.[191] However, the foreman declared that the jurors were in complete agreement from the beginning of their deliberations.[192] "Communism and all that stuff had nothing to do with the case," one juror commented. "We saw right through that. Those defense lawyers didn't stick to the case." Another juror asserted, "What got us was the way those policemen, supposed to be law enforcement officers, went right out and participated in an unlawful act. It was their duty to enforce the law not to break it. It was an outrage. We don't hold with things like that in Polk County." In an apparent reference to former Chief Tittsworth, the jury foreman observed, "We only wish we had the man higher up."[193] Judge Dewell sentenced each of the five men to a four-year prison term, but all remained free on bail, pending appeal.[194]

Many observers believed that the guilty verdicts represented a turning point in Florida justice. "Such a verdict in Missouri, Illinois or New York might go almost unmarked," the *St. Louis Post-Dispatch* declared, but "in Florida, its significance can hardly be overestimated."[195] Upon learning of the decision, Supreme Court Justice Louis D. Brandeis privately called it "among America's most encouraging events of recent years."[196] The American Civil Liberties Union hailed the convictions as "a victory in the fight for civil rights in Florida and the beginning of a drive against the Ku Klux Klan."[197] A Socialist newspaper called the outcome "the most stunning blow against vigilantism ever struck in Florida." This journal warned its readers, however, that the trial was only the first round in the fight to defend civil liberties in Tampa, because the "convicted kidnappers may still be cleared by legal maneuvers in the Florida Supreme Court."[198]

This suspicion proved correct. On July 1, 1937, Florida's highest tribunal overturned the convictions on the ground that Judge Dewell had failed to inform the jury that it could not consider evidence related to the charges of conspiracy to kidnap, which the judge had dismissed. The state's supreme court ordered a new trial for the five former policemen.[199]

During the following year, opponents of vigilantism tried in vain to win conviction of the floggers. In October 1937, after a number of postponements, the state finally prosecuted six men for the murder of Joseph Shoemaker. Five of the defendants were the former policemen whose conviction for kidnapping Poulnot had been recently overturned. The sixth man was Arlie Gilliam, one of the Orlando men charged with participating in the flogging.[200] Despite the presence of the same judge and essentially the same legal teams, the six-day trial in Bartow was scarcely a repeat of the previous one. Taking cognizance of the supreme court's rebuke of his handling of the first trial, Judge Dewell refused to allow any testimony related to events which preceded the kidnapping in front of police headquarters. With the admissible evidence so severely restricted, the state presented its case in four days. Pat Whitaker then moved for a directed verdict of acquittal, which Judge Dewell granted. He ruled that the state had failed to place any of the defendants at the scene of the flogging.[201]

In June 1938, the five defendants were tried again for the kidnapping of Poulnot. The delay in commencing this trial was largely a result of a prolonged campaign to prevent Judge Dewell from presiding. State Attorney Farrior complained to the governor that Dewell was prejudiced against the prosecution, and the Committee for the Defense of Civil Liberties in Tampa agreed. Dewell adamantly refused for months to remove himself, but he finally stepped aside.[202] His replacement, a judge from West Palm Beach, also limited the evidence the state could introduce. At the conclusion of the eleven-day trial in Bartow, the jury found the defendants innocent of kidnapping Poulnot.[203] The foreman explained that the jurors "felt the defense had raised reasonable doubt as to the credibility of Poulnot." Frustrated at the results of two-and-a-half years' work, State Attorney Farrior asserted that "further prosecutions would be useless."[204] Nine days later, legal proceedings against the former Tampa policemen came to an official end when a judge accepted Farrior's motion to dismiss all remaining charges.[205]

The failure to punish any of the vigilantes was widely condemned. The Committee for the Defense of Civil Rights in Tampa charged that the case showed that "murder is safe in Florida if practiced by Klansmen with the support both of a political machine which would make Tammany Hall look like a Sunday School and of employing interests which have established American records in the exploitation of labor."[206] Norman Thomas claimed that "the triumph of Pat Whitaker's city machine and the Ku Klux Klan" represented "a complete breakdown of the processes of justice."[207]

Florida editors were equally outraged because of the stain left on the state's reputation. Calling the second trial "a source of profound disgrace to this state," a Miami editor asserted that "the Shoemaker case would be understandable under a reign of terror in Russia, but not in the United States." A Jacksonville newspaper argued that the inability to convict anyone was "about all the disgrace Florida can stand for awhile."[208] Although the defendants were acquitted, "Florida justice has been found guilty," argued the *Tampa Times*. "Guilty of impotence and incompetency through failure to discover and punish those who committed one of the most sickening crimes in the history of the State." The *Tampa Tribune* observed that "the impotency of Florida justice" had become "a stench and a shame in the nostrils of the nation." As a result, the grave of Joseph Shoemaker remained "a grim and ineradicable indictment of Florida, its courts, its citizenship, its failure to vindicate its good name."[209]

The end of legal proceedings did not halt the outside pressure on Tampa. Indeed, it briefly increased demands for a federal investigation of local vigilantes. The focus of this effort was a Senate committee, chaired by Wisconsin Senator Robert M. La Follette, Jr., which had been probing violations of the civil liberties of trade unionists and radicals. During 1936 and 1937, the La Follette Committee had exposed vigilante violence in several southern communities, notably Birmingham, Alabama, and Harlan County, Kentucky.[210] Following the directed verdict of acquittal in the 1937 trial of Tampa policemen, the Committee for the Defense of Civil Rights in Tampa had organized a campaign to persuade the La Follette Committee to investigate "cases of vigilante terror in Florida."[211] Socialists renewed this effort in 1938, and it picked up broad support, even in Florida.[212] However, limited resources and an unwillingness to pursue additional inquiries in the South prevented the La Follette Committee from undertaking an investigation of Florida.[213]

The three-year crusade for punishment of the Tampa floggers was designed not only to achieve justice in that particular case, but also to prevent further violence. For very different reasons, radicals and important members of the local elite had campaigned to protect leftists and union organizers from vigilante attacks. As a Socialist attorney pointed out after the floggings, "indictments on which men are put to trial even if the accused manage to get loose, are likely to cramp the style and check the activities of the K.K.K. and of mobbers generally."[214] To focus national attention on the community's dismal record, the ACLU branded Tampa one of the country's leading "centers of repression," because it was "under the control of public officials dominated by the Ku Klux Klan."[215]

Although unable to win justice in the flogging case, defenders of civil liberties helped accomplish the larger goal of ending establishment violence in Tampa. "The effort to bring Shoemaker's murderers to justice has at least held in check the sadistic terrorism which was cursing the Tampa area," Norman Thomas noted a year after Shoemaker's death. During 1937, Eugene Poulnot privately expressed concern about the threat of violence by local vigilantes, but he confided that "they don't dare to do anything while the heat is on them."[216]

A 1936 incident had demonstrated the impact of national publicity on repression in Tampa. During the election campaign that year, the Communist party's candidate for President, Earl Browder, tested his right of free speech and found Tampa wanting. Browder went to the cigar city in September to address one of the first public meetings by Communists since the aborted rally of November 7, 1931. After waiting for several hours to gain entry to a locked auditorium that Communists had rented in Ybor City, Browder cancelled his lecture and left Tampa.[217] Citing this as another example of the "gross violations of civil rights in Tampa," Communists blamed "vigilantes, incited by the Ku Klux Klan and the reactionary local press."[218] The custodian in charge of the auditorium claimed that the locked door was due to a misunderstanding by him. Local Socialists and Tampa newspapers thought the Communist party exaggerated the incident, but they supported Browder's right to speak. With backing from the ACLU, the Communist leader scheduled another Tampa speech for October.[219]

On his return visit Browder encountered violence. Despite appeals from ACLU and AFL officials for adequate police protection, Tampa authorities were noticeably absent when Communists staged their rally on a vacant lot in the center of town. As Browder began speaking to about four hundred spectators, fifteen men rushed the platform, wielding blackjacks, revolvers, fists, and brass knuckles. With one man holding Communists at bay with a gun, the rest of the gang tipped over the speakers' platform. During the melee at least five spectators, including two cigarworkers, received cuts and bruises. Browder fled to his hotel room and took a train out of town several hours later.[220]

The ringleaders of the attack were local peace officers, who made no attempt to conceal their identities. Reporters recognized a constable, a deputy constable, and a special deputy sheriff. Displaying his revolver, the constable bragged that he had "cold-cocked" four of the Communists. The attackers, several of whom wore American Legion caps, claimed to represent the Legion and "red-blooded American citizens."[221] When asked about his role in breaking up the rally, one of the constables declared, "I don't think no Communist ought to be allowed to speak anyhow and I don't care who knows it."[222]

The local reaction to the widely publicized assault was swift and decisive. The *Tampa Tribune* bemoaned the extensive media coverage the story received from the press and radio.[223] "Again Tampa is heralded to the world as a community which does not respect the constitutional rights of free speech and peaceable assembly," the *Tribune* complained, noting that "to make it worse, . . . officers of the law lead violent groups in riotous outbreaks of lawlessness." The *Tampa Times* charged that a "handful of self-appointed guardians of the Constitution" had again given the city "a black eye before the nation." On the day after the attack, the three ringleaders were arrested and bound over for trial on charges of aggravated assault and breach of the peace. This response proved to Frank McCallister that the year's "work in the floggings cases [was] bearing fruit." A year earlier, "the local press would have played down the story and by their silence given tacit approval to the mob action."[224]

Evidence pointed to Klan involvement in the attack. Tampa's four American Legion posts immediately denounced the "mob violence" and denied that they planned the assault. Frank McCallister privately reported that the perpetrators and the Tampans who supplied them with bail bonds were identified as prominent Klansmen.[225] Moreover, the Invisible Empire publicly endorsed attacks on Browder. Calling his candidacy "the greatest affront International Communism has ever offered to this country," the Klan described violent disruptions of his speeches as "America's method of voicing disapproval of the Apostle of Revolution."²²⁶ In Tampa an expression of sympathy for the accused vigilantes came from Pat Whitaker, who said he did not approve of breaking up the Browder rally but added that it was "easy to see why people will become over zealous in their attempts to maintain white supremacy and . . . American institutions."²²⁷

The outcome of the Browder incident indicated some continued local support for violent attacks on radicals. After almost a year of legal delays, the charges against two of the accused vigilantes were dismissed. A jury disregarded the testimony of five eyewitnesses and found the last of the three accused men not guilty of assaulting spectators at the Browder rally. The *Tampa Tribune* criticized the failure to convict anyone in the case.²²⁸

Although none of the attackers suffered any punishment, the violence directed at Communists in 1936 was the city's last outburst of vigilantism. The Klan remained active in Tampa, but it avoided violence after 1936. Several months after the attack on Browder, four hundred white-robed and hooded Klansmen held a public rally in a municipal park. In addition to burning a huge wooden cross, local Klansmen boasted that they inducted one hundred new recruits.²²⁹ However, Eugene Poulnot privately dismissed the claim as "just propaganda," designed to "make it appear that they are enjoying prosperity." Poulnot contended that "since the Shoemaker incident many of them have drawn out [including] . . . some of the rank and file that didn't care to go in for that sort of stuff." Poulnot saw evidence of a "process of self distruction [sic] of the Vigilantes."²³⁰ Frank McCallister confided in late 1937 that "we may yet blast the Kluxers from their seats of power."²³¹

Despite prolonged and extensive pressures, the Whitaker machine retained its power. In 1938, local voters returned Pat Whitaker to the state senate, where he had not served since losing his seat four years earlier. In 1939, Robert E. Lee Chancey won reelection to a third term as mayor. The introduction of voting machines, combined with increased public scrutiny, significantly reduced obvious fraud in these elections. They were also conducted without violence.²³²

Tampa was still a wide-open city with illegal gambling and many of the same people in power. In 1938 a local grand jury indicted nine city and county law enforcement officials, including Sheriff McLeod, Deputy Chief of Police Amazon Logan, Chief of Detectives W. D. Bush, and Constable Thomas M. Graves. The men were charged with neglect of duty for failing to enforce laws against gambling. The grand jury's report declared that "Tampa's national reputation for lawlessness and its strangled economic growth [were] largely due to the highly organized and skillfully managed gambling industry."[223] The *Tribune* hailed the indictments as "the answer to a reign of protected lawlessness which has . . . included the murder of Shoemaker, forcible denial of free speech, deliberate theft of elections, ambushed assassinations, private and public corruption, and the unbridled operation of a gambling syndicate."[234] Nothing came of the cases, dismissed on a legal technicality. The indicted officials kept their positions, and one, Constable Hugh Culbreath, was elected sheriff in 1940.[235]

The 1938 grand jury also charged six local men with dominating gambling in Tampa. The accused included Charles McKay ("Charlie") Wall, three Latins, and a black. Charlie Wall, a son of Dr. John P. Wall, had long been considered the "Maestro of Tampa Gambling." Bail money for the six men indicted in 1938 was provided by Wall's cousins, D. B. McKay, Charles A. McKay, Howell T. Lykes, Thompson M. Lykes, and Perry G. Wall, all of whom had been publicly associated with Citizens' Committees in 1910 or 1920. Attorneys for the accused gamblers, who ultimately went free, included Thomas Whitaker and Howard P. Macfarlane, the son of the founder of West Tampa.[236]

In 1950 the celebrated crime committee of U.S. Senator Estes Kefauver held hearings in Tampa. The committee was attracted by warfare among competing syndicates that had left a string of unsolved murders. Public testimony repeated rumors and speculation that linked several local law enforcement officials to payoffs from gamblers, but Police Chief J. L. Eddings, Sheriff Hugh Culbreath, and State Attorney Rex Farrior denied any involvement in illegal activities.[237]

Despite continued political corruption and criminal violence, Tampans avoided vigilantism after 1936. Members of the Tampa elite had first taken an organized stand against some types of vigilante violence during World War I. Concerted opposition was sparked by mob violence directed at jailed criminals who represented no menace to people in positions of power. Instead, lynch law wielded by ordinary "unthinking" Floridians threatened profits and investments. In 1917 and again in 1927, Tampa authorities, backed by vigilance committees of leading citizens, crushed attempts to lynch common criminals who were already behind bars. In both cases, prominent Tampans feared that lynch law would undermine the city's reputation and the potential for new investments.

In the 1930s the conflicting interests of members of the local elite produced sharp disagreements over the propriety of vigilante violence. After a display of class solidarity in repressing the 1931 uprising of cigarworkers, notable members of Tampa's economic elite, including D. B. McKay and other leaders of the Chamber of Commerce, joined most cigar manufacturers in accepting union recognition and collective bargaining under the New Deal. The same drive for profits and stability that had earlier led to vigilante action now dictated reliance on peaceful methods of resolving conflicts. The reaction to the 1934 lynching of a black prisoner reinforced the view that the city had to end mob violence or its image would discourage outside capitalists from investing in Tampa.

In defense of profits and power based on gambling, the Whitaker machine still tolerated vigilante violence to eliminate opponents, especially the Modern Democrats. Most leaders of the city's economic elite, however, denounced the floggings not only because they further tarnished the city's reputation but also because Joseph Shoemaker and local Socialists did not represent a serious threat to D. B. McKay and his allies, who no longer controlled the city government. Moreover, the Socialists had not mobilized cigarworkers, as Communists had in 1931. The employers who went to the defense of the accused floggers were those who continued to resist union recognition and collective bargaining.

The local reaction to the vigilante murder of Joseph Shoemaker showed that little public support remained for a method of control that made Tampa synonymous with "tar and terror." The accused perpetrators of the crime were city employees and Klansmen who, though not members of the elite, were supporters of the status quo. The floggers identified with traditional southern values that equated socialism with communism and race-mixing. The existing distribution of power also provided the indicted policemen with employment and a degree of power as legal and extralegal enforcers of the dominant political faction. The response of higher officials to the flogging cases and the Browder incident demonstrated for the first time that the state would prosecute people who took the law into their own hands. This, combined with increasing opposition from members of the local elite, brought a halt to establishment violence. By 1940, Tampa had disappeared from the ACLU's annual survey of communities which suppressed civil liberties. Indeed, the end of vigilantism in Tampa was part of a temporary national trend. As the ACLU observed in 1939, "Mob violence and vigilante action have sharply declined during the past year."[238]

# Conclusion:
# Violence and Hegemony

Vigilante violence long arbitrated group conflict in Tampa. Originating in the antebellum period, when it was used spontaneously to deal with horse thieves and other common criminals, vigilantism became a systematic means of repressing groups that appeared to challenge the power and interests of the local elite. Tampa well deserved its reputation for "anti-labor, anti-Negro, anti-alien, anti-Communist, anti-Socialist, anti-liberal violence."[1] Members of each of these groups came under attack from the 1880s to the 1930s.

The types and intensity of elite coercion varied widely. The mildest form of intimidation was the threat of violence, used to drive labor organizers, strike leaders, and radicals out of the city. Overt violence included the kidnapping and deportation of union men. In addition to restricting free movement, vigilantes destroyed union property during strikes. For example, private citizens smashed union newspaper presses, overturned soup kitchens, closed labor halls, and seized union records. Vigilantes and their defenders occasionally claimed that union men and radicals were not physically harmed even when they were kidnapped and forcibly deported. This, however, in no way diminished the illegality or effectiveness of the methods. One reason that threats and violence short of physical injury often proved sufficient was that labor organizers did not physically resist. Outnumbered and outgunned, they left town, and their supporters in Tampa relied on legal protests. The shooting of James Wood in 1903 and the lynching of two immigrants in the midst of the 1910 strike also served as vivid lessons of what could happen to anyone who ran afoul of local power brokers. The desired message was reinforced by a photograph of the two lynch victims that was widely circulated on postcards.

The measured application of force and violence demonstrated the planning and purposefulness behind vigilantism. Employing the particular means that seemed necessary to achieve the desired goal, vigilantes acted in a deliberate, controlled manner. The killing of six of their targets between 1882 and 1935 was neither accidental nor unpremeditated. Only in the case of Joseph Shoemaker did the death of a victim appear unplanned, and even then the floggers had intended to inflict serious bodily injury.

Vigilantism was in every sense establishment violence. Employed by members of the local elite, it was designed to enforce dominant values and protect the prevailing distribution of power. Leaders of the lynch mob in 1882 and members of subsequent antilabor Citizens' Committees rarely made any attempt to conceal their identities until the 1930s, when growing opposition and outside pressures forced vigilantes to operate anonymously. The conservative purposes of elite coercion were always clear. Whether the particular target was a black prisoner, a union organizer, a political radical, or a common criminal, extralegal violence was supposed to preserve the status quo.

The local elite crushed mob violence whenever it was initiated by others and threatened to undermine order and stability. In 1927, the suppression of an "unthinking" mob of "hooligans" took the lives of five would-be lynchers and one innocent bystander. In this case and all others involving group violence prior to the 1930s, members of the elite stood together on the same side of the firing line.

After the repression of cigarworkers in 1931, disagreements emerged over the propriety and effectiveness of vigilantism as a means of enforcing order. Nevertheless, the lynchings of Robert Johnson and Joseph Shoemaker in the 1930s were expressions of establishment violence. Even though many prominent Tampans publicly opposed these lynchings, the purpose in both cases was to protect certain vested interests. Moreover, the vigilante killers of Shoemaker escaped punishment largely because of the powerful support they received from a group of Tampa businessmen and the local political boss, Pat Whitaker.

Vigilantes broke the law in order to defend it and destroyed property in order to protect it. This did not, however, represent a contradiction to local notables. Tampa's vigilante tradition was a product of southern culture and politics which restricted formal law and defined community justice to include lynch law. This was reinforced by the southern view of republicanism. "In a democracy with a republican form of government," a 1905 study of lynch law pointed out, "people consider themselves a law unto themselves. They make the laws; therefore they can unmake them. . . . To execute a criminal deserving of death is to act merely in their sovereign capacity, temporarily dispensing with their agents, the legal administrators of the law."[2] Private justice became not merely a legitimate means of preserving order and purity, but a collective duty for southerners who distrusted the state and often took it upon themselves to enforce dominant standards outside regular legal channels. "The mob which punishes the assaulter of female innocence, or executes vengeance upon the perpetrator of any foul crime, may have something said in its favor," the *Tampa Tribune* asserted in 1899.³

The practice of lynch law and other vigilante methods was not, of course, confined to the South. Beginning as a frontier phenomenon in colonial South Carolina, vigilantism spread westward with pioneers who used it to bring order to frontier areas lying beyond the arm of effective law enforcement. Some of the largest vigilante movements occurred in California, Idaho, and Colorado during the latter half of the nineteenth century.⁴ Establishment violence also occasionally erupted in the North and West after the frontier had vanished, but no city outside the South appears to have experienced as many vigilante incidents as Tampa.⁵ For example, the famous San Francisco Vigilante Committee of 1856, which popularized urban vigilantism and served as a model for other communities, operated for only three months. Moreover, vigilantes rarely reappeared in that city during subsequent decades. Confined largely to a brief period in the 1850s, San Francisco Vigilance Committees did not play a continuing role in local power struggles.⁶

In contrast, Citizens' Committees periodically policed Tampa for almost fifty years. Rooted in the Old South, Tampa's vigilante tradition thrived in the New South. When an urban society built on manufacturing generated new challenges to dominant interests, prominent southerners did not hesitate to impose traditional forms of law and order. From 1882 to 1936, the citizens identified as leaders and spokesmen for vigilante movements in Tampa were native-born southerners, with the exception of the Macfarlane brothers and Peter O. Knight, who had relocated in Florida as young men during the 1880s and became staunch defenders of the southern way of life. During labor disputes, vigilantes went to the assistance of Latin cigar manufacturers, but the immigrant capitalists did not lead the Citizens' Committees.

In addition to prominent businessmen and newspaper publishers, southern-born lawyers stand out as the principal organizers of vigilance committees in Tampa. Trained to believe that lynch law was "lawless lawfulness," attorneys accepted it as part of community justice.⁷ This view helps explain why Tampa vigilantes publicly identified themselves for decades, yet suffered no legal penalty. Indeed, many of the most prominent vigilante leaders and their supporters, from Joseph B. Wall to Robert E. Lee Chancey, were former prosecutors. They also usually enjoyed the cooperation of public officials, especially the police. In the view of these officials, a higher law, sometimes referred to as the right of self-preservation, justified citizens with a stake in the community taking the law into their own hands to prevent chaos and enforce order. Six days before formation of the 1910

Citizens' Committee, Wallace Stovall declared that the two-month-old strike by cigarworkers had become "a question of the PRESERVATION OF TAMPA'S CHIEF INDUSTRY." He claimed that "Tampa has never been able to restore or maintain peace in its cigar manufacturing industry while it has permitted the agitator to stand between the workingman and employer." Therefore, he concluded, it was time for "Tampans to say if they will continue to run this town or if they have given its destiny over to the interloper."[8]

Since vigilantes did not consider their actions a violation of the canons of community justice, leading Tampans could simultaneously resort to lynch law and pride themselves on being law-abiding citizens. "In point of an honest, law-abiding citizenship, no community on the American continent can boast of a higher standard than Hillsborough County, Florida," the *Tampa Tribune* trumpeted at the turn of century.[9] The city's growing tradition of vigilantism in no way undercut this perception. There was, however, a double standard. "When labor adopts the employers' tactics, labor goes to jail," observed the local newspaper of cigarworkers.[10]

Despite the frequent resort to vigilante methods, Tampa was not an island of terror in a sea of racial and labor tranquility. In 1884, a group of vigilantes calling themselves the Sara Sota Vigilance Committee killed two men in a neighboring county. And during the first third of the twentieth century, Florida had the largest number of blacks lynched per capita of all the states in the Union. At the same time, the state failed to convict a single person for participating in a lynching. Between 1900 and 1935, a total of twenty-two people (all black) were lynched in the four counties bordering on Hillsborough County.[11] Although these incidents had no direct relation to Tampa or its residents, they reflected the pervasiveness of lynch law in the area.

Tampa itself had nine lynching deaths between 1858 and 1935.[12] Three of the victims were black and the other six were white. Despite differences in race, the nine victims shared several characteristics. In the eyes of the city's establishment, each could be described as an "outsider," a designation resulting not only from caste or class but also from place of birth or residence. Nothing is known of the background of the two horse thieves dispatched in 1858, but they may well have been drifters. None of the six post–Civil War victims was a Tampan by birth, and only the two blacks were probably southerners. Three of the white victims were immigrants, and the fourth, Joseph Shoemaker, was a Yankee. Most of these six men had lived in Tampa only a short time, and the black lynched in 1903 was not even a resident. Surviving records indicate but one man, Ficarrotta, was married, and only two others, Albano and Shoemaker, had any relatives in Tampa.

## Conclusion: Violence and Hegemony

The history of lynching in Tampa shows that no single reason can explain the prevalence of this type of vigilantism. Beginning as a frontier phenomenon related to crime control in the antebellum period, lynching nonetheless persisted long after Tampa had become a large urban center with efficient law enforcement machinery. The situation was further unusual in that only one-third of Tampa's nine recorded lynching victims were black. For the period 1882–1930, 85 percent of the 3,650 people lynched in the South were black, and they were most commonly killed in sparsely settled areas. Tampa's two lynchings of blacks in 1903 and 1934 were, however, typical examples of southern caste violence, except for being executed secretly by small, well-organized groups instead of large mobs. In other respects, these two summary executions followed the southern pattern of antiblack violence, for they were intended to reinforce white supremacy and the dominant belief that no black man could be accused of attacking a white woman and go unpunished.[13]

The South's caste system does not explain two-thirds of Tampa's lynchings. The two horse thieves summarily executed in 1858 were the victims of frontier justice. The 1882 lynching of Charles Owens was a product of the southern code of honor. Occurring in front of the county courthouse during a court recess, the mob killing was defended as the honorable duty of an outraged community which would not tolerate the attempted rape of a prominent woman. The dictates of honor continued to spark personal violence into the twentieth century, but it was not the primary cause of vigilante violence after Tampa became a full-fledged city. Indeed, honor played a diminishing role in all aspects of society. Wallace Stovall, a Kentucky native, observed in 1920 that "the old-time chivalry, deference and honor, reverence and protection, which the Southern gentleman threw about woman has decayed lamentably."[14]

Rather than defending a code of honor, the lynchings of all three whites in the twentieth century were designed to preserve the political and economic order. The summary execution of the two Italian immigrants in 1910 was intended both to eliminate two alleged criminals and to intimidate striking cigarworkers. A cigar industry journal expressed the hope that the double lynching would serve as a lesson to Tampa workers that "the constitutional right of every American citizen does not mean license to openly urge rioting."[15] The flogging of Joseph Shoemaker in 1935 was also designed to suppress a threat to one faction of the local elite. The *Miami News* recognized the situation in Tampa for what it was, branding the fatal flogging as "an example of savage class hatred, one of many such gruesome mass crimes in the Florida cigar-citrus country."[16] Nevertheless, support for this type of repression came from a subsequent Florida governor, Fred P. Cone, who declared in 1937 that "a man ought to be hung on a tree if he advocates overthrow of government."[17]

The Tampa elite took the lead in implementing lynch law. Local notables definitely organized the lynchings of 1860, 1882, and 1910, and they probably participated in each of the other three prior to the 1930s. Other types of vigilantism, which were more common and better publicized than lynchings, demonstrate clearly the class origins of most establishment violence. The Tampa elite enforced order on its own terms through a series of Citizens' Committees organized from 1887 to 1931. Except for the 1899 weight strike which workers won, every industry-wide shutdown of local cigar manufacturing resulted in the formation of a vigilance committee designed to break the strike through force and violence. As "the representative business organization in the city," the Board of Trade initiated these movements, provided the leadership, and supplied the muscle.[18] "The Board of Trade is the business man organized," its president declared at the turn of the century. "It means order in the community and unity of action."[19] The southern-born leadership of the organization had no hesitation in uniting behind the use of violence to protect the economic interests of local businessmen and professionals.

Antilabor vigilantism was a product of both the immediate concern over the economic impact of long strikes and the continuing fear that cigar factory owners might relocate. With small capital investments in plants and none in machinery, cigar manufacturers could easily leave Tampa just as many had earlier abandoned first Havana and then Key West. For this reason, the Board of Trade promised in 1887 to protect manufacturers and their property. Well-organized board members used violent measures to fulfill this pledge for more than forty years. As the cigarworkers' union leaders emphasized in 1920, "The commercial interests of Tampa being so largely dependent upon the wage of the cigar workers, and the Barons of the cigar industry being so stubbornly opposed to organization among the workers, the business element has always arrayed itself on the side of the manufacturers in disputes that threatened to be of long duration. In times past business men have usurped the powers of the police."[20] D. B. McKay, the four-term mayor and member of numerous Citizens' Committees, claimed that "the community [had] a proprietary interest in the [cigar] industry," which had to be protected "by whatever means."[21]

The violent repression of cigarworkers was not simply an expression of antiunion or anti-immigrant attitudes. Other Tampa craftsmen, especially construction workers and printers, operated under union contracts with little opposition. "Unions are allright [sic]," Wallace Stovall observed in the 1890s. "Organization of the laboring men for the betterment of their financial condition is eminently proper."[22] Cigarworkers were placed in a different category not because of their ethnicity, but because of their politics. "Do not think that we object to the organization of labor. Not at all," D. B. McKay's newspaper assured its readers in the midst of the 1920 strike by cigarworkers. "We have always favored union labor, and freely concede the right of collective bargaining. . . . It is only when labor becomes autocratic and dictatorial, attempting to rule . . . its employers, . . . that we object to it." Taking a similar stance, the *Tampa Tribune* declared the following year: "That trade union movement which simply seeks the improvement of the conditions of employment will never lack the support of public opinion; that trade union movement which is nothing but a masque for revolution can never win the support of public opinion."[23] No one ever doubted into which category cigarworkers fell. Unlike other local trade unionists, cigarworkers formed "a class of labor as stubborn as it is misguided," according to the *Tampa Tribune*.[24]

And AFL leaders often agreed. "The cigarmakers of Tampa owing to temperament, environment, and lack of association with those concerned with and familiar with the trade union movement, are easily led, especially so when it comes to the purely speculative theory part of the movement," the national president of the Cigar Makers' International Union complained to Samuel Gompers in 1913. "These people like to be able to strike at any time and dislike any kind of restraint. I am of the opinion that socialists are very active there at present and that the workers lend these people a receptive ear."[25]

Despite political and ethnic differences among workers, the reaction to vigilante violence followed class lines. Except for the 1901 strike, when cigarworkers were split between La Resistencia and the CMIU, Tampa labor displayed a united front during prolonged strikes. Indeed, the very politics of cigarworkers that sometimes made them suspect encouraged class solidarity. "We hold that, above the differences of race and nationality, we should hold the interests we have in common: Capital is our common enemy," *El Internacional* asserted during World War I. "If we were born in different lands it is not our fault. We all labor under the same difficulties; we all have to solve the same problems; we are all the prey of the same evils of Capitalism."[26] Local trade unionists outside the cigar industry were largely native-born whites, but they provided cigarworkers with both moral support and financial assistance during strikes. Some craft unionists paid a high price for thus aligning themselves with cigarworkers: as a result of both the 1910 and 1920 strikes, printers lost union shop agreements they had with Tampa employers. Immigrant cigarworkers also garnered national support from organized labor. Once they abandoned independent unionism after 1901, Samuel Gompers consistently went to their aid, especially when they were victimized by vigilantes.

Labor conflicts in Tampa had an ethnic dimension, but it was muted and rarely verbalized. In the early years of the cigar industry, the CMIU complained about the hostility of Latin operatives toward Americans and American institutions. After 1901, however, immigrant and native-born cigarworkers cooperated in confrontations with employers. Tampa newspapers occasionally engaged in xenophobic denunciations of foreign-born workers, but the growing economic, political, and social alliance between the city's southern elite and immigrant cigar manufacturers defused nativist attitudes. Anti-immigrant rhetoric briefly resurfaced after World War I, when the entire country was gripped by the hysteria of "100 percent Americanism," but the city divided along class rather than ethnic lines during the ten-month strike of 1920–21. "Class consciousness must have been the monstrous malady that lay in the bottom of Pandora's box," the *Tribune* observed in the midst of the strike. The paper claimed that "a clash of classes" was undermining America. "What it lacks of being a class war is slight indeed."[27]

The most significant source of ethnic violence in Tampa, however, was race, not nationality. Although antiblack vigilantism was less common than class violence, it was more vicious. Constituting a smaller proportion of the local population than immigrants and their families, blacks also posed less of a threat. Vigilance committees were not necessary to control blacks, since that group faced legal restrictions and lacked the organization and power of immigrant cigarworkers. In 1917, leading Tampans actually protected a black prisoner from a lynch mob so that he could be legally executed. But when vigilantes took action against blacks, they did so with a viciousness that surpassed the violence directed at other groups. In 1903, for example, Lewis Jackson was castrated and lynched. No immigrant cigarworker nor white radical ever experienced similar treatment. The racism of Tampa vigilantes made mutilation an acceptable punishment only in the case of blacks.

Measured by the frequency of collective violence, class divisions were a more significant force in Tampa than caste divisions. The elite of Tampa more often resorted to extralegal force and violence to repress immigrant workers and white radicals than to control blacks. Moreover, local notables opposed antiblack violence long before they took a similar stand against antilabor violence. White trade unionists also went to the defense of multiracial cigarworkers, and reactions to vigilantism usually followed class lines. Despite attempts to mask repression as a broad community effort, the actions and rhetoric of the

Tampa elite demonstrated that its members were conscious of their collective interests and the need to protect them as a class.

The extensive use of violence to repress workers and radicals was a sign of the elite's weakness, not strength. Studies of hegemony, defined as "the 'spontaneous' consent given by the great masses of the population to the general direction imposed on social life by the dominant fundamental group," emphasize that it is "achieved by consent, not force."[28] A ruling group obtains legitimacy and stability when its values and interests are voluntarily accepted by subordinate groups as those of the society as a whole. Behind the velvet glove of hegemonic control lies the iron hand of public and private force, but a resort to violence is "a sign of the failure of hegemony, the inability of a dominant class to confine conflict to its own chosen political terrain."[29]

Vigilante violence in Tampa indicated the tenuous position of the local elite. From the time class-conscious cigarworkers arrived in the city, they challenged the prevailing distribution of power in the workplace and the community at large, and they denied leading Tampans the loyalty that would have made social harmony possible. "We expect little from the charity or mercy of 'capitalistic rulers,'" the voice of cigarworkers commented during a municipal election campaign in 1920. "Capitalism enslaves the wage workers and the mayor, governor or senator who represents a capitalistic form of government and society can, at best, serve the masters of industry, and from this service we will get—the least our masters are forced by us to give to us."[30] Workers who had their own world view and who acted on it could only be controlled by force.[31] The result in Tampa was over forty years of establishment violence directed primarily at repressing militant workers.

Vigilante violence usually achieved its immediate purpose, but it did not permanently eliminate worker militancy. "Cigar makers are the most radical workers you could find," observed the writer Jose Yglesias, the son of immigrant cigarworkers and a native of Ybor City. "They had many, many strikes."[32] He added that "although they held out and fought hard, they never won a strike. It could not be otherwise—they were a radical Latin island in the south—and when they were not starved out, the authorities sent in the KKK."[33] Establishment violence expelled union leaders from Tampa and helped break strikes by repressing workers, but it did not eradicate class antagonisms or achieve hegemony. As a Resistencia leader pointed out when workers returned to the factory in defeat in 1901, "They have vanquished us but not convinced us."[34]

Economic and political changes achieved the equilibrium that ultimately made vigilante violence unnecessary. Collapse of the handmade cigar industry and dispersal of its labor force undermined the collective strength of cigarworkers. "There is not much hope in Ybor City," a former cigarmaker reflected in the mid-1930s. "The cigar factories are on a continuous decline."[35] As Jose Yglesias pointed out, "Ybor City is not a place where time has stood still, but a town ravaged by time and lost social struggles."[36] The readers' stands were permanently removed in 1931. Factories closed. Cigarmaking machines cheapened labor and opened factory doors to unskilled American women, who posed no immediate threat to manufacturers. In 1933 unionized handworkers gave up the right to strike in return for recognition. Collective bargaining supplanted collective violence.

Occupational and geographic mobility among working-class immigrants also helped the Tampa elite obtain hegemony. Many second-generation immigrants moved away. Jose Yglesias, for example, went to New York and became a writer, although he never abandoned his radicalism.[37] Some of those who remained behind achieved positions of power after the 1930s. By the 1950s, Tampa had an Italian-American mayor who was born and reared in Ybor City by Sicilian parents.[38]

The achievement of hegemony did not, of course, eliminate class and caste divisions. After the 1930s, however, conflicts were managed by the Tampa elite without the use of vigilante violence. The greatest postwar challenge to the local status quo came from blacks in the 1960s, and white Tampans responded nonviolently. When local civil rights demonstrators organized sit-ins and other protests against segregation, beginning in 1960, prominent whites negotiated a gradual end to Jim Crow practices by various businesses. The new "Tampa Technique," emphasizing moderation and cooperation, was a conscious attempt to avoid violence by blacks or whites that would tarnish the city's progressive image.[39] "What new industry would decide to go into a city which seethes with murderous racial conflict?" speculated the *Tampa Tribune* in 1963. Thus, the civic and business elite avoided coercion and repression and relied on persuasion and voluntarism to integrate public facilities. In 1967 the *Tribune* reported with pride that the "Tampa Technique" had paid "high dividends to our community."[40]

The old Tampa method of establishment violence had also once paid high dividends. It had provided an effective means of defending the political power and economic interests of local notables whose use of violence went unchallenged by public authorities. During the 1930s, however, the city began to pay a high price for vigilantism, as state and national resistance to lynch law mounted. Tampa's reputation for "tar and terror" increasingly jeopardized campaigns to lure new investments and tourists to the economically devastated cigar city. Thus, prominent Tampans took a stand against lynch law, and it came to an end in the wake of the furor created by the flogging death of Joseph Shoemaker. Just as vigilantism thrived as long as it seemed necessary to protect the existing order, it disappeared when it threatened to undermine that order.

# Notes

**Introduction**

1. Reed, *The Enduring South: Subcultural Persistence in Mass Society* (Chapel Hill, N.C., 1974), 45.
2. This definition is borrowed from Charles Tilly, Louise Tilly, and Richard Tilly, *The Rebellious Century, 1830–1930* (Cambridge, Mass., 1975), 49. See also Richard Hofstadter, "Reflections on Violence in the United States," in *American Violence: A Documentary History*, ed. Richard Hofstadter and Michael Wallace (New York, 1970), 9.
3. Richard Maxwell Brown, *Strain of Violence: Historical Studies of American Violence and Vigilantism* (New York, 1975), 4–5; Hugh Davis Graham and Ted Robert Gurr, "Conclusion," in *The History of Violence in America: Historical and Comparative Perspectives*, ed. Hugh Davis Graham and Ted Robert Gurr (New York, 1969), 805; Leonard L. Richards, *"Gentlemen of Property and Standing": Anti-Abolition Mobs in Jacksonian America* (New York, 1970); Michael Feldberg, *The Turbulent Era: Riot and Disorder in Jacksonian America* (New York, 1980).
4. Hofstadter, "Reflections on Violence," 11.
5. For a general discussion of the nature of reactionary and revolutionary violence, see Charles Tilly, "Collective Violence in European Perspective," in Graham and Gurr, *Violence in America*, 16–28.
6. Michael Wallace, "The Uses of Violence in American History," *American Scholar* 40 (Winter 1970–71): 82, 96.
7. Hofstadter, "Reflections on Violence," 20; Brown, *Strain of Violence*, 22, 96.
8. Brown, *Strain of Violence*, 95–97. "Vigilantism is a step removed from man-to-man retaliation," John W. Caughey has emphasized. "A one-man vigilance committee would be a contradiction in terms" (*Their Majesties the Mob* [Chicago, 1960], 5).
9. H. Jon Rosenbaum and Peter C. Sederberg, "Vigilantism: An Analysis of Establishment Violence," in *Vigilante Politics*, ed. Jon Rosenbaum and Peter C. Sederberg (Philadelphia, 1976), 3–7, 17 (quotation).
10. Hofstadter, "Reflections on Violence," 9; Richard E. Rubenstein, *Rebels in Eden: Mass Political Violence in the United States* (Boston, 1970), 23–24.
11. The line between legal and extralegal action can be difficult to draw, especially since an act that seemingly violates the law may be widely accepted as legitimate and even officially judged as legal. Nevertheless, vigilantes by definition operate outside the framework of formal written law, and for the historian, as Richard Maxwell Brown has emphasized,

"the most important thing is not whether the actions of officials or vigilantes were legal or illegal but, rather, what the goal was in each case" (*Strain of Violence,* 147).

12. Ibid., 28–31; Hofstadter, "Reflections on Violence," 12. See also Richard C. Wade, "Violence in the Cities: A Historical View," in *Urban Violence,* ed. Charles U. Daly (Chicago, 1969), 7–26.
13. Brown, *Strain of Violence,* 23.
14. Ibid., 127–28; Robert M. Senkewicz, *Vigilantes in Gold Rush San Francisco* (Stanford, Cal., 1985).
15. For general studies of southern violence, see John Hope Franklin, *The Militant South, 1800–1861* (Cambridge, Mass., 1956); Frank E. Vandiver, "The Southerner as Extremist," in *The Idea of the South: Pursuit of a Central Theme,* ed. Frank E. Vandiver (Chicago, 1964), 43–55; Sheldon Hackney, "Southern Violence," *American Historical Review* 74 (Feb. 1969): 906–25; Bertram Wyatt-Brown, *Southern Honor: Ethics and Behavior in the Old South* (New York, 1982)
16. H. V. Redfield, *Homicide, North and South: Being a Comparative View of Crime Against the Person in Several Parts of the United States* (Philadelphia, 1880); H. C. Brearley, *Homicide in the United States* (Montclair, N.J., 1969 [1932]); Raymond D. Gastil, "Homicide and a Regional Culture of Violence," *American Sociological Review* 36 (June 1971): 412–27; William D. Miller, "Myth and New South City Murder Rates," *Mississippi Quarterly* 26 (Spring 1973): 143–53.
17. H. C. Brearley, "The Pattern of Violence," in *Culture in the South,* ed. W. T. Couch (Chapel Hill, N.C., 1934), 678.
18. Albert C. Smith, "'Southern Violence' Reconsidered: Arson as Protest in Black-Belt Georgia, 1865–1910," *Journal of Southern History* 51 (Nov. 1985): 527–64.
19. For studies that view lynching as a type of vigilantism, see James Elbert Cutler, *Lynch-Law: An Investigation into the History of Lynching in the United States* (1905; Montclair, N.J., 1969), 135; Joe B. Frantz, "The Frontier Tradition: An Invitation to Violence," in Graham and Gurr, *Violence in America,* 136; Jacquelyn Dowd Hall, *Revolt Against Chivalry: Jessie Daniel Ames and the Women's Campaign Against Lynching* (New York, 1974), 130–31. Hugh Davis Graham and Ted Robert Gurr have described lynching as "vigilantism's supreme instrument of terror and summary 'justice'" ("Conclusion," 791).
20. Brown, *Strain of Violence,* 24–25, 150–51. The methods of whitecapping could also be employed for reactionary purposes by backward-looking people trying to regain lost rights or power. William F. Holmes, "Whitecapping: Agrarian Violence in Mississippi, 1902–1906," *Journal of Southern History* 35 (May 1969): 165–85; William F. Holmes, "Whitecapping in Mississippi: Agrarian Violence in the Populist Era," *Mid-America* 55 (April 1973): 134–48; William F. Holmes, "Moonshining and Collective Violence: Georgia, 1889–1895," *Journal of American History* 67 (Dec. 1980): 589–611; Paul J. Vanderwood, *Night Riders of Reelfoot Lake* (Memphis, 1969).
21. See, for example, Richard Maxwell Brown, *South Carolina Regulators* (Cambridge, Mass., 1963); Allen W. Trelease, *White Terror: The Ku Klux Klan Conspiracy and Southern Reconstruction* (New York, 1971); Robert P. Ingalls, "Antiradical Violence in Birmingham During the 1930s," *Journal of Southern History* 47 (Nov. 1981): 521–44; Robert P. Ingalls, "Anti-

Labor Vigilantes: The South During the 1930s," *Southern Exposure* 12 (Nov./Dec. 1984): 72–78.
22. American Civil Liberties Union, *Eternal Vigilance! The Story of Civil Liberty, 1937–38* (New York, 1938), 13.
23. Graham and Gurr, "Conclusion," 804. See also Neil J. Smelser, *Theory of Collective Behavior* (New York, 1962). For a classic application of the breakdown theory to the American South as an explanation of its violent past, see Wilbur J. Cash, *The Mind of the South* (New York, 1941), 43–44, 305–11.
24. Tilly, "Collective Violence," 4, 10 (quotation). See also Tilly, Tilly, and Tilly, *Rebellious Century*; H. L. Nieburg, *Political Violence: The Behavioral Process* (New York, 1969).
25. Dickson D. Bruce, Jr., *Violence and Culture in the Antebellum South* (Austin, Tex., 1979), 44–88; Carl Iver Hovland and Robert R. Sears, "Correlation of Lynchings with Economic Indices," *Journal of Psychology* 9 (May 1940): 301–10; James R. McGovern, *Anatomy of a Lynching: The Killing of Claude Neal* (Baton Rouge, La., 1982), 8–11, 15, 149–57; Hackney, "Southern Violence," 924 (quotation).
26. Douglas T. Miller, quoted in Hugh Davis Graham, "The Paradox of American Violence: A Historical Appraisal," in *Collective Violence*, ed. James F. Short, Jr., and Marvin E. Wolfgang (Chicago, 1972), 208.
27. Allen D. Grimshaw, "Interpreting Collective Violence: An Argument for the Importance of Social Structure," ibid., 42.
28. See, for example, Holmes, "Whitecapping, 1902–1906," passim; Holmes, "Moonshining," passim; Hall, *Revolt Against Chivalry*, 129–57; Robert V. Haynes, *A Night of Violence: The Houston Riot of 1917* (Baton Rouge, La., 1976); Charles L. Flynn, Jr., *White Land, Black Labor: Caste and Class in Late Nineteenth-Century Georgia* (Baton Rouge, La., 1983), 25–56.
29. For the origins of the term "New South" and its use by historians to describe the period from 1877 to the 1940s, see Paul M. Gaston, *The New South Creed: A Study in Southern Mythmaking* (New York, 1970), 4–6, 17–20; C. Vann Woodward, *Origins of the New South, 1877–1913* (Baton Rouge, La., 1966), vii–x; George Brown Tindall, *The Emergence of the New South, 1913–1945* (Baton Rouge, La., 1967), x.
30. For overviews of industrialization and urbanization in the South that emphasize the region's distinctive patterns of development, see James C. Cobb, *Industrialization and Southern Society, 1877–1984* (Lexington, Ky., 1984); David R. Goldfield, *Cotton Fields and Skyscrapers: Southern City and Region, 1607–1980* (Baton Rouge, La., 1982).
31. Historians have only begun to investigate local elites in the New South, but community studies have reached similar conclusions about the dominance of upper-class white men. Although the particular distribution of occupations composing a local elite obviously varies, some combination of larger merchants, professionals, bankers and, in some cases, industrialists controlled the levers of power in most communities studied thus far. Historians have found varying degrees of unity among members of local southern elites, but none has discovered a pattern that fits the pluralist model popularized by political scientist Robert A. Dahl in his examination of power in New Haven, Connecticut (*Who Governs? Democracy and Power in an American City* [New Haven, Conn., 1961]). According to Blaine A. Brownell's study of the 1920s, "The 'power struc-

ture' in southern cities was neither monolithic nor open to all significant . . . groups. The white commercial-civil elite was by far the most articulate, influential, and effective leadership group throughout the decade, and its members exercised a dominance in urban affairs that was rarely challenged" (*The Urban Ethos in the South, 1920–1930* [Baton Rouge, La., 1975], 53). In the most detailed investigation of political power in a New South city, Carl V. Harris found evidence of competition among different business interests in Birmingham, but he concluded that "upper-ranking groups," representing 1 percent of the city's population, "prevailed consistently on the issues they considered absolutely essential; they still obtained from the political system everything they really needed from it" (*Political Power in Birmingham, 1871–1921* [Knoxville, Tenn., 1977], 275). See also Floyd Hunter, *Community Power Structure: A Study of Decision Makers* (Chapel Hill, N.C., 1953); Samuel M. Kipp, III, "Old Notables and Newcomers: The Economic and Political Elite of Greensboro, North Carolina, 1880–1920," *Journal of Southern History* 43 (Aug. 1977): 373–94; Eugene J. Watts, *The Social Bases of City Politics: Atlanta, 1865–1903* (Westport, Conn., 1978); Don Harrison Doyle, "Urbanization and Southern Culture: Economic Elites in Four New South Cities (Atlanta, Nashville, Charleston, Mobile), c. 1865–1910," and James M. Russell, "Elites and Municipal Politics and Government in Atlanta, 1847–1890," in *Toward a New South? Studies in Post–Civil War Southern Communities*, ed. Orville Vernon Burton and Robert C. McMath, Jr. (Westport, Conn., 1982), 11–70.

32. Atlanta *Constitution*, June 17, 1887, quoted in Russell, "Elites in Atlanta," 42.
33. Howard N. Rabinowitz, *Race Relations in the Urban South, 1865–1890* (Urbana, Ill., 1980); Goldfield, *Cotton Fields and Skyscrapers*, 6–8, 108–18, 164–66.
34. As one authority has put it, "urban southerners lived in a more violent environment than their urban colleagues in other regions" (Goldfield, *Cotton Fields and Skyscrapers*, 93). A study of homicide rates in the 1920s showed that Tampa had the twenty-fifth highest rate among the ninety-seven southern cities surveyed. Only four of the 727 nonsouthern cities in the sample had homicide rates higher than Tampa (Brearley, *Homicide in the United States*, 209–16; see also Tampa *Daily Times*, June 8, 1927).
35. Tilly, Tilly, and Tilly, *Rebellious Century*, 287.

## 1. The Southern Roots of Lynch Law

1. Tampa *Sunland Tribune*, Aug. 18, 1877, March 9, 1882.
2. Ibid., March 9, 1882; *Bartow Informant*, March 11, 1882; Tallahassee *Weekly Floridian*, March 14, 1882. Court records generated by this case routinely referred to the attacker as "one John," and all newspaper accounts identified him as Charles D. Owens.
3. Tampa *Sunland Tribune*, March 9, 1882.
4. Ibid., *Savannah Morning News*, March 14, 1882; Tallahassee *Weekly Floridian*, March 14, 1882; *Ex Parte Wall*, 107 U.S. 265 (1882).
5. Silvia Sunshine, *Petals Plucked from Sunny Climes* (1880; Gainesville, Fla., 1976), 288–89; Tampa *Sunland Tribune*, Oct. 29, 1881.

## Notes to Pages 2–10

6. George M. Barbour, *Florida for Tourists, Invalids, and Settlers* (New York, 1882), 61.
7. Irving A. Leonard, ed., *The Florida Adventures of Kirk Munroe* (Chuluota, Fla., 1975), 62.
8. Tampa *Sunland Tribune*, Oct. 8, Dec. 3, 1881, Jan. 26, 1882; Leonard, *Kirk Munroe*, 61.
9. Tampa *Sunland Tribune*, Nov. 26, 1881.
10. Ibid., Oct. 15, 1881.
11. Karl H. Grismer, *Tampa: A History of the City of Tampa and the Tampa Bay Region of Florida* (St. Petersburg, Fla., 1950), 157–58, 303, 330.
12. Tampa *Sunland Tribune*, March 9, 1882.
13. Wyatt-Brown, *Southern Honor*, 25–61, 292–324.
14. Jacquelyn Dowd Hall, "'The Mind That Burns in Each Body': Women, Rape and Racial Violence," in *Powers of Desire: The Politics of Sexuality*, ed. Ann Snitow, Christine Stansell, and Sharon Thompson (New York, 1983), 339.
15. Thomas J. Kernan, "The Jurisprudence of Lawlessness," in Report of the Twenty-ninth Annual Meeting of the American Bar Association (Philadelphia, 1906), 451, emphasis added.
16. Charles S. Sydnor, "The Southern and the Laws," *Journal of Southern History* 6 (Feb. 1940): 3–23; James W. Ely, Jr., and David J. Bodenhamer, "Regionalism and the Legal History of the South," in *Ambivalent Legacy: A Legal History of the South*, ed. David J. Bodenhamer and James W. Ely, Jr. (Jackson, Miss., 1984), 3–29; Wyatt-Brown, *Southern Honor*, 362–401.
17. Tampa *Sunland Tribune*, March 16, 1882. See also Tallahassee *Weekly Floridian*, March 14, 1882.
18. Tampa *Sunland Tribune*, March 9, 1882.
19. Ibid., March 23, 1882.
20. *Bartow Informant*, April 1, 1882.
21. *Jacksonville Union* and *Monticello Constitution*, quoted in Tampa *Sunland Tribune*, March 16, 1882.
22. For discussions of southern republicanism, see Edmund S. Morgan, *American Slavery, American Freedom: The Ordeal of Colonial Virginia* (New York, 1976), 369–87; Robert Kelley, *The Cultural Pattern in American Politics: The First Century* (New York, 1979), 84, 99, 271–72; Edward L. Ayers, *Vengeance and Justice: Crime and Punishment in the 19th-Century American South* (New York, 1984), 40–46, 164–65, 245–46.
23. Tallahassee *Weekly Floridian*, March 14, 1882.
24. Jacksonville *Florida Daily Times*, March 10, 1882; Tampa *Sunland Tribune*, March 9, 1882.
25. Lynching, or participation in mob violence, was not a crime under either common law or Florida statutes, but anyone who took part in a lynching could have been charged with related criminal offenses, such as kidnapping or murder (James Harmon Chadbourn, *Lynching and the Law* [Chapel Hill, N.C., 1933], 29; Cutler, *Lynch-Law*, 227–52).
26. Tampa *Sunland Tribune*, April 6, 1882. Local autonomy was accepted by Florida's Governor William D. Bloxham who, according to one historian, took the position that, "regardless of the race of the victim, [he] would not move to bring the perpetrators of a lynching to trial without the support of the local Democratic leaders" (Edward C. Williamson, *Florida Politics in the Gilded Age, 1877–1893* [Gainesville, Fla., 1976], 88).
27. Donald L. Chamberlin, "Fort Brooke: Frontier Outpost, 1824–42," *Tampa*

Bay History 7 (Spring/Summer 1985): 5–29; James W. Covington, "The Armed Occupation Act of 1842," Florida Historical Quarterly 40 (July 1961): 41–52; Janet Snyder Matthews, Edge of Wilderness: A Settlement History of Manatee River and Sarasota Bay, 1528–1885 (Tulsa, 1983), 151–70.

28. John Solomon Otto, "Hillsborough County (1850): A Community in the South Florida Flatwoods," Florida Historical Quarterly 62 (Oct. 1983): 180–93; John Solomon Otto, "Florida's Cattle-Ranching Frontier: Hillsborough County (1860)," Florida Historical Quarterly 63 (July 1984): 71–83; Rodney E. Dillon, Jr., "South Florida in 1860," Florida Historical Quarterly 60 (April 1982): 440–54.
29. Otto, "Hillsborough County (1860)," 80–83; Eirlys Barker, "The Ruling Race in Ante-bellum Hillsborough County," 4–13, manuscript in possession of author; Eighth Census of the United States, 1860, Hillsborough County, Florida, Slave Schedules, National Archives Microcopy No. 653, roll 110, in the University of South Florida Library, Tampa.
30. Tampa Florida Peninsular, March 31, 1860.
31. Ibid., Feb. 23, 1861.
32. James W. Covington, The Billy Bowlegs War, 1855–1858: The Final Stand of the Seminoles Against the Whites (Chuluota, Fla., 1982), 41–49; Anthony P. Pizzo, Tampa Town, 1824–1886: The Cracker Village With a Latin Accent (Miami, 1968), 57–58.
33. Tampa Florida Peninsular, Jan. 21, 1860.
34. Ibid., April 17, 1858.
35. Ibid., April 24, 1858, emphasis in original.
36. Ibid., May 1, 1858, emphasis in original.
37. Ibid., For the use of the term "regulator," see Brown, Strain of Violence, 58.
38. Tampa Florida Peninsular, Sept. 11, 1858.
39. Ibid., Nov. 5, 1859.
40. Ibid., Jan. 21, 1860.
41. Ibid. Neither Adam's race nor his slave status elicited any special comment in this defense of lynching. The value of slaves as property naturally tended to limit the willingness to punish them with death, but Ulrich B. Phillips found several cases of slaves who were lynched for rape and/or murder during the 1840s and 1850s (Phillips, American Negro Slavery [New York, 1918], 460–63, 511).
42. Pizzo, Tampa Town, 65–71; Grismer, Tampa, 139–49.
43. Tampa Sunland Tribune, June 8, 1878.
44. U.S. Census Office, Eleventh Census of the United States: 1890, Population, pt. 1 (Washington, D.C., 1895), 84.
45. Tampa Sunland Tribune, June 8, 1878.
46. Ralph L. Peek, "Lawlessness and the Restoration of Order in Florida, 1868–1871" (Ph.D. diss., University of Florida, 1964), 218; Grismer, Tampa, 150–62.
47. Tampa Florida Peninsular, Jan. 25, 1871.
48. Ibid., July 8, 1871.
49. Ibid., June 17 (second quotation), 24 (first quotation), 1871.
50. Ibid., Aug. 18, 1877.
51. Ibid., Aug. 24, 1877.
52. For studies that emphasize the persistence of antebellum values in the postwar South, see Cash, Mind of the South, 179–85; Jay R. Mandle, The

Roots of Black Poverty: The Southern Plantation Economy After the Civil War (Durham, N.C., 1978), 28–38; Jonathan M. Wiener, Social Origins of the New South: Alabama, 1860–1885 (Baton Rouge, La., 1978), 186–221; Gaston, New South Creed, 153–86; Ayers, Vengeance and Justice, 141–84.

53. Esther J. Crooks and Ruth W. Crooks, The Ring Tournament in the United States (Richmond, Va., 1936), 1–10; Grismer, Tampa, 167–68; Donald B. McKay, Pioneer Florida, 1 (Tampa, Fla., [1959]), 51.
54. Tampa Sunland Tribune, Jan. 6, 1877.
55. Ibid., Jan. 1, 1881; Tallahassee Weekly Floridian, Feb. 17, 1887.
56. Wyatt-Brown, Southern Honor, 440–53; E. P. Thompson, "'Rough Music': Le Charivari anglais," Annales: Economies, Sociétés, Civilisations 27 (March/April 1972): 285–312.
57. McKay, Pioneer Florida, I, 48.
58. Ibid., 49.
59. Ibid., 14–15, 19; Rollin G. Osterweis, Romanticism and Nationalism in the Old South (New Haven, 1949), 41–53, 96–102; Clement Eaton, The Growth of Southern Civilization, 1790–1860 (New York, 1961), 17, 190–91; Wyatt-Brown, Southern Honor, 339–50; 440–50.
60. U.S. Census Office, Compendium of the Tenth Census, Pt. 1 (Washington, D.C., 1883), 495. The data on Tampa's population were derived from manuscript census returns, Tenth Census of the United States, 1880, Hillsborough County, Florida, Population Schedules, National Archives Microfilm Series T-9, roll 128.
61. Makers of America: Florida Edition, 1 (Atlanta, 1909), 281–83; Who Was Who in America, 1 (Chicago, 1942), 739.
62. Ex Parte Wall, 107 U.S. 269; National Cyclopedia of American Biography, 6 (New York, 1929), 147; Grismer, Tampa, 331.
63. Ex Parte Wall, 107 U.S. 266, 269.
64. Ibid., 267–68.
65. Ibid.
66. Ibid., 267.
67. Ibid., 270.
68. In re Wall, 13 F. 814 (1882), 817–20.
69. Tampa Sunland Tribune, March 23, 1882.
70. Ibid., March 23 (first quotation), April 13 (second quotation), 1882.
71. Ibid., March 23, 1882.
72. Tallahassee Weekly Floridian, March 21, 1882.
73. Monticello Constitution, quoted in Tampa Sunland Tribune, March 30, 1882.
74. Tampa Guardian, quoted in ibid., March 23, 1882.
75. Bartow Informant, April 1, 1882; Tampa Sunland Tribune, April 6, 20, 1882.
76. Ayers, Vengeance and Justice, 19–26.
77. In re Wall, 13 F. 820. The Tennessee case was Smith v. State, 1 Yeager 228 (1829).
78. Tampa Sunland Tribune, April 13, 1882.
79. Key West Democrat, quoted in ibid., March 30, 1882.
80. Ibid., March 23, 1882.
81. Tampa Guardian, quoted in ibid., March 16, 1882.
82. Ibid.
83. Charles E. Harrision, Genealogical Records of the Pioneers of Tampa

and of Some Who Came After Them (Tampa, 1915), 24–28; James M. Ingram, "John Perry Wall: A Man for All Seasons," Tampa Historical Society Sunland Tribune 2 (Oct. 1975): 9–19.
84. Tampa Sunland Tribune, Oct. 10, 1881; Harrison, Genealogical Records, 28–30; National Cyclopedia of American Biography, VI, 147.
85. The wives of John P. Wall and Howell T. Lykes were the sisters of John A. McKay, whose home was invaded by Charles Owens. Grismer, Tampa, 319, 330, 331; Donald B. McKay, Pioneer Florida, 3 (Tampa, 1959), 3–5; Tampa Sunland Tribune, May 4, 1882.
86. George B. Church, Jr., The Life of Henry Laurens Mitchell, Florida's 16th Governor (New York, 1978), 1–4.
87. Tampa Florida Peninsular, April 20, 1861.
88. Church, Mitchell, 9–32; National Cyclopedia of American Biography, 11 (New York, 1909), 383.
89. Harrison, Genealogical Records, 57; Biographical Directory of the American Congress, 1774–1961 (Washington, 1961), 1635; Tampa Sunland Tribune, Nov. 26, 1881, April 6, 1882. Stephen Sparkman was a cousin of Tampa's mayor, George B. Sparkman (Grismer, Tampa, 316).
90. For a discussion of the significance of titles in the old South, see Wyatt-Brown, Southern Honor, 157–58.
91. Ibid., 354; Cash, Mind of the South, 111–12.
92. See, for example, Tampa Sunland Tribune, March 23, April 13, 1882.
93. Wyatt-Brown, Southern Honor, 397.
94. Ex Parte Wall, 107 U.S. 265.
95. Ibid., 271. According to Richard Maxwell Brown, New Jersey was an "Eastern non-vigilante state" (Brown, Strain of Violence, 170).
96. Ex Parte Wall, 107 U.S. 271, 272.
97. Ibid., 272.
98. Ibid., 288.
99. Ibid., 275.
100. Ibid., 274.
101. Ibid., 290, 291.
102. Allen Morris, The People of Lawmaking in Florida, 1822–1983 (Tallahassee, Fla., 1982); National Cyclopedia of American Biography, vol. 6, 147.
103. Tampa Morning Tribune, Jan. 2, 1900.
104. McKay, Pioneer Florida, II, 439–40. McKay's aunt was John P. Wall's second wife (Grismer, Tampa, 319, 332).
105. Tampa Morning Tribune, May 12, 1899.
106. Ibid., Feb. 2, 1911.
107. Ibid., Feb. 9, 1911.
108. Address of Herbert S. Phillips, [Feb. 8, 1911], p. 2, typescript in box 3, Herbert S. Phillips Papers, University of South Florida Special Collections, Tampa, Fla.
109. Letter to the Editor, Nation 36 (Feb. 22, 1883): 170.
110. "The Southern Street Duel," Outlook 90 (Dec. 5, 1908): 773.
111. Jacksonville Florida Times-Union, June 17, 1885. See also Redfield, Homicide, 204; Woodward, Origins of the New South, 158–60.
112. Tampa Guardian, May 26, 1886; Jacksonville Florida Times-Union, April 19, 1887.
113. Tampa Morning Tribune, Sept. 5, 1895.
114. Redfield, Homicide, 197.

115. Tallahassee *Floridian*, Oct. 27, 1865, quoted in Jerrell H. Shofner, *Nor Is It Over Yet: Florida in the Era of Reconstruction, 1863–1877* (Gainesville, Fla., 1974), 41.
116. See, for example, Tampa *Florida Peninsula*, Feb. 6, May 11, 1870, Jan. 4, Feb. 18, March 15, April 5, 1871.
117. U.S. Census Office, *Ninth Census: The Statistics of the Population of the United States*, 1 (Washington, D.C., 1872), 98.
118. Tampa *Sunland Tribune*, May 26, 1877.
119. *Webb's Jacksonville and Consolidated Directory of the Representative Cities of East and South Florida, 1886* (Jacksonville, 1886), 523, 552, 530.
120. *Tampa Journal*, June 23, 1887.
121. *Tampa Tribune*, May 31, 1888.
122. Ibid., July 13, 1892.
123. Tampa's biracial society was complicated by the presence of Afro-Cubans, who represented 13 percent of Cuban immigrants in Tampa at the turn of the century. Under increased pressure to observe local segregation, Afro-Cubans formed their own social institutions, but they remained integrated in the work force of the cigar factories (Susan D. Greenbaum, "Afro-Cubans in Exile: Tampa, Florida, 1886–1984," *Cuban Studies/Estudios Cubanos* 15 [Winter 1985]: 59–72).
124. U.S. Census Bureau, *Thirteenth Census of the United States: 1910, Population*, 2 (Washington, D.C., 1913), 330.
125. *Tampa Morning Tribune*, Dec. 14, 1900.
126. Jesse Jefferson Jackson, "The Negro and the Law in Florida, 1821–1921: Legal Patterns of Segregation and Control in Florida, 1821–1921" (M.A. thesis, Florida State University, 1960), 86–106; J. Morgan Kousser, *The Shaping of Southern Politics: Suffrage Restriction and the Establishment of the One-Party South* (New Haven, Conn., 1974), 91–103; Jerrell H. Shofner, "Custom, Law, and History: The Enduring Influence of Florida's 'Black Code,'" *Florida Historical Quarterly* 55 (Jan. 1977): 277–98. For racial practices in other New South cities, see Howard N. Rabinowitz, *Race Relations in the Urban South, 1865–1890* (New York, 1978).
127. *Tampa Tribune*, Oct. 5, 1892.
128. *Tampa Morning Tribune*, Aug. 14, 16, 18, 23, 1895.
129. Ibid., Sept. 13, 1895. In 1895, Tampa avoided a lynching after Harry Singleton, a twenty-five-year-old "negro desperado," was arrested for killing a white policeman. When a lynch mob gathered, local authorities quickly arrested one ringleader and called out the militia. After being convicted of the crime and exhausting his appeals, Singleton was executed in 1898. This was Tampa's first legal execution since 1860 (ibid., Sept. 27, Oct. 6, 1895, Jan. 8, 1898).
130. Ibid., June 23, 1899.
131. Ibid., Jan. 22, 1921.
132. Hall, "'Mind That Burns,'" 339.
133. *Tampa Morning Tribune*, Aug. 4, 1901.
134. *St. Petersburg Times*, June 8, 1901.
135. *Tampa Morning Tribune*, Aug. 24, Nov. 21, 1901.
136. Ibid., Nov. 21, 1901.
137. Ibid., Dec. 3, 1903. For the Houston incident, see ibid., July 31–Aug. 2, 1903; Gainesville *Sun*, Aug. 4, 1903.
138. *Tampa Morning Tribune*, Dec. 5, 1903. See also *Chicago Tribune*, Dec. 6, 1903.

224  Notes to Pages 30–33

139. Cutler, *Lynch-Law*, 176; George M. Frederickson, *The Black Image in the White Mind: The Debate on Afro-American Character and Destiny, 1817–1914* (New York, 1971), 256–82; Joel Williamson, *The Crucible of Race: Black-White Relations in the American South Since Emancipation* (New York, 1984), 185–89, 306–10.
140. *Tampa Morning Tribune*, Dec. 5, 1903. See also Jacksonville *Florida Times-Union*, Dec. 6, 1903.
141. *Tampa Morning Tribune*, Dec. 6, 1903.
142. Ibid., Dec. 9, 1903.
143. *Tampa Tribune*, May 14, 1891.

### 2. The Origins of Antilabor Vigilantism

1. *Tampa Journal*, June 23, 1887.
2. Grismer, *Tampa*, 170–81; Durward Long, "The Historical Beginnings of Ybor City and Modern Tampa," *Florida Historical Quarterly* 45 (July 1966): 31–35; Minutes of the Tampa Board of Trade, May 7, 1885, Tampa Chamber of Commerce, Tampa, Fla.
3. L. Glenn Westfall, "Don Vicente Martínez Ybor, The Man and His Empire: Development of the Clear Havana Industry in Cuba and Florida in the Nineteenth Century" (Ph.D. diss., University of Florida, 1977), 17–26, 38–75; Jean Stubbs, *Tobacco on the Periphery: A Case Study in Cuban Labour History, 1860–1958* (Cambridge, 1985), 17–20; Jesse L. Keene, "Gavino Gutiérrez and His Contributions to Tampa," *Florida Historical Quarterly* 36 (July 1957): 38–39.
4. L. Glenn Westfall, "Latin Entrepreneurs and the Birth of Ybor City," *Tampa Bay History* 7 (Fall/Winter 1985): 5–10; Minutes of the Tampa Board of Trade, October 5, 1885.
5. Stanley Buder, *Pullman: An Experiment in Industrial Order and Community Planning, 1880–1930* (New York, 1967), 38–74, 92–104; *Tampa Journal*, December 29, 1886; *Tampa Tribune*, February 23, 1888; *Tampa Morning Tribune*, January 21, 1900; *Tampa Guardian*, May 5, 1886.
6. Horace B. Davis, "Company Towns," *Encyclopedia of the Social Sciences*, 4 (New York, 1942), 119.
7. A. Stuart Campbell, *The Cigar Industry of Tampa, Florida* (Gainesville, Fla., 1939), 13–14, 19; Stubbs, *Tobacco on the Periphery*, 68–72.
8. WPA Federal Writers' Project, "Life History of Fernando Lemos," manuscript copy in Univ. of South Florida Special Collections, Tampa, Fla.
9. Campbell, *Cigar Industry of Tampa*, 19–20. Hereinafter, the term "cigarworker" is used to describe any employee involved in the production process, regardless of the particular skill involved. "Cigarmaker" refers to a worker responsible for rolling cigars. From the beginning of Ybor City, immigrant women were employed as cigarworkers, especially as "strippers" to remove the stems from tobacco leaves. By the 1920s, women had moved into most other cigar trades, including cigarmaking (*Tampa Guardian*, May 5, 1886; Nancy A. Hewitt, "Women in Ybor City: An Interview with a Woman Cigarworker," *Tampa Bay History* 7 [Fall/Winter 1985]: 161–65). For a discussion of the similar production process used by hand cigarworkers in northern factories, see Patricia Ann Cooper, "From Hand Craft to Mass Production: Men, Women and Work Culture in American

Cigar Factories, 1900–1919" (Ph.D. diss., University of Maryland, 1981), 48–87.

10. Campbell, *Cigar Industry of Tampa*, 4–5; David A. McCabe, *The Standard Rate in American Trade Unions* (Baltimore, 1912), 185–88, 212–25; U.S. Bureau of Labor Statistics, Bulletin 161, *Wages and Hours of Labor in the Clothing and Cigar Industries, 1911 to 1913* (Washington, D.C., 1915), 66; *Cigar Makers' Official Journal* (hereinafter *CMOJ*), June 1890; *Tampa Daily Times*, Dec. 28, 1921. Unlike other factory workers in the South who were historically paid less than similar workers in the North, Florida's cigarmakers had wage rates that were equal to or higher than those of their northern colleagues during the 1880s (Melton Alonza McLaurin, *The Knights of Labor in the South* [Westport, Conn., 1978], 18–20).

11. Campbell, *Cigar Industry of Tampa*, 8, 19 (quotation). Cigarmakers had a certain degree of control over the workplace, but they also labored in a distinctly unhealthy environment where employees spat on dirty floors and factory windows were commonly kept closed in order to maintain the warm, moist atmosphere necessary for working the tobacco. A 1904 report by a Florida health official found that there was "no hygienic precaution" in any of Tampa's cigar factories. Similar conditions around the country help explain why cigarworkers ranked second only to stone cutters in the national mortality rate for tuberculosis at the turn of the century (Durward Long, "An Immigrant Co-Operative Medicine Program in the South, 1887–1963," *Journal of Southern History* 17 [Nov. 1965]: 422 (quotation); *El Internacional*, April 19, 1918; Cooper, "From Hand Craft to Mass Production," 55).

12. Louis A. Pérez, Jr., "Reminiscences of a *Lector*: Cuban Cigar Workers in Tampa," *Florida Historical Quarterly* 53 (April 1975): 445–46, 446–47. See also Stubbs, *Tobacco on the Periphery*, 97–99.

13. Jose Yglesias, *The Truth About Them* (New York, 1971), 207.

14. *Tampa Journal*, December 29, 1886.

15. Richard Price, "The Labour Process and Labour History," *Social History* 8 (Jan. 1983): 62; David Montgomery, *Workers' Control in America: Studies in the History of Work, Technology, and Labor Struggles* (Cambridge, 1979), 25. The militancy of cigarworkers throughout the United States is reflected in strike data which show that of leading industries, the tobacco industry had the highest number of strikes per employee for the period 1881–1905. P. K. Edwards, *Strikes in the United States, 1881–1974* (New York, 1981), 105–06.

16. *El Internacional*, Nov. 23, 1921.

17. Campbell, *Cigar Industry of Tampa*, 1, 5.

18. Local boosters chose to overlook the brief delay that V. M. Ybor & Company experienced in starting production in Ybor City, reportedly because cigarworkers struck in protest against the hiring of a Spanish foreman (*Tobacco Leaf*, February 5, 1887; José Rivero Muniz, *The Ybor City Story, 1885–1954*, trans. by Eustasio Fernandez and Henry Beltran [Tampa, 1976], 11). One historian has claimed that the absence of stripped tobacco prevented Martínez Ybor's firm from commencing production when originally scheduled, but he provides no documentation for this claim (Long, "Beginnings of Ybor City," 35).

19. *Tampa Guardian*, June 9, 30, 1886; *Tampa Journal*, Dec. 29, 1886.

20. Gerald Eugene Poyo, "Cuban Émigré Communities in the United States and the Independence of Their Homeland, 1852–1895" (Ph.D. diss., University of Florida, 1983), 247; McLaurin, *Knights of Labor*, 48–49. In addition to the local assembly of cigarworkers in Ybor City, the Knights of Labor had two other mixed locals in Tampa, and all three of these locals were organized in 1886 (Jonathan Garlock and N. C. Builder, "Knights of Labor Data Bank: User's Manual and Index to Local Assemblies" [1973], computer printout in Department of Archives and Manuscripts, Catholic University of America Library, Washington, D.C.).
21. *Tampa Journal*, Feb. 2, 1887.
22. Ibid. See also *Tobacco Leaf*, Feb. 5, 1887.
23. *Tobacco Leaf*, Jan. 29, Feb. 5, 1887; Jacksonville *Florida Times-Union*, Jan. 28, 29, Feb. 2, 1887.
24. Jacksonville *Florida Times-Union*, Feb. 2, 15, 1887; *Tampa Journal*, Feb. 2, 9, 1887.
25. *Tobacco*, Jan. 28, 1887.
26. *Tampa Journal*, Jan. 26, Feb. 9, 1887. In the wake of the strike, the Tampa correspondent for a Jacksonville newspaper reported: "The temporary suspension of business in the great cigar factory [of V. M. Ybor] affected business somewhat throughout the city [of Tampa]" (Jacksonville *Florida Times-Union*, Feb. 15, 1887).
27. *Tampa Journal*, Feb. 9, 1887.
28. Minutes of the Tampa Board of Trade, March 8, 1887.
29. *United States Tobacco Journal*, March 19, 1887.
30. Minutes of the Tampa Board of Trade, March 8, 1887.
31. "Statement of the Committee of Fifteen," March 9, 1887, in *Tampa Tribune*, March 12, 1887.
32. *Tobacco Leaf*, March 19, 1887.
33. Ibid.
34. *Tampa Tribune*, March 12, 1887; *New York Herald*, March 13, 1887. The two Cubans charged with murder were subsequently tried in Tampa and found not guilty (*Tampa Tribune*, Feb. 16, 1888).
35. *Tampa Tribune*, March 12, 1887.
36. Ibid.
37. Ibid., emphasis added. For the background of Thomas K. Spencer, see Harrison, *Genealogical Records*; Grismer, *Tampa*, 181, 318. For the Haymarket bombing and Tampa's reaction to it, see Paul Avrich, *The Haymarket Tragedy* (Princeton, N.J., 1984); *Tampa Guardian*, May 12, 19, 1886.
38. See supra, 11–12.
39. *Tampa Journal*, March 24, 1887. For the background of William N. Conoley, see *Tampa Guardian*, Oct. 13, 1886; *Tampa Journal*, June 23, 1887.
40. Jacksonville *Florida Times-Union*, March 22, 1887.
41. Minutes of the Tampa Board of Trade, May 19, 1886; *Florida State Gazetteer and Business Directory, 1883–84* (Jacksonville, n.d.), 362–65; Grismer, *Tampa*, 178–80; *Tampa Tribune*, September 15, 1887.
42. *Tampa Journal*, Jan. 26, June 23, 1887. Between 1880 and 1890, the assessed value of property in Hillsborough County went from $751,347 to $4,317,844, which represented an increase of 574 percent (U.S. Census Office, *Eleventh Census, 1890: Report on Wealth, Debt, and Taxation*, 2 [Washington, D.C., 1895], 66). For a discussion of rising property values

as a source of capital accumulation, see Maurice Dobb, *Studies in the Development of Capitalism* (New York, 1963), 176–81.
43. *Key West Democrat*, quoted in *Tampa Journal*, March 24, 1887.
44. *New York Herald*, March 14, 1887.
45. Resolutions of the Cuban Federation of Cigar Makers of Key West, April 5, 1887, L. W. Bethel to the Attorney General, May 17, 1887, box 315 (2929/1887), Central Files, Department of Justice Records, R.G. 60, National Archives, Washington, D.C.
46. Tilly, Tilly, and Tilly, *The Rebellious Century*, 46.
47. *Tampa Journal*, March 31, June 2 (quotation), 1887; *Tampa Tribune*, April 29, May 15, 1887. In January 1888, the Board of Trade formally thanked local cigar manufacturers "for their successful efforts in inducing other wealthy factories" to relocate in Tampa, and the board "welcome[d] heartily the new comers reiterating the assurances of last summer that they shall be protected in their persons and property" (Minutes of the Tampa Board of Trade, Jan. 10, 1888, Tampa Board of Trade Records).
48. *Tampa Tribune*, April 22, 1887.
49. Ibid., June 17, 1887.
50. Minutes of the Tampa City Council, July 15, 18, August 16, 1887, Tampa City Clerk's Office, Tampa, Fla.
51. Long, "Beginnings of Ybor City," 42; U.S. Census Office, *Eleventh Census, 1890: Population of the U.S.*, pt I (Washington, D.C., 1895), 454.
52. *Tampa Tribune*, May 25, 1894.
53. *CMOJ*, March and April, 1889; Poyo, "Cuban Émigré Communities," 245–318; Stubbs, *Tobacco on the Periphery*, 86–87, 105. The geographic mobility of cigarmakers, "the traveling fraternity" as they referred to themselves, was common to the trade. One study of Tampa's Afro-Cubans, most of whom were cigarworkers, found "a pattern of circulatory migration" which removed over 90 percent of this relatively small group from the city between 1899 and 1900. The Afro-Cubans who departed were replaced by a comparable number of new arrivals (Greenbaum, "Afro-Cubans in Exile," 63–64; see also Patricia A. Cooper, "The 'Traveling Fraternity': Union Cigar Makers and Geographic Mobility, 1900–1919," *Journal of Social History*, 17 [Fall 1983]: 127–38).
54. Poyo, "Cuban Émigré Communities," 245–83; Gerald E. Poyo, "Tampa Cigarworkers and the Struggle for Cuban Independence," *Tampa Bay History* 7 (Fall/Winter 1985): 94–105.
55. José Rivero Muniz, "Tampa at the Close of the Nineteenth Century," *Florida Historical Quarterly* 41 (April 1963): 339; *La Revista de Flórida*, quoted in Poyo, "Cuban Émigré Communities," 252.
56. Poyo, "Cuban Émigré Communities," 245–312; Joan Marie Steffy, "The Cuban Immigrants of Tampa, Florida, 1886–1898" (M.A. thesis, University of South Florida, 1975), 61–70.
57. *Tampa Tribune*, May 7, 1891. By the end of 1892, in the wake of the founding of the Cuban Revolutionary Party, the cause of *Cuba Libre* had attracted the public support of several leading Spanish anarchists and a number of Cuban anarchists living in Florida's émigré communities (Poyo, "Tampa Cigarworkers," 101).
58. *Tampa Tribune*, Aug. 1–3, 8, 1892.
59. Ibid., Aug. 15, 1892.
60. Ibid., Aug. 18, 1892.
61. Ibid., Aug. 16, 20, 22, 25, 26, 1892.

62. Ibid., Aug. 1, 1892.
63. Ibid., Aug. 27, 1892. For discussion of the hysterical fear of anarchists in the United States during this period, see John Higham, *Strangers in the Land: Patterns of American Nativism, 1860–1925* (New York, 1963), 52–56, 78; Avrich, *Haymarket Tragedy*, 215–19, 428–31.
64. *Tampa Tribune*, Sept. 1, 1892.
65. Ibid., Sept. 2, 1892, emphasis added.
66. Ibid., Sept. 6, 1892.
67. Ibid., Sept. 7, 1892. Other members of the "committee of five" were: J. C. McNeill, an architect and contractor who owned a store in Ybor City and also served as president of the Tampa City Council; and C. E. Parcell, an architect and contractor who had built several large projects in Ybor City. *The Gate-to-the-Gulf City Directory, 1893* (Tampa, 1893), 121, 164, 173, 177, 196; *Tampa Morning Tribune*, Jan. 21, 1900; Grismer, *Tampa*, 183, 191.
68. *Tampa Tribune*, Sept. 8, 1892. This attack on Latin cigarworkers was unusual in that it reflected nativist attitudes. Members of the Tampa elite generally refrained from publicly expressing such prejudice at a time when they were courting Latin capitalists.
69. *Tampa Tribune*, Oct. 11–12, 1892; *Tobacco Leaf*, Sept. 14, Oct. 12, 1892.
70. The antilabor stance of Tampa's elite was in marked contrast to the support given strikers by local property owners, including merchants and professionals, in some northern communities studied by Herbert G. Gutman. Focusing on responses to industrialization in several small cities during the 1870s, Gutman found that new industrialists encountered criticism and even opposition from nonindustrial capitalists who held local positions of power and prestige. According to Gutman, members of the existing elite initially perceived the new industrialist as "a disruptive outsider," whereas "the discontented worker still was viewed by his fellow citizens as an individual and was not yet the stereotyped 'labor agitator'" (*Work, Culture and Society in Industrializing America: Essays in American Working-Class and Social History* [New York, 1976], 256, 319). In Tampa, however, cigarworkers were not only militant trade unionists who acted collectively, but they were also largely aliens who lacked political power. For evidence that members of local elites sided with factory owners in other towns in the South, even when the labor force was composed of native-born whites, see Melton Alonza McLaurin, *Paternalism and Protest: Southern Cotton Mill Workers and Organized Labor, 1875–1905* (Westport, Conn., 1971), 56–57, 145–47, 150–51, 207–09.
71. *Tampa Tribune*, Oct. 19, 1891.

### 3. "Pro Bono Publico": The Citizens' Committee of 1901

1. U.S. Census Office, *Twelfth Census of the United States: 1900, Population*, pt. 1 (Washington, D.C., 1901), 612; Durward Long, "The Making of Modern Tampa: A City of the New South, 1885–1911," *Florida Historical Quarterly* 49 (April 1971): 337–41; *Tampa Morning Tribune*, June 30, 1896, quoted in Gary R. Mormino, "Tampa and the New Urban South: The Weight Strike of 1899," *Florida Historical Quarterly* 60 (Jan. 1982): 339.
2. Grismer, *Tampa*, 204–05, 340; Steffy, "Cuban Immigrants," 55–56.

3. "West Tampa's Cigar Factories Reminders of Area's Past Boom," Tampa Historical Society *Sunland Tribune* 7 (Nov. 1981): 112–18, 146; Arsenio M. Sanchez, "Incentives Helped to Build West Tampa," ibid., 11 (Dec. 1985): 9–13.
4. Tony Pizzo, "The Italian Heritage in Tampa," ibid., 3 (Nov. 1977): 24–33; WPA Federal Writers' Project, "Life History of John Cacciatore," 1, typescript in University of South Florida Special Collections, Tampa, Fla.; Gary R. Mormino and George E. Pozzetta, *The Immigrant World of Ybor City: Italians and Their Latin Neighbors in Tampa, 1885–1985* (Urbana, Ill., 1987), 81–91. For examples of the common local usage of the word "Latin" to describe people living in Tampa who came from Latin America, Spain and Italy, see *El Internacional*, March 14, 1919; *Tampa Morning Tribune*, Oct. 22, 1920.
5. *U.S. Tobacco Journal*, Dec. 9, 1899; U.S. Census Office, *Twelfth Census of the United States: 1900: Manufacturers*, vol. 8, pt. 2 (Washington, D.C., 1902), 128. Data on numbers of cigar factories vary widely since "factory" could include everything from a plant with hundreds of workers to a small shop (*chinchale* or "buckeye") run by a cigarmaker and his family. In addition, cigar factories required little capital investment for the plant or equipment which meant that smaller owners regularly went in and out of business with little notice. However, the number of cigars produced was carefully recorded by the U.S. Bureau of Internal Revenue for tax purposes (Stubbs, *Tobacco on the Periphery*, 77; Campbell, *Cigar Industry of Tampa*, 31, 46–47).
6. U.S. Immigration Commission, *Immigrants in Industries*, pt. 14 (Washington, D.C., 1911), 187.
7. Mormino and Pozzetta, *Immigrant World*, 175–205; Greenbaum, "Afro-Cubans in Exile," 61–62; Long, "Co-Operative Medicine," 417–34.
8. Poyo, "Cuban Émigré Communities," 205–353; George E. Pozzetta, "Immigrants and Radicals in Tampa, Florida," *Florida Historical Quarterly* 57 (Jan. 1979): 337–39.
9. Angelo Massari, *The Wonderful Life of Angelo Massari* (New York, 1965), 56.
10. Louis A. Pérez, Jr., "Cubans in Tampa: From Exiles to Immigrants, 1892–1901," *Florida Historical Quarterly* 57 (Oct. 1978): 133–35.
11. *Tobacco*, July 14, 1899. See also *Tobacco Leaf*, Aug. 23, 1899; Cooper, "From Hand Craft to Mass Production," 151.
12. *Tobacco*, May 12, 19, 1899.
13. Montgomery, *Workers' Control*, 98.
14. Mormino, "Weight Strike," 350–51; *Tampa Guardian*, May 5, 1886; WPA Federal Writers' Project, "Ybor City: Latin Populations," 164, 168, typescript in P. K. Yonge Library of Florida History, University of Florida, Gainesville.
15. *Tampa Morning Tribune*, Aug. 6, 15, 1899; Stubbs, *Tobacco on the Periphery*, 24–26; WPA Federal Writers' Project, "Life History of José Ramon Sanfeliz," 4, typescript in University of South Florida Special Collections, Tampa.
16. *Tobacco*, July 14, 1899.
17. Ibid., July 21, 1899.
18. *Tampa Morning Tribune*, July 8, 1899; Patricia A. Cooper, *Once a Cigar Maker: Men, Women, and Work Culture in American Cigar Factories, 1900–1919* (Urbana, Ill., 1987), 100, 104–07, 134–38, 294–99.

19. *Tobacco*, July 14, 1899.
20. *Tampa Morning Tribune*, May 4, 1899.
21. Dudley Haddock, *Wallace F. Stovall, A Publisher's Publisher* (n.p., 1949), 8–12, 15.
22. *Tampa Morning Tribune*, Oct. 18, 1898.
23. Ibid., Jan. 1, 1921; Haddock, *Stovall*, 6, 8, 12–13; Grismer, *Tampa*, 353–54.
24. *Tampa Morning Tribune*, July 14, 1899.
25. Ibid., June 17, 1899.
26. Ibid., July 7, 1899.
27. Ibid., Aug. 6, 8, 1899.
28. Ibid., Aug. 15, 1899; *CMOJ*, Sept. 1899. The Ybor-Manrara factory opposed a settlement for several more weeks, but the firm finally capitulated in September and reopened on the same terms (*Tobacco*, Sept. 22, 1899).
29. *Tobacco*, Aug. 18, 1899.
30. *Tobacco Leaf*, Aug. 23, 1899.
31. *Tobacco*, Aug. 18, 1899.
32. Ibid.
33. *Tobacco Leaf*, Aug. 23, 1899.
34. *Tampa Morning Tribune*, Aug. 9, 1899.
35. Ibid., July 13, 1899. See also ibid., July 11, 1899.
36. U.S. Department of Commerce, *Report of the Commissioner of Corporations on the Tobacco Industry*, pt. 1 (Washington, D.C., 1909), 153–54; *CMOJ*, Oct. 1899. By 1900, at least seventeen of Tampa's cigar manufacturers had their headquarters outside Florida, primarily in New York (R. G. Dun & Company, *Reference Book [and Key] Containing Ratings of Merchants, Manufacturers and Traders Generally, Throughout the United States and Canada* 127 [Jan. 1900], copy in Dun & Bradstreet, Inc., Library, New York).
37. *CMOJ*, April 1892.
38. Samuel Gompers, *Seventy Years of Life and Labor: An Autobiography*, 1 (New York, 1967 [1925]), 106–33, 164–82, 385; Cooper, "From Hand Craft to Mass Production," 3–5, 8. Gompers' ideas may have been more radical than commonly assumed, but at the time they certainly seemed conservative to most of Tampa's cigarworkers. For an examination of Gompers and the AFL "in the context of a Marxian tradition," see Stuart B. Kaufman, *Samuel Gompers and the Origins of the American Federation of Labor, 1848–1896* (Westport, Conn., 1973), 222 and passim.
39. *CMOJ*, June 1890.
40. Ibid., April, June, July and Aug. 1892, April 1893, April 1894, Feb. 1895, May 1896, May 1898, April 1899; John C. Appel, "The Unionization of Florida Cigarmakers and the Coming of the War With Spain," *Hispanic American Historical Review* 36 (Feb. 1956): 38–49.
41. *CMOJ*, Feb. 1900.
42. Ibid., Nov. 15, 1900.
43. Durward Long, "'La Resistencia': Tampa's Immigrant Labor Union," *Labor History* 6 (Fall 1965): 196.
44. *La Federación*, Dec. 14, 1900.
45. *American Federationist* 7 (Dec. 1900): 387.
46. *Tampa Morning Tribune*, Nov. 2, 19, 1900.
47. Ibid., Nov. 7, 1900.
48. *Tobacco Leaf*, Nov. 7, 1900.

49. *Tampa Morning Tribune*, Nov. 11, 1900. See also *U.S. Tobacco Journal*, Nov. 17, 1900; *Tobacco*, Nov. 23, 1900.
50. *Tampa Morning Tribune*, Nov. 16, 1900.
51. Ibid., Nov. 18, 1900.
52. Ibid., Nov. 21, 1900. See also ibid., Nov. 24, Dec. 1, 1900.
53. Ibid., Nov. 29, 1900. See also ibid., Nov. 23, 1900.
54. *Tobacco Leaf*, Nov. 24, 1900.
55. *Tampa Morning Tribune*, Nov. 16, 18, 20, 1900.
56. *Tobacco Leaf*, Nov. 28, 1900; *Tampa Morning Tribune*, Nov. 23, 1900.
57. *Tampa Morning Tribune*, Nov. 27, 1900.
58. Ibid.
59. Ibid., Dec. 2, 8, 11, 1900.
60. Ibid., Oct. 23, 1901; U.S. Dept. of Commerce, *Report on the Tobacco Industry*, pt. 1, 6–10, 26–27, 150–55, 291–92, 419–23.
61. Willis N. Baer, *The Economic Development of the Cigar Industry in the United States* (Lancaster, Pa., 1933), 103.
62. U.S. Department of Commerce, *Report of the Commissioner of Corporations on the Tobacco Industry*, pt. 2 (Washington, D.C., 1911), 31, 272. The successful antitrust suit that broke up the American Tobacco Company in 1911 had little impact on the firm's cigar interests since the company was allowed to retain ownership of the American Cigar Company (U.S. Department of Commerce, *Report of the Commissioner of Corporations on the Tobacco Industry*, pt. 3 [Washington, D.C., 1915], 210–216).
63. E. T. Ware, quoted in Durward Long, "Labor Relations in the Tampa Cigar Industry, 1885–1911," *Labor History* 12 (Fall 1971): 552.
64. *CMOJ*, Dec. 1901.
65. *U.S. Tobacco Journal*, June 8, 1901. See also *Tampa Morning Tribune*, June 12, 1901.
66. *U.S. Tobacco Journal*, June 23, 1901.
67. Ibid., June 8, 1901; *CMOJ*, Nov. 1901.
68. *Tampa Morning Tribune*, July 24, 1901; *U.S. Tobacco Journal*, July 13, 1901.
69. *Tampa Morning Tribune*, July 27, 1901.
70. Ibid., July 25, 1901.
71. *Tobacco Leaf*, July 31, 1901.
72. Ibid., Aug. 7, 1901.
73. *Mulberry Era*, quoted in *Tampa Morning Tribune*, July 28, 1901.
74. *Tampa Morning Tribune*, July 31, 1901; *Tobacco Leaf*, Aug. 7, 1901.
75. *Tampa Morning Tribune*, Aug. 6, 1901.
76. Ibid., Aug. 7, 1901. According to a subsequent report, Padilla had fled to Havana (ibid., Aug. 11, 1901).
77. *U.S. Tobacco Journal*, Aug. 10, 1901.
78. *Tampa Morning Tribune*, Aug. 7, 1901. See also *New York Herald*, Aug. 7, 1901.
79. *Tampa Morning Tribune*, Aug. 23, 1901. The Tampa correspondent for *Tobacco Leaf* had reported the destination was Honduras even before the ship had left Tampa (*Tobacco Leaf*, Aug. 7, 1901).
80. Jacksonville *Florida Times-Union and Citizen*, Aug. 8, 1901. The San Francisco Vigilance Committees of the 1850s also deported "undesirables," but there is no evidence that Tampa vigilantes were aware of this precedent (Senkewicz, *Vigilantes in San Francisco*, pp. 84, 169, 173).

81. *Tampa Morning Tribune*, Aug. 7, 1901.
82. Ibid., Aug. 8, 1901.
83. Ibid., Aug. 11, 1901; *Tobacco Leaf*, Aug. 7, 1901; *U.S. Tobacco Journal*, Aug. 10, 1901; Jacksonville *Florida Times-Union and Citizen*, Aug. 7, 1901.
84. *La Federación* "Suplemento," Aug. 1901.
85. Grismer, *Tampa*, 332–33; Keene, "Gavino Gutierrez," 40.
86. *Tampa Morning Tribune*, March 25, 1910.
87. Jacksonville *Florida Times-Union and Citizen*, Aug. 9, 1901.
88. *Tobacco*, Sept. 20, 1901.
89. *Tobacco Leaf*, Aug. 14, 1901; *Weekly Tallahassean*, Aug. 8, 1901.
90. *Tobacco Leaf*, Aug. 14, 1901.
91. Ibid., Aug 17, 1901. See also *Tobacco*, Aug. 9, 1901.
92. *U.S. Tobacco Journal*, Aug. 31, 1901.
93. Jacksonville *Florida Times-Union and Citizen*, Aug. 8, 1901. The International Typographical Union (ITU) local in Tampa formally protested the Labor Assembly's "hasty endorsement," emphasizing that one of the men kidnapped was a printer who belonged to the ITU. This referred to Luis Barcia who worked for *La Federación* (*Tampa Morning Tribune*, Aug. 9, 1901; *New York Herald*, Aug. 25, 1901).
94. *CMOJ*, Aug. 1901. See also ibid., Sept. and Nov. 1901. Despite such denials, indirect evidence strongly suggests that CMIU leaders in Tampa had advance knowledge of the plans of the Citizens' Committee. Nevertheless, they probably did not participate in the kidnappings which would have occurred regardless of the position of the CMIU. For evidence of the probable foreknowledge of CMIU officers, see James S. Jones to George Perkins, March 12, 1903, American Federation of Labor Records: The Samuel Gompers Era (microfilm edition, 1979), reel 139 (hereinafter cited as AFL Records); Perkins to Gompers, Dec. 22, 1909, ibid., reel 36; *Tampa Morning Tribune*, March 25, 1910.
95. St. Augustine *Evening Record*, Aug. 8, 1901.
96. Jacksonville *Florida Times-Union and Citizen*, Aug. 8, 1901.
97. Pensacola *Daily News*, Aug. 17, 1901, emphasis added.
98. *Gainesville Sun* quoted in *Tampa Morning Tribune*, Sept. 8, 1901.
99. *Kissimmee Gazette* quoted in *Tampa Morning Tribune*, Aug. 11, 1901.
100. *Savannah Morning News* quoted in *Tampa Morning Tribune*, Aug. 9, 1901. For an isolated criticism of the vigilante activities in Tampa during the strike, see *Cresent City News*, Sept. 12, 1901.
101. Jacksonville *Florida Times-Union and Citizen*, Aug. 8, 16, 1901. The men deported to Honduras were Luis Barcia, Pedro Casellas, Gabriel Grillo, José Fueyo, Cresencio Gonzales, Charles Kelly (an Afro-American cigarmaker), Estanislao Lanza, Félix Menendes, Belen Parrondo, Ramon Piquero, Severino Prieto, Francisco Rodriquez and Eustacio Valdes (*La Federación* "Suplemento," Aug. 1901; *New York Herald*, Aug. 8, 1901; *Sholes' Directory of the City of Tampa, 1901* [Tampa, n.d.], 267).
102. *New York Herald*, Aug. 11, 1901.
103. *Tampa Morning Tribune*, Aug. 11, 1901.
104. "Manifesto to the Workers and the People of Tampa," Aug. 1901, in microfilm collection of assorted Ybor City newspapers, University of South Florida Library, Tampa.
105. *L'Alba Sociale*, Aug. 15, 1901, reprinted in Pozzetta, "Radicals in Tampa," 348.

106. *U.S. Tobacco Journal*, Aug. 10, 1901; *Tobacco Leaf*, Aug. 21, 1901; Stubbs, *Tobacco on the Periphery*, 75.
107. *Tobacco Leaf*, Sept. 11, 1901.
108. Jacksonville *Florida Times-Union and Citizen*, Aug. 19, 1901; *Tampa Morning Tribune*, Aug. 18, 21, 1901; *Tobacco*, Aug. 23, 1901.
109. *Tobacco Leaf*, Aug., 28, 1901.
110. *Tampa Morning Tribune*, Aug. 27, 28, 1901; *U.S. Tobacco Journal*, Aug. 31, 1901.
111. *Tobacco Leaf*, Sept. 4, 1901.
112. *El Despertar*, Sept. 10, 1901; *Tobacco Leaf*, Sept. 25, 1901; *Tobacco*, Sept. 20, 27, 1901.
113. *U.S. Tobacco Journal*, Sept. 28, 1901.
114. Ibid., Oct. 5, 12, 1901; *Tobacco Leaf*, Sept. 25, 1901.
115. *Tampa Morning Tribune*, Sept. 19, 1901.
116. *Tobacco*, Sept. 30, 1901.
117. *Tampa Morning Tribune*, Sept. 21, 1901.
118. Ibid., Sept. 25, 1901.
119. *Pensacola News*, quoted in *Tampa Morning Tribune*, Sept. 29, 1901.
120. *Tampa Morning Tribune*, Sept. 22, 29, 1901.
121. Ibid., Oct. 3, 1901.
122. Ibid., Oct. 6, 1901.
123. *U.S. Tobacco Journal*, Oct. 12, 1901.
124. *Tampa Morning Tribune*, Oct. 3, 5, 1901.
125. *U.S. Tobacco Journal*, Oct. 12, 1901.
126. *Tobacco*, Oct. 11, 1901.
127. *Tobacco Leaf*, Oct. 9, 1901.
128. *Tobacco*, Oct. 25, 1901.
129. *U.S. Tobacco Journal*, Nov. 16, 1901.
130. *Tampa Morning Tribune*, Nov. 21, 1901.
131. *U.S. Tobacco Journal*, Nov. 23, 1901; *Tampa Morning Tribune*, Nov. 24, 1901.
132. *CMOJ*, Dec. 1901.
133. Isabel Otero, Loretta Casellas and Carolina Barcia to William S. Jennings, Aug. 12, 1901, box 6, William S. Jennings Papers, Florida State Archives, Tallahassee. See also Louisa Kelly to Jennings, Aug. 16, 1901, box 15, ibid.
134. For letters of protest, see box 6, ibid.
135. Department of Justice to J. N. Stripling, Oct. 9, 1901, box 128 (12993/1901), Year Files, Department of Justice Records.
136. J. N. Stripling to P. C. Knox, Oct. 14, 1901, ibid. See also *Tampa Morning Tribune*, Oct. 16, 1901.
137. *Tampa Morning Tribune*, Oct. 25, 1901.
138. Knight to William S. Jennings, Oct. 25, 1901, box 6, Jennings Papers. Knight's close association with the cigar industry dated to the beginning of the enterprise in Tampa when he served as attorney for the Ybor City Land and Improvement Co. In 1889, a Spanish-language labor newspaper described him as "the captain of the lynchers," because he headed a committee that forced a strike leader to leave Key West (*Tampa Morning Tribune*, May 10, 1899, Jan. 21, 1900; *El Productor*, quoted in Poyo, "Cuban Émigré Communities," 264).
139. William S. Jennings to Richard T. Hicks, Oct. 25, 1901, box 6, Jennings Papers.

140. *Tampa Morning Tribune*, Oct. 26, 1901.
141. Ibid., Nov. 1, 1901.
142. C. S. Wilson to William S. Jennings, Oct. 29, 1901, box 6, Jennings Papers.
143. *U.S. Tobacco Journal*, Oct. 19, 1901.
144. *Tobacco*, Aug. 16, 1901.
145. *U.S. Tobacco Journal*, Sept. 28, 1901. See also *Tobacco*, Sept. 20, 1901.
146. The consolidation of Tampa's ruling elite took a variety of forms during the early twentieth century. One that continues as a tradition today began in 1904 as a festival celebrating the exploits of a mythical pirate, José Gaspar, who had supposedly plundered ships sailing near his hideaway along Florida's Gulf coast. The annual festival was organized by members of the local elite who formed "Ye Mystic Krewe of Gasparilla" to lead the celebration. "Disguised as Latin pirates, members of the Anglo establishment invaded the city, acting out violence that was as much a part of themselves as the pirates they played," according to the recent interpretation of a French anthropologist. The mock invasion was followed by the mayor's surrendering the city to the "pirates" for a day of festivities. In addition to providing "the elite with the opportunity to display its wealth and self-assurance," the Gasparilla celebration served another purpose. "The ritual of the festival tried to open a safety valve to release the ethnic and social tensions in a city where the relations between the different classes and the different ethnic groups were marked by repressive violence in which a largely Anglo elite confronted mostly Latin and particularly militant workers" (André-Marcel d'Ans, "The Legend of Gasparilla: Myth and History on Florida's West Coast," trans. Marie-Joèle Ingalls, *Tampa Bay History* 2 [Fall/Winter 1980], 25, 26). One of the original members of the Gasparilla Krewe was a cigar manufacturer, Augustine A. Martínez (Edwin D. Lambright, *The Life and Exploits of Gasparilla, Last of the Buccaneers, With the History of Ye Mystic Krewe* [Tampa, 1936], 48, 187).
147. *New York Herald*, Aug. 25, 1901; *American Industries*, Aug. 15, 1903, quoted in U.S. Senate, Committee on Education and Labor, 76 Cong., 1 Sess., *Report Pursuant to S. Res. 266, Violations of Free Speech and Rights of Labor*, pt. 6 (Washington, D.C., 1939), 11. See also David Montgomery, "Violence and the Struggle for Unions in the South, 1880–1930," in *Perspectives on the American South: An Annual Review of Society, Politics and Culture*, by Merle Black and John Shelton Reed, 1 (New York, 1981), 45.
148. W. A. Platt to Gompers, Nov. 19, 1902, AFL Records, reel 36.
149. "Committee of Tampa and Surrounding Country" to Wood, March 1903, ibid., reel 139. See also *Tampa Morning Tribune*, March 5, 1903. Wood was one of the CMIU's best organizers, and he had previously been in Tampa in 1895. Cooper, "From Hand Craft to Mass Production," 179; *CMOJ*, Feb. 1895.
150. George Perkins to Samuel Gompers, March 12, 1903, ibid.
151. Perkins to Tampa Chief of Police, March 12, 1903, box 1285 (12993/1901), Department of Justice Records.
152. Perkins to P. C. Knox, March 12, 1903, Perkins to Roosevelt, March 12, 1903, ibid.
153. James S. Jones to Perkins, March 12, 1903, AFL Records, reel 139.
154. Gompers to Jones, March 19, 1903, Jones to Gompers, March 20, 1903, ibid.

155. Wood to Gompers, March 20, 1903, ibid.
156. *Palatka News*, April 3, 1903. Wood's injury appeared minor at first, but it eventually cost him the amputation of his left arm. Frank Morrison to Perkins, July 12, 1906, AFL Records, reel 36.
157. D. G. Sanford to Gompers, April 1, 1903, AFL Records, reel 36; Jacksonville *Florida Times-Union*, April 2, 1903.
158. *CMOJ*, April 15, 1903.
159. Ibid., April 15, 1904.

### 4. "The Cossacks of Tampa": The Citizens' Committee of 1910

1. *CMOJ*, April 15, 1907.
2. Page, "A Journey Through the Southern States," *World's Work* 14 (June 1907): 9033.
3. U.S. Bureau of the Census, *Thirteenth Census of the United States: 1910, Population*, 2 (Washington, D.C., 1913), 305, 330; U.S. Immigration Commission, *Immigrants in Industries*, pt. 14, 187; *Tobacco*, Oct. 27, 1910; Baer, *Cigar Industry*, 107.
4. U.S. Immigration Commission, *Immigrants in Industries*, pt. 14, 192.
5. *El Internacional*, Oct. 28, 1910.
6. Perkins Report to CMIU Executive Board, Dec. 7, 1909, AFL Records, reel 36. A government study of the average hourly wage of male cigarmakers found that in 1912 Tampa ranked behind all but one of the five northern cities surveyed (U.S. Bureau of Labor Statistics, Bulletin 161, *Wages and Hours of Labor in the Clothing and Cigar Industries, 1911 to 1913* [Washington, D.C., 1915], 75).
7. Perkins to Samuel Gompers, Nov. 2, 1909, AFL Records, reel 36.
8. *CMOJ*, April 15, 1909, April 15, 1910.
9. Perkins Report, Dec. 7, 1909.
10. Perkins to "Fellow Workmen of the City of Tampa," *CMOJ*, Dec. 15, 1909.
11. Perkins Report, Dec. 7, 1909.
12. *Tobacco*, Dec. 29, 1909; *El Internacional*, June 3, 1910; *U.S. Tobacco Journal*, July 16, 23, 1910.
13. *U.S. Tobacco Journal*, July 30, Aug. 8, 1910.
14. *Tobacco Leaf*, Oct. 20, 1910.
15. *Tampa Morning Tribune*, Aug. 5, 1910.
16. *U.S. Tobacco Journal*, Aug. 6, 1910.
17. *Tampa Morning Tribune*, Aug. 12, 1910.
18. Ibid. For the role of Italian workers in the 1910 cigar strike, see George E. Pozzetta, "Italians and the Tampa General Strike of 1910," in *Pane e Lavoro: The Italian American Working Class*, ed. George E. Pozzetta (Toronto, 1980), 29–46.
19. *Tampa Morning Tribune*, Sept. 6, 1910.
20. Ibid., Sept. 8, 1910. Although domestic production of clear Havana cigars was concentrated in Tampa, the plants were increasingly operated by absentee owners. In 1910, twenty-five of Tampa's largest thirty-six factories were branches of companies with headquarters in the North, especially New York (*Tobacco*, Oct. 20, 27, 1910; Dun & Co., *Reference Book* 167 [Jan. 1910]).
21. *Tampa Morning Tribune*, March 18, 1910. See also ibid., Nov. 21, 1910.

22. The other Board of Trade members appointed to the committee were Thomas C. Taliaferro, a founding member of the board and president of First National Bank; Alonzo C. Clewis, president of Exchange National Bank; Melville W. Carruth, a founder of the Board of Trade and president of American National Bank; C. E. Allen, cashier and a director of Citizens Bank and Trust Company; Eugene Holtsinger, a lawyer and real estate developer; William H. Beckwith, a real estate developer; and Wallace F. Stovall, owner of the *Tampa Morning Tribune* (ibid., Aug. 14, 1910). For biographical information on these men, all of whom were born in the South, see *R. L. Polk & Co.'s Tampa City Directory, 1910* (Tampa, 1910), 3, 120, 180, 384; Grismer, *Tampa*, 180–81, 330–31, 336–38, 340, 344–45, 379.
23. *Tampa Morning Tribune*, Aug. 14, 1910.
24. Ibid., Sept. 1, 1910.
25. Ibid., Aug. 23, 1910; *U.S. Tobacco Journal*, Aug. 20, 27, 1910.
26. *El Internacional*, Oct. 28, 1910.
27. *Tampa Morning Tribune*, Sept. 4, 1910; *U.S. Tobacco Journal*, Sept. 3, 10, 1910; *Tobacco Leaf*, Sept. 8, 22, 1910.
28. *Tampa Morning Tribune*, Aug. 15, 1910; *Tobacco*, Aug. 18, 1910.
29. *Tampa Morning Tribune*, Aug. 27, 1910.
30. Ibid., Sept. 14, 1910.
31. Ibid.; *Tobacco*, Sept. 15, 1910.
32. *Tampa Morning Tribune*, Sept. 15, 1910. Sources sympathetic to cigar manufacturers offered several possible explanations for the shooting of Easterling, suggesting that he might have been a target of strikers. In July, Easterling had reportedly scared a committee of union organizers away from the factory of his employer by firing shots, which hit no one. He later allegedly received a threatening letter after he had taken a group of Tampa cigarworkers to work at a branch factory in Jacksonville (*U.S. Tobacco Journal*, July 16, 1910; *Tampa Morning Tribune*, Sept. 15, 1910).
33. *Tampa Morning Tribune*, Sept. 21, 1910.
34. Ibid.
35. Ibid., Sept. 22, 1910.
36. Ibid., Sept. 21, 1910.
37. Ibid., Sept. 23, 1910; *U.S. Tobacco Journal*, Sept. 24, 1910; *Tobacco*, Sept. 29, 1910.
38. *Tampa Morning Tribune*, Sept. 21, 23, 1910. For the nature of the Black Hand, see Humbert S. Nelli, "Italians and Crime in Chicago: The Formative Years, 1890–1920," *American Journal of Sociology* 74 (Jan. 1969): 373–91.
39. *Tampa Morning Tribune*, Sept. 22, 1910; *Miami News-Record*, quoted in *Ocala Banner*, Sept. 30, 1910.
40. *Tampa Morning Tribune*, Sept. 22, 1910. Easterling's condition seemed to be improving at the time of the lynching, but he died from his wound a week after the murder of Albano and Ficarrotta (ibid., Sept. 29, 1910).
41. Ibid., Sept. 22, 1910.
42. Ibid., emphasis added. For endorsements of this point of view, see *Jacksonville Metropolis*, quoted in ibid., Sept. 24, 1910; *Pensacola Journal*, Sept. 25, 1910.
43. *CMOJ*, Jan. 1912.
44. *Tobacco*, Sept. 22, 1910.
45. *Tobacco Leaf*, Sept. 29, 1910.

## Notes to Pages 98–102

46. *CMOJ*, Oct. 15, 1910.
47. *El Internacional*, Sept. 23, 1910.
48. Montigliari to Secretary of State, Oct. 1, 1910, box 3671 (311.651/T15), State Decimal File, Department of State Records, R.G. 59, National Archives, Washington, D.C.
49. G. Moroni to Cusani Confalonieri, Oct. 11, 1910, ibid.
50. R. A. Jackson to Albert W. Gilchrist, Oct. 8, 1910, ibid. By an interesting coincidence, the presiding judge in the subsequent grand jury investigation of the double lynching was Joseph B. Wall, who had been disbarred in federal court for leading the 1882 mob that had lynched Charles Owens. In his charge to the grand jury in 1910, Judge Wall complained that criminals escaped justice as a result of legal technicalities. The grand jury failed to indict anyone for the murder of Albano and Ficarrotta (*Tampa Morning Tribune*, Dec. 15, 23, 1910). Under pressure from the Italian government, the federal government subsequently paid an indemnity of $6,000 to Albano's mother, "out of humane considerations" (William J. Bryan to Cusani Confalonieri, Nov. 14, 1913, box 3671, Department of State Records).
51. *Tampa Morning Tribune*, Sept. 23, 1910.
52. Ibid., Sept. 28, 1910.
53. Ibid., Oct. 1, 1910.
54. *Tobacco Leaf*, Sept. 22, 1910.
55. Ibid., Sept. 29, 1910. See also *U.S. Tobacco Journal*, Oct. 8, 1910.
56. *Tampa Morning Tribune*, Oct. 4, 1910.
57. Ibid., Oct. 5, 1910.
58. Grismer, *Tampa*, 340–41; *Tobacco*, Oct. 6, 1910; *Tampa City Directory, 1910*, 281.
59. *Tampa Morning Tribune*, Oct. 5, 1910.
60. *U.S. Tobacco Journal*, Oct. 8, 1910.
61. Robinson, *Hillsborough County*, 159–61 (quotation).
62. *Tampa Morning Tribune*, Sept. 17, 1899, Dec. 9, 1903; Campbell, *Cigar Industry of Tampa*, 44; Placie, *Prominent Personalities of Tampa*; Grismer, *Tampa*, 348.
63. *Plant City Courier*, n.d., clipping, Knight Scrapbooks, vol. 1, Peter O. Knight Papers, P. K. Younge Library of Florida History, University of Florida, Gainesville. A leading cigar manufacturer later described Knight as "one of the 'strong men' in Tampa" (WPA Federal Writers' Project, "Life History of Enrique Pendas," 4, typescript in University of South Florida Special Collections, Tampa).
64. Grismer, *Tampa*, 330.
65. *Tampa Morning Tribune*, Oct. 5, 1910.
66. Ibid.
67. Ibid.
68. *U.S. Tobacco Journal*, Oct. 15, 1910.
69. The names of 432 men who endorsed the Citizens' Committee are listed in *Tampa Morning Tribune*, Oct. 5, 1910. The occupations of 322 signatories can be found in the city directory. (Most others cannot be positively identified due to carelessness in printing initials or full names correctly.) Of these 322 Tampans, the largest single group (31 percent) was engaged in various services, especially real estate, insurance and banking. The second largest group (25 percent) was composed of merchants. Nine percent were lawyers. Six percent were public officials, in-

cluding Tampa's mayor, police chief, assistant police chief, two city detectives, and the marshal of West Tampa. The five men (1.5 percent) clearly identified with the cigar industry included two manufacturers, a factory manager, a foreman and a cashier. Only seven of the total 432 signatories had Spanish or Italian surnames, and four of these were cigar manufacturers or bankers (*Tampa City Directory, 1910*).

70. *Tampa Morning Tribune*, Oct. 5, 1910.
71. Ibid., Oct. 3, 1910.
72. Ibid., Oct. 13, 1910.
73. Ibid., Oct. 5, 1910.
74. *Tobacco*, Oct. 13, 1910. See also *Tampa Morning Tribune*, Oct. 8, 12, 1910.
75. *U.S. Tobacco Journal*, Oct. 15, 1910. For a list of the firms that agreed to reopen, see *Tobacco*, Oct. 20, 1910.
76. *Tampa Morning Tribune*, Oct. 17, 1910. See also *Tobacco*, Oct. 20, 1910.
77. *Tampa Morning Tribune*, Oct. 17, 1910; *Tobacco*, Oct. 20, 1910; *Tobacco Leaf*, Oct. 20, 1910. In addition to Macfarlane, Melville W. Carruth and Howell T. Lykes, all of whom had served on the Board of Trade committee that had tried unsuccessfully to mediate the strike in August, the delegation that went to the Labor Hall was composed of the following Board of Trade members: John H. Drew, a West Tampa real estate developer; Thomas D. Fisher, the owner of a Tampa cigar box company; and Curren E. Webb, a general contractor (*Tampa Morning Tribune*, Oct. 17, 1910). For biographical information on these men, see supra, 236, n. 22; *Tampa City Directory*, 1910, 232; Robinson, *Hillsborough County*, 243, 405.
78. *Tobacco*, Oct. 20, 1910.
79. *Tampa Morning Tribune*, Oct. 17, 1910.
80. Ibid., Jan. 21, 1900, Oct. 18, 1910.
81. Ibid.
82. *Tobacco Leaf*, Oct. 27, 1910.
83. *Tampa Morning Tribune*, Oct. 18, 1910.
84. Ibid.; *Tobacco*, Oct. 20, 27, 1910; *Tobacco Leaf*, Oct. 27, 1910; *CMOJ*, Nov. 15, 1910.
85. *Tampa Morning Tribune*, Oct. 19, 1910; Thomas J. Turner to Samuel Gompers, Oct. 25, 1910, Samuel Gompers Letterbooks (microfilm edition), reel 150.
86. *Tobacco Leaf*, Oct. 27, 1910.
87. J. V. Mock to Samuel Gompers, Oct. 22, 1910, Gompers Letterbooks, reel 150.
88. *Tampa Morning Tribune*, Oct. 19, 1910.
89. Ibid., Oct. 20, 1910.
90. *El Internacional*, Oct. 21, 1910.
91. Ibid., Nov. 18, 1910.
92. Ibid., Oct. 28, 1910.
93. Ibid.
94. Ibid., Nov. 4, 1910.
95. Tampa Joint Advisory Board to Gompers, Oct. 17, 1910, Gompers to Gilchrist, Oct. 20, 1910, Gompers Letterbooks, reel 149.
96. R. R. Cone to Gompers, Oct. 23, 1910, ibid. Cone was an AFL organizer in La Grange, Georgia, where the frightened CMIU official sought refuge after fleeing Tampa.

97. McKay to Gilchrist, Oct. 22, 1910, in *Tampa Morning Tribune*, Oct. 23, 1910.
98. JAB Statement, Nov. 15, 1910, in *CMOJ*, Nov. 15, 1910.
99. Ernest Bohm to Taft, Oct. 21, 1910, file 16–20, box 3359, Department of Justice Records. Other protests against antilabor violence in Tampa included a mass rally by trade unionists in Boston and a statement of condemnation by Jacksonville's central labor council (*Tampa Morning Tribune*, Nov. 16, 1910).
100. John M. Cheney to Attorney General, Nov. 23, 1910, file 16–20, box 3369, Department of Justice Records.
101. *Tobacco Leaf*, Nov. 3, 1910.
102. *Tobacco*, Oct. 27, 1910.
103. *Tampa Morning Tribune*, Oct. 25, 27, 1910.
104. Ibid., Nov. 24, 1910.
105. Ibid., Nov. 29, 1910. After failing to have their convictions overturned on appeal in 1911, the three union men each served about one month of their sentences, and then they received pardons from the state, over the objections of Tampa political and business leaders. De la Campa's pardon was granted on the condition that he leave the state for at least six years. Ibid., Aug. 9–10, 1911; Edward Stanly, Jr., to Samuel Gompers, July 1, 1911, AFL Records, reel 36.
106. *Tampa Morning Tribune*, Nov. 25, 1910.
107. Ibid., Dec. 7, 1910.
108. *CMOJ*, Dec. 15, 1910, emphasis added.
109. *Tobacco Leaf*, Dec. 1, 1910.
110. *Tampa Morning Tribune*, Nov. 26, 1910.
111. Ibid., Dec. 12, 1910.
112. Ibid., Nov. 26, 1910.
113. *Report of the Proceedings of the 30th Annual Convention of the American Federation of Labor* (Washington, D.C., 1910), 299.
114. Gompers to Gilchrist, Nov. 25, 1910, Gompers Letterbooks, reel 151.
115. *Tampa Morning Tribune*, Oct. 28, 1910.
116. The resolutions had been prepared by a subcommittee whose members were Hugh Macfarlane; Wallace Stovall; Frank C. Bowyer, a Tampa businessman, former mayor (1898–1900) and current president of the Board of Trade; Julius A. Trawick, manager of Tampa Electric Company, a utility headed by Peter O. Knight; and Kenneth I. McKay, the brother of Mayor D. B. McKay and the law partner of John P. Wall, Jr. (ibid., Nov. 28, 1910). For biographical information on these men, see *Tampa City Directory, 1910*, 176, 569; Grismer, *Tampa*, 348.
117. *Tampa Morning Tribune*, Nov. 30, 1910.
118. Ibid., Dec. 3, 1910.
119. Ibid., Dec. 7, 1910.
120. Ibid., Dec. 8, 1910.
121. Ibid., Dec. 19, 1910.
122. Gompers to George Perkins, Dec. 12, 1910, in *CMOJ*, Dec. 15, 1910.
123. *El Internacional*, Nov. 25, 1910.
124. Ibid., Dec. 16, 1910.
125. *Tampa Morning Tribune*, Dec. 12, 1910.
126. *Tobacco*, Jan. 12, 1911.
127. *Tampa Morning Tribune*, Jan. 2, 3, 1911; *CMOJ*, Jan. 15, 1911.
128. *Tampa Morning Tribune*, Dec. 23, 1910.

240  Notes to Pages 110–117

129. *El Internacional*, Jan. 20, 1911. See also *CMOJ*, Jan. 15, 1911.
130. *El Internacional*, Jan. 27, 1911.
131. *Tampa Morning Tribune*, Jan. 26, 1911; *CMOJ*, Feb. 15, 1911.
132. *CMOJ*, Feb. 15, 1911.
133. Report of J. E. Farrell and C. S. Marsh, Feb. 7, 1911, in ibid.
134. Ibid.
135. Ibid., July 15, 1911.
136. Ibid., March 15, 1911. For a similar complaint at the beginning of the strike, see Perkins to Samuel Gompers, June 27, 1910, AFL Records, reel 36.
137. *CMOJ*, Nov. 15, 1910.
138. Ibid., March 15, 1911. For CMIU strength in the North, see Baer, *Cigar Industry*, 94–98; Cooper, "From Hand Craft to Mass Production," 111–14, 140–81.
139. *El Internacional*, Nov. 11, 1910.
140. *CMOJ*, July 15, 1911.
141. Ibid., Nov. 15, 1910.
142. *Tobacco Leaf*, Nov. 24, 1910.
143. *El Internacional*, Nov. 18, 1910.
144. *CMOJ*, July 15, 1911.
145. *Tobacco Leaf*, Dec. 1, 1910.
146. *Tampa Morning Tribune*, Jan. 2, 1911.
147. Ibid., March 6, 7, 1911.
148. *Tobacco*, March 16, 1911.
149. *Tampa Morning Tribune*, Feb. 2, March 8, 1911.
150. Ibid., emphasis added.
151. Ibid., April 4, May 4, June 5, Aug. 9, 1911.
152. JAB Statement, Nov. 5, 1910, in *CMOJ*, Nov. 15, 1910.
153. *El Internacional*, Dec. 3, 1910.
154. One of Tampa's most exclusive social clubs was the Tampa Yacht and Country Club, organized in 1904. By 1912 its membership included eight Latin cigar manufacturers and five other Latin entrepreneurs, including the son of Vicente Martínez Ybor. At least 22 other club members were prominent leaders of the 1910 Citizens' Committee or the Citizens' Association of 1911 (Pauline Browne Hazen, *The Blue Book: Tampa, Florida, 1912– 1913* [Tampa, 1912], 54–59).
155. *Tampa Morning Tribune*, Dec. 13, 1910.

### 5. From "Stern Repression" to Collective Bargaining

1. Christopher L. Tomlins, *The State and the Unions: Labor Relations, Law, and the Organized Labor Movement in America, 1880–1960*, (Cambridge, 1985), 10–95.
2. Bing, *War-Time Strikes and Their Adjustment* (1921; New York, 1971), 273.
3. Ibid., 151.
4. Ibid., 275–76.
5. Irving Bernstein, *The Lean Years: A History of the American Worker, 1920–1933* (Baltimore, 1966), 190–243; Irving Bernstein, *The New Deal Collective Bargaining Policy* (Berkeley, 1950), 129–31, 148–49, et passim.
6. *CMOJ*, April 15, 1910, April 1913, April 1915, April 1916, April 1917.

7. "Rules of the Cigar Manufacturers' Bureau of the Board of Trade," Feb. 28, 1917, Tampa Board of Trade Records.
8. Minutes of the Board of Governors, April 4, 1917, ibid.
9. "Business Men of Tampa to the Employees of the Cigar Factories," n.d. [Sept. 1917], ibid. See also *El Internacional*, April 19, 26, 1918; *Tampa Daily Times*, April 29, 30, 1918.
10. Jerome Jones to H. L. Kerwin, May 22, 1918, file 33/1380, Federal Mediation and Conciliation Service Records, R.G. 280, Federal Records Center, Suitland, Md. Hereinafter cited as FMCS Records.
11. *Tampa Daily Times*, May 17, 1918.
12. *El Internacional*, July 11, 1919.
13. Ibid., March 26, 1920.
14. *Tampa Daily Times*, May 21, 24, 1918.
15. Statement of Manuel Corral, May 20, 1918, in file 33/1380, FMCS Records.
16. *Tobacco Leaf*, June 20, 27, 1918.
17. *Tampa Morning Tribune*, Aug. 10, 1918.
18. *Tobacco*, Aug. 22, 1918.
19. *Tobacco Leaf*, Aug. 22, 1918.
20. Laureano Torres et al., to the President of the Board of Trade, Aug. 12, 1918, Tampa Board of Trade Records.
21. *Tampa Morning Tribune*, Aug. 12, 1918.
22. Ibid.
23. Minutes of a Special Meeting, Aug. 14, 1918, Tampa Board of Trade Records.
24. *Tampa Morning Tribune*, Aug. 15, 1918. For information on Watson, see *R. K. Polk & Co.'s Tampa City Directory, 1918* (Tampa, 1918), 27, 824; Placie, *Prominent Personalities of Tampa*. Watson later served as Florida's attorney general (1940–48) and was largely responsible for adoption of the state's "right-to-work" law banning the union shop (John G. Shott, *How "Right-to-Work" Laws Are Passed: Florida Sets the Pattern* [Washington, D.C., 1956], 18–43).
25. *Tobacco Leaf*, Aug. 15, 1918.
26. *Tampa Morning Tribune*, Aug. 15, 1918.
27. Ibid., Aug. 16, 1918.
28. *Tobacco*, Aug. 22, 1918.
29. *El Internacional*, Aug. 23, 1918.
30. Ibid., Aug. 30, 1918.
31. J. Hernandez to Gompers, Aug. 14, 1918, Gompers to Hernandez, Aug. 18, 1918, AFL Records, reel 36; Gompers, *Seventy Years*, Vol. 2, 350–76.
32. Report of Grace Coates, n.d., in H. L. Kerwin to Frank Morrison, Oct. 23, 1918, AFL Records, reel 36.
33. Ibid.
34. Ibid.; *El Internacional*, Sept. 20, 27, 1918.
35. R. S. Sexton and Henry Sterling to Frank Morrison, n.d., AFL Records, reel 36.
36. U.S. Bureau of the Census, *Fourteenth Census of the United States: 1920, Population*, 3 (Washington, D.C., 1922), 196.
37. *U.S. Tobacco Journal*, Aug. 9, 23, 1919; *El Internacional*, Aug. 1, 1919; George Perkins to Samuel Gompers, Dec. 24, 1919, AFL Records, reel 36. After the enrollment of additional members in 1920, Tampa had the largest group of unionized cigarmakers of any city in the country (Gompers to R. S. Sexton and Sol Sontheimer, Sept. 1, 1920, ibid.).

38. *U.S. Tobacco Journal,* Nov. 19, 1919. For the hysterical reaction against workers and unions after the war, see Robert K. Murray, *Red Scare: A Study in National Hysteria, 1919–1920* (Minneapolis, 1955), 82–121, 267–69; Wayne Flynt, "Florida Labor and Political 'Radicalism,' 1919–1920," *Labor History* 9 (Winter 1968): 73–90.
39. *Tampa Morning Tribune,* April 27, 1919.
40. *Tampa Daily Times,* May 27, 1919; *Tampa Morning Tribune,* July 14, 1919.
41. Ibid., June 29, 1919.
42. Ibid., April 27, May 1, 1919; *Tampa Daily Times,* May 1, 1919; *El Internacional,* May 9, 1919.
43. *El Internacional,* May 9, 1919.
44. Ibid., May 23, 1919.
45. Ibid., May 30, 1919; *Tampa Morning Tribune,* May 2, 1919.
46. Tampa Cigar Manufacturers' Association to the Secretary of Labor, Dec. 21, 1920, file 170/1145A, FMCS Records; *Tobacco Leaf,* April 8, 1920; *El Internacional,* Sept. 24, 1920; Robinson, *Hillsborough County,* 348. In addition to the large factories that constituted the Cigar Manufacturers Association, Tampa had over 200 small ("buckeye") shops. The CMIU charged that one reason the Manufacturers' Association refused to settle the 1920 strike was to force small plants out of business (*Tampa Morning Tribune,* Sept. 12, Dec. 19, 1920; *El Internacional,* Nov. 6, 13, 1920).
47. For the planning of employers with assistance from the Board of Trade, see Minutes of the Board of Governors, March 26, Dec. 3, 1919, Tampa Board of Trade Records.
48. *El Internacional,* Jan. 16, 1920.
49. Ibid., Jan. 23, 1920.
50. Ibid., March 19, 1920.
51. Ibid., April 16, 1920; *Tampa Daily Times,* April 14, 1920.
52. *Tampa Daily Times,* April 15, 1920.
53. Ibid., April 19, 1920. For an overview of the 1920 strike, see Durward Long, "The Open-Closed Shop Battle in Tampa's Cigar Industry, 1919–1921," *Florida Historical Quarterly* 47 (Oct. 1968): 101–21.
54. *El Internacional,* June 11, 1920.
55. Ibid., April 23, 1920.
56. *Tobacco Leaf,* Jan. 20, 1921.
57. Ibid., April 29, 1920.
58. *Tampa Morning Tribune,* Aug. 8, 1920. For national developments, see Allen M. Wakstein, "The Origins of the Open Shop Movement, 1919–1920," *Journal of American History* 51 (Dec. 1964): 460–75.
59. *U.S. Tobacco Journal,* April 17, 1920.
60. *Tampa Morning Tribune,* July 18, 1920.
61. Ibid., Oct. 10, 1920.
62. *Tobacco Leaf,* July 1, 1920.
63. *CMOJ,* Dec. 15, 1920.
64. "Tampa JAB Appeal for Financial Assistance," May 19, 1920, AFL Records, reel 36.
65. *Tampa Citizen,* July 16, Aug. 27, 1920.
66. *El Internacional,* July 16, 1920.
67. Tampa JAB to CMIU, n.d., in *CMOJ,* Sept. 15, 1920; R. S. Sexton to Samuel Gompers, Aug. 5, 1920, AFL Records, reel 36.

68. R. S. Sexton to Samuel Gompers, Oct. 15, 1920, AFL Records, reel 36.
69. *Tampa Morning Tribune*, July 7, 1920; *Tobacco Leaf*, July 8, 1920.
70. *Tampa Morning Tribune*, July 18, 1920.
71. Minutes of the Board of Governors, July 14, 1920, Tampa Board of Trade Records. For biographical information on Bize, Griffin, Taliafero and Wall, see Grismer, *Tampa*, 330, 337, 357, 363.
72. Resolutions Adopted by the Board of Governors, July 26, 1920, Tampa Board of Trade Records. Celestino Vega, a cigar manufacturer, sat on the Board of Governors (Minutes of the Board of Governors, Sept. 8, 1920, ibid.).
73. *Tobacco*, Aug. 5, 1920.
74. Kenneth I. McKay to H. L. Kerwin, Aug. 16, 1920, file 170/1145, FMCS Records.
75. *Tampa Morning Tribune*, July 31, 1920.
76. Ibid., Aug. 7, 1920.
77. *El Internacional*, Aug. 13, 1920.
78. Ibid., Aug. 20, 1920.
79. *Tampa Morning Tribune*, Aug. 10, 1920.
80. Lovett to L. P. Dickey (secretary to the Board of Trade), July 28, 1920, in *Tampa Citizen*, July 30, 1920. See also Lovett to Samuel Gompers, Sept. 13, 1920, AFL Records, reel 36.
81. R. S. Sexton to Samuel Gompers, July 31, 1920, AFL Records, reel 36. For Catts' relations with labor generally and cigarworkers' favorable opinion of him, see Wayne Flynt, *Cracker Messiah: Governor Sidney J. Catts of Florida* (Baton Rouge, La., 1977), 143, 221–35, 255–59; *El Internacional*, July 11, 1919.
82. Sontheimer to Samuel Gompers, July 27, 1920, AFL Records, reel 36.
83. Catts to A. J. White, July 21, 1920, ibid.
84. *Tampa Morning Tribune*, Aug. 1, 1920; R. S. Sexton to Samuel Gompers, Aug. 21, 1920, AFL Records, reel 36.
85. Perkins to W. B. Wilson, May 6, June 23, 1920, file 170/1145, FMCS Records.
86. H. L. Kerwin to Perkins, July 3, 1920, ibid. The Division of Conciliation had been established as part of the new Department of Labor in 1913, but the division's function was purely "diplomatic," in that it had no legal power to intervene in labor disputes or enforce any settlement. Nevertheless, it succeeded through "its good offices" in adjusting the majority of disputes it handled between 1913 and 1920 (George S. Watkins, *Labor Problems and Labor Administration in the United States During the World War* [1920; New York, 1970], 124–26 [quotations]).
87. Buchanan to Cunningham, July 8, 1920, file 170/1145, FMCS Records.
88. Buchanan to H. L. Kerwin, Aug. 7, 1920, ibid.
89. H. S. Foley to H. L. Kerwin, Aug. 11, 1920, ibid.
90. McKay to Duncan U. Fletcher, July 23, 1920, Buchanan to H. L. Kerwin, Aug. 7, 1920, ibid.
91. Buchanan to H. L. Kerwin, July 29, 1920, ibid., emphasis in original.
92. Kenneth I. McKay to John R. Collings, Aug. 12, 1920, ibid.
93. *Tampa Citizen*, Aug. 13, 1920.
94. *Tobacco Leaf*, Sept. 2, 1920.
95. R. S. Sexton to Gompers, Aug. 14, 1920, AFL Records, reel 36.
96. *Tampa Morning Tribune*, Aug. 15, 1920.
97. Ibid., Aug. 19, 1920.
98. Ibid., Aug. 23, 1920.

99. R. S. Sexton to Gompers, Aug. 24, 1920, AFL Records, reel 36. Parkhill was a sixty-year-old public servant who had held a variety of local, state and federal positions, including city attorney, state supreme court judge, and major in the Judge Advocate General's Department of the U.S. Army during World War I. He was also the son-in-law of Joseph B. Wall, who had died in 1912 (Robinson, *Hillsborough County*, 343–44).
100. *Tampa Morning Tribune*, Aug. 26, 1920.
101. Ibid., Aug. 30, 1920.
102. H. L. Kerwin to Kenneth I. McKay, Sept. 17, 1920, file 170/1145, FMCS Records.
103. Kenneth I. McKay to H. L. Kerwin, Sept. 2, 1920, ibid.
104. *Tampa Morning Tribune*, Sept. 3, 1920.
105. Ibid., Oct. 12, 1920; *U.S. Tobacco Journal*, Oct. 23, 1920.
106. R. S. Sexton to Gompers, Oct. 15, 1920, AFL Records, reel 36.
107. *Tampa Morning Tribune*, Nov. 18, 1920.
108. Ibid., Nov. 29, 1920.
109. Ibid., Nov. 26, 28, Dec. 2, 1920; *Tampa Citizen*, Dec. 3, 1920.
110. *Tampa Daily Times*, Dec. 1, 1920.
111. *R. L. Polk & Co.'s Tampa City Directory, 1920* (Jacksonville, 1920), 538; Robinson, *Hillsborough County*, 260–61. Griffin was active enough in the 1910 committee to become treasurer of the Citizens' Association created in 1911. (*Tampa Morning Tribune*, March 8, 1911; see also supra, 113).
112. Minutes of the Board of Governors, Oct. 27, 1920, Tampa Board of Trade Records.
113. *Tampa Morning Tribune*, Dec. 2, 1920. See also *Tampa Daily Times*, Dec. 1, 1920. For biographical information on Charles McKay, see Robinson, *Hillsborough County*, 329; Placie, *Prominent Personalities of Tampa*; Grismer, *Tampa*, 334–35.
114. *Tobacco Leaf*, Dec. 9, 1920.
115. *U.S. Tobacco Journal*, Dec. 11, 1920.
116. *Tampa Morning Tribune*, Dec. 3, 1920; *Tampa Daily Times*, Dec. 2, 1920.
117. *Tampa Morning Tribune*, Dec. 2, 1920, emphasis added.
118. *Tampa Citizen*, Dec. 3, 1920.
119. Ibid., Dec. 10, 1920.
120. Ibid., Dec. 17, 1920.
121. Ibid., Dec. 10, 1920.
122. Gompers to Catts, Dec. 4, 1920, AFL Records, reel 36.
123. *Tampa Daily Times*, Dec. 11, 1920.
124. *Tampa Morning Tribune*, Dec. 18, 19, 21, 1920.
125. *Tampa Citizen*, Dec. 24, 1920.
126. *Tampa Morning Tribune*, Jan. 19, 1921. See also Oscar F. Nelson to H. L. Kerwin, Jan. 24, 1921, file 170/1145A, FMCS Records.
127. Kenneth I. McKay to R. B. Mahaney, Jan. 31, 1921, file 170/1145A, FMCS Records.
128. Jose M. Muniz to W. B. Wilson, Feb. 7, 1921, ibid.; *Tampa Citizen*, Feb. 4, 1921; *El Internacional*, Feb. 5, 1921; *Tampa Morning Tribune*, Feb. 6, 1921; *Tobacco Leaf*, Feb. 10, 1921.
129. *Tampa Morning Tribune*, Feb. 5, 1921. In the wake of the 1920 strike, the *Tribune* and most other local employers of printers ended union-shop

agreements and adopted "that sound principle of Americanism, the 'open shop'" (ibid., Jan. 1, 1922).
130. *El Internacional*, Feb. 12, 1921.
131. *CMOJ*, Feb. 15, 1921.
132. *El Internacional*, Feb. 5, 1921.
133. Ibid., Feb. 12, 19, 1921.
134. Perkins to Samuel Gompers, Jan 5, [1922], AFL Records, reel 36.
135. Perkins to Samuel Gompers, Nov. 29, 1921, ibid.; *Tampa Daily Times*, Nov. 17, 19, 1921; *Tampa Morning Tribune*, Nov. 18, 1921; *El Internacional*, Nov. 25, 1921.
136. *Tampa Daily Times*, Nov. 21, 1921; Minutes of a Special Meeting of the Board of Governors, Nov. 19, 1921, Tampa Board of Trade Records.
137. *Tampa Morning Tribune*, Nov. 19, 1921.
138. Ibid., Nov. 21, 1921; *Tampa Daily Times*, Nov. 22, 1921.
139. *Tampa Daily Times*, Nov. 23, 1921. See also *Tampa Morning Tribune*, Nov. 24, 1921.
140. Perkins to Gompers, Nov. 29, 1921, AFL Records, reel 36; *El Internacional*, Dec. 23, 1921; *Tobacco Leaf*, Nov. 24, 1921.
141. *Tampa Morning Tribune*, Nov. 23, 1921.
142. Ibid., Nov. 24, 1921; *Tampa Daily Times*, Nov. 28, 1921, emphasis added.
143. *El Internacional*, Nov. 23, 1921.
144. *Tampa Daily Times*, Nov. 25, 1921.
145. Ibid., Nov. 26–29, 1921.
146. *Tampa Morning Tribune*, Dec. 28, 1921.
147. *Tampa Daily Times*, Nov. 30, 1921; *Tampa Morning Tribune*, Nov. 30, 1921.
148. *Tampa Daily Times*, Dec. 28, 1921.
149. *Tampa Morning Tribune*, Dec. 28, 1921; *Tampa Daily Times*, Dec. 28, 1921.
150. *Tampa Daily Times*, Dec. 30, 1921.
151. Tampa JAB to Carey [sic] Hardee, Dec. 31, 1921, Perkins to Gompers, Jan. 25, 1922, AFL Records, reel 36.
152. Perkins to Gompers, Jan. 5, 1922, AFL Records, reel 36.
153. JAB to Hardee, Dec. 31, 1921, Gompers to Hardee, Jan. 5, 1922, Hardee to Francisco Fuente, Jan. 5, 1922, ibid.
154. *El Internacional*, Jan. 7, 1922.
155. *Tobacco Leaf*, Dec. 5, 1931; "Industrial Survey of Tampa, Florida" (typescript, 1930), 104, in Special Collections, University of South Florida Library, Tampa; U.S. Bureau of the Census, *Fifteenth Census of the United States: 1930, Population*, 4 (Washington, D.C., 1933), 361–63. For criticism of Tampa locals by national CMIU officials and threats of "secession" by union members during the 1920s, see *CMOJ*, June 15, 1923, June 1926; Manuel Gonzalez to I. M. Ornburn, Sept. 28, Dec. 15, 1927, Cigar Makers' International Union of America Papers, reel 19 (Local 336), McKeldin Library, University of Maryland, College Park (hereinafter cited as CMIU Papers).
156. Campbell, *Cigar Industry of Tampa*, 140–41; WPA Federal Writers' Project, "Life History of Fernando Lemos," 4. See also Baer, *Cigar Industry*, 80–89, 196–209; "Technological Changes in the Cigar Industry and Their Effects on Labor," *Monthly Labor Review* 33 (Dec. 1931): 11–17.
157. *CMOJ*, May 1929, April and July (quotation), 1930, Oct. 1931.

158. *CMOJ*, Jan. 1931.
159. *Tampa Morning Tribune*, July 24, 1930; Campbell, *Cigar Industry of Tampa*, 59.
160. Tampa Chamber of Commerce, "Report: Growth and Prosperity of the City of Tampa" (1931), 16, typescript in box 85, Doyle E. Carlton Papers, Florida State Archives, Tallahassee, Fla. During the 1920s, the Tampa Board of Trade was reorganized to form the Tampa Chamber of Commerce.
161. *Tampa Morning Tribune*, July 7, 1930.
162. William Z. Foster, *From Bryan to Stalin* (New York, 1937), 216–20, 243; Anita Brenner, "Tampa's Reign of Terror," *Nation* 135 (Dec. 7, 1932): 555. Even before arrival of the TWIU in Tampa, a report to the governor from an informant in Tampa declared: "There is no doubt but what the Communist [sic] are attempting to organize here, among the negroes and Cubans" (George B. Helmer to Doyle E. Carlton, Dec. 5, 1930, box 16, Carlton Papers).
163. *CMOJ*, Jan. 1932.
164. *Southern Worker*, June 20, 27, Aug. 15, Sept. 19, 1931; *Tampa Morning Tribune*, Nov. 9, Dec. 27, 1931.
165. *La Gaceta*, Oct. 31, Nov. 1, 1931. The men arrested were Nilo Lima, Jim Nine and Jack Nabo (*Tampa Morning Tribune*, Nov. 1, 1931).
166. *Tampa Morning Tribune*, Nov. 1, 1931; *Tampa Daily Times*, Nov. 4, 1931; *Daily Worker*, Nov. 13, 1931.
167. *Tampa Morning Tribune*, Nov. 5, 1931.
168. Brenner, "Reign of Terror," 556.
169. *Tampa Morning Tribune*, Dec. 6, 1931.
170. Ibid., Nov. 8, 1931.
171. *La Gaceta*, Nov. 6, 1931.
172. *Tampa Morning Tribune*, Nov. 8, 1931, Jan. 16, 1932.
173. *La Gaceta*, Nov. 9, 1931; *Daily Worker*, Nov. 13, 1931; Edwin L. Bryan to American Civil Liberties Union, Jan. 7, 1932, vol. 564, American Civil Liberties Union Papers, Princeton University Library, (hereinafter cited as ACLU Papers).
174. *Tampa Daily Times*, Nov. 9, 1931. Local AFL officials immediately disavowed any connection with the Nov. 7 rally, and the president of Tampa's Central Trades and Labor Assembly declared that Frederick Crawford would be expelled from the painters' union (ibid.; Jacksonville *Florida Times-Union*, Nov. 10, 1931).
175. *Tampa Morning Tribune*, Nov. 10, 1931.
176. Ibid., Nov. 13, 1931.
177. Ibid., Nov. 10, 1931.
178. Ibid., Nov. 11, 1931.
179. Ibid., Nov. 12, 1931.
180. Jacksonville *Florida Times-Union*, Nov. 12, 1931.
181. *Tampa Morning Tribune*, Nov. 11, 1931. The fifteen men and two women charged were Juan Hidalgo (alias Jim Nine), Carlos Lezama, Nilo Lima, J. E. McDonald, Frederick Crawford, Angel Cabrera, José Campo, Cesario Alvarez, Ismael Cruz, Joe Hevia, Mario Lopez, Grady Manasco, Félix Marero, Eugene Cabrera, F. L. Rodriguez, Frances Romero, and Carolina Vasquez (*Tampa Daily Times*, Nov. 11, 1931).
182. *Tampa Morning Tribune*, Nov. 12, 13, 1931; *Daily Worker*, Nov. 14, 1931; Fred G. Biedenkapp to ACLU, Jan. 23, 1932, vol. 653, ACLU Papers. For the history of the International Labor Defense, see Charles H. Martin, "The

International Labor Defense and Black America," *Labor History* 26 (Spring 1985): 165-94.
183. *Daily Worker,* Nov. 17, 25, 1931; Brenner, "Reign of Terror," 557.
184. *Tampa Morning Tribune,* Nov. 27, 1931. Attacks on the institution were not new. Previous attempts to do away with the reader included a 1910 experiment by a Tampa manufacturer who hired a harpist to play popular and classical music (*Tobacco Leaf,* Nov. 14, 1900, Nov. 17, 1910).
185. *Tampa Morning Tribune,* Nov. 28, 29, 1931; *Jacksonville Florida Times-Union,* Nov. 29, 30, 1931; *Daily Worker,* Nov. 30, 1931; *New York Times,* Nov. 30, 1931; *Tobacco Leaf,* Dec. 5, 1931.
186. *Daily Worker,* Dec. 2, 1931.
187. *Tobacco Leaf,* Dec. 5, 1931.
188. *Tampa Daily Times,* Dec. 1, 1931; *U.S. Tobacco Journal* Dec. 5, 1931.
189. *Tampa Morning Tribune,* Dec. 4, 1931.
190. *Tobacco Leaf,* Dec. 12, 1931; *Tampa Morning Tribune,* Dec. 5, 1931, emphasis added.
191. *Tampa Morning Tribune,* Dec. 5, 1931; *Tampa Daily Times,* Dec. 4, 1931.
192. *Jacksonville Florida Times-Union,* Dec. 5, 1931.
193. *Tampa Morning Tribune,* Dec. 5, 1931.
194. *Daily Worker,* Dec. 14, 1931.
195. Ibid., Dec. 5, 1931; *Tampa Daily Times,* Dec. 2, 5, 18, 1931. See also supra, 148.
196. *Tampa Morning Tribune,* Dec. 6, 1931.
197. Ibid., Dec. 7, 1931. See also ibid., March 23, 1932; *Who's Who in America, 1930-1931* (Chicago, 1930), 158.
198. *Tampa Morning Tribune,* Dec. 8, 1931; *Tampa Daily Times,* Dec. 8, 1931.
199. *Tampa Morning Tribune,* Dec. 7, 1931.
200. Ibid., Dec. 9-12, 15, 1931; *CMOJ,* Jan. 1932.
201. *Tobacco Leaf,* Dec. 19, 1931.
202. Although the TWIU temporarily ceased public activities which were prohibited under the federal court injunction, the union was reportedly holding meetings in Tampa several months later (*Tampa Morning Tribune,* April 8, 1932).
203. *Tobacco Leaf,* Dec. 19, 1931; *Tampa Morning Tribune,* Dec. 13, 1931. See also *New York Times,* Dec. 13, 1931.
204. *Tampa Morning Tribune,* Dec. 11, 1931.
205. Ibid., Jan. 16, 17, 1932.
206. Ibid., Jan. 22, 1932. Those convicted and the sentences imposed were ten years for Enrique Bonillo (alias Nilo Lima), Carlos Lezama, J. E. McDonald and Jim Nine; three years for Cesario Alvarez and Félix Marero; one year and a day for Angel Cabrera, José Campo, Ismael Cruz, Joe Hevia, F. L. Rodriguez, Frances Romero and Carolina Vasquez (ibid., Feb. 2, 1932; Herbert J. Jacobi Memorandum, Feb. 14, 1933, vol. 653, ACLU Papers).
207. *Lezama et al. v. State,* 148 So. 304 (1933). Despite the court's decision voiding the convictions, the last of the three prisoners were not released from jail until July 1933 (Edwin L. Bryan to ACLU, July 11, 1933, vol. 653, ACLU Papers).
208. ACLU Press Release, May 25, 1933, vol. 653, ACLU Papers. Due to a shortage of funds, the International Labor Defense had turned over appeal of the Tampa cases to the ACLU (Lucille B. Milner to Edwin L. Bryan, March 1, 1933, Fred G. Biedenkapp to Bryan, March 22, 1933, ibid.).

209. *Tobacco Leaf,* Jan. 16, 1932.
210. Ibid., Jan. 9, 1932.
211. The two men were Carl D. Brorein and James W. Morris. *Tampa Morning Tribune,* Jan. 3, 15, 1932. The President of the Chamber of Commerce during 1931 was a cigar manufacturer, A. L. Cuesta, Jr. Minutes of the Board of Governors, April 8, 1931, Tampa Board of Trade Records.
212. Thomas M. Finn to H. L. Kerwin, Dec. 12, 1933, A. L. Cuesta, Jr., to Finn, Sept. 7, 1934, file 182/295, FMCS Records; Russell H. Mack, *The Cigar Manufacturing Industry: Factors of Instability Affecting Production and Employment* (Philadelphia, 1933), 1–21, 50–59; W. D. Evans, "Effects of Mechanization in Cigar Manufacture," *Monthly Labor Review* 46 (May 1938): 1100–21.
213. *Business Week,* March 8, 1933, July 20, 1932. See also Campbell, *Cigar Industry of Tampa,* 46; Stubbs, *Tobacco on the Periphery,* 132–36.
214. I. M. Ornburn to Leo Wolman, Oct. 12, 1933, Consolidated Approved Code Industry File, National Recovery Administration Records, R.G. 9, National Archives, Washington, D.C. (hereinafter cited as CACI File, NRA Records); Campbell, *Cigar Industry of Tampa,* 140. In 1930, Tampa's 11,222 cigarworkers represented 24.3 percent of the city's total work force. By 1940 the city had only 6,300 cigarworkers, who composed 13.7 percent of the local work force (U.S. Bureau of the Census, *Fifteenth Census of the United States: 1930, Population* 4 [Washington, D.C., 1933], 339–46; U.S. Bureau of the Census, *Sixteenth Census of the United States: 1940, Population,* 3 [Washington, D.C., 1943], 666–70).
215. WPA Federal Writers' Project, "Life History of Enrique Pendas," 8, typescript in University of South Florida Special Collections, Tampa.
216. A Tampa CMIU officer claimed that the independent union had "Communistic tendencies" (Manuel Gonzalez to R. E. Van Horn, Aug. 9, 1933, CACI File, NRA Records). However, leaders of the new union publicly denied that their organizatioin had any connection with the Communist party (*Tampa Morning Tribune,* Aug. 14, 1933). An official of the party's Trade Union Unity League later declared privately that the Tampa union "was independent and was in no way connected with the TUUL and was very moderate" (Jack Stachel to Lucille B. Milner, Dec. 21, 1933, vol. 653, ACLU Papers).
217. *Tampa Morning Tribune,* Aug. 9–11, 16, 17, 1933; William E. Sullivan to William Green, Aug. 10, 1933, Green to George Googe, Aug. 22, 1933, AFL Records, reel 36; Sullivan to I. M. Ornburn, Sept. 1, 1933, CMIU Papers, reel 20 (Local 500); *CMOJ,* Oct.–Dec. 1933.
218. Kenneth I. McKay to Robert K. Strauss, Aug. 2, 1933, CACI File, NRA Records.
219. Finn to H. L. Kerwin, Dec. 9, 1933, file 182/295, FMCS Records.
220. Finn to H. L. Kerwin, Dec. 14, 1933, ibid.
221. Finn to H. L. Kerwin, Dec. 20, 1933, ibid.
222. R. E. Van Horn to H. L. Kerwin, Dec. 19, 1933, ibid. For CMIU complaints about continued radical activity among Tampa cigarworkers, see I. M. Ornburn to H. L. Kerwin, June 18, 1934, ibid.
223. *Tobacco Leaf,* Dec. 30, 1933.
224. Transcript of Conference between Cigar Manufacturers Committee and Workers' Committee, May 25, 1935, file 182/295B, FMCS Records.
225. WPA Federal Writers' Project, "Life History of John Cacciatore," 5, typescript in University of South Florida Special Collections, Tampa.

226. Finn to H. L. Kerwin, March 1, 1934, file 182/295, ibid. For evidence of Hav-A-Tampa's continued refusal to comply with provisions of the NRA code for the cigar industry, see Finn to Kerwin, April 6, 1935, file 182/295B, ibid.; Memorandum from NRA Legal Division to Regional Compliance Council No. 4, March 13, 1935, "Cigar Industry—Complaints," NRA Records.
227. McKay to Finn, Sept. 9, 1935, Finn to Kerwin, Sept. 10, 1935, file 182/295, FMCS Records.
228. Finn to H. L. Kerwin, April 6, 8, 1935, file 182/295B, ibid.; "Life History of Fernando Lemos," 3–4.
229. Finn to H. L. Kerwin, April 15, 16, 17, 1935, file 182/295B, FMCS Records.
230. Finn to H. L. Kerwin, April 13, 1935, ibid.
231. *Tampa Daily Times*, April 17, 1935.
232. José Martinez and Isidor B. Velasco to Frances Perkins, Sept. 8, 1935, file 182/295, FMCS Records. See also *La Gaceta*, Sept. 6, 1935.
233. WPA Federal Writers' Project, "History of Ybor City as Narrated by José García," 11, typescript in P. K. Yonge Library of Florida History, University of Florida, Gainesville.
234. Finn to H. L. Kerwin and Francis J. Haas, Sept. 27, 1935, file 182/295, FMCS Records.
235. WPA Federal Writers' Project, "Life History of John Cacciatore," 4–5.
236. WPA Federal Writers' Project, "Life History of Domingo Ginesta," 5.
237. Tomlins, *The State and the Unions*, 102–47; Philip Taft and Philip Ross, "American Labor Violence: Its Causes, Character, and Outcome," in *Violence in America*, ed. Graham and Gurr, 378–86.

### 6. "Tar and Terror"

1. *Tampa Morning Tribune*, Dec. 30, 1920; *Tampa Daily Times*, Dec. 29, 1921.
2. *Tampa Morning Tribune*, April 21, 1917; *Tampa Daily Times*, April 22, 1917 (quotations).
3. *Tampa Morning Tribune*, April 22, 1917.
4. Ibid., April 23, 1917.
5. *Tampa Daily Times*, April 23, 1917.
6. Sumter L. Lowry, *Ole 93* (Tampa, 1970), 39–42.
7. *Tampa Daily Times*, May 30, 1927.
8. Ibid., May 21, 1927; *Tampa Morning Tribune*, May 30, 1927.
9. *Tampa Daily Times*, May 31, 1927.
10. *Tampa Morning Tribune*, June 2, 1927.
11. *New York Times*, June 2, 1927; *Report of the Adjutant General of the State of Florida For the Years 1927 and 1928* (Tallahassee, Fla., [1928]), 10–11.
12. *Tampa Daily Times*, June 1, 1927. See also Lowry, *Ole 93*, 43–45.
13. *Tampa Morning Tribune*, June 2, 1927.
14. Ibid., June 6, 1927.
15. *Tampa Daily Times*, June 1, 1927.
16. Ibid., June 7, 1927.
17. *Tampa Morning Tribune*, June 1, 1927.
18. Ibid., June 4, 1927.
19. Ibid., Jan. 11, 1921.

20. Ibid., Nov. 20, 1920.
21. Arthur Raper, J. H. McGrew, and Benjamin E. Mays, "A Study of Negro Life in Tampa" (typescript, 1927), 2, in University of South Florida Special Collections, Tampa. See also Benjamin E. Mays, *Born to Rebel: An Autobiography* (New York, 1971), 106–24.
22. *Tampa Morning Tribune*, Jan. 30, 1926.
23. For the decline of public lynchings in the presence of large mobs, see Jessie Daniel Ames, *The Changing Character of Lynching* (Atlanta, 1942), 2, 5; McGovern, *Anatomy of a Lynching*, 140–41.
24. Surviving sources contain no biographical information about Johnson except his approximate age (*Atlanta World*, Feb. 2, 1934).
25. *Tampa Daily Times*, Jan. 30–31, 1934; Jacksonville *Florida Times-Union*, Jan. 31, 1934; *Tampa Morning Tribune*, Jan. 31, 1934; Walter Howard, "'A Blot on Tampa's History': The 1934 Lynching of Robert Johnson," *Tampa Bay History* 6 (Fall/Winter 1984): 5–18.
26. Merlin G. Cox, "David Sholtz: New Deal Governor of Florida," *Florida Historical Quarterly* 43 (Oct. 1964): 142–43; James William Dunn, "The New Deal and Florida Politics" (Ph.D. diss., Florida State University, 1971), 89–99.
27. Jessie Daniel Ames to David Sholtz, Jan. 30, 1934, Sholtz to J. Rex Farrior and W. C. Spencer, Jan. 30, 1934, box 72, David Sholtz Papers, Florida State Archives, Tallahassee.
28. *Tampa Daily Times*, Jan. 31, 1934; W. C. Spencer to David Sholtz, Jan. 31, 1934, box 72, Sholtz Papers. Spencer's willingness to follow the governor's orders may be explained in part by the fact that he was facing trial on extortion charges and was subject to removal by the governor. On Feb. 9, 1934, a jury acquitted Spencer of the charge, but he was finally removed by Sholtz in 1935 (*Tampa Daily Times*, Jan. 29, Feb. 3, 10, 1934; *Tampa Morning Tribune*, Oct. 11, 1935).
29. *Tampa Daily Times*, Feb. 1, 1934.
30. "Report of the Grand Jury for the Fall Term A.D. 1933," n.d., box 72, Sholtz Papers.
31. Farrior to Sholtz, March 14, 1934, ibid.
32. *Tallahassee Daily Democrat*, Jan. 31, 1934.
33. Emile Durkheim's concept of "repressive justice" and its relation to lynching are discussed in Hall, *Revolt Against Chivalry*, 138–39.
34. Of the eighty-four lynchings for the period 1931–35, only four occurred in southern cities. The cities were Vicksburg, Jackson, Birmingham and Tampa (Commission on Interracial Cooperation, *The Mob Still Rides: A Review of the Lynching Record, 1931–35* [Atlanta, n.d.], 15).
35. *Tampa Daily Times*, Jan. 30, 1934; *Tampa Morning Tribune*, Feb. 1, 1934.
36. *Tampa Daily Times*, Jan. 31, 1934. The Scottsboro case had begun in 1931, when nine black youths were convicted of raping two white women. Eight had been sentenced to death in what promised to be a legal lynching until outside groups took up the case which became a cause celebre as it worked its way through the courts. The lynching of Robert Johnson briefly attracted national attention, including in Congressional hearings, where witnesses used it to prove the need for federal antilynching legislation, but the Tampa case was soon overshadowed by other mob killings, especially the brutal lynching of Claude Neal in north Florida in October 1934 (Dan T. Carter, *Scottsboro, A Tragedy of the American South* [New York, 1969]; *Pittsburgh Courier*, Feb. 17, 1934; U.S. Senate, *Punishment for the Crime of Lynching: Hearings before a Subcommittee*

of the Committee on the Judiciary, 73rd Cong., 2nd Sess., on S. 1978, Feb. 20–21, 1934, pt. 1 [Washington, D.C., 1934], 66, 77, 160; Robert L. Zangrando, *The NAACP Crusade Against Lynching, 1909–1950* [Philadelphia, 1980], 117–23; McGovern, *Anatomy of a Lynching*).

37. *Tampa Morning Tribune*, Feb. 1, 1934.
38. Ibid., Feb. 23, 1934.
39. Leading black newspapers, which had originally reported Johnson's lynching, did not even mention the subsequent failure to indict anyone for the crime. The Association of Southern Women for the Prevention of Lynching, which had followed the Johnson case closely, limited its response to quiet pressure on the governor to launch another inquiry. The NAACP officially protested the lynching when it occurred, but the organization's records show no subsequent action (Jessie Daniel Ames to Jane Cornell, Feb. 28, March 6, 26, 1934, box 17, Association of Southern Women for the Prevention of Lynching Papers, Special Collections, Woodruff Library, Atlanta University Center, hereinafter cited as ASWPL Papers; Walter White to David Sholtz, Feb. 2, 1934, box 72, Sholtz Papers; Catherine T. Freeland to May White Ovington, Feb. 15, 1934, microfilm reel 12, National Association for the Advancement of Colored People Papers, Library of Congress, Washington, D.C.).
40. *Tampa Daily Times*, Feb. 28, 1936; Robinson, *Hillsborough County*, 408; Grismer, *Tampa*, 408; "Pat Whitaker," in *Prominent Personalities*, ed. Placie.
41. Robinson, *Hillsborough County*, 212.
42. *Tampa Morning Tribune*, March 25, April 5, 1910.
43. *Tampa Daily Times*, Feb. 28, 1936.
44. Grismer, *Tampa*, 282.
45. Will C. Spencer to J. P. Newell, Aug. 30, 1935, Sholtz to Vivian Collins, Sept. 2, 1935, box 56A, Sholtz Papers; *Tampa Morning Tribune*, Sept. 4, 1935.
46. James A. Clendinen, quoted in "Tampa's Most Turbulent Election," by Leland Hawes, *Tampa Tribune*, March 31, 1984.
47. K. I. McKay to David Sholtz, Sept. 11, 1935, box 56A, Sholtz Papers.
48. *Tampa Morning Tribune*, Sept. 4, 1935 (first quotation), Jan. 1, 1936 (second quotation). For examples of the national publicity generated by the primary election, see ibid., Sept. 4, 1935; *New York Times*, Sept. 4, 1935.
49. *Tampa Morning Tribune*, Oct. 24, 1935.
50. Ibid., Sept. 4, 1935.
51. Ibid., Dec. 4, 1935.
52. Ibid., Sept. 19, 1935.
53. *Tampa Daily Times*, Feb. 27, 1936.
54. Ibid. See also Adiel J. Moncrief, Jr., to the Editor, *Christian Century* 53 (March 25, 1936): 469.
55. Jack Jameson, *Night Riders in Sunny Florida: The K.K.K. Murder of Joseph Shoemaker* (New York, 1936), 9; Alice C. Voorhis to Norman Thomas, Dec. 23, 1935, Norman Thomas Papers, New York Public Library; *Polk's Tampa City Directory, 1932* (n.p., 1932), 540; *Polk's Tampa City Directory, 1935* (n.p., 1935), 509, 571; *Tampa Morning Tribune*, Dec. 13, 1935.
56. Norman Thomas to Mary Sanford, Dec. 30, 1935, Thomas Papers.
57. Shoemaker, quoted in *New Leader*, April 4, 1936.
58. Henry B. Walbridge to Gretchen J. Garrison, Nov. 1, 1934, Walbridge to Mary Sanford, Jan. 2, 1936, Thomas Papers.

59. *Tampa Morning Tribune*, Nov. 1, 1935. These proposals were drawn in large part from a plan distributed by *Common Sense*, a socialist journal which had Shoemaker as its Florida agent. He also served as the Florida agent for Upton Sinclair's *National EPIC News* (Herman Wold, "And Southern Death," *Common Sense* 5 [Feb. 1936]: 12).
60. *Tampa Morning Tribune*, Oct. 27–29, 31, Nov. 5, 1935. See also ibid., Sept. 19, Oct. 11, 1935.
61. Ibid., Nov. 4, 1935.
62. Ibid., Oct. 27, 1935.
63. Ibid., Oct. 13, 15, 28, 29, 1935.
64. Ray F. Robbins, "The Socialist Party in Florida, 1900–1916" (M.A. thesis, Samford University, 1971), 9, 11, 20; Frank McCallister to Norman Thomas, Dec. 2, 1935, Thomas Papers; *Tampa Morning Tribune*, Oct. 16, 18, 1931; *Tampa Daily Times*, Nov. 5, 1931. The Socialist party had virtually disappeared in Florida during the 1920s, but it claimed 188 members in the state by 1935. This exceeded the party membership in any other southern state. Tampa's local chapter, reorganized in 1931, was one of the more active, providing much of the leadership for the Socialist party in Florida during the 1930s (Report of M. E. Edson, May 1931, box 537, Socialist Party of America Papers, Duke University Library, Durham, N.C.; Membership Report by State, 1928–1935, box 145, ibid.).
65. Clarence Senior form letter, March 19, 1936, box 148, Socialist Party Papers; David Lasser, "Socialists and the Unemployed," *American Socialist Monthly* 5 (June 1936): 10–14; *New Leader*, Jan. 11, 1936; D. M. Benson to ACLU, May 11, 1934, vol. 741, ACLU Papers; *Tampa Daily Times*, Feb. 26, 1936.
66. J. Edgar Hoover, "Memorandum for the Attorney General," Dec. 14, 1935, file 109-18-6, Classified General File, Department of Justice Records.
67. R. E. L. Chancey to Aubrey Williams, Nov. 17, 1936, folder 641-P, Florida State File, Works Projects Administration Records, R.G. 69, National Archives, Washington, D.C.
68. Norman Thomas to Robert Alexander, Jan. 13, 1936, Thomas Papers.
69. *Tampa Daily Times*, Feb. 26, 1934.
70. *New Leader*, Jan. 11, 1936.
71. "Tampa's Opportunity For Honest Gov't" [Nov. 4, 1935], circular in folder 2, box 142, Workers Defense League Papers, Walter P. Reuther Library, Wayne State University, Detroit.
72. *Tampa Morning Tribune*, Nov. 5, 1935.
73. Ibid., Nov. 5, 1935.
74. Ibid., Nov. 9, 11, 13, 14, 16, 18, 20, 26, 1935.
75. Wolf, "Southern Death," 12.
76. J. Rex Farrior to David Sholtz, Dec. 12, 1935, box 56A, Sholtz Papers. See also *Tampa Morning Tribune*, Dec. 13, 17, 1935.
77. *Tampa Morning Tribune*, Dec. 13, 1935.
78. *Tampa Daily Times*, Dec. 2, 1935. Reports subsequently surfaced revealing that it was not unusual for Tampa police to question people about possible "Communist" beliefs. In October 1935, a Tampa high school teacher, Walter T. Burrell, was picked up by police after he had told a class that "if the American people had as much interest in political economy as they had in the world's series [sic], this country would not be run today by a bunch of political racketeers with 15 to 20 million unemployed." After Sergeant C. A. Brown questioned Burrell's students

about these comments, the chief of police had Burrell taken into custody and questioned him for several hours. Burrell was then released, and police kept no record of his arrest (*Tampa Morning Tribune*, Dec. 20, 1935).
79. D. M. Benson to David Lasser, Dec. 2, 1935, vol. 835, ACLU Papers; *Tampa Morning Tribune*, Dec. 10, 12, 1935.
80. Farrior to Sholtz, Dec. 12, 1935.
81. Ibid.; *Tampa Daily Times*, Dec. 2, 14, 1935; [David Lasser] to Mary Fox, n.d. [Dec. 7, 1935], folder 10, box 143, Workers Defense League Papers (hereinafter cited as Lasser Report); Interview of Eugene F. Poulnot by Ian Van Buskirk, Sept. 1973, tape recording in possession of author.
82. Lasser Report. See also Hoover, "Memorandum."
83. *Tampa Morning Tribune*, Dec. 3, 1935.
84. Benson to Lasser, Dec. 2, 1935; Lasser Report.
85. *Tampa Morning Tribune*, Dec. 4, 1935.
86. Ibid., Dec. 10, 1935. Reports circulated that Shoemaker had been castrated, but according to his brother, he had not been "mutilated" (George Clifton Edwards to Norman Thomas, Jan. 6, 1936, Thomas Papers).
87. Ames, *Changing Character of Lynching*, 33. Ames and others who kept track of lynching had no doubt that Shoemaker's murder qualified as a lynching. See also Commission on Interracial Cooperation, *The Mob Still Rides*, 15.
88. "A Man Is Killed," *New Republic* 85 (Dec. 25, 1935): 187.
89. *Bradenton Herald*, Dec. 18, 1935. See also *Nation* 141 (Dec. 25, 1935): 726.
90. Fredrickson, *Black Image*, 273; Williamson, *Crucible of Race*, 185–89.
91. Wyatt-Brown, *Southern Honor*, 435–61.
92. *Tampa Daily Times*, Dec. 24, 1920; *Tampa Morning Tribune*, 24, 1920.
93. *Tampa Morning Tribune*, Nov. 1–2, 1923.
94. Committee for the Defense of Civil Rights in Tampa, *Tampa—Tar and Terror* (New York, [1936]),9 (hereinafter cited as CDCRT; *Tampa Daily Times*, Dec. 14–15, 1931; Roy Wilkins to David Sholtz, Jan. 16, 1933, box C351, NAACP Papers. For the 1931 flogging of Frederick Crawford in Tampa, see supra 00.
95. *St. Petersburg Times*, March 23, 1935 (quotation); R. Carlton Wright to Norman Thomas, Jan. 3, 1936, Thomas Papers.
96. *Tampa Daily Times*, March 2, 1936.
97. *St. Petersburg Times*, Dec. 11, 1935; "What is Americanism?" *Common Sense* 5 (Feb. 1936): 5.
98. *Socialist Call*, Dec. 28, 1935. See also CDCRT, *Tar and Terror*, 15; Hubert Herring, "Tampa Warns America," *Christian Century* 53 (March 4, 1936): 359–60.
99. ACLU Press Release, Dec. 8, 1935, vol. 835, ACLU Papers; *Daily Worker*, Dec. 11, 1935. See also "Vigilante Brutality," *Common Sense* 5 (Jan. 1936): 5.
100. *Tampa Daily Times*, Dec. 3, 1935. See also *Tampa Morning Tribune*, Dec. 3, 1935.
101. Benson to Lasser, Dec. 2, 1935.
102. McCallister to Roger N. Baldwin, Dec. 2, 1935, vol. 835, ACLU Papers; Aaron Levenstein, "A Fighter for Freedom," *New Republic* 93 (Dec. 8, 1937): 122; *St. Petersburg Times*, April 22, 1937.
103. McCallister to Thomas, Dec. 1, 1935, vol. 835, ACLU Papers; Thomas to

254  *Notes to Pages 185–187*

R. E. L. Chancey, Dec. 2, 1935, Thomas to J. R. McLeod, Dec. 2, 1935, Thomas Papers. Thomas also tried to get the federal government to intervene, but "a discreet" investigation by the Federal Bureau of Investigation "fail[ed] to disclose a violation of any Federal law," according to Attorney General Homer T. Cummings (Thomas to Cummings, Dec. 5, 1935, Cummings to Thomas, Dec. 17, 1935, Thomas Papers; Hoover, "Memorandum"). Groups around the country, especially union locals, continued to press for federal prosecutions in the case (See file 109-18-6, Classified General File, Department of Justice Records).

104. Minutes of CDCRT, Dec. 5, 1935, folder 1, box 142, Workers Defense League Papers; *New Leader,* Dec. 7, 1935; CDCRT, *Tar and Terror,* 15–16; CDCRT, *Smash the Power of the Ku Klux Klan* (n.p. [1936]), a pamphlet in vol. 931, ACLU Papers; *Daily Worker,* Dec. 6, 11, 1935. During the following year, the committee raised over $7,600, which was used to finance extensive publicity and to pay staff members and investigators (CDCRT, Financial Statement, Nov. 1, 1936, vol. 931, ACLU Papers).
105. ACLU Press Release, Dec. 2, 1935, vol. 835, ACLU Papers; *American Federation of Labor Weekly News Service,* Dec. 14, 1935.
106. Tallahassee *Daily Democrat,* Dec. 16, 1935; *Miami Herald,* Dec. 13, 1935.
107. *Tampa Daily Times,* Dec. 3, 4, 1935. See also ibid., Dec. 9, 11, 13, 14, 16, 1935.
108. *Tampa Morning Tribune,* Dec. 13, 1935.
109. Ibid., Dec. 11, 1935. See also ibid., Dec. 4, 6, 8, 1935.
110. CDCRT, *Tar and Terror,* 14.
111. *Tampa Morning Tribune,* Dec. 6, 11, 18, 1935; Jose Martinez and I. B. Valasco to Sholtz, Dec. 5, 1935, box 56A, Sholtz Papers.
112. *Tampa Morning Tribune,* Dec. 11, 1935.
113. Edward Miraglia to Clifton Reed, Dec. 13, 1935, vol. 835, ACLU Papers; *Tampa Morning Tribune,* Dec. 19, 1935.
114. Robbins Ralph, quoted in "Tampa Church Marks Centennial," by Leland Hawes, *Tampa Tribune,* March 23, 1985.
115. McCallister to Norman Thomas, Jan. 3, 1936, Thomas Papers; Metcalf to Roger N. Baldwin, Sept. 22, 1936, vol. 931, ACLU Papers.
116. Lasser Report.
117. *Tampa Morning Tribune,* Dec. 9, 1935.
118. Ibid. See also Walter Metcalf, "Tampa Repents," *Fellowship* 2 (Feb. 1936): 4, clipping in vol. 931, ACLU Papers.
119. Aron S. Gilmartin to Frank McCallister and Charles E. Jensen, Dec. 6, 1935, folder 3, box 143, Workers Defense League Papers; McCallister to Mary Fox, Jan. 10, 1936, folder 1, box 144, ibid.; Lasser Report; *Socialist Call,* Jan. 25, 1936.
120. Metcalf to David Sholtz, Jan. 13, 1936, box 56A, Sholtz Papers. Metcalf's interest appeared to wane during 1936 and 1937, and he was privately criticized by local Socialists (Frank McCallister to Aron S. Gilmartin, Sept. 2, 15, 1936, folder 4, box 144, Workers Defense League Papers; Eugene Poulnot to Gilmartin, Sept. 15, 1937, folder 31, box 143, Workers Defense League Papers).
121. George Clifton Edwards, "Memorandum as to the Shoemaker Case," Feb. 28, 1936, folder 14, box 142, Workers Defense League Papers.
122. Thomas to the Editor of the *Tampa Tribune,* Dec. 19, 1935, Thomas Papers; *Tampa Morning Tribune,* Dec. 22, 1935.

123. Mrs. Harry Howard to Roger Baldwin, Dec. 5, 1935, vol. 835, ACLU Papers.
124. Lasser Report; *Sebring News*, quoted in *Tampa Morning Tribune*, Dec. 16, 1935.
125. *Tampa Morning Tribune*, Dec. 14, 1935.
126. Ibid., June 28, 1934, Jan. 24, 1936.
127. Ibid., Dec. 6, 1935.
128. Ibid., Dec. 11, 1935. Sholtz backed up his public directive by "confidentially" giving $500 from a state contingency fund to assist the investigation (Sholtz to Farrior, Dec. 19, 1935, box 56A, Sholtz Papers).
129. *Tampa Morning Tribune*, Oct. 11, 1935.
130. Farrior to Sholtz, Dec. 12, 1935, box 56A, Sholtz Papers.
131. *Tampa Morning Tribune*, Dec. 17, 1935.
132. Ibid., Dec. 5, 10–12, 1935.
133. Ibid., Dec. 10, 17, 18, 1935.
134. Ibid., Dec. 19, 1935. The men arrested were Charles A. Brown, John P. Bridges, Carl W. Carlisle, Robert L. Chappell and F. W. Switzer.
135. Ibid., Oct. 20, Nov. 17, Dec. 1, 25, 1935, Jan. 24, 1936.
136. *St. Louis Post-Dispatch*, Jan. 12, 1936.
137. Lasser Report; CDCRT, *Tar and Terror*, 10; Jameson, *Night Riders*, 15. A Tampa acquaintance of Shoemaker confided to the ACLU that prior to the floggings he had been approached by a Klan member who said the KKK was after Shoemaker (W. A. Sallade to Arthur Garfield Hays, n.d. [Dec. 1935], vol. 835, ACLU Papers).
138. R. Charlton Wright, "In Florida—The Klan Again," Dec. 25, 1935, typescript in folder 3, box 143, Workers Defense League Papers. Both contemporary observers and historians have emphasized that the KKK wielded strong influence in Tampa during this period (Roger N. Baldwin to George B. Parker, Dec. 19, 1935, vol. 835, ACLU Papers; David Lasser to George Clifton Edwards, Dec. 21, 1935, folder 14, box 142, Workers Defense League Papers; Edwards to Norman Thomas, Jan. 6, 1936, Thomas Papers; *Detroit News*, March 24, 26, 27, 1936; Jameson, *Night Riders*, 11–16; Arnold Rice, *The Ku Klux Klan in American Politics* [Washington, D.C., 1962], 96; David M. Chalmers, *Hooded Americanism: The First Century of the Ku Klux Klan, 1865–1965* [Garden City, N.Y., 1965], 312). For a Klan statement of its popularity in Tampa, see *Kourier* 10 (March 1936): 43.
139. Edward Miraglia to Roger N. Baldwin, Dec. 17, 1935, vol. 835, ACLU Papers.
140. *Tampa Morning Tribune*, Dec. 20, 1935. The head of the KKK, Hiram Wesley Evans, denied from his Atlanta headquarters Klan involvement in the Tampa floggings, but such denials were routinely issued in cases of Klan-related violence, over which national leaders exercised little control (ibid.; Chalmers, *Hooded Americanism*, 297).
141. *Tampa Morning Tribune*, Dec. 23, 25, 1935.
142. *Tampa Daily Times*, Dec. 23, 1935.
143. *Tampa Morning Tribune*, Dec. 29, 1935, Jan. 11, 1936. The third Orlando man indicted was James Dean.
144. Ibid., Feb. 15, 1935. Menendez was never brought to trial (ibid., July 20, 1937).
145. Ibid., Dec. 20, 1935, Feb. 26, 1936. The same group of attorneys had successfully defended Sam Crosby and several other men against charges of vote fraud in the September primary (ibid., Dec. 20, 1935).
146. Ibid., Dec. 20, 24, 29, 1935; *Tampa Daily Times*, Feb. 28, 1936; *Tampa*

City Directory, 1935; "Edward W. Spencer" and "Eli Witt," in *Prominent Personalities*, ed. Placie; Grismer, *Tampa*, 388–89, 398–99; Earl J. Brown, "Eli Buchanan Witt: The South's Most Outstanding Tobacco Merchant," Tampa Historical Society *Sunland Tribune* 7 (Nov. 1981): 85–94. Woodbery had also provided bonds for Sam Crosby and several other men accused of vote fraud in September 1935 (*Tampa Morning Tribune*, Sept. 4, 1935).
147. See supra, 159–60.
148. CDCRT, *Tar and Terror*, 8, emphasis in original.
149. Farrior to Sholtz, Dec. 12, 1935; *Daily Worker*, March 26, May 22, 1936; Jameson, *Night Riders*, 14, 18.
150. Jameson, *Night Riders*, 18–19, emphasis in original.
151. George Clifton Edwards to Norman Thomas, Jan. 6, 1936, Thomas Papers.
152. David Lasser to George Clifton Edwards, Dec. 21, 1935, Edwards to Lasser, Jan. 5, 1936, folder 14, box 142, Workers Defense League Papers; CDCRT, "Memorandum on the Tampa Affair," n.d. [Dec. 1935], Norman Thomas to Paul Pierce, Jan. 24, 1936, Thomas to Jerry McLeod, Jan. 28, 1936, Thomas Papers.
153. *Tampa Morning Tribune*, Jan. 20, 1936.
154. *Tampa Daily Times*, Jan. 20, 1936 (quotation); *Tampa Morning Tribune*, Jan. 21, 1936.
155. *Wauchula Herald* quoted in *Tampa Morning Tribune*, Jan. 10, 1936; George Clifton Edwards, "Memorandum as to the Shoemaker Case," Feb. 28, 1936, folder 14, box 142, Workers Defense League Papers. See also *Socialist Call*, Dec. 28, 1935.
156. *Tampa Morning Tribune*, Feb. 22, 1936.
157. Ibid., Jan. 24, 25, 27, 28, 1936.
158. *Socialist Call*, Feb. 1, 1936. See also CDCRT, *Tar and Terror*, 10.
159. *Tampa Morning Tribune*, Jan. 27, Feb. 2, 1936.
160. Ibid., Feb. 28, 29, 1936; *Socialist Call*, March 21, 1936; *Daily Worker*, March 26, 1936; "Florida: Body and Limbs," *Time* 30 (Oct. 25, 1937): 17.
161. *Miami Herald*, quoted in *Tampa Morning Tribune*, March 13, 1936.
162. Sholtz to Farrior, Feb. 19, 1936, box 56A, Sholtz Papers, emphasis added.
163. *Tampa Morning Tribune*, Feb. 25, 28, 1936.
164. Ibid., March 3, 17, 18, 1936.
165. Ibid., March 19, 23, 1936.
166. Dewell to J. P. Newell, March 23, 1936, box 56A, Sholtz Papers. For a biographical sketch of Dewell, see M. F. Hetherington, *History of Polk County, Florida: Narrative and Biographical* (1928; Chuluota, Fla., 1971), 227.
167. *Tampa Morning Tribune*, March 25, 26, April 1, 1936.
168. *Polk County Democrat*, April 3, 1936.
169. *Polk County Record*, April 14, 15, 24, 1936; *St. Louis Post-Dispatch*, April 14, May 19, 1936. For examples of coverage in northern newspapers, see *New York Post*, April 15–May 24, 1936. *New York Times*, April 19–May 24, 1936; *Chicago Daily Tribune*, April 24, May 24, 1936; *St. Louis Post-Dispatch*, April 13–May 24, 1936. The Socialist and Communist press also sent reporters to cover the trial, and the ACLU and the CDCRT jointly hired both a newspaperman to publicize the trial and a legal observer to monitor the proceedings (*Socialist Call*, April 23–May 30, 1936; *Daily Worker*, April 13–May 25, 1936; Mary Fox to ACLU,

March 23, 30, 1936, vol. 931, ACLU Papers; CDCRT Press Release, April 16, 1936, box 150, Socialist Party Papers).
170. *Tampa Morning Tribune*, April 15, 16, 1936.
171. Ibid., April 21–24, 1936.
172. *St. Louis Post-Dispatch*, May 25, 1936.
173. *Tampa Morning Tribune*, April 14, 1936.
174. *St. Louis Post-Dispatch*, April 14, 1936.
175. Ibid., April 15, 1936.
176. *Tampa Morning Tribune*, April 15, 1936.
177. Ibid., April 17, 1936.
178. *St. Louis Post-Dispatch*, April 17, 1936.
179. *Tampa Morning Tribune*, April 22, 1936.
180. Ibid., May 8, 1936.
181. Ibid. For the history of the Herndon case, see Charles H. Martin, *The Angelo Herndon Case and Southern Justice* (Baton Rouge, La., 1976).
182. *St. Louis Post-Dispatch*, May 8, 1936.
183. *Tampa Morning Tribune*, April 23, 1936.
184. Ibid., April 28, 30, May 1, 5, 6, 1936.
185. Ibid., April 29, 1936.
186. Ibid., May 1, 1936. Following the testimony of Eddings and Bush, Mayor Chancey fired six defendants who had been suspended from their jobs as city employees since the previous December. Bridges, Brown, Crosby and Switzer were dismissed from the police department; Carlisle lost his job as assistant tax collector; and Chappell was dismissed from the city waterworks (ibid., May 2, 1936).
187. *St. Louis Post-Dispatch*, May 13, 14, 18, 19, 1936.
188. Ibid., May 21, 1936.
189. *Tampa Morning Tribune*, May 22, 1936.
190. Ibid., May 23, 1936.
191. *Polk County Democrat*, May 29, 1936. See also *Polk County Record*, May 25, 1936.
192. *Tampa Morning Tribune*, May 24, 1936; Marie Gill to Norman Thomas, n.d. [June 1936], folder 14, box 143, Workers Defense League Papers.
193. *St. Louis Post-Dispatch*, May 23, 24, 1936.
194. *Tampa Morning Tribune*, Aug. 8, 1936.
195. *St. Louis Post-Dispatch*, May 25, 1936.
196. Brandeis to Felix Frankfurter, May 23, 1936, box 28, Felix Frankfurter Papers, Library of Congress, Washington, D.C. The author thanks William E. Leuchtenburg for bringing this document to his attention.
197. ACLU Press Release, June 5, 1936, vol. 931, ACLU Papers.
198. *Socialist Call*, May 30, 1936.
199. *Brown et al. v. State*, 175 So. 515 (1937).
200. At the request of State Attorney Farrior, charges were dismissed against the two other Orlando men arrested in December 1935 (*St. Louis Post-Dispatch*, Oct. 6, 1937).
201. Ibid., Oct. 5, 8, 12, 14, 15, 1937.
202. J. Rex Farrior to Fred P. Cone, Nov. 4, Dec. 6, 1937, Jan. 11, 1938, box 44, Fred P. Cone Papers, Florida State Archives, Tallahassee; Walter Metcalf to Cone, n.d., ibid.; *St. Louis Post-Dispatch*, May 31, 1938.
203. *Tampa Morning Tribune*, June 7, 12, 1938. The jury's verdict received national newspaper coverage (see, for example, *Atlanta Constitution*, June

11, 1938; *Milwaukee Journal,* June 11, 1938; New Orleans *Times-Picayune,* June 11, 1938; *New York Post,* June 11, 1938; *New York Times,* June 11, 1938).
204. *St. Louis Post-Dispatch,* June 12, 1938.
205. *Tampa Morning Tribune,* June 21, 1938.
206. CDCRT Press Release, Oct. 15, 1937, folder 2, box 143, Workers Defense League Papers.
207. *Socialist Call,* June 25, 1938.
208. *Miami Herald,* Nov. 24, 1937; *Jacksonville Journal,* quoted in *Tampa Morning Tribune,* June 25, 1938.
209. *Tampa Daily Times,* June 11, 1938; *Tampa Morning Tribune,* June 12, 1938.
210. Jerold S. Auerbach, *Labor and Liberty: The La Follette Committee and the New Deal* (Indianapolis, 1966), 67–68, 94–96.
211. *Socialist Call,* Oct. 16, 1937. See also *New York Post,* Oct. 21, 1937; Norman Thomas, et al., to "Dear Friend," n.d. [Oct. 1937], folder 4, box 142, Workers Defense League Papers; Virginius Dabney to Robert M. La Follette, Oct. 29, 1937, Norman Thomas to La Follette, May 23, 1938, folder 6, box 143, Workers Defense League Papers.
212. Frank McCallister to Aron S. Gilmartin, June 11, 1938, folder 22, box 26, Workers Defense League Papers; *St. Louis Post-Dispatch,* June 16, 23, 1938; *Socialist Call,* July 2, 1938.
213. Robert Wohlforth to Roger N. Baldwin, Nov. 10, 1937, vol. 1035, ACLU Papers; Auerbach, *Labor and Liberty,* 95–96. For correspondence related to the campaign to get an investigation of Tampa, see folder 6, box 143, Workers Defense League Papers. In a last attempt to win justice in the flogging case, Norman Thomas tried unsuccessfully in 1939 to interest the Department of Justice in prosecuting Shoemaker's killers under federal civil rights statutes (Brien McMahon to Thomas, March 23, 1939, file 109-18-6, Classified General File, Department of Justice Records).
214. George Clifton Edwards, "Memorandum as to the Shoemaker Case," Feb. 28, 1936, folder 14, box 142, Workers Defense League Papers.
215. ACLU, *Eternal Vigilance,* 13. See also ACLU, *Let Freedom Ring? The Story of Civil Liberty, 1936–37* (New York, 1937), 2.
216. *Socialist Call,* Dec. 19, 1936; Poulnot to Aron S. Gilmartin, March 4, 1937, folder 10, box 144, Workers Defense League Papers.
217. *Daily Worker,* Sept. 19, 1936; *Tampa Morning Tribune,* Sept. 14, 1936.
218. *Daily Worker,* Sept. 14 (second quotation), 15 (first quotation), 1936.
219. *Tampa Morning Tribune,* Sept. 15, 22, 1936; *Tampa Daily Times,* Sept. 17, 1936; Frank McCallister to Aron S. Gilmartin, Sept. 15, Oct. 23, 1936, folders 4 and 5, box 144, Workers Defense League Papers; Roger N. Baldwin to Alexander Trachtenberg, Sept. 16, 1936, vol. 931, ACLU Papers.
220. Arthur Garfield Hays to R. E. L. Chancey, Sept. 14, 1936, vol. 931, ACLU Papers; *Daily Worker,* Oct. 26, 1936; *Tampa Daily Times,* Oct. 26, 1936.
221. The men identified as leaders of the vigilantes were Constable Fred W. Newberger, Deputy Constable John R. Parrish and Lawrence Ponder, a special deputy sheriff, who claimed he had resigned his commission the previous day. *Tampa Morning Tribune,* Oct. 26, 1936.
222. *Tampa Daily Times,* Oct. 26, 1936.
223. *Tampa Morning Tribune,* Oct. 26, 1936. *Daily Worker,* Oct. 30, 1936; *New York Times,* Nov. 1, 1936.
224. *Tampa Morning Tribune,* Oct. 27, 1936; *Tampa Daily Times,* Oct. 26,

1936; McCallister to Aron S. Gilmartin, Oct. 26, 1936, folder 5, box 144, Workers Defense League Papers.
225. *Tampa Morning Tribune,* Oct. 27, 1936; McCallister to Aron S. Gilmartin, folder 5, box 144, Workers Defense League Papers.
226. "How Americans Handle Communist Earl Browder," *Kourier* 12 (Nov. 1936): 7.
227. *Tampa Morning Tribune,* Oct. 28, 1936.
228. Ibid., Sept. 16–18, 1937.
229. McCallister to Aron S. Gilmartin, Oct. 30, 1936, folder 5, box 144, Workers Defense League Papers; *Tampa Morning Tribune,* Feb. 23, 24, 1937. See also "The Klan in Florida," *New Republic* 91 (June 9, 1937): 118.
230. Poulnot to Aron S. Gilmartin, March 4, 15, 1937, folder 10, box 144, Workers Defense League Papers.
231. McCallister to Aron S. Gilmartin, Nov. 18, 1937, folder 18, box 144, ibid.
232. *Tampa Morning Tribune,* May 4, June 6, 11, 1938; Hawes, "Tampa's Turbulent Election."
233. *Tampa Morning Tribune,* April 5, 1938.
234. Ibid., April 6, 1938.
235. Ibid., July 19, 1938, Oct. 6, 1947.
236. *Tampa Morning Tribune,* June 21, July 19, 1938. Rick Barry, "Tampa's Gambling Past," *Tampa Tribune,* May 8, 1978. For biographical information on H. P. Macfarlane, see Grismer, *Tampa,* 341.
237. U.S. Senate, *Investigation of Organized Crime in Interstate Commerce: Hearings Before a Special Committee to Investigate Organized Crime in Interstate Commerce,* 81st Cong., 2d Sess. and 82d Cong., 1st Sess., on S. Res. 202, pt. 1-A (Washington, D.C., 1951), passim; Kefauver, *Crime in America* (Garden City, N.Y., 1951), 69–73; William Howard Moore, *The Kefauver Committee and the Politics of Crime, 1950–52* (Columbia, Mo., 1974), 127–30.
238. ACLU, *The Bill of Rights—150 Years After: The Story of Civil Liberty, 1938-1939* (New York, 1939), 29.

**Conclusion: Violence and Hegemony**

1. Anita Brenner and S. S. Winthrop, *Tampa's Reign of Terror* (n.p., n.d. [1933]), 16.
2. Cutler, *Lynch-Law,* 269.
3. *Tampa Morning Tribune,* Aug. 24, 1899.
4. Brown, *Strain of Violence,* 98–112. Brown largely limits his study to pre–twentieth-century vigilante movements and specifically avoids the "protean" task of examining urban vigilantism in the twentieth century (ibid., 128).
5. Other southern cities with reputations for vigilante violence in the twentieth century included Atlanta, Birmingham, Memphis and New Orleans. All four (in addition to Tampa) were cited by the ACLU as "centers of repression" during the 1930s (Tindall, *Emergence of the New South,* 524–30). See also Goldfield, *Cotton Fields and Skyscrapers,* 93–94; William D. Miller, *Memphis During the Progressive Era* (Memphis, 1957), 8–9, 191–95; Kenneth T. Jackson, *The Ku Klux Klan in the City, 1915-1930* (New York, 1967), 25–58; Ingalls, "Anti-Labor Vigilantes," 72–78; Ingalls, "Antiradical Violence in Birmingham," 521–44.

6. Brown, *Strain of Violence*, 134–43; Senkewicz, *Vigilantes in San Francisco*, 156–77. Vigilantes briefly reorganized in San Francisco in 1877, when a Committee of Safety violently disrupted peaceful protests by workers (Peter R. Decker, *Fortunes and Failures: White Collar Mobility in Nineteenth-Century San Francisco* [Cambridge, Mass., 1978], 245–49).
7. Brown, *Strain of Violence*, 144–79. In contrast to Tampa, where lawyers led a number of vigilance committees, the San Francisco Vigilance Committee of 1856 contained no lawyers among its thirty-seven leaders (Senkewicz, *Vigilantes in San Francisco*, 170).
8. *Tampa Morning Tribune*, Sept. 28, 1910.
9. Ibid., Jan. 21, 1900.
10. *El Internacional*, March 26, 1920.
11. Janet Synder Matthews, "'He Has Carried His Life in His Hands': The 'Sarasota Assassination Society' of 1884," *Florida Historical Quarterly* 58 (Jan. 1979): 1–21; McGovern, *Anatomy of a Lynching*, 12; "Lynchings by Counties—Florida," box 6, ASWPL Papers.
12. Lynching data are sometimes unreliable, especially in terms of specific details such as the actual locations for reported lynchings. The standard published sources for annual data are: National Association for the Advancement of Colored People, *Thirty Years of Lynching in the United States, 1889–1918* (New York, 1969 [1919]); Monroe Work, ed., *Negro Year Book*, 11 vols. (Tuskegee, Ala., 1912–56). *Thirty Years of Lynching* (p. 56) attributed four lynch deaths to Tampa in March 1910 and April 1912, that in fact occurred in other nearby counties. For more precise information on these cases, see *Tampa Morning Tribune*, March 8–10, 1910, and April 15, 1912.
13. Hall, *Revolt Against Chivalry*, 134–35, 138–42; Arthur F. Raper, *The Tragedy of Lynching* (Montclair, N.J., 1969 [1933]), 6, 28–29, 43–51.
14. *Tampa Morning Tribune*, Sept. 21, 1920.
15. *Tobacco*, Sept. 22, 1910.
16. *Miami News*, Oct. 11, 1937, clipping in folder 2, box 145, Workers Defense League Papers.
17. *New York Times*, Oct. 22, 1937.
18. *Tampa Morning Tribune*, Sept. 28, 1900.
19. Minutes of the Tampa Board of Trade, Feb. 1, 1899, Tampa Board of Trade Records.
20. Joint Advisory Board to AFL Officers, May 5, 1920, AFL Records, reel 36.
21. *Tampa Daily Times*, Nov. 28, 1921.
22. *Tampa Morning Tribune*, Oct. 24, 1896.
23. *Tampa Daily Times*, Nov. 10, 1920; *Tampa Morning Tribune*, Feb. 10, 1921.
24. *Tampa Morning Tribune*, July 19, 1899.
25. George Perkins to Samuel Gompers, Jan. 25, 1913, AFL Records, reel 36.
26. *El Internacional*, Sept. 15, 1916.
27. *Tampa Morning Tribune*, July 18, 1920.
28. Antonio Gramsci, quoted in T. J. Jackson Lears, "The Concept of Cultural Hegemony: Problems and Possibilities," *American Historical Review* 90 (Oct. 1985): 568 (first quotation); Eugene D. Genovese, *In Red and Black: Marxian Explorations in Southern and Afro-American History* (New York, 1973), 406 (second quotation).
29. Wiener, *Social Origins of the New South*, 221.
30. *El Internacional*, March 26, 1920.

31. Lears, "Cultural Hegemony," 574–75, 579.
32. Studs Terkel, *Hard Times: An Oral History of the Great Depression in America* (New York, 1970), 109.
33. Yglesias, "The Radical Latino Island in the Deep South," *Tampa Bay History* 7 (Fall/Winter 1985): 168.
34. Yglesias, *The Truth About Them*, 209.
35. WPA Federal Writers' Project, "Life History of John Cacciatore," 4.
36. Yglesias, "Latino Island," 166.
37. Ben Brown, "In His Own Write: Ybor City's Native Son," *Tampa Tribune*, April 1, 1979. When asked his politics in the 1970s, Yglesias responded pointedly: "Should like to overthrow capitalism" (Ann Evory, ed., *Contemporary Authors*, vols. 41–44 [Detroit, 1979], 792).
38. Gary R. Mormino, "Tampa: From Hell Hole to the Good Life," in *Sunbelt Cities: Politics and Growth Since World War II*, ed. Richard M. Bernard and Bradley R. Rice (Austin, Tex., 1983), 143–45.
39. Steven F. Lawson, "From Sit-in to Race Riot: Businessmen, Blacks, and the Pursuit of Moderation in Tampa, 1960–1967," in *Southern Businessmen and Desegregation*, ed. Elizabeth Jacoway and David R. Colburn (Baton Rouge, La., 1982), 257–81; "Civil Rights Protests in Tampa: Oral Memoirs of Conflict and Accommodation," *Tampa Bay History* 1 (Spring/Summer 1979): 37–54.
40. *Tampa Tribune*, Sept. 18, 1963, Dec. 1, 1967, quoted in Lawson, "Sit-in to Race Riot," 280.

# Bibliography

**Manuscript Collections**

American Civil Liberties Union Papers. Princeton University Library, Princeton, N.J.
American Federation of Labor Records: The Samuel Gompers Era. Microfilm edition, 1979.
Association of Southern Women for the Prevention of Lynching Papers. Special Collections, Woodruff Library, Atlanta University Center, Atlanta.
Doyle E. Carlton Papers. Florida State Archives, Tallahassee.
Cigar Makers' International Union of America Papers. Microfilm. McKeldin Library, University of Maryland, College Park.
Fred P. Cone Papers. Florida State Archives, Tallahassee.
Department of Justice Records. Record Group 60. National Archives, Washington, D.C.
Department of State Records. Record Group 59. National Archives, Washington, D.C.
Federal Mediation and Conciliation Service Records. R.G. 280. Federal Records Center, Suitland, Md.
Samuel Gompers Letterbooks. Microfilm edition. Library of Congress, Washington, D.C.
William S. Jennings Papers. Florida State Archives, Tallahassee.
Peter O. Knight Papers. P. K. Yonge Library of Florida History, University of Florida, Gainesville.
National Association for the Advancement of Colored People Papers. Library of Congress, Washington, D.C.
National Recovery Administration Records. Record Group 9. National Archives, Washington, D.C.
Herbert S. Phillips Papers. University of South Florida Special Collections, Tampa.
David Sholtz Papers. Florida State Archives, Tallahassee.
Socialist Party of America Papers. Duke University Library, Durham, N.C.
Tampa Board of Trade Records. Tampa Chamber of Commerce, Tampa, Fla.
Norman Thomas Papers. New York Public Library, New York.
Workers Defense League Papers. Walter P. Reuther Library, Wayne State University, Detroit, Mich.
Works Projects Administration Records. Record Group 69. National Archives, Washington, D.C.

## Government Documents

Eighth Census of the United States, 1860. Hillsborough County, Florida, Slave Schedules. National Archives Microcopy No. 653, roll 110.
Report of the Adjutant General of the State of Florida For the Years 1927 and 1928. Tallahassee, Fla., [1928].
Tenth Census of the United States, 1880. Hillsborough County, Florida, Population Schedules. National Archives Microfilm Series T-9, roll 128.
U.S. Bureau of Labor Statistics. Bulletin 161. *Wages and Hours of Labor in the Clothing and Cigar Industries, 1911 to 1913.* Washington, D.C., 1915.
U.S. Bureau of the Census. *Fifteenth Census of the United States: 1930, Population.* Vol. 4. Washington, D.C., 1933.
———. *Fourteenth Census of the United States: 1920, Population.* Vol. 3. Washington, D.C., 1922.
———. *Sixteenth Census of the United States: 1940, Population.* Vol. 3. Washington, D.C., 1943.
———. *Thirteenth Census of the United States: 1910, Population.* Vol. 2. Washington, D.C., 1913.
U.S. Census Office. *Compendium of the Tenth Census.* Washington, D.C., 1883.
———. *Eleventh Census, 1890: Population of the U.S.* Pt. 1. Washington, D.C., 1895.
———. *Eleventh Census, 1890: Report on Wealth, Debt, and Taxation.* Vol. 2. Washington, D.C., 1895.
———. *Ninth Census: The Statistics of the Population of the United States.* Vol. 1. Washington, D.C., 1872.
———. *Thirteenth Census of the United States: 1910, Population.* Vol. 2. Washington, D.C., 1913.
———. *Twelfth Census of the United States: 1900: Manufacturers.* Vol. 8, pt. 2. Washington, D.C., 1902.
———. *Twelfth Census of the United States: 1900, Population.* Pt. 1. Washington, D.C., 1901.
U.S. Department of Commerce. *Report of the Commissioner of Corporations on the Tobacco Industry.* 3 pts. Washington, D.C., 1909, 1911, 1915.
U.S. Immigration Commission. *Immigrants in Industries.* Pt. 14: *Cigar and Tobacco Manufacturing.* Washington, D.C., 1911.
U.S. Senate. *Investigation of Organized Crime in Interstate Commerce: Hearings Before a Special Committee to Investigate Organized Crime in Interstate Commerce.* 81st Cong., 2d Sess. and 82d Cong., 1st Sess. Pt. 1-A. Washington, D.C., 1951.
U.S. Senate. *Punishment for the Crime of Lynching: Hearings before a Subcommittee of the Committee on the Judiciary.* 73d Cong., 2d Sess. Pt. 1. Washington, D.C., 1934.
U.S. Senate Committee on Education and Labor. *Report Pursuant to S. Res. 266, Violations of Free Speech and Rights of Labor.* 76 Cong., 1 Sess. Pt. 6. Washington, D.C., 1939.

## Court Cases

*Brown et al. v. State.* 175 So. 515 (1937).
*Ex Parte Wall,* 107 U.S. 265 (1882).
*In re Wall,* 13 F. 814 (1882).
*Lezama et al. v. State,* 148 So. 304 (1933).
*Smith v. State,* 1 Yeager 228 (1829).

## Newspapers and Periodicals

*Atlanta Constitution.* 1938.
*Atlanta World.* 1934.
*Bartow Informant.* 1882.
*Bradenton Herald.* 1935.
*Chicago Tribune.* 1903, 1936.
*Cigar Makers' Official Journal,* 1887–1935.
*Crescent City News.* 1901.
*Daily Worker.* 1931, 1935–1936.
*Detroit News.* 1936.
Dun, R. B., & Company. *Reference Book (and Key) Containing Ratings of Merchants, Manufacturers and Traders Generally, Throughout the United States and Canada.* 1900, 1910, 1920.
*El Desperatar.* 1901.
*El Internacional,* 1910–11, 1918–22.
Jacksonville *Florida Daily Times.* 1882.
Jacksonville *Florida Times-Union.* 1885, 1887, 1903–04, 1931, 1934.
Jacksonville *Florida Times-Union and Citizen.* 1901.
*Kourier.* 1936.
*La Federación.* 1900–01.
*La Gaceta.* 1931, 1935.
*Miami Herald.* 1935, 1937.
*New Leader.* 1935–36.
New Orleans *Times-Picayune.* 1938.
*New York Herald.* 1887, 1901.
*New York Post.* 1936–38.
*New York Times.* 1927, 1931, 1935–38.
*Ocala Banner.* 1910.
*Palatka News.* 1903.
Pensacola *Daily News.* 1901.
Pensacola *Journal.* 1910.
*Pittsburgh Courier.* 1934.
*Polk County Democrat.* 1936.
*Polk County Record.* 1936.
*Savannah Morning News.* 1882.
*Socialist Call.* 1935–38.
*Southern Worker.* 1931.
St. Augustine *Evening Record.* 1901.
*St. Louis Post-Dispatch.* 1936–38.
*St. Petersburg Times.* 1901, 1935, 1937.
Tallahassee *Daily Democrat.* 1934–35.
Tallahassee *Weekly Floridian.* 1882, 1887.
*Tampa Citizen.* 1919–21.

*Tampa Daily Times.* 1917–39.
*Tampa Florida Peninsula.* 1858–61, 1871, 1877.
*Tampa Guardian.* 1886.
*Tampa Journal.* 1886–87.
*Tampa Tribune,* 1886–92.
*Tampa Sunland Tribune.* 1877–78, 1881–82.
*Tampa Morning Tribune.* 1895–1940.
*Tobacco.* 1887, 1892, 1899–1901, 1909–11, 1920.
*Tobacco Leaf.* 1887, 1899–1901, 1910, 1918, 1920–21, 1931–33.
*U.S. Tobacco Journal.* 1899, 1900–1901, 1910, 1919–20, 1931.
*Weekly Tallahassean.* 1901.


## Books

American Civil Liberties Union. *The Bill of Rights—150 Years After: The Story of Civil Liberty, 1938–1939.* New York, 1939.
———. *Eternal Vigilance! The Story of Civil Liberty, 1937–38.* New York, 1938.
———. *Let Freedom Ring! The Story of Civil Liberty, 1936–37.* New York, 1937.
American Federation of Labor. *Report of the Proceedings of the 30th Annual Convention of the American Federation of Labor.* Washington, D.C., 1910.
Ames, Jessie Daniel. *The Changing Character of Lynching.* Atlanta, 1942.
Auerbach, Jerold S. *Labor and Liberty: The La Follette Committee and the New Deal.* Indianapolis, 1966.
Avrich, Paul. *The Haymarket Tragedy.* Princeton, N.J., 1984.
Ayers, Edward L. *Vengeance and Justice: Crime and Punishment in the 19th-Century American South.* New York, 1984.
Baer, Willis N. *The Economic Development of the Cigar Industry in the United States.* Lancaster, Pa., 1933.
Barbour, George M. *Florida for Tourists, Invalids, and Settlers.* New York, 1882.
Bernstein, Irving. *The Lean Years: A History of the American Worker, 1920–1933.* Baltimore, 1966.
———. *The New Deal Collective Bargaining Policy.* Berkeley, 1950.
Bing, Alexander M. *War-Time Strikes and Their Adjustment.* 1921; New York, 1971.
*Biographical Directory of the American Congress, 1774–1961.* Washington, 1961.
Brearley, H.C. *Homicide in the United States.* 1932; Montclair, N.J., 1969.
Brenner, Anita, and S. S. Winthrop. *Tampa's Reign of Terror.* New York, n.d. [1933].
Brown, Richard Maxwell. *South Carolina Regulators.* Cambridge, Mass., 1963.
———. *Strain of Violence: Historical Studies of American Violence and Vigilantism.* New York, 1975.
Brownell, Blaine A. *The Urban Ethos in the South, 1920–1930.* Baton Rouge, La., 1975.

———, and David R. Goldfield, eds. *The City in Southern History: The Growth of Urban Civilization in the South.* Port Washington, N.Y., 1977.
Bruce, Dickson, D., Jr. *Violence and Culture in the Antebellum South.* Austin, Tex., 1979.
Buder, Stanley. *Pullman: An Experiment in Industrial Order and Community Planning, 1880–1930.* New York, 1967.
Campbell, A. Stuart. *The Cigar Industry of Tampa, Florida.* Gainesville, Fla., 1939.
Carter, Dan T. *Scottsboro: A Tragedy of the American South.* Baton Rouge, La., 1969.
Cash, Wilbur J. *The Mind of the South.* New York, 1941.
Caughey, John W. *Their Majesties the Mob.* Chicago, 1960.
Chadbourn, James Harmon. *Lynching and the Law.* Chapel Hill, N.C., 1933.
Chalmers, David M. *Hooded Americanism: The First Century of the Ku Klux Klan, 1865–1965.* Garden City, N.Y., 1965.
Church, George B., Jr. *The Life of Henry Laurens Mitchell, Florida's 16th Governor.* New York, 1978.
Cobb, James C. *Industrialization and Southern Society, 1877–1984.* Lexington, Ky., 1984.
Commission on Interracial Cooperation. *The Mob Still Rides: A Review of the Lynching Record, 1931–1935.* Atlanta, n.d.
Committee for the Defense of Civil Rights in Tampa. *Tampa—Tar and Terror.* New York, n.d. [1936].
Cooper, Patricia A. *Once a Cigar Maker: Men, Women, and Work Culture in American Cigar Factories, 1900–1919.* Urbana, Ill., 1987.
Covington, James W. *The Billy Bowlegs War. 1855–1858: The Final Stand of the Seminoles Against the Whites.* Chuluota, Fla., 1982.
Crooks, Esther J., and Crooks, Ruth W. *The Ring Tournament in the United States.* Richmond, Va., 1936.
Cutler, James Elbert. *Lynch-Law: An Investigation into the History of Lynching in the United States.* 1905; Montclair, N.J., 1969.
Dahl, Robert A. *Who Governs? Democracy and Power in an American City.* New Haven, Conn., 1961.
Dobb, Maurice. *Studies in the Development of Capitalism.* New York, 1963.
Dollard, John. *Caste and Class in a Southern Town.* 1937; Garden City, N.Y., 1957.
Eaton, Clement. *The Growth of Southern Civilization, 1790–1860.* New York, 1961.
Edwards, P. K. *Strikes in the United States, 1881–1974.* New York, 1981.
Feldberg, Michael. *The Turbulent Era: Riot and Disorder in Jacksonian America.* New York, 1980.
*Florida State Gazetteer and Business Directory, 1883–84.* Jacksonville, n.d.
Flynn, Charles L., Jr. *White Land, Black Labor: Caste and Class in Late Nineteenth-Century Georgia.* Baton Rouge, La., 1983.
Flynt, Wayne. *Cracker Messiah: Governor Sidney J. Catts of Florida.* Baton Rouge, La., 1977.

Foster, William Z. *From Bryan to Stalin*. New York, 1937.
Franklin, John Hope. *The Militant South, 1800–1861*. Cambridge, Mass., 1956.
Fredrickson, George M. *The Black Image in the White Mind: The Debate on Afro-American Character and Destiny, 1817–1914*. New York, 1971.
Gaston, Paul M. *The New South Creed: A Study in Southern Mythmaking*. New York, 1970.
*The Gate-to-the-Gulf City Directory, 1893*. Tampa, 1893.
Genovese, Eugene D. *In Red and Black: Marxian Explorations in Southern and Afro-American History*. New York, 1973.
Goldfield, David R. *Cotton Fields and Skyscrapers: Southern City and Region, 1607–1980*. Baton Rouge, La., 1982.
Gompers, Samuel. *Seventy Years of Life and Labor: An Autobiography*. 2 vols. 1925; New York, 1967.
Graham, Hugh Davis, and Ted Robert Gurr, eds. *The History of Violence in America: Historical and Comparative Perspectives*. New York, 1969.
Grismer, Karl H. *Tampa: A History of the City of Tampa and the Tampa Bay Region of Florida*. St. Petersburg, Fla., 1950.
Gutman, Herbert G. *Work, Culture and Society in Industrializing America: Essays in American Working-Class and Social History*. New York, 1976.
Haddock, Dudley. *Wallace F. Stovall, A Publisher's Publisher*. N.P., 1949.
Hall, Jacquelyn Dowd. *Revolt Against Chivalry: Jessie Daniel Ames and the Women's Campaign Against Lynching*. New York, 1974.
Harris, Carl V. *Political Power in Birmingham, 1871–1921*. Knoxville, 1977.
Harrison, Charles E. *Genealogical Records of the Pioneers of Tampa and of Some Who Came After Them*. Tampa, 1915.
Haynes, Robert V. *A Night of Violence: The Houston Riot of 1917*. Baton Rouge, La., 1976.
Hazen, Pauline Browne. *The Blue Book: Tampa, Florida, 1912–1913*. Tampa, 1912.
Hetherington, M. F. *History of Polk County, Florida: Narrative and Biographical*. 1928; Chuluota, Fla., 1971.
Higham, John. *Strangers in the Land: Patterns of American Nativism, 1860–1925*. New York, 1963.
Hunter, Floyd. *Community Power Structure: A Study of Decision Makers*. Chapel Hill, N.C., 1953.
Jackson, Kenneth T. *The Ku Klux Klan in the City, 1915–1930*. New York, 1967.
Jameson, Jack. *Night Riders in Sunny Florida: The K.K.K. Murder of Joseph Shoemaker*. New York, 1936.
Kaufman, Stuart B. *Samuel Gompers and the Origins of the American Federation of Labor, 1848–1896*. Westport, Conn., 1973.
Kefauver, Estes. *Crime in America*. Garden City, N.Y., 1951.
Kelley, Robert. *The Cultural Pattern in American Politics: The First Century*. New York, 1979.
Kousser, J. Morgan. *The Shaping of Southern Politics: Suffrage Restric-*

tion and the Establishment of the One-Party South. New Haven, 1974.
Lambright, Edwin D. *The Life and Exploits of Gasparilla, Last of the Buccaneers, With the History of Ye Mystic Krewe.* Tampa, 1936.
Leonard, Irving A., ed. *The Florida Adventures of Kirk Munroe.* Chuluota, Fla., 1975.
Lowry, Sumter L. *Ole 93.* Tampa, 1970.
Mack, Russell H. *The Cigar Manufacturing Industry: Factors of Instability Affecting Production and Employment.* Philadelphia, 1933.
*Makers of America: Florida Edition.* Vol. 1. Atlanta, 1909.
Mandle, Jay R. *The Roots of Black Poverty: The Southern Plantation Economy After the Civil War.* Durham, N.C., 1978.
Martin, Charles H. *The Angelo Herndon Case and Southern Justice.* Baton Rouge, La., 1976.
Massari, Angelo. *The Wonderful Life of Angelo Massari.* New York, 1965.
Matthews, Janet Snyder. *Edge of Wilderness: A Settlement History of Manatee River and Sarasota Bay, 1528–1885.* Tulsa, 1983.
Mays, Benjamin E. *Born to Rebel: An Autobiography.* New York, 1971.
McCabe, David A. *The Standard Rate in American Trade Unions.* Baltimore, 1912.
McGovern, James R. *Anatomy of a Lynching: The Killing of Claude Neal.* Baton Rouge, La., 1982.
McKay, D.B. *Pioneer Florida.* 3 vols. Tampa, n.d. [1959].
McLaurin, Melton Alonza. *The Knights of Labor in the South.* Westport, Conn., 1978.
———. *Paternalism and Protest: Southern Cotton Mill Workers and Organized Labor, 1875–1905.* Westport, Conn., 1971.
Montgomery, David. *Workers' Control in America: Studies in the History of Work, Technology, and Labor Struggles.* Cambridge, 1979.
Moore, William Howard. *The Kefauver Committee and the Politics of Crime, 1950–52.* Columbia, Mo., 1974.
Morgan, Edmund S. *American Slavery, American Freedom: The Ordeal of Colonial Virginia.* New York, 1976.
Mormino, Gary R., and George E. Pozzetta. *The Immigrant World of Ybor City: Italians and Their Latin Neighbors in Tampa, 1885–1985.* Urbana, Ill., 1987.
Morris, Allen. *The People of Lawmaking in Florida, 1822–1983.* Tallahassee, Fla., 1982.
Muniz, José Rivero. *The Ybor City Story, 1885–1954.* Trans. Eustasio Fernandez and Henry Beltran. Tampa, 1976.
Murray, Robert K. *Red Scare: A Study in National Hysteria, 1919–1920.* Minneapolis, 1955.
National Association for the Advancement of Colored People. *Thirty Years of Lynching in the United States, 1889–1918.* 1919; New York, 1969.
*National Cyclopedia of American Biography.* Vol. 6. New York, 1929.
Nieburg, H.L. *Political Violence: The Behavioral Process.* New York, 1969.
Osterweis, Rollin G. *Romanticism and Nationalism in the Old South.* New Haven, 1949.

Phillips, Ulrich B. *American Negro Slavery.* New York, 1918.
Pizzo, Anthony P. *Tampa Town, 1824–1886: The Cracker Village With a Latin Accent.* Miami, 1968.
Placie, William J., ed. *Prominent Personalities of Tampa.* Tampa, 1942.
*R. L. Polk & Co.'s Tampa City Directory, 1910.* Tampa, 1910.
*R. L. Polk & Co.'s Tampa City Directory, 1918.* Tampa, 1918.
*R. L. Polk & Co.'s Tampa City Directory, 1920.* Jacksonville, 1920.
*R. L. Polk & Co.'s Tampa City Directory, 1932.* N.P., n.d.
*R. L. Polk & Co.'s Tampa City Directory, 1935.* N.P., n.d.
Rabinowitz, Howard N. *Race Relations in the Urban South, 1865–1890.* New York, 1978.
Raper, Arthur F. *The Tragedy of Lynching.* 1933; Montclair, N.J., 1969.
Redfield, H.V. *Homicide, North and South: Being a Comparative View of Crime Against the Person in Several Parts of the United States.* Philadelphia, 1880.
Reed, John Shelton. *The Enduring South: Subcultural Persistence in Mass Society.* Chapel Hill, N.C., 1974.
Rice, Arnold. *The Ku Klux Klan in American Politics.* Washington, D.C., 1962.
Richards, Leonard L. *"Gentlemen of Property and Standing": Anti-Abolition Mobs in Jacksonian America.* New York, 1970.
Rosenbaum, H. Jon, and Peter C. Sederberg, eds. *Vigilante Politics.* Philadelphia, 1976.
Rubenstein, Richard E. *Rebels in Eden: Mass Political Violence in the United States.* Boston, 1970.
Senkewicz, Robert M. *Vigilantes in Gold Rush San Francisco.* Stanford, Cal., 1985.
Shofner, Jerrell H. *Nor Is It Over Yet: Florida in the Era of Reconstruction, 1863–1877.* Gainesville, Fla., 1974.
*Sholes' Directory of the City of Tampa, 1901.* Tampa, n.d.
Shott, John G. *How "Right-to-Work" Laws Are Passed: Florida Sets the Pattern.* Washington, D.C., 1956.
Smelser, Neil J. *Theory of Collective Behavior.* New York, 1962.
Stubbs, Jean. *Tobacco on the Periphery: A Case Study in Cuban Labour History, 1860–1958.* Cambridge, 1985.
Sunshine, Silvia. *Petals Plucked from Sunny Climes.* 1880; Gainesville, Fla., 1976.
Terkel, Studs. *Hard Times: An Oral History of the Great Depression in America.* New York, 1970.
Tilly, Charles, Louis Tilly, and Richard Tilly. *The Rebellious Century, 1830–1930.* Cambridge, Mass., 1975.
Tindall, George Brown. *The Emergence of the New South, 1913–1945.* Baton Rouge, La., 1967.
Tomlins, Christopher L. *The State and the Unions: Labor Relations, Law and the Organized Labor Movement in America, 1880–1960.* Cambridge, 1985.
Toplin, Robert Brent. *Unchallenged Violence: An American Ordeal.* Westport, Conn., 1975.
Trelease, Allen W. *White Terror: The Ku Klux Klan Conspiracy and Southern Reconstruction.* New York, 1971.
Vanderwood, Paul J. *Night Riders of Reelfoot Lake.* Memphis, 1969.

Watkins, George S. *Labor Problems and Labor Administration in the United States During the World War.* 1920; New York, 1970.
Watts, Eugene J. *The Social Bases of City Politics: Atlanta, 1865–1903.* Westport, Conn., 1978.
*Webb's Jacksonville and Consolidated Directory of the Representative Cities of East and South Florida, 1886.* Jacksonville, 1886.
*Who Was Who in America.* Vol. 1. Chicago, 1942.
Wiener, Jonathan M. *Social Origins of the New South: Alabama, 1860–1885.* Baton Rouge, La., 1978.
Williamson, Edward C. *Florida Politics in the Gilded Age, 1877–1893.* Gainesville, Fla., 1976.
Williamson, Joel. *The Crucible of Race: Black-White Relations in the American South Since Emancipation.* New York, 1984.
Woodward, C. Vann. *Origins of the New South, 1877–1913.* Baton Rouge, La., 1966.
Work, Monroe, ed. *Negro Year Book.* 11 vols. Tuskegee, Ala., 1912–56.
Wyatt-Brown, Bertram. *Southern Honor: Ethics and Behavior in the Old South.* New York, 1982.
Yglesias, Jose. *The Truth About Them.* New York, 1971.
Zangrando, Robert L. *The NAACP Crusade Against Lynching, 1909–1950.* Philadelphia, 1980.


### Articles and Essays

Ans, André Marcel d'. "The Legend of Gasparilla: Myth and History on Florida's West Coast." Trans. Marie-Joèle Ingalls. *Tampa Bay History* 2 (Fall/Winter 1980): 5–29.
Appel, John C. "The Unionization of Florida Cigarmakers and the Coming of the War With Spain." *Hispanic American Historical Review* 36 (Feb. 1956): 38–49.
Brearley, H.C. "The Pattern of Violence." In *Culture of the South*, ed. W. T. Couch. Chapel Hill, N.C., 1934.
Brenner, Anita. "Tampa's Reign of Terror." *Nation* 135 (Dec. 7, 1932): 555.
Brown, Ben. "In His Own Write: Ybor City's Native Son." *Tampa Tribune*, April 1, 1979.
Brown, Earl J. "Eli Buchanan Witt: The South's Outstanding Tobacco Merchant." Tampa Historical Society *Sunland Tribune* 7 (Nov. 1981): 85–94.
Chamberlin, Donald L. "Fort Brooke: Frontier Outpost, 1824–42." *Tampa Bay History* 7 (Spring/Summer 1985): 5–29.
"Civil Rights Protests in Tampa: Oral Memoirs of Conflict and Accommodation." *Tampa Bay History* 1 (Spring/Summer 1979): 37–54.
Cooper, Patricia A. "'The Traveling Fraternity': Union Cigar Makers and Geographic Mobility, 1900–1919." *Journal of Social History* 17 (Fall 1983): 127–38.
Covington, James W. "The Armed Occupation Act of 1842." *Florida Historical Quarterly* 40 (July 1961): 41–52.
Cox, Merlin G. "David Sholtz: New Deal Governor of Florida." *Florida Historical Quarterly* 43 (Oct. 1964): 142–52.

Davis, Horace B. "Company Towns." *Encyclopedia of the Social Sciences*. Vol. 4. New York, 1942.
Dillon, Rodney E., Jr. "South Florida in 1860." *Florida Historical Quarterly* 60 (April 1982): 440–454.
Doyle, Don Harrison. "Urbanization and Southern Culture: Economic Elites in Four New South Cities (Atlanta, Nashville, Charleston, Mobile), c. 1865–1910." In *Toward a New South? Studies in Post–Civil War Southern Communities*, eds. Orville Vernon Burton and Robert C. McMath, Jr. Westport, Conn., 1982.
Ely, James W., Jr., and David J. Bodenhamer. "Regionalism and the Legal History of the South." In *Ambivalent Legacy: A Legal History of the South*, eds. David J. Bodenhamer and James W. Ely, Jr. Jackson, Miss., 1984.
Evans, W. D. "Effects of Mechanization in Cigar Manufacture." *Monthly Labor Review* 46 (May 1981): 1100–21.
Flynt Wayne. "Florida Labor and Political 'Radicalism,' 1919–1920." *Labor History* 9 (Winter 1968).
Frantz, Joe B. "The Frontier Tradition: An Invitation to Violence." In *Violence in America: Historical and Comparative Perspectives*, ed. Hugh Davis Graham and Ted Robert Gurr. New York, 1969.
Gastil, Raymond D. "Homicide and a Regional Culture of Violence." *American Sociological Review* 36 (June 1971): 412–27.
Graham, Hugh Davis. "The Paradox of American Violence: A Historical Appraisal." In *Collective Violence*, eds. James F. Short, Jr., and Marvin E. Wolfgang. Chicago, 1972.
Greenbaum, Susan D. "Afro-Cubans in Exile: Tampa, Florida, 1886–1984." *Cuban Studies/Estudios Cubanos* 15 (Winter 1985): 59–72.
Grimshaw, Allen D. "Interpreting Collective Violence: An Argument for the Importance of Social Structure." In *Collective Violence*, eds. James F. Short, Jr. and Marvin E. Wolfgang. Chicago, 1972.
Hackney, Sheldon. "Southern Violence." *American Historical Review* 74 (Feb. 1969): 906–25.
Hall, Jacquelyn Dowd. "The Mind That Burns in Each Body." In *Powers of Desire: The Politics of Sexuality*, eds. Ann Snitown, Christine Stansell, and Sharon Thompson. New York, 1983.
Hawes, Leland. "Tampa Church Marks Centennial." *Tampa Tribune*, March 23, 1985.
———. "Tampa's Most Turbulent Election." *Tampa Tribune*, March 31, 1984.
Herring, Hubert. "Tampa Warns America." *Christian Century* 53 (March 4, 1936): 359–60.
Hewitt, Nancy A. "Women in Ybor City: An Interview with a Woman Cigarworker." *Tampa Bay History* 7 (Fall/Winter 1985): 161–65.
Hofstadter, Richard. "Reflections on Violence in the United States." In *American Violence: A Documentary History*, ed. Richard Hofstadter and Michael Wallace. New York, 1970.
Holmes, William F. "Moonshining and Collective Violence: Georgia, 1889–1895." *Journal of American History* 67 (Dec. 1980): 589–611.
———. "Whitecapping: Agrarian Violence in Mississippi, 1902–1906." *Journal of Southern History* 35 (May 1969): 165–85.

———. "Whitecapping in Mississippi: Agrarian Violence in the Populist Era." *Mid-America* 55 (April 1973): 134–48.
Hovland, Carl Iver, and Robert R. Sears. "Correlation of Lynchings with Economic Indices." *Journal of Psychology* 9 (May 1940): 301–10.
Howard, Walter. "'A Blot on Tampa's History': The 1934 Lynching of Robert Johnson." *Tampa Bay History* 6 (Fall/Winter 1984): 5–18.
Ingalls, Robert P. "Anti-Labor Vigilantes: The South During the 1930s." *Southern Exposure* 12 (Nov./Dec. 1984): 72–78.
———. "Antiradical Violence in Birmingham During the 1930s." *Journal of Southern History* 47 (Nov. 1981): 521–44.
———. "General Joseph B. Wall and Lynch Law in Tampa." *Florida Historical Quarterly* 63 (July 1984): 51–70.
———. "Lynching and Establishment Violence in Tampa, 1858–1935." *Journal of Southern History* 53 (Nov. 1987): 613–44.
———. "The Murder of Joseph Shoemaker." *Southern Exposure* 8 (Summer 1980): 64–68.
———. "Radicals and Vigilantes: The 1931 Strike of Tampa Cigar Workers." In *Southern Workers and Their Unions, 1880–1975: Selected Papers, the Second Southern Labor History Conference, 1978*, ed. Merl E. Reed, Leslie S. Hough, and Gary M. Fink. Westport, Conn., 1981.
———. "The Tampa Flogging Case, Urban Vigilantism." *Florida Historical Quarterly* 56 (July 1977): 13–27.
———. "Vanquished But Not Convinced: Worker Militancy and Vigilante Violence in Tampa." *Southern Exposure* 14 (Jan./Feb. 1986): 51–58.
Ingram, James M. "John Perry Wall: A Man for All Seasons." Tampa Historical Society *Sunland Tribune* 2 (Oct. 1975): 9–19.
Keene, Jesse L. "Gavino Gutierrez and His Contributions to Tampa." *Florida Historical Quarterly* 36 (July 1957): 33–41.
Kernan, Thomas J. "The Jurisprudence of Lawlessness." *Report of the Twenty-ninth Annual Meeting of the American Bar Association*. Philadelphia, 1906.
Kipp, Samuel M., III. "Old Notables and Newcomers: The Economic and Political Elite of Greensboro, North Carolina, 1880–1920." *Journal of Southern History* 43 (Aug. 1977): 373–94.
"The Klan in Florida." *New Republic* 91 (June 9, 1937): 18.
Lasser, David. "Socialists and the Unemployed." *American Socialist Monthly* 5 (June 1936): 10–14.
Lawson, Steven F. "From Sit-in to Race Riot: Businessmen, Blacks, and the Pursuit of Moderation in Tampa, 1960–1967." In *Southern Businessmen and Desegregation*, eds. Elizabeth Jacoway and David R. Colburn. Baton Rouge, La., 1982.
Lears, T. J. Jackson. "The Concept of Cultural Hegemony: Problems and Possibilities." *American Historical Review* 90 (Oct. 1985): 567–93.
Levenstein, Aaron. "A Fighter for Freedom." *New Republic* 93 (Dec. 8, 1937): 122.
Long, Durward. "The Historical Beginnings of Ybor City and Modern Tampa." *Florida Historical Quarterly* 45 (July 1966): 31–44.

———. "An Immigrant Co-Operative Medicine Program in the South, 1887–1963." *Journal of Southern History* 17 (Nov. 1965): 417–34.
———. "Labor Relations in the Tampa Cigar Industry, 1885–1911." *Labor History* 12 (Fall 1971): 551–59.
———. "The Making of Modern Tampa: A City of the New South, 1885–1911." *Florida Historical Quarterly* 49 (April 1971): 333–45.
———. "The Open-Closed Shop Battle in Tampa's Cigar Industry, 1919–1921." *Florida Historical Quarterly* 47 (Oct. 1968): 101–21.
———. "'La Resistencia': Tampa's Immigrant Labor Union." *Labor History* 6 (Fall 1965): 193–213.
Martin, Charles H. "The International Labor Defense and Black America." *Labor History* 26 (Spring 1985): 165–94.
Matthews, Janet Snyder. "'He Has Carried His Life in His Hands': The 'Sarasota Assassination Society' of 1884." *Florida Historical Quarterly* 58 (Jan. 1979): 1–21.
Miller, William D. "Myth and New South City Murder Rates." *Mississippi Quarterly* 26 (Spring 1973): 143–53.
Montgomery, David. "Violence and the Struggle for Unions in the South, 1880–1930." In *Perspectives on the American South: An Annual Review of Society, Politics and Culture*, vol. 1, ed. Merle Black and John Shelton Reed. New York, 1981.
Mormino, Gary R. "Tampa and the New Urban South: The Weight Strike of 1899." *Florida Historical Quarterly* 60 (Jan. 1982): 337–56.
———. "Tampa: From Hell Hole to the Good Life." In *Sunbelt Cities: Politics and Growth Since World War II*, ed. Richard M. Bernard and Bradley R. Rice. Austin, Tex., 1983.
Muniz, José Rivero. "Tampa at the Close of the Nineteenth Century." *Florida Historical Quarterly* 41 (April 1963): 332–42.
Nelli, Humbert S. "Italians and Crime in Chicago: The Formative Years, 1890–1920." *American Journal of Sociology* 74 (Jan. 1969): 373–91.
Otto, John Solomon. "Florida's Cattle-Ranching Frontier: Hillsborough County (1860)." *Florida Historical Quarterly* 63 (July 1984): 71–83.
———. "Hillsborough County (1850): A Community in the South Florida Flatwoods." *Florida Historical Quarterly* 62 (Oct. 1983): 180–93.
Page, Walter H. "A Journey Through the Southern States." *World's Work* 14 (June 1907): 9007–42.
Pérez, Louis A., Jr. "Cubans in Tampa: From Exiles to Immigrants, 1892–1901." *Florida Historical Quarterly* 57 (Oct. 1978): 129–40.
———. "Reminiscences of a *Lector*: Cuban Cigar Workers in Tampa." *Florida Historical Quarterly* 53 (April 1975): 443–49.
Pizzo, Tony. "The Italian Heritage in Tampa." Tampa Historical Society *Sunland Tribune* 3 (Nov. 1977): 24–33.
Poyo, Gerald E. "Tampa Cigarworkers and the Struggle for Cuban Independence." *Tampa Bay History* 7 (Fall/Winter 1985): 94–105.
Pozzetta, George E. "Immigrants and Radicals in Tampa, Florida." *Florida Historical Quarterly* 57 (Jan. 1979): 337–48.
———. "Italians and the General Strike of 1910," In *Pane e Lavoro: The Italian American Working Class*, ed. George E. Pozzetta. Toronto, 1980.

Price, Richard. "The Labour Process and Labour History." *Social History* 8 (Jan. 1983): 57–75.
Sanchez, Arsenio M. "Incentives Helped to Build West Tampa." Tampa Historical Society *Sunland Tribune* 11 (Dec. 1985): 9–13.
Shofner, Jerrell H. "Custom, Law, and History: The Enduring Influence of Florida's 'Black Code.'" *Florida Historical Quarterly* 55 (Jan. 1977): 277–98.
Smith, Albert C. "'Southern Violence' Reconsidered: Arson as Protest in Black-Belt Georgia, 1865–1910." *Journal of Southern History* 51 (Nov. 1985): 527–64.
"The Southern Street Duel." *Outlook* 90 (Dec. 5, 1908): 773.
Sydnor, Charles S. "The Southern and the Laws." *Journal of Southern History* 6 (Feb. 1940): 3–23.
Taft, Philip, and Philip Ross. "American Labor Violence: Its Causes, Character, and Outcome." In *Violence in America: Historical and Comparative Perspectives*, ed. Hugh Davis Graham and Ted Robert Gurr. New York, 1969.
"Technological Changes in the Cigar Industy and Their Effects on Labor." *Monthly Labor Review*. 33 (Dec. 1931): 11–17.
Thompson, E. P. "'Rough Music': Le Charivari anglais." *Annales: Économies, Sociétés, Civilisations* 27 (March/April 1972): 285–312.
Vandiver, Frank E. "The Southerner as Extremist." In *The Idea of the South: Pursuit of a Central Theme*, ed. Frank E. Vandiver. Chicago, 1964.
Wade, Richard C. "Violence in the Cities: A Historical View." In *Urban Violence*, ed. Charles U. Daly. Chicago, 1969.
Wakstein, Allen M. "The Origins of the Open Shop Movement, 1919–1920." *Journal of American History* 51 (Dec. 1964): 460–475.
Wallace, Michael. "The Uses of Violence in American History." *American Scholar* 40 (Winter 1970–71): 81–102.
Westfall, L. Glenn. "Latin Entrepreneurs and the Birth of Ybor City." *Tampa Bay History* 7 (Fall/Winter 1985): 5–21.
Wold, Herman. "And Southern Death." *Common Sense* 5 (Feb. 1936): 12.
Yglesias, Jose. "The Radical Latino Island in the Deep South." *Tampa Bay History* 7 (Fall/Winter 1985): 166–69.

## Theses and Dissertations

Cooper, Patricia Ann. "From Hand Craft to Mass Production: Men, Women and Work Culture in American Cigar Factories, 1900–1919." Ph.D. diss., University of Maryland, 1981.
Dunn, James William. "The New Deal and Florida Politics." Ph.D. diss., Florida State University, 1971.
Jackson, Jesse Jefferson. "The Negro and the Law in Florida, 1821–1921: Legal Patterns of Segregation and Control in Florida, 1821–1921." M.A. thesis, Florida State University, 1960.
Peek, Ralph L. "Lawlessness and the Restoration of Order in Florida, 1868–1971." Ph.D. diss., University of Florida, 1964.
Poyo, Gerald Eugene. "Cuban Émigré Communities in the United

States and the Independence of Their Homeland, 1852–1895." Ph.D. diss., University of Florida, 1983.
Steffy, Joan Marie. "The Cuban Immigrants of Tampa, Florida, 1886–1898." M.A. thesis, University of South Florida, 1975.
Westfall, L. Glenn. "Don Vicente Martínez Ybor, The Man and His Empire: Development of the Clear Havana Industry in Cuba and Florida in the Nineteenth Century." Ph.D. diss., University of Florida, 1977.

**Oral Histories**

Poulnot, Eugene F. Interview by Ian Van Buskirk. September 1973. Tape recording, in possession of author.
WPA Federal Writers' Project. "History of Ybor City as Narrated by José García." Typescript in P. K. Yonge Library of Florida History, University of Florida, Gainesville.
———. "Life History of Domingo Ginesta." Typescript in University of South Florida Special Collections, Tampa.
———. "Life History of Enrique Pendas." Typescript in University of South Florida Special Collections, Tampa.
———. "Life History of Fernando Lemos." Typescript in University of South Florida Special Collections, Tampa.
———. "Life History of John Cacciatore." Typescript in University of South Florida Special Collections, Tampa.
———. "Life History of José Ramón Sanfeliz." Typescript in University of South Florida Special Collections, Tampa.

# Index

Afro-Cubans, xix, 56, 223 n.123, 227 n.53
Akerman, Alexander, 155, 156
Alabama, 15
Albano, Angelo, 96, 97, 98, 105, 115, 236 n.40, 237 n.50
Allen, C. E., 236 n.22
Alvarez, Cesario, 246 n.181, 247 n.206
American Cigar Company, 71, 82, 83, 231 n.62
American Civil Liberties Union (ACLU), 186, 187, 195, 255 n.137; condemns Tampa, xvii, 200, 259 n.5; on decline of vigilantism, 204; defends accused Communists, 247 n.208; and Earl Browder rally, 201; and flogging cases, 184, 185, 198, 256 n.169; and strikes (1931), 157
American Commonwealth Federation, 181
American Federation of Labor (AFL), 120, 150; affiliates in Tampa, 70, 77, 90, 102–3, 105, 136, 210, 211; and floggings (1935), 185; nature of, 61–62; and strikes (1910), 108; and strikes (1920), 137, 139; see also Central Trades and Labor Association
American Legion, 151, 152, 154, 186
American Tobacco Company, 101, 120; and antiunionism, 71, 112; and cigar industry, 70–71, 149, 231 n.62; closes Tampa factories, 158, 161; and "trust factories" in Tampa, 71; see also American Cigar Company
Ames, Jessie Daniel, 253 n.87
anarchism, 57, 101

anarchists: attitudes toward, 50, 52, 75, 80, 84, 122; and Cuba Libre, 227 n.57; in Tampa, 34, 43
Anderson, John B., 69–70
antilynching legislation, 250 n.36
Association of Southern Women for the Prevention of Lynching, 167, 251 n.39
Atlanta, Ga., 259 n.5

Barcia, Luis, 232 n.93, 232 n.101
Bartlum, Joseph F., 107
Bartow, Fla., 192–93, 199
Beckwith, William H., 236 n.22
Benitez, Santos, 36
Bianco, Pietro, 148, 149
Bing, Alexander M., 116
Birmingham, Ala., 200, 217 n.31, 250 n.34, 259 n.5
Bize, Louis A., 119, 135, 136
"Black Hand," 97
blacks, 151, 157, 206; and civil rights movement, 214; discrimination against, 27–28, 166, 177, 195, 196, 212, 223 n.123; lynching of, in the South, 3, 28, 183, 209, 220 n.41; lynching of, in Tampa, 12, 29–30, 166–68, 204, 208–9, 212; number of, in Tampa, 27, 166; during post–Reconstruction era, 26–28; during Reconstruction, 26; as slaves, 10, 12, 20; as vigilante victims, 163, 184, 205; see also Afro-Cubans
Bloxham, William D., 219 n.26
Bolshevism, 120, 122, 146; see also communism
Bonillo, Enrique, 247 n.206
Boston, Mass., 112
Bowyer, Frank C., 239 n.116

Bradley, Joseph P., 22
Brandeis, Louis D., 198
Bridges, John P., 182, 194, 196, 255 n.134, 257 n.186
Brorein, Carl D., 248 n.211
Browder, Earl, 200–1, 204
Brown, Charles A. ("Smitty"), 194, 196, 252 n.78, 255 n.134, 257 n.186
Buchanan, Joseph R., 137–38
Buffalo, N.Y., 80
Burrell, Walter T., 252 n.78
Bush, W. D., 196, 202, 257 n.186

Cabrera, Angel, 246 n.181, 247 n.206
Cabrera, Eugene, 246 n.181
California, 23, 207
Campo, José, 246 n.181, 247 n.206
Carlisle, Carl W., 182, 194, 196, 255 n.134, 257 n.186
Carlton, Doyle E., 168
Carruth, Melville W., 236 n.22, 238 n.77
Casellas, Pedro, 232 n.101
cattle ranching, 10
Catts, Sidney J., 137, 143, 149
Cedar Key, Fla., 2
Central Labor Union of New York, 41
Central Trades and Labor Assembly, 70, 77, 105, 120, 186, 232 n.93, 246 n.174
Centro Asturiano, 56
Centro Espanõl, 56
Chancey, Robert E. Lee, 207; biography, 177; and Communists, 151, 152; and election of 1935, 177, 180, 181; and flogging cases, 185, 188–89, 257 n.186; and reelection (1939), 202; and strikes (1931), 154–55, 156
Chappell, Robert L. 182, 194, 197, 255 n.134, 257 n.186
charivari, 14, 15
Chicago, Ill., 61
cigarettes, 71
cigar industry: arrival in Tampa, 31, 32; collective bargaining in, 158–59, 160–61; decline of, 149, 158, 161, 162, 213–14; in Havana, 33, 58, 78, 158, 210; in Jacksonville, 72; in Key West, 32, 33, 37, 73, 78, 86, 210; and machinery, 150, 158, 159, 161, 214; number of employ-

cigar industry (continued)
ees in, 56, 87, 121, 149, 248 n.214; number of factories, 229 n.5; output of, 87, 121, 149, 158; and Tampa's economy, 35, 37, 41, 55, 69, 76, 87, 90, 95, 112, 117, 135, 136, 146, 150, 179, 208, 210, 226 n.26; in West Tampa, 55–56
cigarmakers, 224 n.9; see also cigarworkers
Cigar Makers' International Union (CMIU): and government mediation, 118, 137; locals in Tampa, 61, 62, 133; membership in Tampa, 62, 81, 84, 87, 88, 117, 121, 145, 149, 150, 159, 241 n.37; and NRA code, 158–59; nature of 61–62; organizing in Tampa, 62, 84–85, 86, 88, 158–59; and radicals, 150, 248 n.222; and La Resistencia, 69, 70, 71, 72, 77, 211; and strike benefits, 110–11, 134, 144; and strikes (1900), 63, 69–70; and strikes (1901), 72, 77, 81; and strikes (1910), 107, 110–11; and strikes (1920), 133, 135, 139; and vigilantism, 77, 85, 98, 232 n.94; see also Joint Advisory Board
cigar manufacturers: as absentee owners, 61, 71, 90, 99–100, 133, 155, 160, 230 n.36, 235 n.20; antiunionism of, 32, 58–59, 71, 73, 79–80, 85–86, 112, 133, 134, 156, 186, 210; appeals for aid, 38, 51, 73, 89, 119, 135; ban readers, 145, 153; competition among, 58, 61, 158, 159–60, 242 n.46; consolidation among, 61; guarantees of protection for, 38, 41–42, 51, 55, 83, 101, 114, 136, 139, 210, 227 n.47; and injunctions, 143–44, 155; organize in Tampa, 58–59; threaten to leave Tampa, 73, 100, 148, 160, 210; and union recognition, 159, 203; see also Cigar Manufacturers' Association of Tampa, and names of individual companies
Cigar Manufacturers' Association of Tampa, 113, 142, 149, 178; antiunionism of, 58–59, 71, 89–90, 133, 134, 137, 138; membership, 89, 133, 157–58, 159, 242 n.46; origins of, 58; and strikes (1899), 58, 59; and strikes (1901), 73, 79;

Cigar Manufacturer's Association of Tampa (continued)
and strikes (1910), 89, 95, 99–100, 103; and strikes (1920), 133–34, 135, 137–38, 140, 144; and strikes (1921), 145; and strikes (1935), 160; and wage cut, 150

cigarworkers: in Boston, 112; conflicts among, 36–37, 43, 50, 61–63, 211, 212; in Cuba, 42–43, 135; customs of, 33–34, 35, 161; definition of, 224 n.9; different skills of, 33, 63, 88, 89, 224 n.9; hours, 33; in Key West, 42–43, 82–83; in New York, 112; occupational diseases of, 225 n.11; and radicalism, 31, 34, 36, 37, 43, 56–57, 62–63, 114–115, 122, 150, 151, 159, 204, 211, 213, 248 n.222; and readers (lectores), 34, 145, 149, 153, 156, 158, 214, 247 n.184; and unemployment, 149–50, 158, 161–62; and unions, 61–63, 150, 158; unity of, 35, 56–57, 58, 78, 82–83, 135, 144, 153, 211, 212; and vigilantes, 38–39, 52, 74, 78, 79, 85, 95, 96, 104, 105, 110, 120, 121, 142, 143, 146, 147, 148, 154, 157, 186, 210; violence among, 36, 43, 50, 53, 63, 95, 109, 141, 154, 226 n.34; wages, 33, 60, 88, 89, 117, 118, 145, 149–50, 225 n.10, 235 n.6; in West Tampa, 56, 145; and workers' control, 34–35, 36–37, 57–58, 60–61, 71–72, 73, 225 n.18; *see also* Cigar Makers' International Union, Cuban Federation of Cigar Makers, Knights of Labor, La Resistencia, strikes

Círculo Cubano, 56
Citizens' Association, 113–14, 240 n.154, 244 n.111
Citizens' Committees, 114, 206, 207; of 1887, 38–40, 42, 135; of 1892, 51–52, 101, 108, 135; of 1901, 73, 74–81, 83, 85, 86, 232 n.94; of 1910, 99, 100–13, 122, 135, 136, 138, 141, 203, 207–8, 237 n.69, 240 n.154, 244 n.111; of 1918, 119–21; of 1920, 141–43, 144, 203; of 1931, 153–54, 155–56
Civil War, 12, 13, 15, 17, 20, 21, 22, 26, 30

Clear Havana Cigar Manufacturers' Association of Tampa, 83; *see also* Cigar Manufacturers' Association of Tampa
clear Havana cigars, 33, 71, 87, 88, 235 n.20; *see also* cigar industry
Clewis, Alonzo C., 236 n.22
Coates, Grace E., 120–21
Colorado, 19, 207
Committee to Defend Civil Liberties in Tampa, 187, 191, 199
Committee to Defend Civil Rights in Tampa, 185, 186, 187, 191, 199, 200, 254 n.104, 256 n.169
communism, 180, 189, 195, 197, 201, 204; *see also* Bolshevism
Communist party, 153, 179, 200–1, 248 n.216; organizing in Tampa, 150–51, 155
Communists, 52, 159, 182, 194, 195, 196; activities of, 200–1, 204, 246 n.162; repression of, 150–51, 152, 154, 155, 156, 202, 252 n.78
Cone, Fred P., 210
Confederacy, 11, 20, 21, 24–25
Conoley, William N., 37–42 passim
Craft, D. Isaac, 2, 5, 17
Crawford, Frederick, 150–51, 152, 246 n.174, 246 n.181
Crosby, Sam, 194, 196, 255 n.145, 255 n.146, 257 n.186
Cruz, Ismael, 246 n.181, 247 n.206
Cuba: independence movement, 31, 32, 36, 43, 57, 277 n.57; trade with Tampa, 10; tobacco from, 33
Cuban Federation of Cigar Makers, 36, 39, 41, 61
Cuban Revolutionary Party, 43, 57, 227 n.57
Cubans: and anarchism, 227 n.57; arrival in Tampa, 30, 32, 56; conflicts with Spaniards, 36–37, 43; expelled from Tampa, 38–39; in Key West, 83; and radicalism, 57; *see also* cigarworkers, immigrants
Cuesta, A. L., Jr., 248 n.211
Cuesta-Rey factory, 72
Culbreath, Hugh, 203
Cummings, Homer T., 253 n.103

Davis, Fred J., 160
Davis, Jefferson, 11

Dean, James, 255 n.143
Debs, Eugene V., 180
de la Campa, José, 90, 95, 96, 98, 103, 105, 107, 111, 239 n.105
Democratic party, 13, 14, 18, 26, 180; see also White Municipal party
Detroit, Mich., 148
Dewell, Robert T., 193, 194, 197, 198, 199
Díaz, Luis, 146, 147
Drew, John H., 238 n.77
Duke, James B., 71

Easterling, J. F., 95–96, 97, 98, 105, 236 n.32, 236 n.40
Eddings, J. L., 196, 203, 257 n.186
Egmont Key, 29
Elks Club, 154
Ellinger factory, 61
Emilio Pons & Company, 50
Evans, Hiram Wesley, 255 n.140

Fariss, Robert P., 192
Farrior, J. Rex: and flogging cases, 188, 189, 193, 196, 199, 257 n.200; and Kefauver Committee, 203; and lynching (1934), 167–68
Federación Cubana de Tabaqueros. See Cuban Federation of Cigar Makers
Ficarrotta, Castenge, 96–97, 98, 105, 115, 236 n.40, 236 n.50
Field, Stephen J., 23
Finn, Thomas, 159, 160, 161
Fisher, Thomas D., 238 n.77
flogging cases (1935-38): investigation of, 188–89; prosecution of, 190, 193-99
floggings, xvi, xvii; in 1931, 151; in 1935, 163, 177, 183; purpose of 184; see also flogging cases
Florida State Bar Association, 23, 53
Florida State Federation of Labor, 136
Fort Brooke, 5
Fuente, Francisco, 148
Fueyo, José, 232 n.101

gambling, 14–15, 178–79, 202–3, 204
García, José, 161
Garfield, James A., 44
Gaspar, José, 234 n.146
Gasparilla, 234 n.146
Georgia, 15

Georgia State Federation of Labor, 118
Germany, 118
Gil, J. M., 110
Gilchrist, Albert W., 98, 108, 109
Gillian, Arlie F., 190, 198
Glenn, Clyde, 100
Gompers, Samuel, 84, 140, 211; and Cigar Makers' International Union, 61; ideas of, 230 n.38; protests vigilantism, 85, 106, 108, 109, 120, 143, 149, 212; and strikes (1920), 139
Gonzales, Cresencio, 232 n.101
Graves, Thomas M., 167, 168, 202
Green, William, 185
Griffin, J. Arthur, 135, 141, 142, 244 n.111
Grillo, Gabriel, 232 n.101
Guiteau, Charles J., 4
Gutiérrez, Aurora, 76
Gutman, Herbert, 228 n.70
Guzman, Gonzalo Perez, 33

Hamilton County, 20
Hardee, Cary A., 149
Harlan County, Ky., 200
Havana, 32, 58, 81, 135, 210
Havana-American Company, 61, 63, 71
Hav-A-Tampa Cigar Company, 159–60, 162, 190, 191, 249 n.226
Haya, Ignacio, 32, 42
Haymarket bombing, 40
hegemony, 31, 213, 214
Henderson, Frank, 191
Hernando County, 13, 20, 21
Herndon, Angelo, 196
Hevia, Joe, 246 n.181, 247 n.206
Hildalgo, Juan, 246 n.181
Hillsborough County: economy, 10, 226 n.42; lynching record of, 208
Hillsborough County Bar Association, 177, 186
Hofstadter, Richard, xv
Holtsinger, Eugene, 236 n.22
Home Guards, 122
Honduras, 74, 84, 231 n.79, 232 n.101
honor: and community justice, 30, 40; and the Confederacy, 24–25; decline of, 53, 209; and lynching, 3–5, 21–22, 209; northern views of, 18–19; and personal violence,

honor (continued)
  25–26; and rape, 23, 28, 209; and women, 25
Houston, George, 29

Idaho, 84, 207
Illinois, 198
immigrants: xix, 15; arrival in Tampa, 27, 31, 42; attitudes toward, 52, 53, 76–77, 212; 228 n.68; as cigar-workers, 87; conflicts among, 36, 37, 53, 115, 212; institutions of, 42, 56; mobility of, 214; and radicalism, 56–57; as vigilante victims, 184, 205, 208, 212; see also Cubans, Italians, Spaniards
Indiana, 191
Industrial Workers of the World (IWW), 118–19, 120
International Labor Defense, 152–53, 185, 247 n.208
International Longshoremen's Association, 191
International Typographical Union, 102, 134–35, 136, 232 n.93

Jackson, Lewis, 29–30, 212
Jackson, Miss., 250 n.34
Jacksonville, Fla., 146
Jacksonville, Tampa and Key West Railway, 20
Jensen, Charles E., 180, 182, 195
Johnson, Robert, 166–67, 168, 183, 206, 250 n.36, 251 n.39
Johnston, J. C., 107–8, 109
Joint Advisory Board (JAB), 148; organization of, 88; protests vigilantism, 114, 149; and strikes (1910), 89–90, 101, 105, 110, 111, 112; and strikes (1920), 133, 134, 135, 139, 144

Kefauver, Estes, 203
Kelly, Charles, 232 n.101
Key West, Fla., 15, 32, 38, 41, 58, 62; see also cigar industry
Kiwanis Club, 136, 165, 168
Knight, Peter Oliphant, 207, 232 n.138, 237 n.63, 239 n.116; biography, 101; and Citizens' Committee of 1910, 101; condemns "agitators," 122; and strikes (1901), 83

Knights of Hillsborough, 14
Knights of Labor, 35, 36, 61, 226 n.20
Ku Klux Klan (KKK), xvii, 213; attacks on Earl Browder, 201–2; and floggings (1923), 184; and floggings (1935), 189–90, 191, 192, 198, 199, 204, 255 n.137, 255 n.140; influence in Tampa, 200, 255 n.138

La Follette, Robert M., Jr., 199
La Follette Committee, 200
Lanza, Estanisalo, 232 n.101
Lasser, David, 185, 187
Levins, Benjamin Frank, 164
Lezama, Carlos, 246 n.181, 247 n.206
Liceo Cubano, 42
Lima, Nilo, 246 n.181, 247 n.206
Local Independent Union of the Cigar Industry of Tampa, 158
Locke, James W., 15–19, 22
Locke, William, 11
Logan, Amazon C., 146, 148, 154, 202
Lopez, Mario, 246 n.181
Lovett, Richard B., 136
Lowry, Sumter L., 164, 165
Lykes, Frederica, 20
Lykes, Howell T. (1846–1906), 20, 222 n.85
Lykes, Howell T. (1879–1942), 90, 113, 159, 203, 238 n.77
Lykes, Thompson, M., 203
Lykes Brothers, 90
Lynch, Charles, xvii
lynching, xvi, 146; in cities, 250 n.34; and community justice, 1, 21–22, 30, 97–98; in 1858, 11, 208, 209; in 1860, 12, 210; in 1882, 1–5, 15–19, 22–23, 24, 40, 209, 210; and Florida law, 219 n.25; in 1903, 29–30, 166, 208, 209, 212; in 1910, 96–97, 114, 115, 205, 209, 210; in 1934, 166–67, 209, 250 n.36, 251 n.39; in 1935, 183, 208, 209, 253 n.87; northern views of, 17, 18–19, 22–23; prevention of, 28–29, 163–66, 223 n.129; and rape, 3–4, 28–29, 163, 220 n.41; record in Florida, 165; record in the South, 183; record in Tampa, 183; and vigilantism, xvii, 216 n.19; in the West, 19–20; see also blacks, flogging cases

McCallister, Frank, 185, 201, 202
McCarty, Ada, 2, 14
McCarty, Mitchell, 4
McCaskill, John A., 182, 189
McDonald, J. E., 246 n.181, 247 n.206
Macfarlane, Howard P., 203
Macfarlane, Hugh Campbell, 90, 119, 207, 239 n.116; biography, 55; and Citizens' Association, 113; and Citizens' Committee of 1910, 100–1, 103, 104, 108; and West Tampa, 55–56
Macfarlane, Matthew B., 90, 119, 177, 207
McKay, Charles Angus, 142, 203
McKay, Donald Brenham, 110, 142, 146, 154, 203, 211, 239 n.116; biography, 24; and Cigar Manufacturers' Association, 158; and cigarworkers, 161; and Citizens' Association, 113; and Citizens' Committee of 1892, 51; and Citizens' Committee of 1901, 76; and Citizens' Committee of 1910, 100, 106–7, 109, 112; and Citizens' Committee of 1931, 158; and collective bargaining, 159, 162, 203; on lynching, 24, 163, 165; marriage of, 76; and mayoral elections, 76, 150, 177, 178; on southern culture, 14, 25; and strikes (1910), 104, 105; and strikes (1918), 121; and strikes (1920), 135, 138, 141; and strikes (1935), 160; on vigilantism, 121, 210
McKay, James, 10, 20
McKay, John A., 222 n.85
McKay, Kenneth I., 113, 178, 239 n.116
McKay, Matilda, 20
McKinley, William, 80
McLeod, Jerry R., 188, 189, 191
McNeill, J. C., 228 n.67
Magbee, James T., 19
Manasco, Grady, 246 n.181
Manrara, Eduardo, 36, 58
Marero, Félix, 246 n.181, 247 n.206
Martí, José, 43
Martínez Ybor, Candido, 42, 59
Martínez Ybor, Vicente, 42, 240 n.154; and *Cuba Libre*, 57; death of, 58; and Ybor City, 32–33, 34
Martínez Ybor factory, 37, 50, 51, 52, 58

May Day, 43, 122
Memphis, Tenn., 259 n.5
Menendes, Félix, 232 n.101
Menendez, Manuel, 190, 255 n.144
Metcalf, Walter, 187, 191, 254 n.120
Mexico, 164
Missouri, 198
Mitchell, Henry Laurens, 4, 14, 20–21
Modern Democrats, 183, 184, 188, 189, 190, 191, 204; activities of, 180–81, 196, 197; organization of, 180; police raid on, 182, 194
Morris, James, 248 n.211
Munroe, Kirk, 3

National Association for the Advancement of Colored People (NAACP), 185, 251 n.39
National Association of Manufacturers, 84
National Guard, 164, 165, 178
National Industrial Recovery Act, 158
National Recovery Administration (NRA), 158, 159, 249 n.226
Neal, Claude, 250 n.36
Newberger, Fred W., 258 n.221
New Deal, 180; collective bargaining under, 116, 158, 161, 162, 203
New Jersey, 22, 222 n.95
New Mexico, 19
New Orleans, La., 30, 56, 259 n.5
New South, xix, xx, 207, 217 n.31
New York, N.Y., 61, 71, 100, 112, 160, 161, 182, 185, 214
New York State, 198
Nine, Jim, 246 n.165, 246 n.181, 247 n.206

Old South, xix, 10, 14–15, 20, 24, 53, 207
Orlando, Fla., 190
Owens, Charles D., 1–5, 14, 15, 16, 19, 21, 209, 218 n.2, 222 n.85, 237 n.50

Padilla, José Gonzalez, 73, 74, 78
Page, Walter Hines, 87
Palatka, Fla., 85
Parcell, C. E., 228 n.67
Parkhill, Charles B., 139–40, 244 n.99
Parrish, John R., 258 n.221
Parrondo, Belen, 232 n.101

Pendas, Enrique, 103, 113, 133, 158
Perkins, George W., 90; on conditions in Tampa, 85–86, 88–89, 145; protests vigilantism, 84–85, 86, 148–49; and radicals, 88, 111, 211; and strikes (1910), 111–12; and strikes (1920), 137
Pinellas County, 184
Piquero, Ramon, 232 n.101
Plant, Henry B., 31
Polk County, 1, 13, 193, 197, 198
Ponder, Lawrence, 258 n.221
Pons, Emilio, 59
Poulnot, Eugene, 194; biography, 180–81, 182; on decline of vigilantism, 200, 202; flogging of, 183; kidnapping of, 182, 186, 194; and prosecution of flogging cases, 185, 195, 197, 199
Prieto, Severino, 232 n.101
Pullman, George, 32

readers. *See* cigarworkers
Reconstruction, xviii, 17, 21, 22, 26, 30
Red Scare, 122
Reed, John Shelton, xv
Regensburg, Jerome, 155
Regensburg & Sons, Inc., 155
Relief Work Council, 181
republicanism: and community justice, 38, 102, 115, 142, 146; and lynching, 30; and vigilantism, 12, 77, 86, 141
Republican party, 10, 13, 15, 18, 26
La Resistencia, 111, 211, 213; conflict with the Cigar Makers' International Union, 63, 69, 70, 71, 72; demise of, 81, 82; leaders kidnapped, 74, 79, 80, 84; membership, 62, 63, 72, 82; origins of, 62; threats against, 69; and strikes (1901), 72–82
"right to work" law, 241 n.23
ring tournaments, 14
Roberts, Charles Homer, 180
Rodriguez, F. L., 246 n.181, 247 n.206
Rodriquez, Francisco, 232 n.101
Rogers, Samuel J.: arrest of, 182; biography, 181; flogging of, 183; kidnapping of, 182, 194; and prosecution of flogging cases, 185, 195

Romero, Frances, 246 n.181, 247 n.206
Roosevelt, Theodore, 85
Rotary Club, 136
Rotureau, Eugene L., 190
Roush, Walter, 182
Rubiera, Ramón, 39, 41
Russell, Brit, 107
Russian revolution, 122, 151, 152

St. Petersburg, Fla., 184, 185
Sánchez & Haya, 32, 38, 43, 50, 59
San Francisco, Calif., 260 n.6
San Francisco Vigilance Committee, xvi, 207, 231 n.80, 260 n.7
Sara Sota Vigilance Committee, 208
Savannah, Ga., 5
Schwab-Davis Company, 160
Scottsboro case, 168, 195, 250 n.36
Seidenberg factory, 61, 63
Shoemaker, Joseph A., 162, 189, 199, 203, 208, 209; activities of, 180, 181–82, 252 n.59; biography, 179; flogging and death of, 183, 205–6, 252 n.86, 253 n.87, 255 n.137; kidnapping of, 182; reactions to death of, 184–87, 204, 214, 253 n.103; and Socialist party, 179–80; *see also* flogging cases
Shoemaker, Leroy T. ("Jack"), 179, 183, 189
Sholtz, David: biography, 167; and elections of 1935, 178; and flogging cases, 188, 193, 255 n.128; and lynching (1934), 167; and removal of sheriff, 188, 250 n.28
Sicily, 56, 57
Sinclair, Upton, 180, 252 n.59
Singleton, Harry, 223 n.129
slavery, 10, 14, 26
socialism, 43, 57, 179–80, 185
Socialist party, 106, 182, 191; in Florida, 180–81, 185, 252 n.64; *see also* Socialists
Socialists, 52, 57, 122, 211; defend Earl Browder, 200; and flogging cases, 187, 191, 200; in Tampa, 106, 180–81, 204; as vigilante victims, 163
La Sociedad de Torcedes de Tampa. *See* La Resistencia
Sontheimer, Sol, 137, 142, 143
South Carolina, 15, 181, 206
South Florida Railroad, 31

Soviet Union, 155
Spaniards: and anarchism, 43, 50; arrival in Tampa, 32, 56; as cigar manufacturers, 32, 36; as cigarworkers, 35, 36–37, 56, 63; and radicalism, 57; see also immigrants
Spanish-Cuban-American War, 57
Sparkman, George Bascom, 17, 222 n.89
Sparkman, Stephen M.: biography, 21, 222 n.89; and Citizens' Committee of 1887, 38; and Citizens' Committee of 1892, 51; and lynching (1882), 16; and strikes (1901), 82
Spencer, Edward W., 190
Spencer, Thomas K., 18, 39–40, 42
Spencer, Will C., 167, 188, 250 n.28
Spivey, Edward, 190
Stephens, Miller A., 180, 181
Stovall, Wallace F., 109, 120: antiunionism of, 103; biography, 59; and Citizens' Association, 113; and Citizens' Committee of 1910, 102, 107–8, 112; and honor, 209; and strikes (1899), 60; and strikes (1910), 95, 105, 236 n.22, 239 n.116; and strikes (1920), 136, 139–40; and vigilantism, 60, 69, 74, 75, 83, 97–98, 99, 100, 103, 122, 139–40, 140–41, 147–48, 163, 208
strikes: in 1886, 58, 225 n.18; in 1887, 36, 58; in 1892, 43, 50, 51, 52; in 1899, 55, 57–61, 82, 210; frequency of, 225 n.15; in Key West, 32; in 1900, 70, 82; in 1901, 55, 72–81; in 1910, 89–90, 95–112, 138, 205, 209, 211; in 1918, 118; in 1919, 121; in 1920, 121–22, 133–45, 211, 212; in 1921, 145–47; in the 1920s, 149; in 1931, 153–56, 158; in 1933, 158; in 1935, 160
Switzer, F. W., 182, 184, 194, 255 n.134, 257 n.186

Taft, William Howard, 107
Taliaferro, Thomas Carson, 135, 236 n.22
Tampa: and antebellum culture, 13–15, 30; antebellum economy of, 10; as "center of repression," xvii, 200; characteristics of, xviii, xix;

Tampa (continued)
during the Civil War, 10–11, 12–13; crime in, 1–2, 3, 11, 13, 28–29, 36, 164, 166–67, 218 n.34; in the 1880s, 1–3, 25, 31–32, 35–42; in the late 1890s, 43, 50–52, 55–62; elite, xix, 10, 32, 53, 104, 210, 213, 234 n.146; incorporation of, 11, 13; lynching record of, 208, 260 n.12; in the 1920s, 121–22, 133–48, 164–66; in the 1930s, 149–62, 166–68, 177–204; and the Old South, 5, 10; and the open shop, 90, 102–3; origins of, 5, 10, politics, 10–11, 42, 177–79, 180, 181, 202, 203, 204, 214; population, 3, 5, 10, 15, 26, 27, 32, 42, 55, 87, 121, 149, 168; population table, 27; during Reconstruction, 13, 14, 26; and the union shop, 90; during World War I, 117–21, 163–64; see also cigar industry
Tampa Board of Trade, 40, 50 76, 113, 236 n.22, 238 n.77, 239 n.116; Cigar Manufacturers' Bureau of, 117; and founding of Ybor city, 32; guarantees to protect cigar manufacturers, 38, 41–42, 51, 55, 83, 135, 136, 210, 227 n.47; membership, 32, 42, 90; origins of, 32; reorganized as Tampa Chamber of Commerce, 246 n.160; and strikes (1899), 59; and strikes (1900), 69–70; and strikes (1901), 73, 75–76, 82; and strikes (1910), 90, 95; and strikes (1918), 119; and strikes (1920), 135–36, 137, 138, 141; and vigilantism, 37–38, 39, 41, 51, 53, 148, 210
Tampa Chamber of Commerce, 35, 150, 155, 158, 203, 246 n.160, 248 n.211
Tampa Junior Chamber of Commerce, 178, 186
Tampa Ministerial Association, 187
Tampa Retail Merchants Association, 142
Tampa Stevedoring Company, 190
Tampa Wholesale Grocers' Association, 136
Tampa Yacht and Country Club, 240 n.154

tar-and-feathering, xvi, xvii, 163, 183, 184
Tennessee, 19
Ten Years' War, 32
Third Seminole War, 11, 12
Thomas, Norman, 192, 194; on decline of vigilantism, 200; and flogging cases, 179, 185, 187, 191, 199, 253 n.103, 258 n.213
Tilly, Charles, xviii
Tittsworth, Richard G., 188, 189, 190, 194, 196, 197, 198
Tobacco Workers Industrial Union (TWIU), 150, 153-57 passim, 246 n.162, 247 n.202
Tompkins, H. Carl, 192
Trade Union Unity League, 150, 248 n.216
Trawick, Julius A., 113
Trenton, N.J., 158
"trust factories," 71

L'Unione Italiana, 56
La Unión Martí-Maceo, 56
United Spanish War Veterans, 154
U.S. Department of Labor, 116, 161; Division of Conciliation, 137, 159, 243 n.86; mediates 1933 agreement, 159; and strikes (1918), 118, 120; and strikes (1920), 137-38, 140, 144; and strikes (1935), 160

Valdes, Eustacio, 232 n.101
Vasquez, Carolina, 246 n.181, 247 n.206
Vermont, 179
Vicksburg, Miss., 250 n.34
vigilance committees, 24; in 1858, 11, 12, 40; in 1892, 51; in 1903, 84, 85; in 1918, 119-20, 121; in 1927, 165, 166; see also Citizens' Committees
vigilantism: and cities, xvi, 259 n.5; and community justice, xix, 4, 5, 11-12, 18-19, 24, 40, 51-52, 53-54 74-75, 76-78, 86, 102, 113-14, 141, 145-46, 147-48, 155, 206-7, 209-10, 215 n.11; decline of, 117, 160, 162, 163, 200, 202, 203-4, 214; definition of, xv; economic justifications of, 37, 39-40, 50, 53, 75, 76, 77, 84, 86, 97, 98, 99, 114, 115, 139, 140-41, 146-47, 148, 208, 209,

vigilantism (continued)
210; effectiveness of, 12, 52, 78, 81-82, 111-13, 147, 157, 213; in 1887, 37-39; in 1892, 51-52; and the frontier, xvi, 207, 209; in 1901, 73-76, 79, 80; in 1903, 84-85; in 1910, 103-4, 106, 107-8, 110; in 1918, 121; in 1921, 146, 148; in 1931, 150-51; in 1936, 201; and the South, xvii; and the state, xviii, 162, 204, 207, 219 n.26; and the state (1860), 12; and the state (1882), 5, 12, 16-17, 21, 22-23; and the state (1887), 41; and the state (1901), 82, 83, 85, 86; and the state (1910), 87, 98, 99, 106-7, 108, 109-10, 115; and the state (1918), 119, 120-21; and the state (1920), 137, 138, 139-40, 143, 145, and the state (1921), 147, 148-49; and the state (1934), 167-68; and the state (1935-38), 187-89, 193-99, 201, 202; and the state (1939), 258 n.213; and Tampa's image, 28-29, 164, 165-66, 168, 186, 188, 200, 201, 202-4, 205, 214; see also flogging, flogging cases, lynching, tar-and-feathering
violence: definition of, xv; explanations of, xvii-xviii; and the South, xvi, xviii; see also cigarworkers

Wall, Charles McKay, 203
Wall, J. Edgar, 135
Wall, John P., 203, 222 n.85; biography, 20; and lynching (1882), 3, 4, 17-18, 19; and Tampa Board of Trade 42; and Tampa Tribune, 59
Wall, John P., Jr., 101, 239 n.116
Wall, Joseph Baisden, 42, 90, 101, 207, 244 n.99; biography, 15, 20, 21, 23-24; and Citizens' Committee of 1887, 38-41 passim; and Citizens' Committee of 1892, 51-52, 53; disbarment of, 16-19, 22-23; and lynching (1882), 15-19; and lynching (1910), 237 n.50; wealth of, 40-41
Wall, Perry G. (1846-1906), 20
Wall, Perry G. (1879-1942), 90, 165, 203
War Labor Board, 121

Watson, J. Thomas, 119–20, 121, 241 n.23
Webb, Curren E., 238 n.77
Weir, Thomas M., 51–52, 108
West Palm Beach, Fla., 199
West Tampa: annexation of, 149; and lynching (1910), 96, 99; origins of, 55–56; population of, 56, 87, 121
Whitaker, Charles C., 104, 108, 113
Whitaker, Patrick Crisp, 204; biography of, 177; and flogging cases, 190, 193–98 passim, 206
Whitaker, Thomas, 177, 203
whitecapping, xvii, 216 n.20
White Municipal party, 177, 181
white primary, 27–28
Williams, Peter A., 16
Wilson, Woodrow, 138
Witt, Eli B., 190
women: as cigarworkers, 63, 158, 159, 214, 224 n.9; and honor, 3–4
Wood, James, 84–85, 205, 235 n.156

Woodbery, Daniel Hoyt, 160, 190, 191, 255 n.146
Workers Alliance of America, 180, 181, 185, 187
Works Progress Administration, 188
World War I, 117, 163, 211; government support for labor during, 116; and Home Guards, 122; impact of, 203, 212; service in, 164, 165

Ybor & Company, 32, 36, 38, 225 n.18
Ybor City: annexation of, 42; growth of, 35, 42; origins of, 32–33, 34, 35; and West Tampa, 56
Ybor City Land and Development Company, 32, 101, 233 n.138
Ybor-Manrara factory, 57, 59, 61, 230 n.28
Ye Mystic Krewe of Gasparilla, 234 n.146
Yglesias, Jose, 213, 214, 261 n.37

www.ingramcontent.com/pod-product-compliance
Lightning Source LLC
Chambersburg PA
CBHW022105150426
43195CB00008B/273